About the author

Christina Fink is a program associate and lecturer at the International Sustainable Development Studies Institute and program coordinator and lecturer in the Foreign Affairs Training Program, Chiang Mai, Thailand. She is also honorary assistant professor in the Department of Sociology, Hong Kong.

LIVING SILENCE IN BURMA
Surviving under military rule

Christina Fink

second edition

Silkworm Books
CHIANG MAI, THAILAND

Zed Books
LONDON | NEW YORK

Living silence in Burma: surviving under military rule, second edition, was first published in 2009

Published in Thailand, Burma, Laos, Cambodia and Vietnam by Silkworm Books, 6 Sukkasem Road, T. Suthep, Chiang Mai 50200, Thailand

www.silkwormbooks.com

Published in the rest of the world by Zed Books Ltd, 7 Cynthia Street, London N1 9JF, UK and Room 400, 175 Fifth Avenue, New York, NY 10010, USA

www.zedbooks.co.uk

The first edition, *Living Silence: Burma under military rule*, was first published in 2001.

Set in OurType Arnhem and Futura Bold by Ewan Smith, London
Cover designed by Rogue Four Design
Index: ed.emery@thefreeuniversity.net
Printed and bound in Great Britain by CPI Antony Rowe, Chippenham and Eastbourne

Distributed in the USA exclusively by Palgrave Macmillan, a division of St Martin's Press, LLC, 175 Fifth Avenue, New York, NY 10010, USA

A catalogue record for this book is available from the British Library
Library of Congress Cataloging in Publication Data available

ISBN   978 1 84813 271 9 hb
ISBN   978 1 84813 272 6 pb
ISBN   978 974 9511 81 7 pb (Silkworm Books)

Contents

Illustrations

All photographs are by Nic Dunlop/Panos Pictures

Acknowledgements

First and foremost, I would like to thank those who shared their stories with me. For some it was a painful experience, bringing up feelings of suffering and loss. For others it was risky, because to speak against the government is a crime in Burma. Unfortunately I could not include everyone's stories here, but each and every one helped me to understand Burma better. I would also like to express my gratitude to all who helped to arrange interviews for me, to those who interpreted and translated interviews, often at short notice and late hours, and to those who have answered so many questions for me over the past several years. Although I would like to name everyone here, for their safety, I cannot.

I am grateful to Nic Dunlop for working with me to create the photo essay, to Ko Sitt Nyein Aye for allowing me to use the title of one of his articles, 'In the dark, every cat is black', as a chapter title, and to Ko Maing Kyaw Khin for agreeing to let me use one of his cartoons. Also to Ko Mun Awng for his song of defiance, and to the former political prisoner who shared his song of sadness with me. Thanks to Moe Kyaw for making the maps and to Ko Zaw Oo and U Aung Saw Oo for their help in reconstructing a list of student protests and school closures from 1962 to 1999.

The book has benefited greatly from the comments and suggestions made by several people who read earlier drafts; most especially, Hadley Arnold, Nancy Chen, Min Zin, Josef Silverstein, Martin Smith, NC, and Win Min, as well as CT, Mathea Falco, KK and UTZ. Needless to say, any mistakes are my responsibility alone.

I am deeply grateful to the Open Society Institute for providing me with a fellowship to research and write this book. Robert Molteno, my editor, was also wonderfully supportive. And Chris Beyrer and Edith Mirante gave me much helpful advice throughout the writing process.

I am indebted to Maureen Aung-Thwin, who first stimulated my interest in Burma with her infectious enthusiasm. And I will never forget the Burmese residents of the two houses where I was based while conducting much of my research. Their generosity, good humour and fantastic cooking deepened an already great love for Burma.

For the second edition, I would like to thank my editor, Tamsine O'Riordan, for her helpful suggestions, and Win Min for all his assistance during the interviews and the writing process.

Author's note

Burmese prefixes

In Burma it is polite to put a prefix in front of the name of the person to whom one is talking. The speaker chooses the prefix according to the age of the other person, relative to one's own age. Thus if a woman's name were Mee Mee, and she were about forty years old, a girl would call her 'Daw Mee Mee', but someone in his or her thirties would call that same woman 'Ma Mee Mee'.

Daw – for aunts, older women
U – for uncles, older men
Ma – for older sisters, women slightly older than oneself
Ko – for older brothers, men slightly older than oneself
Nyi ma – for younger sisters, girls
Maung – for younger brothers, boys
There are also specialized terms for military officers, teachers, doctors and abbots which are put in front of individuals' respective names.

A note on pronunciation

'ky' is pronounced 'ch', thus 'kyi', as in the name Aung San Suu Kyi, is pronounced 'chee'.

'gy' is pronounced 'j', thus 'gyi' is pronounced 'jee'.

'ye' is pronounced 'yay'.

'we' is pronounced 'way', thus 'shwe' is pronounced 'shway'.

Acronyms

AAPP	Assistance Association for Political Prisoners
ABFSU	All Burma Federation of Students' Unions
ABMA	All Burma Monks' Alliance
ABSDF	All Burma Students' Democratic Front
AFPFL	Anti-Fascist People's Freedom League
ASEAN	Association of South-East Asian Nations
BBC	British Broadcasting Corporation
BSPP	Burma Socialist Programme Party
CNF	Chin National Front
CNLD	Chin National League for Democracy
CPB	Communist Party of Burma
CRPP	Committee Representing the People's Parliament
DDSI	Directorate of Defence Services Intelligence
DKBA	Democratic Karen Buddhist Army
DPNS	Democratic Party for a New Society
DVB	Democratic Voice of Burma
GONGO	government-organized non-governmental organization
ICRC	International Committee of the Red Cross
ILO	International Labour Organization
KIO	Kachin Independence Organization (armed wing: Kachin Independence Army)
KMT	Kuomintang (anti-communist Chinese force)
KNPLF	Karenni State Nationalities People's Liberation Front
KNPP	Karenni National Progressive Party
KNU	Karen National Union (armed wing: Karen National Liberation Army)
MI	military intelligence
MMCWA	Myanmar Maternal and Child Welfare Association
MWEA	Myanmar Women's Entrepreneurial Association
NCGUB	National Coalition Government of the Union of Burma
NGO	non-governmental organization
NLD	National League for Democracy
NMSP	New Mon State Party (armed wing: Mon National Liberation Army)

NUP	National Unity Party
PVO	People's Volunteer Organization
RFA	Radio Free Asia
RIT	Rangoon Institute of Technology
SLORC	State Law and Order Restoration Council
SNLD	Shan Nationalities League for Democracy
SNPLO	Shan State Nationalities People's Liberation Organization
SPDC	State Peace and Development Council
SSA	Shan State Army
UNDP	United Nations Development Programme
UNICEF	United Nations International Children's Emergency Fund
UNLD	United Nationalities League for Democracy
USDA	Union Solidarity and Development Association
UWSA	United Wa State Army
VOA	Voice of America

Glossary

ah nah	a feeling of obligation to or concern for others that makes one act in a restrained way
awza	influence, the ability to command others
Bogyoke	General
Coco Island	a penal colony where political prisoners were sent under the Ne Win regime
Daw	a term of respect for older women
Dobama Asiayone	'We Burmans' association; emerged in the colonial period
Four Cuts	military strategy of cutting enemy access to food, money, recruits and intelligence
gahta	a magical incantation
haw pyaw bwe	a public lecture
kamauk	a wide-brimmed farmer's hat, used by the NLD as its symbol
kaung ma	derogatory term for a woman, akin to 'bitch'
kyat	Burmese currency
kyet su	physic nut (also called jatropha), used for making bio-diesel
Lanzin Youth	the youth wing of the Burma Socialist Programme Party
longyi	a sarong, or piece of cloth sewn into a tube, worn by women and men
metta sutta	Buddhist verses of compassion or loving kindness
nat	a spirit in nature or of a dead person
ngapi	fish paste, a staple food for many in Burma
pinni	a traditional cotton jacket
Pyu Saw Hti	a paramilitary force named after a legendary hero
sangha	the Buddhist monkhood
sawbwa	the title for hereditary Shan princes
Swan Arr Shin	'Masters of Force', the name of a paramilitary group established by the authorities in the early 2000s
tat	militia
tatmadaw	the Burmese government's armed forces
thakin	master
thanaka	a yellowish powder made from various types of wood which is applied to the face and arms

thangyat	chorus songs mocking authorities, sung at Burmese new year
thingyan	Burmese new year, which takes place in mid-April
Thirty Comrades	thirty young men who went to Japan for military training before the Second World War
U	a term of respect for older men
yadaya	cheating fate by the use of magic to ward off undesirable occurrences
Zaw Gyi	a legendary wizard who lives in the forest

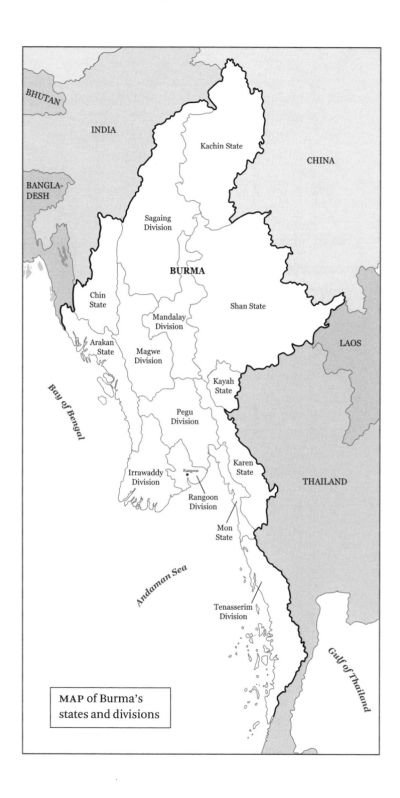

BHUTAN

INDIA

BANGLA-
DESH

Bay of Bengal

Chin
State

Arakan
State

Sagaing
Division

Kachin State

CHINA

BURMA

Mandalay
Division

Magwe
Division

Shan State

LAOS

Kayah
State

Pegu
Division

Irrawaddy
Division

Rangoon

Karen
State

THAILAND

Rangoon
Division

Mon
State

Andaman Sea

Tenasserim
Division

Gulf of Thailand

MAP of Burma's
states and divisions

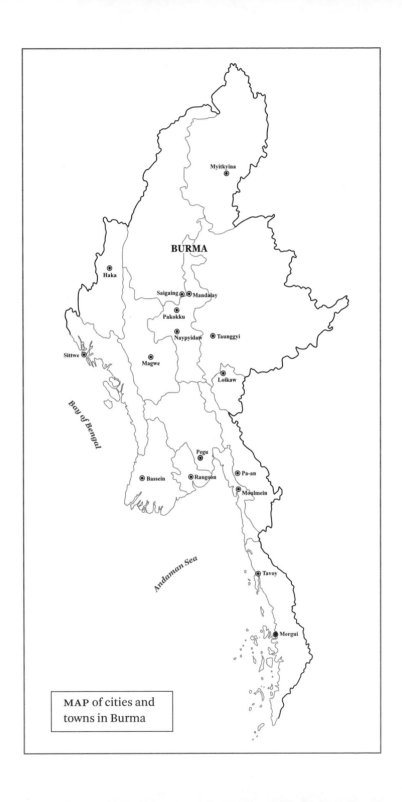

Myitkyina

BURMA

Haka

Saigaing Mandalay

Pakokku

Naypyidaw Taunggyi

Sittwe

Magwe

Loikaw

Bay of Bengal

Pegu

Bassein Rangoon Pa-an

Moulmein

Andaman Sea

Tavoy

Mergui

MAP of cities and
towns in Burma

To friends in Burma

Introduction

Burma is a surprising country. Boasting emerald-green rice fields, a multitude of tropical flowers and fruits, and brilliantly painted temples and shops, it is awash with colour. Many Burmese, men and women, continue to wear *longyis* – tube-shaped pieces of cloth tucked or knotted at the waist – decorated in striking patterns. Meanwhile, children run around with *thanaka*, a sweet-smelling paste made from ground wood, smeared on their faces. A carefree cheerfulness seems to characterize the people, but if you mention 'democracy' or Aung San Suu Kyi, people freeze.

Burma is blessed with abundant natural resources, including oil and natural gas, yet it is one of the least developed countries in the world. In the rural areas, oxcarts are still in use and candles are a necessity rather than a decorative item, as less than 25 per cent of rural houses have electricity.[1]

The lovely port-city of Rangoon is dominated by the shimmering golden Shwedagon Pagoda, although high-rise hotels now clutter the view. Rangoon's markets and tea shops bustle with activity, but its main universities are quiet as most classes have been moved to campuses outside the city, where university students cannot easily organize mass demonstrations.

Although Rangoon served as the capital from the British colonial period, in 2005 the regime suddenly moved the seat of government to an undeveloped area in the middle of the country. Removed from the trials and tribulations of ordinary citizens, the leading generals can enjoy their modern homes and perhaps believe that they are ruling wisely.

For tourists, one of the most striking images in Burma is that of crimson- and saffron-robed monks walking serenely down the streets single file on their early-morning alms rounds. Pious Buddhist men and women step out of their homes to offer food, grateful for the opportunity to make merit. But in September 2007, monks marched by the thousands down the streets of some of Burma's largest towns for a different reason: to try to awaken a spirit of compassion in the hearts of the military leaders. In August 2007, the regime had suddenly removed subsidies on diesel and compressed natural gas, resulting in massive price increases. The impact on the poor was disastrous: some people could literally no longer afford to take the bus to work. After a few bold activists were arrested for marching in protest, the monks decided they had to make an effort on the people's behalf. The regime, however, had no tolerance for such actions, particularly when lay people started joining in. Soldiers and other paramilitary groups brought the movement to an end through a combination of beatings, shootings, midnight temple raids and mass arrests.

Burma has been under military control since 1962. In 1988, pro-democracy demonstrations broke out nationwide, shattering the silence that had largely characterized political life for so many years. Students, professionals, civil servants and even some soldiers took to the streets to celebrate their new-found freedom. But after six weeks, the military was able to re-establish control, in part by promising multiparty elections for a new government. In 1990, the National League for Democracy, led by Aung San Suu Kyi, won a landslide victory, and change seemed imminent. But the regime refused to transfer power and instead began arresting some of those who had been elected. Aung San Suu Kyi herself had been put under house arrest in 1989 and was not released until 1995. She was soon rearrested and has spent most of the years since trapped in her house, only rarely able to communicate with family, friends or the outside world. Meanwhile thousands of other Burmese citizens have spent years behind bars for the 'crime' of daring to speak out against the regime.

Today, there are two key political issues in Burma: the restoration of democracy and the resolution of the political rights of ethnic nationalities. Despite domestic and international calls for democratization, the top generals have insisted on keeping power for themselves. At the same time, the regime has remained committed to the concentration of political power at the centre so as to prevent what it calls 'the disintegration of the union'. While the military regime has insisted that it is working to unify the country, its promotion of Burman culture, the Burmese language and Buddhism at the expense of other cultures, languages and religions has in many ways exacerbated pre-existing divisions.

Civil war broke out soon after independence, with ethnic minorities seeking greater autonomy in their areas. Since 1962, however, the regime has sought to bring all the ethnic areas, which make up half the country, under centralized control and to limit the teaching of ethnic minority languages. Resentment towards these policies, as well as anger over the brutal counter-insurgency campaigns in the ethnic states, drove tens of thousands of young men to join ethnic nationalist armies bent on maintaining territory under their own control.

Resistance to military rule, then, has come from both pro-democracy supporters and ethnic nationalist groups that seek greater autonomy.

These struggles, however, have overlapped only partially. Some ethnic nationalist leaders worry that a democratic government would not safeguard minority rights. At the same time, some Burman pro-democracy activists are uncomfortable with the ethnic nationalists' demands for autonomy, which they perceive as potentially leading to the break-up of the country. In recent years, many of the opposition groups have come to see the creation of a federal, democratic union as the best solution for all, but the regime's divide-and-rule tactics have made it difficult for them to work together.

Many Burmese citizens readily admit their dissatisfaction with military rule. They are tired of the political repression, the widespread extortion and the inability of the regime to manage the economy. They are also frustrated by the constant uncertainties they face. What is permitted by the authorities today may be considered unacceptable tomorrow. This is equally true for businesses involved in importing and exporting goods, non-governmental organizations carrying out programmes in rural communities, and writers dealing with the censorship board.

But most Burmese hesitate to take action, for even being caught with an opposition newspaper can land them in prison for years. In addition, their families may face trouble because of their actions. As a result, most Burmese attempt to get on with their lives as best they can while indulging in the dream that perhaps one day the United States or the United Nations will swoop in and remove the regime for them.

Such a scenario is extremely unlikely. While international interest in Burma has increased significantly since 1990, no government or international body has proposed any kind of military action to remove the regime. Instead, various foreign governments have tried both sanctions and persuasion to compel the regime to take a more conciliatory approach to its opposition. But the leading generals have bristled at what they see as outside interference in Burma's internal affairs. As the foreign minister, Win Aung, put it in 1998 when the UN tried to offer large-scale financial assistance in return for political concessions, 'Giving a banana to a monkey and asking it to dance is not the way. We are not monkeys.'[2]

Despite the regime's tenacity, it has to be asked how the military has managed to stay in power for so many years. Many factors have combined to keep Burma under military rule, including fear, the difficulties of organizing and sustaining an opposition movement, and successful propaganda by the regime, particularly with regard to the need for the military to hold the country together. In the 1990s, international players also contributed to the regime's staying power, with China providing

3

massive military support to Burma's armed forces and foreign companies investing significant amounts of money in joint ventures with military-owned businesses. Yet Burma's economic mismanagement, ongoing counter-insurgency campaigns and inability or unwillingness to stop the drug trade also had serious impacts for Burma's neighbours. Migrant workers, refugees and drugs have flowed out of Burma, but the regime has never offered an apology.

Modern authoritarian regimes have held power in countries of widely diverse religious and cultural backgrounds, suggesting that there is nothing particular about Burmese culture which makes Burma more susceptible to military rule. The leaders of authoritarian regimes, however, naturally seek to emphasize those historical, cultural and religious traditions which help legitimize or bolster their power. This book illustrates how successive regimes in Burma have manipulated Burmese history and exploited certain cultural norms and popular beliefs both to legitimize military rule and to marginalize detractors. The book will also show how successive regimes have used violence and a climate of insecurity to instil fear and political passivity in the people they have ruled.

Before going any farther, it should be made clear that while it is possible to talk about 'the military' and 'the people' as separate categories, in fact the reality is much more complicated. Many families have members in both the military and the pro-democracy movement. A significant percentage of soldiers do not approve of military rule even though they continue to carry out their superiors' commands. And a number of students who became pro-democracy activists in 1988 originally intended to become military officers. Most adults in Burma are members of the pro-regime Union Solidarity Development Association, whether willingly or not. At a deeper level, the military's propaganda and ways of operating have profoundly shaped even those opposed to military rule.

Nevertheless, it is not without irony that I have selected *Living Silence in Burma* as the title of this book. Burma is such a vibrant and lively place, yet many subjects are off limits, or talked about only in whispers, behind closed doors. People in Burma are reluctant to speak up because they are never sure who is listening. To protect themselves and their families, Burmese participate in creating the silence that constrains many aspects of their lives.

The first five chapters of this book offer an overview of Burma's modern history, with a focus on the political resistance movements that have emerged. Chapters 6 to 12 consider the stresses people in Burma face, the accommodations they have made, and the forms that individual acts of defiance have taken in people's daily lives. How has the military regime created techniques of control that lead people to act in ways that foster continued military rule? What kinds of resistance have emerged and in what spaces? By looking into households and communities, prisons, schools, barracks and religious centres, the penetration of military rule into all facets of people's lives becomes clear. But in all of these settings, there are also people who have tried to live by different rules and, in doing so, reaffirm their commitment to bringing about political change.

Since 1988, international players have had a growing role in Burma's political conflicts. The impacts of their policies and actions are considered in Chapter 13, as are the consequences of Burma's policies for its neighbouring countries. The final chapter looks at how Burma's political conflicts might be resolved in the future.

Throughout the book, I have used Burma rather than Myanmar, as the military regime unilaterally changed the English name of the country to Myanmar in 1989 without consulting the country's citizens. In Burmese, 'Bama' and 'Myanma' are used interchangeably for the name of the country.

In preparing this edition, some sections from the first edition were cut and other sections were reworked. Sections have been added throughout the book to bring it up to date and to further clarify how military rule has lasted so long. In the eight years since the first edition was published, little has changed in terms of the regime's desire to maintain power, its brutal treatment of dissidents and its inability to take care of its citizens. What has changed, however, is the greater level of international involvement in Burma's affairs and the expansion of private business and independent organizations. In addition, more and more Burmese have travelled out of the country for education or work, and small but significant numbers of people now have access to the Internet. Many now know how far their country lags behind other countries, and they do not accept the regime's claims that military rule is necessary. At the same time, a growing number of Burmese realize that all modern governments have certain responsibilities to provide basic services to their populations, and that the regime has failed to meet these. A variety of civil society organizations have emerged to try to tackle the country's social welfare problems themselves, albeit generally in small-scale ways.

I first came to know about Burma's political struggles through meeting members of the resistance movement on the Thai–Burma border. While conducting anthropological research with the Karen ethnic minority group in Thailand in 1992–93, I visited Manerplaw, the headquarters of the Karen National Union's resistance army, which had been fighting for political autonomy since 1949. This was also a coordinating centre for other ethnic nationalist groups as well as the Burmese students and elected politicians who had fled central Burma between 1988 and 1991. I was struck by the fact that they were risking their lives for demands that I took for granted: democracy, human rights and freedom of expression. But why had the struggle gone on for so long, and what kind of a role should the international community be playing? I looked for a job that would help me learn more.

From mid-1995 until 1997, I worked for the Open Society Institute's Burma Project, running an online newspaper called *The BurmaNet News* and meeting with the Burma Project's grantees. Spending much of my time on the Thai–Burma border, I also travelled into Burma and along Burma's other borders. With the support of an Open Society Institute fellowship, I left my job at the end of 1997 to devote a year to carrying out more extensive interviews with Burmese from all walks of life. Most of the interviews were conducted in Burma's neighbouring countries as well as in Australia and the United States.

While the military regime carefully watches foreigners' activities in Burma, at any one time there are more than one million Burmese abroad, including undocumented migrant workers, traders and businessmen who regularly go back and forth. Not only farmers but also civil servants have ended up seeking work in other countries as they have found it impossible to support their families in Burma. There are also students and members of religious orders who travel outside the country, refugees and political activists living on Burma's borders, and thousands of Burmese who have settled abroad to escape military repression or simply to live a more comfortable life.

For the first edition, I interviewed over 150 people, including students, farmers, soldiers, teachers, doctors, lawyers, politicians, civil servants, writers, artists, musicians, monks and priests. This updated edition is based on dozens more interviews and conversations with Burmese from a wide variety of backgrounds. The interview dates are not given in the endnotes although other references are. The names of all except prominent public figures have been changed in order to protect their identities.

I found it much easier to conduct interviews outside Burma, even with some of the people I had previously met inside the country, because in general none of us was worried that the conversation was being overheard by an informer. Many were eager to tell their stories, to revel in moments of triumph and to pour out feelings that had been held inside for so long.

But for some, the telling was painful, as it brought up difficult moral questions and feelings of despair.

What is a life well lived under military rule? Survival depends on submitting to those in power. Truth is often irrelevant. And people have to face choices that are hardly imaginable in a free society. Should you take the high road and refuse to cooperate with the authorities' demands or should you go along with them, like everyone else seems to be doing? Should you raise your children to accept military rule as normal or should you encourage them to resist and risk years of imprisonment? Is seizing a Burmese embassy abroad justified if the world seems to be ignoring your people's call for help?

While this book deals with the specifics of life under military rule in Burma, it raises questions about the human condition in general. Repression is not unique to Burma. And at various times, people everywhere have participated in uncomfortable silences with regard to political and social issues, when speaking up was a very difficult thing to do. Yet momentous changes do occur, often catching us by surprise. Burma, then, has a place in a broader history of people's struggles for political systems that can guarantee both prosperity and justice.

1 | Historical legacies

The problems in Burma have not been brought on by the military alone. Everyone is responsible. (A Burmese professor)

Burma is inhabited by a mix of people whose past historical relations were often contentious. In the pre-colonial days, Burman kings routinely conquered other peoples, and in three periods consolidated their rule over a number of neighbouring kingdoms and principalities. The successes of such expansionist campaigns brought pride to the victors, but in some cases involved terrible massacres. Under British colonial rule, ethnic minority groups – including Chinese and Indian immigrants as well as indigenous groups – were often privileged politically and economically over the Burman majority. Later, successive Burmese military regimes attempted to erase the humiliation of colonialism and shore up their own legitimacy by linking their political and religious activities to the accomplishments of great Burmese kings in the past. The legacies of both the pre-colonial and colonial periods have partially shaped the way that politics and ethnic relations are understood by people in Burma today.

Pre-colonial principalities and kingdoms

Burma consists of a flat heartland encircled by mountain ranges to the north, east and west. The country is dissected by the Irrawaddy, Salween and Chindwin rivers, and the Irrawaddy delta in the lower part of Burma offers particularly rich soil and bountiful rice harvests. To the south lies the sea. The largest population groups on the plains are the Burmans, Karens, Mons and Arakanese (or Rakhines). It should be noted that 'Burman' refers to the ethnic group, while 'Burmese' refers to the language that Burman people speak, as well as to all citizens of Burma. 'Burmese' is, however, often used interchangeably by outsiders and native speakers to refer to ethnic Burmans and all people living in Burma.

Burma's great kingdoms evolved in the lowlands, where much wealth was put into the construction of great Buddhist monasteries and pagodas, many of which are still standing. Most people survived as farmers and fishermen, and Buddhism, mixed with spirit worship, was the dominant religion. The Shans, living primarily in the north-eastern hills, are also predominantly Buddhist and developed principalities centred around prosperous rice-growing valleys. They were often linked in tributary relations to Burman rulers on the plains, but Burman officials never directly administered their territory.

A number of different peoples also live in the mountains, including the Chins, Kachins, Karennis (also known as Kayah), Nagas, Pa'os, Palaungs and Was, as well as many smaller groups. Hundreds of thousands of Karens can also be found in the eastern mountains along the Thai–Burma border. Because of the difficulties of food production in the hills, upland communities have tended to be small and scattered and only loosely connected to larger political centres. Today members of some upland minority groups practise Christianity, while others are Buddhists or continue to worship ancestral and territorial spirits.

In pre-colonial times, there were numerous kingdoms in the territory now known as Burma. Burman kings were periodically able to build empires stretching across much of modern-day Burma, but at other times, Mon and Arakanese rulers presided over flourishing kingdoms of their own in what is now lower Burma. The size of the kingdoms fluctuated dramatically, depending on the number of tributary relations kings could establish and maintain. When kings were weak, appointed princes, pretenders and tributaries often revolted and sought the throne for themselves or looked for alliances with other rising powers.

One of the primary strategic concerns for rulers throughout mainland South-East Asia was acquiring more manpower to till the land, expand the army, and build temples, palaces and irrigation works.[1] In many war campaigns, the victorious army returned not only with loot but also with thousands of captives who were compelled to join the local workforce.[2] As a result, there was a tremendous mixing of people, particularly around the capitals.

Unlike neighbouring India, Burma never had a fixed class structure. Social and political relationships were, however, ordered by status considerations. Older people were considered higher in status to younger people, monks to lay people, and kings' appointees to commoners. In each case, the senior person in the relationship expected to be heeded by the junior person. Much of political life operated according to a patron–client model with inferiors providing goods and services to superiors in return for protection.

Rulers of lowland kingdoms often claimed suzerainty over surrounding mountainous regions, and in some cases patron–client relationships were established, with local chiefs and princes sending tribute to the kings.

But kings typically exerted little effort in trying to bring these sparsely inhabited areas under their control. Some mountainous areas were seen as buffer zones between lowland kingdoms and were generally traversed only in times of war.[3]

Burmese kingdoms were characterized by great social mobility, permitting people of ability to move from humble origins to high positions without much difficulty. Downward mobility was also common, however, because there was no permanent bureaucracy. The power of kings was absolute, and they could remove or even execute their officials at any time, for the slightest offence.[4] Upon the death or dethronement of a king, his officials often lost their jobs too. In such a fluid political environment, elites at every level watched carefully for the emergence of rivals who could threaten their precarious control.

Resulting feelings of fear, jealousy and suspicion come across vividly in the legends of the thirty-seven *nats*, spirits who were propitiated in the pre-colonial period and continue to be cultivated by many Burmese today. Most of the *nats* were talented individuals who were killed by kings because they or one of their relatives had slighted the king or appeared to be a potential threat. After becoming *nats*, they were understood to be powerful but capricious beings who could influence human affairs.

To give just one example, the legend of the Mahagiri (King of the Mountain) spirit claims he was originally a handsome and strong blacksmith with a growing reputation for his might. The king worried that the blacksmith might eventually try to usurp the throne, so he devised a plan to get rid of him. The king married the blacksmith's sister, and after some time asked the blacksmith to come to the palace so that he could confer an official title on him. The poor blacksmith arrived suspecting nothing, and was immediately hurled into a fire and burned to death. Upon hearing his anguished cries, his sister was overcome with grief, threw herself in the flames and died too. The brother and sister spirits were so angry at the king's betrayal that they killed anyone who came near the tree in which they had taken up residence. The king had the tree cut down and discarded in the river. The trunk floated downstream to the territory of another king, who decided to give the spirits a proper home. He built them a shrine on Mount Popa and had images of the pair carved, covered in gold and attired in courtly robes.[5]

Mount Popa is an old volcano which juts straight out of the plains behind the ancient capital of Pagan, and the two *nats* became known as the protector spirits for Pagan and all who came to worship them. Eventually, the Mahagiri *nat* became the household guardian spirit, with many rural Burmese even today presenting coconut offerings for him in their homes.

The cultivation of the *nats*, which represented separate and uncontrollable sources of power, marked a symbolic challenge to the kings, who were trying to unify power under their own rule. Burma's first empire-building king, Anawrahta, went so far as to chain up a set of the thirty-seven *nat* images in a cave to signify that their power had been contained. Beginning with Anawrahta, Burmese kings promoted Theravada Buddhism, which emphasized the need for each individual to focus on his or her own spiritual path in order to achieve a higher rebirth and, eventually, freedom from the cycle of birth and death altogether. Kings served as the patrons of the Buddhist religion, supporting the Buddhist clergy and commissioning the construction of pagodas and monasteries.

Although Burman kings ultimately depended on the threat of force to maintain their rule, they were still believed to have obtained such high positions because of meritorious deeds in their past lives. Moreover, through their support of the monkhood and pagoda-building projects, they were seen as providing spiritual benefits to their subjects.

Burman kings often waged war in the name of Buddhism, and Anawrahta invaded the Mon kingdom in lower Burma in 1057 with the justification that the Mon king had refused to give him a copy of the Theravada Buddhist scriptures. After sacking the Mon capital, he moved large numbers of Mon scholars and monks back to his capital in Pagan to disseminate Theravada Buddhist teaching and culture. The Burmese script and Burmese literature were subsequently developed from Mon, which had its origins in the Pali and Sanskrit languages of India. As Theravada Buddhism spread throughout the plains, monks began teaching boys in the villages to read and write so they could deepen their knowledge of Buddhist teachings. As a result, literacy in pre-colonial Burma was widespread.

Like the predominantly Buddhist Mons and Arakanese, Burmans later associated the rule of their kings with the glorification of the Buddhist faith. After the British conquered Burma, some of the most prominent resisters were monks, who felt that their religion was being slighted.

British rule

British merchants first entered Burmese waters in the 1600s, and they soon began to exchange weapons in return for trading concessions. In 1824, the British seized the Tenasserim and Arakan regions (now south-eastern and south-western Burma), after Burman forces entered British-controlled territory in pursuit of fleeing political opponents. The British went on to annex lower Burma in 1852–53 and central and northern Burma in 1885–86, in part to counterbalance growing French influence in the region.[6]

The British originally ruled Burma as an appendage of India, but they also brought with them Western notions of states as fixed and bounded, and they quickly set about delineating their territory. Parts of the mountainous 'frontier areas', which had never been under any lowland kingdom's direct rule, were mapped into Burma and many hill populations ended up split between Burma and neighbouring countries.[7] This was of little concern to the colonial officials, who relied on existing princes, chiefs and headmen to collect taxes, but otherwise rarely interfered in local affairs. In the plains, however, the British ruled directly, banishing the king and his immediate family to exile in India.

In the mountainous areas, after initial resistance to British rule had been quelled, acceptance of colonial government was surprisingly widespread. In part, this was because the British froze local rulers' power, rather than eliminating them. While most Burmans bitterly resented colonial domination, some Karens and other upland minorities considered the period of British rule as a golden age, because lowland armies no longer came through on war campaigns against neighbouring realms.[8] Moreover, the colonial regime allowed missionaries to establish schools and hospitals throughout the country, including in the hill areas, providing hill peoples with much-appreciated access to education and healthcare. Many Karens, Karennis, Kachins and Chins converted to Christianity.[9] The British also encouraged ethnic minorities to join the colonial defence force, which was organized into ethnic-based battalions, while limiting and later dismissing ethnic Burman troops.[10] From the British perspective, by keeping the peoples in the hills divided from the people in the plains, it was easier to maintain control.

The British were able to generate substantial revenue from Burma's rich agricultural lands and natural resources. Besides exporting great quantities of rice, the colonial government and the British East India Company focused their energies on extractive industries such as teak, petroleum, tin and gems. To move these goods, they established a network of roads, railroads and river transport. Eager for more manpower, they encouraged the immigration of Chinese and Indians, particularly men. Indian peasants flocked to newly opened cultivation areas in lower Burma, while Indian clerks were brought in to staff the civil service and to serve in the defence force. Many Indians and Chinese also created niches for themselves in the commercial sector, transporting goods and setting up their own shops and businesses.

In the plains, the British government introduced a civil service and legal codes so that administration and justice would operate efficiently and uniformly. Although determined to maintain law and order so business could flourish, the British also believed that the new system offered the Burmese an improvement over what they saw as the arbitrary exercise of power by kings and their officials in the past. Nevertheless, most Burmans were not happy to be under foreign rule, and the colonial government faced opposition from several quarters. During the first years of British occupation, guerrilla forces sprang up throughout the countryside to attack British troops and their garrisons. Even after the rural revolts had been quelled, resentment simmered.

Monks and lay people were particularly incensed by what they perceived as British disrespect towards Buddhism. The British refused to take off their shoes in monasteries, as was required by local custom. Many Burmese were also upset that the colonial administration would not instal a new religious patron to replace the banished king. In 1906, the Young Men's Buddhist Association, modelled on the Young Men's Christian Association (YMCA), was formed to address religious and social issues. In 1917, the more political General Council of Burmese Associations (GCBA) was established. This association set up chapters around the country and provided gathering places for monks, intellectuals and others committed to nationalist causes.

U Ottama and U Wisara, two monks who had travelled abroad, took up politics to promote the protection of Buddhism. The colonial government arrested them for making seditious speeches against the British, but the arrests served only to increase their support. To protest against the colonial government's regulation forbidding the wearing of monks' robes in prison, U Wisara engaged in a hunger strike, which lasted 166 days, until his death.[11] This ultimate sacrifice profoundly moved many Burmese who had not concerned themselves with politics before.

Resistance to the British in the early days tended to look to the past for inspiration, recalling the days when Burmese kings had promoted Buddhism for the benefit of all. As students began to return from studies in the West, however, they brought back new ideas about representative government and democratic practices. Lending libraries opened with wide assortments of books. Those with a thirst for knowledge could plunge into Western philosophy, history and economics. Over time, Burmese demands shifted from seeking the restoration of the monarchy to calling for the establishment of an independent Burmese state with a modern form of government.

University and high-school students played an instrumental role in developing a new political consciousness, which combined a commitment to Buddhism with a desire for independence and a progressive form of government. In 1920, students organized a strike when the colonial government proposed to establish Rangoon University, but limit entrance to an elite few who would be trained as bureaucrats for the colonial regime. The students demanded wider access and a more comprehensive curriculum. On 5 December 1920, they gathered at the symbolic centre of Rangoon, the Shwedagon Pagoda, where relics of the Buddha were believed to be enshrined. Refusing to return to school until their demands were met, they camped out at the pagoda and set up their own classes. Finally, the administration relented, but the strike served as the impetus for the development of National Schools, Burmese-run institutions which were independent of the British educational system.

Resentment about being treated as second-class citizens in their own country led a group of students to begin calling themselves *thakin*, or 'master', to emphasize that Burmese were the rightful rulers of their country. The *thakin* movement, which also encouraged wearing traditional homespun clothing rather than Western apparel, was formalized through the establishment of the Dobama Asiayone, or 'We Burmans Association', in the early 1930s. As local chapters formed throughout the country, they became hubs of political activity.[12]

In 1936, student demonstrations broke out again after two university students, both of whom later became prominent political figures, were expelled. Nu, the head of the student union, publicly called for an overhaul of the university's teaching staff and curriculum. Aung San, the editor of the student magazine, refused to divulge the identity of the author of an article entitled 'Hellhound at large', which defamed one of the university administrators. Demanding their reinstatement, fellow students refused to return to classes and again headed to the Shwedagon Pagoda. The strike continued for several months and spread to colleges and high schools in other parts of the country.

In 1938, university student union members and Dobama Asiayone chapters joined with industrial workers to organize a march from the oilfields in central Burma to the capital in Rangoon. Such strikes, boycotts and demonstrations reflected the growing organizational strength of the Burmese nationalists. The newspapers, magazines and independent associations which emerged helped to spread their message.

Peasants also took action after the worldwide depression hit Burma in 1929. Burmese farmers suffered tremendously as rice prices dropped and taxes became harder to pay. Many lost their land, in some cases to Indian moneylenders. A charismatic former monk named Saya San spearheaded a mass revolt against British rule which lasted from 1930 to 1932. Thousands of armed peasants attacked colonial offices throughout rural Burma. The British brutally repressed the rebellion and publicly displayed the severed heads of some of their captives. Saya San was captured and hanged, while many more peasants died in battle, some because they had believed their magical tattoos and charms would make them invulnerable to bullets. Although the revolt was unsuccessful, Saya San and his followers' audacity further stimulated nationalist feelings.

Nationalist passions were also aroused because of the way in which the British had privileged foreigners over the indigenous population. Many Indians and Chinese were prospering through their association with the British, often at the expense of the Burmese. In addition, some Burmese were upset that Burmese women were marrying foreign men or becoming their mistresses. Burmese anger and resentment periodically exploded in the form of anti-Indian and anti-Chinese riots.[13]

The British introduced new ethnic tensions to Burma, and through their exploitative economic practices turned many against capitalism. The British did eventually introduce limited representative government, however, permitting elected politicians to participate in governance. In 1923, the British handed over some minor decision-making powers to an elected domestic assembly, with the provision that the British governor could veto any decision he did not like. Burmese politicians heatedly debated whether there was any point in participating in such an administration. Conflicts also arose over the reservation of a number of the domestic assembly seats for British commercial interests, Indians and Karens living in the plains. Later, when the issue of separating Burma from India came up, some Burmese opposed it, fearing that the Burmese would be granted fewer political rights than the Indians. Nevertheless, the two countries were separated in 1937, and the British put into effect a new constitution which provided for an elected House of Representatives and an Upper House, half of whose members were elected. Although a number of Burmese politicians enthusiastically contested the elections, the British government's continued refusal to grant full self-government infuriated many others.

By the late 1930s, young urban nationalists were beginning to look to Asian powers for assistance in establishing an armed resistance movement. In early 1941, student leader Aung San and twenty-nine colleagues secretly left the country. Later calling themselves the Thirty Comrades, they were given military training by the Japanese army. In January 1942, they crossed from western Thailand into Burma with Japanese troops to free the country from British rule. The British and local forces under British control unsuccessfully fought the Japanese advance into the plains and finally had to make a hasty retreat to India.

Although many Burmese initially viewed the Japanese as their liberators, the Japanese ruled Burma like a conquered territory and their military police terrorized the local population. Aung San, by then a general, and other nationalists became increasingly disillusioned. On 27 March 1945, they began a coordinated resistance movement in cooperation with Allied troops, who marched back into northern Burma from India. Burmese from many different political backgrounds joined together under the Anti-Fascist People's Freedom League (AFPFL) to help drive the Japanese out. Once the war was over, the British tried to reinstate colonial rule. But the Burmese nationalists were insistent on independence and organized widespread strikes to make their point. With limited troops available to compel submission, the British began to negotiate with the Burmese nationalists and in January 1947 signed an agreement promising independence within a year.

British colonial rule ended with a mixed legacy for Burma. The transportation infrastructure – in the form of roads, railways and steamships for inland waterways – had been greatly extended, but much of it had been destroyed during the war. A professional civil service had been created and the idea of representative government introduced. The British encouragement of Indian and Chinese immigration, however, and the use of ethnic minorities in the colonial army and police forces, engendered new forms of ethnic tension. Because the British had governed the frontier areas separately from the plains, the peoples in the hills felt little connection to Ministerial Burma, while many Burman leaders were dismissive of the hill people's concerns and interests.

Independence

Before the British government handed over power, it insisted that the political status of the peoples in the frontier areas be resolved. Burman politicians wanted the frontier areas to join the new union of Burma, but not all ethnic leaders were eager to do so. During the Second World War, some of the ethnic nationalities, such as the Kachins and the Karens, had fought with the British against the Japanese. After the British had fled,

16

there were incidences of Burman soldiers massacring Karen villagers, and Karens retaliating by killing Burmans. By the end of the war, the Burmans had shifted their support to the Allies, but animosity remained between Burmans and Karens in particular. Moreover, some ethnic leaders had hoped that the British would support their demands for independent statehood.

The one person who seemed to have the vision and diplomatic skills to resolve this problem was General Aung San. The most widely respected Burmese nationalist leader at the time, General Aung San reached out to non-Burmans. He made trips to the hill areas to meet with ethnic leaders, and organized a multi-ethnic conference at the Shan town of Panglong to come up with a political structure which both Burmans and the ethnic nationalities in the frontier areas could accept. Although the Karens attended only as observers and several other minorities were not invited, Kachin, Shan and Chin representatives participated. The concept of a federal union was agreed upon, and ethnic states were to be created with autonomy over their internal affairs.

Burmese leaders were worried that the British would renege on their promise to grant independence, so the constitution for the new union was hurriedly written by an elected constituent assembly dominated by the AFPFL under General Aung San. The constitution stipulated that the new Union of Burma would be ruled by a democratically elected parliament and prime minister. The ethnic states would have their own state councils, whose members would also serve in the union government's parliament, and the head of each state would automatically be a member of the union government's cabinet.

Originally, four ethnic states were to be created. The Karenni and Shan states were accorded the right to secede after ten years if they were not happy with their status in the union.[14] The Kachin State was not allowed to secede because it consisted partly of territory that had been under Burman control in the past. The Karen State was to be established but, at the time of drafting the constitution, there were still serious disagreements over its boundaries. Much of the Karen population was scattered across lower Burma, but Burman leaders would not agree to incorporate these areas, which also contained significant Burman and other populations, into Karen State. The Chins did not ask for a state, and the Mons and Arakanese were not offered states. A provision was included, however, for the possible formation of new states in the future.[15] The states had little real autonomy in practice, in part because they depended on financial support from the central government.[16]

Within most of the ethnic groups, there were people who were willing to join the new union as well as people who were adamantly opposed to it. Thus, as the constitution drafting took place, groups of Karens, Karennis, Mons, Buddhist Arakanese and Muslims in Arakan territory began preparing for armed struggle, while the leading Burmese politicians looked for more moderate ethnic representatives with whom they could forge agreements. The failure to resolve adequately the ethnic nationalities' demands through the constitutional drafting process set the conditions for outbreaks of violence later.

Had General Aung San lived, perhaps Burma's history would have been different. On 19 July 1947, U Saw, an ambitious senior politician, had his gunmen assassinate the thirty-two-year-old general and most of his cabinet. Apparently expecting the British to ask him to form a new government, U Saw was instead immediately arrested and executed the following year. Whether other individuals or organizations were also involved in the plot remains a mystery.[17]

Despite the loss of some of its foremost leaders, Burma became independent on 4 January 1948, at 4.20 a.m. This early hour was selected by Burmese astrologers as the most propitious for the country's new beginning. The AFPFL took power with the devoutly Buddhist statesman U Nu as the country's first prime minister.

The decade from 1948 to 1958 was Burma's first experiment with full democracy. Citizens were able to elect their own representatives, and policies were widely debated in the parliament as well as in independent newspapers and tea shops. People could speak freely, and hopes were high that Burma would prosper. Nevertheless, Burma's new political leaders faced enormous problems. There were not enough trained Burmese professionals, because most government posts had been held by foreigners. Many Indian civil servants had fled during the Second World War, afraid of what the Burmans might do to them once the British were gone. The country was still recovering from the massive destruction and displacement caused during the war, guns were readily available, and banditry was wreaking havoc in much of the countryside.[18]

Of even greater concern, several groups sought to bypass the electoral process and wrest power by force, challenging the stability of the new government. The Communist Party, originally a member of the AFPFL, split into two factions and both went underground. The Red Flag branch had decided to take up arms even before independence, and the much larger White Flag branch followed suit in March 1948. Determined to institute a communist state through an armed revolution, both groups relocated to jungle strongholds and sought to mobilize local populations around issues of land reform. The armed People's Volunteer Organization (PVO), which had been set up by General Aung San for Second World War veterans, also turned into an insurgent group.

Meanwhile, on 31 January 1949, Karen forces turned on the struggling government. Karen and Burman leaders had been unable to agree on the boundaries of a new Karen State and communal tensions had been growing, leading many Karens in the Burma Army to mutiny and join local Karen defence forces in an armed rebellion. At one point in 1949, the central government controlled little more than the capital city of Rangoon. General Ne Win, however, who replaced a Karen as commander-in-chief of the army, led government troops in slowly pushing the various anti-government forces away from the towns in the plains. Many of the government troops were actually ethnic minorities who were committed to the new federal union. Local militias, or *tats*, working with the socialist faction of the AFPFL, also helped retake control of some of the districts. By 1952, much of the countryside was back in the government's hands, although it was still too dangerous for trains to run after dark. Passengers had to get off at sunset and could continue their journey only when the sun rose the next morning.

During this period, the Burma Army had to contend with Chinese troops as well. After Mao Zedong took power in 1949, anti-communist Kuomintang troops fled to northern Burma. Hoping to regroup and launch counter-offensives into China, they operated in Burmese territory with the covert support of the United States' military but without the Burmese government's permission. Meanwhile, the Chinese government was printing maps showing large parts of northern Burma as belonging to China, and Mao Zedong's troops were making incursions to chase down the Kuomintang. The government in Rangoon tried to use diplomacy to settle its problems with China, while also sending Burmese troops on operations to root out the Kuomintang in Shan State. The Burmese troops acted like a conquering force, however, mistreating Shan villagers and causing many Shans to question whether joining the union had been the right decision.[19]

In central Burma, the government set about trying to rebuild the economy and introducing development projects. Committed to the idea of a welfare state, the government initiated a mass education programme in the rural areas and made public education free. Land reform programmes redistributed some of the land that had ended up in the hands of foreigners and absentee landlords during the colonial period. Low-interest loans were issued to farmers, and money was allocated for communities to build wells, roads, schools and reading rooms.

Despite the government's good intentions, many of the social welfare programmes had little impact because of problems of implementation. The national leaders saw the need to help communities, but they did not incorporate people at the community level into the design of the programmes. Thus, the projects did not always fit with community needs, and villagers felt little commitment to the programmes. At the same time, some politicians tied the provision of welfare programmes to political allegiance. If local leaders could bring in the vote for a certain politician, he would reward them with government projects.[20]

The concept of a legal opposition was still new and often resisted. The political parties of the day sought to monopolize power and eliminate their opposition altogether. The idea that the opposition could play a constructive role in offering different points of view had no roots in Burma. Opposition in the past had always been understood as insubordination, and politicians in the 1950s found it difficult to negotiate, compromise or work together with political representatives from other factions and parties.

Too often, politicians undermined democratic principles in order to maintain their positions. Political debates in parliament often degenerated into mud-slinging and name-calling, and some politicians even resorted to underhanded techniques to disempower their rivals. Members of the ruling party sometimes accused more left-leaning rivals of being communists and had them imprisoned, although the courts would release them if there was a lack of evidence. Politicians even tried to use student organizations as proxies in their struggles against rival political parties. In the 1950s, there were two university student unions: the Democratic Students' Organization, which strongly supported the ruling party, and the Students' United Front, which was more leftist-leaning and had some associations with communists. The activities of university students became absurdly politicized, with even a demand for the extension of a university holiday becoming a 'leftist–rightist' issue.

Meanwhile, in towns and rural areas, private armies in the pay of politicians were sometimes used to intimidate and even murder opposition party members and their supporters. Villagers found that the best way to survive the violence and political rivalries was to stay as neutral as possible, and to demonstrate political allegiance only to the party that was clearly going to win.

Nevertheless, U Nu's government managed the country's foreign relations wisely. Given Burma's geographical position between two powerful neighbours, India and China, the government adopted a neutralist foreign policy. Burma was outward-looking in its trade policies and participated actively in international affairs.[21]

At the same time, U Nu often intertwined his deeply Burmese religious and cultural sensibilities with the country's politics. He devoted much energy to promoting Buddhism through sponsoring meditation programmes for lay people and organizing a Buddhist synod, which brought together monks from all over Burma and other Buddhist countries. Although the state was officially secular, U Nu was establishing himself as the patron of Buddhism in much the same way that Burmese kings had in the past.

U Nu's willingness to place religious concerns above ongoing political crises irritated more educated, urban politicians and intellectuals but did not bother less worldly villagers. At one point, U Nu took a forty-five-day leave of absence from his job as prime minister to meditate at Mount Popa, the home of the Mahagiri *nat* discussed earlier. Despite the fact that the country was facing urgent problems, villagers in upper Burma reportedly supported his decision. Because U Nu's horoscope indicated that this period was inauspicious for him, the villagers believed U Nu was doing the country a favour by temporarily removing himself from national politics.[22]

Thus, although Burma was nominally a democracy, earlier authoritarian traditions partly informed the way that politics operated in post-independence Burma. The establishment of a freer society had permitted the proliferation of newspapers, independent associations and political parties. Still, a winner-takes-all mentality remained the norm, and frequent instances of political violence and abuse of power hampered the development of a democratic culture.

Beginnings of militarization

Most Burmese citizens in the 1950s viewed the Burmese armed forces, or the *tatmadaw*, with respect. Along with the AFPFL, the *tatmadaw* was credited with playing a significant role in bringing about independence and in rescuing the country from dismemberment by insurgent forces. The Burmese population in the lowlands was eager to see peace restored in their towns and villages, and most were relieved when the various forces were pushed back by the *tatmadaw*.

The *tatmadaw* had begun as a small, disorganized army, but it was quickly professionalized through intensive battle experience and institutional development initiated by military men who had trained at military academies abroad. To guarantee a degree of financial independence, the military set up its own profit-making corporation. The corporation originally ran shops selling bulk goods, but it soon expanded into the import–export business and became a major player in the domestic economy.[23] Boosted by its military and economic successes, the *tatmadaw* increasingly identified itself as playing an essential role in the country's internal affairs.

Meanwhile, as 1958 approached, hereditary Shan *sawbwas*, or princes, and young Shan leaders began debating the status of the Shan states in public meetings. According to the 1947 constitution, the Shan *sawbwas* could continue to govern their territories as principalities and could serve in one of the two houses in the state council, with elected representatives serving in the other. They also had the right to leave the union in 1958 if political integration wasn't working out. The central government wanted Shan State to stay in the union, but among the Shans feelings were mixed. Some princes close to the government supported the union, while a number of Shan university students and others favoured independence. Many Karennis felt the same. This concerned *tatmadaw* leaders, who did not want any of the ethnic states to secede.

At the same time, some military officers were openly voicing discontent with parliamentary rule. They disliked the government's willingness to rehabilitate insurgent left-wing politicians and resented civilian interference in their affairs. They were also disturbed by the disorderliness of the parliamentary system, in which politicians were constantly attacking each other and seemingly doing little to resolve the country's problems. The AFPFL continued to dominate the parliament, but it split into two antagonistic groups, the Clean and the Stable AFPFL, in April 1958. Each group tried to outmanoeuvre the other by wooing army and militia leaders and ethnic representatives in the government. Rumours spread that a group of military officers were plotting a coup.

In September 1958, General Ne Win and two other senior officers, Maung Maung and Aung Gyi, took power. Prime Minister U Nu tried to limit the damage to the constitutional government by inviting General Ne Win to form a caretaker government. U Nu announced that the handover had been voluntary, but it became clear later that he had had little choice in the matter.[24] The public did not initially oppose the caretaker government, because the elected parliament was in such disarray. Rangoon was filled with squatters who had fled the dangers of life outside the capital. Huts lined many of the city's thoroughfares and covered vacant lots, and the drains were like open latrines. If a military government could do a bit to clean up the cities and restore order, it was welcome.

Under the caretaker government, known in Burmese as the *Bogyoke* (General's) government, General Ne Win achieved several successes. He concluded a significant border demarcation agreement with China which led to better relations between the two governments. He also convinced the Shan and Karenni hereditary leaders to give up their powers and allow for the election of all political representatives in their states. Most importantly to those in the cities, he kept food prices low and moved the squatter communities to newly established satellite towns.[25]

Thoughtful individuals, however, viewed the government's handling of the squatters with concern. The squatters were given only twelve to twenty-four hours' notice before military trucks picked them up, and many were unable to bring all their things with them. The new sites were not adequately prepared as residential areas, and the new residents had to make do as best they could. In this and other projects, the army showed little respect for the people it was supposedly helping.

The caretaker government was sensitive to criticism and imprisoned numerous journalists for daring to critique its actions. And much to civil servants' annoyance, battlefield commanders were brought in to replace or work alongside bureaucrats. After the general's government extended its term twice beyond the original six-month period, pressure increased for an election to restore democracy.

General Ne Win complied, and the election date was set for February 1960. Nevertheless, some military leaders hoped to influence the outcome, and some Stable AFPFL politicians flaunted their connections with high-ranking officers, thinking this would win them the support of the people. But they miscalculated, for the voters wanted the military to return to barracks and were annoyed by its attempts to manipulate the election. At the same time, many Burmese Buddhist voters were drawn by U Nu's pledge to make Buddhism the state religion. They gave a landslide victory to his 'Clean' faction of the AFPFL, which had been reorganized as the *Pyidaungsu*, or Union, Party.

Among the ethnic nationalities, however, discontent with U Nu and other senior Burmese politicians was growing. Despite their promises, the parliamentary governments of the 1950s had done very little to develop the minority regions. Moreover, the central government had relinquished few powers to the ethnic states, and the *tatmadaw*'s presence in areas of insurgency had often resulted in the suspension of the rule of law. Most upsetting to Christian minorities, U Nu pushed a law through parliament making Buddhism the state religion. In doing so, he went against General Aung San's insistence on keeping the state secular. With majority rule, it seemed that the ethnic minorities could do little to stop measures supported by the far more numerous Burman representatives. Frustrated Kachins began talking about armed resistance.

In the meantime, U Nu continued to meet with ethnic leaders to discuss their demands. He offered amnesties to ethnic fighters who surrendered, but he was finding it difficult to work out a settlement with the Shans and Karennis, who were considering seceding. Most Burman politicians continued to oppose increased political autonomy for the ethnic minorities. As Dr Ba Maw, a Burman who served as prime minister during the Japanese occupation, put it: 'The Burmese as a rule show a big-race mentality in their dealings with the smaller native races; they find it hard to forget their long historical domination over those races.'[26] Even though some of the ethnic areas had never been under Burman domination, most Burmans still very much wanted the minority areas to remain part of modern Burma.

By 1961, Shan and Kachin nationalists were organizing resistance armies along the lines of the Karen. They increasingly felt that negotiating with the government was pointless. Still, older and more prominent minority leaders remained committed to working out a solution with the elected government. It was on 2 March 1962, during a high-level seminar on federal issues attended by Prime Minister U Nu and senior Shan representatives, that General Ne Win again seized power. This time, U Nu, members of his government and many Shan leaders were arrested.

General Ne Win's colleague, Brigadier Aung Gyi, justified the coup by insisting that the union was in danger of disintegrating. A month after the coup, General Ne Win declared that parliamentary democracy, as practised so far, had not worked. The new military government, it was implied, could manage the country's affairs more effectively.

Even though most people had voted against the military-backed Stable AFPFL in 1960, two years later they were willing to give the military another chance. In part, people were disappointed with how democratic rule had functioned, and there was hope that General Ne Win would act in the nation's best interest. Others were cynical about government in general. Burmese have traditionally identified the government as one of the five enemies, the others being fire, water (floods and storms), thieves and malevolent people. Ordinary people had never had much control over the political process and felt it was best just to get on with life regardless of who was in power.

The major political parties stayed quiet, but some student groups did make statements against the coup. Within the military itself, particularly among those who had worked with the British before independence, there was also some opposition. One man who was a high-ranking naval officer at the time later said: 'Some of us worried that now Ne Win was here to stay. We did get from the British the idea of the separation of politics and the military.' Bo Let Ya, a popular member of the Thirty Comrades, sent out word that all former military comrades should state as a group that the military should not stay in power. He was arrested.

General Ne Win had already eliminated many of his rivals within the military the year before. Telling U Nu that they had been involved in election irregularities in 1960, he had eleven senior officers expelled from the army and others transferred to inactive posts. Although General Ne Win had started life with little promise, having dropped out of university and worked as a postal clerk, he had come a long way. He was admired for being a man of action and, as one of the Thirty Comrades, he was viewed as untouchable. He had expanded the army from a few thousand men in 1948 to 100,000 in 1962, and with his close rivals removed, the lower ranks were willing to follow him obediently, whether out of respect or fear.

In retrospect, one can ask how things might have been different if General Aung San had lived. Perhaps democratic norms would have gradually developed, and the ethnic groups' political demands would have been resolved at the negotiating table. But growing political tensions and a legacy of authoritarianism had inhibited the development of a stable, open society. Having rid themselves of the British, the Burmans had found a renewed pride in their numerical dominance and their heritage as a conquering race, and this hindered their ability to understand and resolve the ethnic nationalities' demands. Because of the civil war, the military often ignored due process in areas where it operated, and politicians were able to use pocket armies not only to go after bandits but also to intimidate their opposition. Although the government did seek to develop the country, there was little substantive dialogue between politicians and the people in their constituencies, and too many politicians were consumed with their own personal interests. As a result, democracy was only superficially rooted in Burma, and the military was able to take over with little resistance.

2 | The Ne Win years, 1962–88

One Energy Minister said, 'To spare the wood, use charcoal.' But you
see charcoal is made from wood. Those kind of people were governing.
(U Po Khin)

The Revolutionary Council, 1962–74

After the 1962 coup, General Ne Win and his Revolutionary Council
immediately set about imposing order, and the universities were one of
the first targets. The military regime announced stricter regulations for
university students, one particularly irksome rule being that dormitories
were locked at 8 p.m. to prevent students from going out to visit friends
or chat in tea shops. Angry students broke through the locked doors to
shout in protest for three successive nights. As the protests continued,
the students' union took over the leadership.

On the afternoon of 7 July, students held a mass meeting in the
assembly hall of the Rangoon University student union building. Then,
they went out to demonstrate for about an hour. Just as they were dispersing, riot police stormed the campus and took over the student union.
According to witnesses, a riot began, with the police firing tear-gas and
students throwing stones. Some students also lit fireworks, increasing
the chaos. Students shouted insulting slogans against General Ne Win,
while soldiers entered the campus with their guns ready. When the protest
did not immediately break up, they began shooting. Over one hundred
students were apparently killed, although the government admitted to
only fifteen deaths.[1] In the early hours of the next morning, the military
blew up the student union building, the centre of student activism since
colonial days.

While General Ne Win succeeded in stopping the student protests,
his recourse to such extreme measures provoked bitterness against the
regime. U Pyone Cho, a university student at the time, recalled:

> You didn't find a lot of students that were really political at that stage.
> But because of the killing and all, that really made students start think-
> ing. And from then on, every month there would be a book of poems.
> And every 7th [July], people would wear black [in commemoration of the
> killings]. I won't say all the students, but quite a few.

The university was closed for four months, and as students travelled back to their home towns, they brought with them news of what had happened. The event was kept alive through the memorial song 'Old Union', set to the tune of a popular song, 'Old City of Pagan'. But the crackdown on students was just a taste of what was to come.

Through his Revolutionary Council, General Ne Win sought to remake Burmese politics and society. Land and wealth were to be redistributed, foreigners stripped of their assets, and self-serving politicians and capitalists replaced with loyal army men dedicated to serving the nation. Approximately two thousand civilian members of the country's administration lost their jobs to military personnel.[2] Security and administrative councils were also set up at the divisional, township and village levels in central Burma. The ethnic states lost what autonomy they had had, with security and administrative councils established there as well. These new military-guided councils served as the primary structure through which the Revolutionary Council interacted with society.

The Revolutionary Council instituted what it called 'the Burmese Way to Socialism', a programme that was originally supported by some intellectuals and politicians who felt that the AFPFL's watered-down socialist policies had not gone far enough. For them, capitalism was linked with foreign exploitation, and they supported the regime's decision to seal the country off from foreign investment. Between 1963 and 1965, all banks, industries and large shops were nationalized. Most of the businesses were run by Indians and Chinese; by taking state control, the government intended to return the profits to indigenous Burmese. In March 1964, the Revolutionary Council demonetized 50-kyat and 100-kyat notes, also with the intention of removing wealth from foreign hands. As a result, hundreds of thousands of Indian and Chinese business people lost everything and left the country. Those businesses that did not collapse came under state ownership.

Military men were brought in to run the businesses, but with little education or relevant experience, they found it difficult to handle their new jobs. In cases where skilled civilians remained on staff, the new bosses often felt threatened by them. With no other opportunities available, many experienced professionals and bright young people emigrated, starting the brain drain which has continued ever since. The Revolutionary Council appeared to be unconcerned by the departure of so many of its most talented people, but the effect on industry was devastating. Burma had been ahead of both Malaysia and Thailand in industrial production in the 1950s, but declined steadily from 1964 onwards.

Agricultural production was also profoundly affected. While land reform programmes carried through by the regime gave agricultural plots
to many landless farmers, farmers were told that they had to sell their
rice to the government, at below market prices. Frustrated with the new
system, some farmers put less effort into their cultivation while others
hoarded as much rice as possible and sold or bartered it surreptitiously
on the black market. Because rice exports were one of Burma's primary
sources of foreign exchange, the dramatic fall in rice exports, from 1.8
million tons in 1963 to 0.3 million tons in 1968, made it impossible for
the government to pay for necessary imports.[3] Both industrial and agricultural production suffered. The regime responded not by liberalizing
the sale of rice but by cutting imports, including machinery and spare
parts. This further hindered agricultural development.

With the nationalization of shops also came the establishment of
cooperatives, where people could buy their daily necessities at subsidized
prices. At first the shops were well stocked and the government prided
itself on taking care of the people. But soon stocks of even the most
basic goods were insufficient, and waiting in line for rations became a
part of daily life. To make up for the inadequacies of the cooperatives,
a thriving black market emerged, with goods coming from Thailand and
other neighbouring countries.[4]

In what at first seemed a positive development, the military regime
announced that it would hold peace talks in Rangoon for all groups willing to participate. Safe passage to and from the talks was guaranteed. In
1963, many representatives of armed ethnic groups as well as communist
leaders came to Rangoon, but the regime took a hard line with all of
them. The communists were told to give up their armed struggle, and
the regime refused to consider various ethnic nationalist demands for
increased autonomy. When the talks broke down in November, students
and others staged demonstrations. The universities were closed, and a
number of students were arrested and sent to a penal colony on Coco
Island.[5] When the universities reopened a year later, a new system was
introduced. One of the most significant changes was that teachers were
made more responsible for the conduct of the students. The regime
hoped to use the teachers as their eyes and ears to reduce the likelihood
of more protests.

In the meantime, independent associations also started to come under
pressure. Even library clubs, such as Pyone Cho's in Rangoon, were forced
to shut down. Pyone Cho and his university friends had established their
library club in Pyone Cho's father's garage on 141st Street shortly before

the coup. The club had begun by having its members sweep the street and clear the drains every weekend. Members took turns volunteering for night shifts to watch out for fire, a frequent problem in those days. When people in the neighbourhood saw that the club was working for the good of the community, they began giving monthly contributions. The club boasted over one hundred members and rented out all kinds of books, including the anti-government poetry books and other literature written in commemoration of the 7 July killings. The club also staged citywide essay-writing competitions, sending announcements to all the schools and publicizing the winning essays in newspapers.

With police permission, the club held public lectures on big stages in the streets. People from all over Rangoon would come to listen. The club was so popular that many debate teams and writers' clubs wanted to join, so they were taken on as affiliate members. Gradually, though, it became more difficult to acquire permits for public talks. When the library club committee decided to hold a debate between several famous writers at Gandhi Hall, with the provocative title 'Man is worse than a dog', they were originally denied permission by the police. The permit was granted only when a higher-ranking military officer overruled the police chief, thinking the club was planning to attack the deposed prime minister U Nu. Instead, the speakers discussed the dangers of military rule. Not long after, the regime announced that private associations had to register with the government or close down. After a visit from a government official in which they were told their club did not meet the new regulations, Pyone Cho and his friends had to shut the library and stop their activities.

As the Revolutionary Council expanded its control, most independent associations and newspapers were either absorbed by the government or forced out of existence. All publications had to pass through a newly formed censorship board. Private schools were nationalized, and a government-controlled Burmese-language curriculum was imposed throughout the country. Meanwhile most foreign missionaries, scholars and Western foundations were forced to leave and foreigners' access to Burma was tightly restricted.

Independent trade unions were outlawed, and existing political parties were also compelled to disband, with the only legal political party being the government's Burma Socialist Programme Party (BSPP). Originally, membership in the BSPP was restricted to the military and the administration; the regime later expanded membership, however, and established other mass organizations under state control. As time went on, people's avenues for participation in civic life were increasingly limited, although citizens were welcome to join regime-sponsored organizations which were primarily dedicated to maintaining military rule. In these associations, there was little room for personal initiative or creative thought. The regime was looking for passive supporters, not freethinkers. This was the beginning of the constriction of civil society in Burma for many years to come.

Meanwhile, the effects of the government's mismanagement of the economy became clear in 1967 when the scarcity of rice in Rangoon became a severe problem. Civil servants would sign in at their offices in the morning and then leave to spend the day searching for rice in villages outside the city. Although the government's inappropriate procurement and distribution policies were largely to blame for the shortage, people's anger turned against Chinese merchants, who controlled much of the black-market rice trade. Merchants were stockpiling rice, knowing they could sell it for a higher price as the crisis worsened. Some Burmese had also been irritated by the fact that the Chinese embassy was encouraging support for the Cultural Revolution among Sino-Burmese, including the wearing of Mao badges. Riots broke out, and the Chinese embassy and many Chinese-owned shops and homes were attacked. The military regime declared martial law and solved the problem by ordering all the warehouses to be opened and the surplus rice to be distributed. Dissidents have argued that this was an early example of how General Ne Win was able to deflect the people's anger away from the regime and channel it into communal riots.[6]

The military regime sought to demonstrate its commitment to ensuring public safety by announcing sweeps to rid the streets of crime. The police were ordered to round up a certain number of criminals during each sweep, and in order to meet their quotas they often arrested people against whom they had no evidence. The detainees' families were not informed, and victims were usually not tried. The prisoners could only hope that for one reason or another they would eventually be released.

Tint Zaw, a Rangoon University professor who was imprisoned for his connections with student activists and for his refusal to join the regime's Burma Socialist Programme Party, met many such hapless prisoners during his years in prison. He remembered one bizarre case where the wife of a man who was arrested assumed that her husband had gone off with another woman. She put an announcement in the newspaper stating that he was her legal husband and anyone keeping him would be sued. In those days, prisoners were still allowed to read the newspaper, and the man saw the announcement about himself and showed it to the prison officer. An intelligence officer was sent to question him and only then was he released. Tint Zaw himself was never charged for his 'crimes'. When he was arrested he was invited 'to stay for some time' in prison. That 'some time' turned out to be nine years.

Although General Ne Win had hoped to win popular support with his nationalization and land reform programmes, they led to economic disaster. In order to establish a more legitimate administration, he decided to reorganize his government. He and nineteen other senior officers resigned from the military in 1972 and assumed civilian titles. He also announced that the regime planned to draw up a new constitution and institute a one-party system, with elections for a People's Assembly (*pyithu hluttaw*) and local councils. In theory, the one-party system would give people a voice in managing the country's affairs, but that was to prove illusory from the start.

The BSPP era, 1974–88

While the new constitution was being drafted, government authorities announced that citizens were welcome to send in their suggestions. But when several Chins wrote in recommending the adoption of federalism and a multiparty system, they were arrested. Perhaps because the Chins had always been loyal to the government and there were no *tatmadaw* troops in Chin State, the authorities felt they had to act particularly harshly to stifle such demands. As a result, a member of a Chin youth group who signed his name on a letter calling for a federal union spent ten months in solitary confinement, a Chin major in the *tatmadaw* served a two-year prison sentence, and a Chin public health assistant was imprisoned for several months, with his family having no idea what had happened to him.[7] When the public health assistant was released, he was given a letter stating that he would never be permitted to work in Chin State again.

In December 1973 there was a national referendum in which people had to vote for or against the new constitution, which called for a unitary state under one-party rule. It received 90 per cent support with an astounding 95 per cent of eligible voters voting.[8] Were people that delighted with the idea of one-party rule? Did so many ethnic minority voters support a unitary state? Many Burmese say that few understood the new system, but at least it offered the possibility of popular participation. Certainly some people hoped that greater civilian involvement would result in improvements. There were also instances of intimidation and ballot-box tampering, however, which appear to have helped to produce such resoundingly positive results.

Saw Tu, a high-school headmaster and a member of the election commission in Karen State, explained how the results were obtained in the remote area of the country where he worked. Saw Tu was the first from his township in Karen State ever to attend university. After graduating, he came back and taught in a district high school and was later promoted to headmaster. In 1973, he was appointed to the district commission responsible for overseeing the referendum.

He explained that, starting in the mid-1960s, the regime conducted a population survey of the distant hill villages through the cooperative shop in town. All the mountain villagers had to buy their goods at their designated cooperative shop (which carried no coffee, milk or sugar, because the authorities said mountain people didn't need these luxuries). Whenever a villager came to the shop, the clerk asked for the names of all the residents in that person's village. Because the villages were small, with only twenty or thirty families, the villager could easily name everyone. After some time, the authorities were able to obtain almost all the names of the villagers and villages, without ever having to travel there themselves. When the referendum was held, the government was able to use the name lists to their advantage. Everyone eighteen years old and over was supposed to vote in the referendum, but ballot boxes never reached the hill people in Saw Tu's district. Yet when the results came out, he was astounded to see that they had all apparently voted for the constitution.

Saw Tu also spoke of a case in one village where everyone put their votes in the black box, meaning they were against the constitution. Military authorities went to the village and asked the residents, 'Are you for us or against us?' Then they made the villagers vote again. That time, they all put their votes in the white box.

In town, the military authorities could not easily order people to vote again, but they made it clear that there could be consequences for those who dared to vote against the constitution. In Saw Tu's district, how people voted was obvious to the officials on duty because of the way the ballot boxes were arranged. The curtain around the voting area reached only to about knee height and the two boxes were placed far apart. It was not possible to stand next to the box for 'yes' votes and reach the box for 'no' votes. Saw Tu remembered that some townspeople who voted against the constitution were put under watch, but the clerks were able to protect some 'no' voters by pretending not to know who they were. The clerks were reluctant to turn in their friends, particularly since many of them were not all that hopeful about the new constitution themselves.

Bertil Lintner reported a similar occurrence in Shan State, where some of the student vote-counters took it upon themselves to move ballots from the 'no' box to the 'yes' box, because they didn't want anybody to get in trouble.[9]

With the development of a one-party system, General Ne Win sought to use the BSPP to cement the allegiance of civil servants and others to his military-backed government. In the 1970s, party membership was open to all, and not joining carried negative consequences. Party members took over many of the administrative posts at all levels of government, and civil servants were expected to become members.

Saw Tu said he had no interest in joining the party and just wanted to put his energy into teaching. But the officials kept after him, and he finally gave in. He said he was pressured more than most, because the officials hoped that if they could win him over, they could use him to bring in more Karen members. Although he didn't even bother to fill out the entire application form, he was soon presented with his party membership card. Following that, on many ceremonial occasions, such as Independence Day and Union Day, he and other civil servants were ordered to give speeches praising the BSPP and denouncing the Karen National Union (KNU), which had been fighting for autonomy since 1949. Many Karen in his district had sons or relatives who had joined the KNU.

I asked him whether he didn't feel as if he was promoting the BSPP government by making such speeches. He replied that the speeches were meaningless, because everyone knew they had been written by the party. Even if you wrote the speech yourself, he said, you had to give it to the BSPP for editing. Still, I wanted to know, didn't he feel anything when he read those speeches? He replied, 'Actually, internally I didn't feel quite right.' He had been a university student in Rangoon then and had joined his friends at the 7 July demonstration. He had also seen his fellow students shot down. But he felt that he had to go along with the authorities now that he was a headmaster. He explained, 'You had to act in a certain way so that they would trust you. Only then could you work safely for your people.'

Saw Tu travelled to mountain villages, encouraging young Karen to get an education. But the authorities suspected he was trying to link up with the rebels. Finally he did just that. He and his family joined the KNU.

There were civil servants who refused to join the BSPP, but they often suffered as a consequence. Because healthcare was nationalized, all doctors and nurses belonged to the civil service and were expected to become party members. Dr Aye Win, who did not join, talked about having to attend monthly indoctrination sessions for the first two years of his service. But he felt that medicine, not politics, was his business. He knew that if he didn't join, he might not get a promotion or he might get transferred to a remote area, but he decided that wasn't important. His first supervisor didn't mind, but he warned Dr Aye Win, 'It may be hard for you in your next posting.'

His next assignment was at a hospital in a Karen town in a 'brown' area. The military refers to districts where both government and anti-government forces operate as 'brown' areas. 'White' areas are totally under government control and 'black' areas under opposition control. Dr Aye Win remembered that, at first, the BSPP members there thought he was a member and treated him well. But once they found out he wasn't a member, they began pressuring him. They reported that he wasn't doing his job properly and criticized him for treating all patients without asking whether they belonged to an insurgent organization. The local party authorities told him that as a township medical officer, he was expected to be a role model for the community.

One day the BSPP authorities announced that there should be a hospital clean-up with community participation the following Sunday. Dr Aye Win said that was not necessary because the staff were already taking care of the cleaning. But the party members told him that the people should feel that they were helping others. Dr Aye Win asked, 'Why are you forcing people to volunteer? I'll take any real volunteers, but not people who are forced to do this work.' This only exacerbated his problems with the party authorities. Eventually, he had to leave the district.

As much as the BSPP government encouraged people to join the party in most areas of the country, in the predominantly Chin town of Kalaymyo, Chin citizens were often prevented from joining. At that time, there was no anti-government insurgency movement in the area, and relations between the Christian Chins and Buddhist Burmans in Kalaymyo were good, with frequent cases of intermarriage. 'But', said Salai Zal Seng, a Chin church leader living in Kalaymyo, 'the administrative body wanted to split us.' Chin citizens found it difficult to become BSPP members, with the result that less than a quarter of the 900 BSPP members in the township were Chins. The township committee was also dominated by Burmans, with only an occasional Chin member. Frustrated by this, Salai Zal Seng's father, a civil servant, asked the township military commander, Captain Soe Win, why the distribution of power was so uneven. Captain Soe Win replied, 'Do you think that power is given by the sharing method?' Salai

Zal Seng's father insisted that he saw no reason why power couldn't be shared since everyone was living together without any problems. The captain didn't say anything but had Salai Zal Seng's father transferred to a remote district on the Indian border.

In central Burma, many people who became party members also had high ideals and were committed to working for their country, but they found they could do little. Ohn Myint was a third-generation BSPP member who lived in a large town in central Burma. Both his parents and his grandfather were members of the party. He himself attended many of the training courses given by the party's youth organization. But, by the time he was in high school, he realized the BSPP wasn't really working for the people. He recalled, 'My grandpa was one of the leaders of our BSPP unit, and they had to hold meetings every month.' He explained that at first they took the job seriously. They would discuss local problems and write reports for their superiors, but there was never any response, so later they stopped holding meetings, and Ohn Myint helped write the reports for his grandfather. He said: 'I could just copy the old one and change the date.'

The judicial system also offered little hope of a fair hearing. Under the Revolutionary Council, courts were run by a panel of three judges, at least one of whom had to have some legal training. During the BSPP period, the three judges were elected, but had to be party members. The chairman of the three judges was generally a military officer, while the other two judges came 'from the people' and frequently included individuals with little education. From the government's perspective, a lack of education was not a problem. Loyalty and honesty were more important. Good people could be taught what they needed to know, but smart people could be tricky and less reliable.

Daw Mi Mi, a female lawyer during this period, explained that a lawyer would usually be there to act as an adviser to the people's judges, but they generally took their advice from the BSPP township council instead. Besides the political influence of the council, corruption was a constant problem. In non-political cases, rich men could often pay off everyone involved: doctors doing autopsies, police and judges. At a minimum, they could get their sentences reduced, if not thrown out. Sometimes the police took bribes from both sides, and tried to confuse the case by bringing in fake evidence or destroying real evidence. With civil servants' salaries too low to cover monthly living expenses, corrupt practices soon permeated many interactions between the public and the administration.

Although many civil servants did attempt to perform their jobs well, the system favoured those who did not challenge their superiors. Corruption was a far smaller crime than insubordination.

General Ne Win had originally governed with the promise of efficiency and improving national welfare, but things were falling apart. Lower-level officials realized it was safer to report only what their superiors wanted to hear, often masking the severity of problems under their jurisdiction. At the same time, no one wanted to take responsibility for making decisions, for fear of being punished. Thus, civil servants and party functionaries tended to send even small issues up to higher levels, with the result that little effective work was actually carried out.

The increasing presence of military intelligence agents, or MI, who functioned like a secret police in other countries, also dampened people's desire to speak out about problems. Besides plainclothes intelligence agents, there were also informers in neighbourhoods and many work-places. As a result, most people appeared to be obedient even if they didn't have faith in the government's policies.

General Ne Win had originally shunned bringing religion into state affairs, both because of his government's socialist ideology and because he wanted to rein in the influence of the monks. In 1962, monks were ordered to register with the government, a stipulation that was rejected on religious grounds as monks are perceived to be above the realm of worldly affairs. When some monks protested in Mandalay, the demonstration was broken up by troops, who shot several of the protesters.[10] In 1965, the regime organized a *sangha* (monks) conference, which established an official monks' organization, the *Sangha Maha Nayaka*, and began registering all monks. Protesting monks were arrested, and several mon-asteries, where dissent was most fervent, were closed down.

By the late 1960s, however, General Ne Win was beginning to demon-strate a more public interest in Buddhism. While this may have been a reflection of his faith, it was also a way to gain some legitimacy with the majority Burman Buddhist population, for whom religious practice was central to their identity.[11] General Ne Win also began looking to Buddhist merit-making, astrology and sympathetic magic in support of his political ambitions. This was not particularly surprising to most Burmese, who frequently turn to such practices themselves. As much as Buddhism might ask people to recognize that all attachment is suffering, most people are still concerned with their daily affairs; in particular, job security, health and the well-being of loved ones. They are looking for meaning and control over their lives, and by building pagodas and making merit in other ways, they hope to maintain or improve their status.

At the same time, a belief in spirits, astrology and fortune-telling helps people make sense of why they get sick, why they get into trouble, and how to get out of these situations or prevent them altogether. Burmese parents have the astrological charts of their children calculated and written out soon after their birth. These charts indicate the general course of the child's life, but mothers continue to have readings done at significant times for more specific predictions. Astrologers are consulted about the appropriate date for weddings, shop openings and Buddhist ordination ceremonies. People also seek out the services of other types of fortune-tellers, who make their predictions based on palm reading, intuition or other signs. Unlike in the West where fortune-tellers and astrologers almost exclusively emphasize the positive, fortune-tellers in Burma often predict life-threatening dangers, illness and other serious problems. Luckily, they also suggest measures (*yadaya*) that individuals can take to ward off these troubles.

General Ne Win frequently appealed to fortune-tellers for advice on how to prolong his rule. On one occasion, he reportedly shot his image in a mirror so that he himself wouldn't be killed. Similarly, he had the lovely *go go* trees that provided shade along the road to his birthplace near Prome cut down, because the expression *go go that*, 'cut down the *go go* trees', also means to kill yourself. By removing the trees he believed that he could prevent his own political death. Most dramatically, in the mid-1970s he suddenly ordered cars to be driven on the right instead of the left. This was reportedly meant to stop the threat of a political attack from the right. Even today, a number of old cars in Burma sport steering wheels on the wrong side, making driving a precarious experience.

For many people, such actions, no matter how bizarre, suggested that General Ne Win had special powers on his side. This only reinforced a feeling of the futility of resisting. And despite dissatisfaction with many aspects of BSPP rule, some of the regime's propaganda did appeal to Burmese citizens. In particular, the regime was successful in convincing most people that a strong unitary state was necessary and that the ethnic nationalist armies had to be defeated. In the press, the ethnic nationalist armies were portrayed as rapists and murderers, and, having never visited the remote areas themselves, many readers believed the accounts.

Also, General Aung San's name still carried tremendous meaning for Burmese people, and General Ne Win claimed to represent Aung San's legacy. Both members of the Thirty Comrades, they had fought for independence together, and General Ne Win sought to play up this connection. General Ne Win presented his regime as carrying out the socialist policies General Aung San would have wanted to implement, and portrayed the army, founded by General Aung San, as continuing to sacrifice for the people in order to maintain the country's integrity.

At the time, few Burmese could travel outside the country, and foreign journalists could not easily come in. Even tourists could obtain only seven-day visas to Burma. Lacking information about how other countries were developing, most Burmese took military-backed, one-party rule as a given and tried to make the best of their situation. In many cases this meant joining the party or at least trying to benefit from connections to government officials. Becoming a military officer was also enticing, as higher-ranking officers could obtain cars (models assigned by rank) at a time when most people got around by oxcart or bicycle.

Resistance in the cities

Despite the general population's overall passivity, the BSPP regime under General Ne Win did face occasional resistance from monks, students and urban workers. It was generally only the most idealistic and brave members of each of these groups, however, who initiated such activities, for they risked torture and imprisonment if they were caught. Each demonstration started with a specific grievance, and although the protests sometimes widened into calls for the overthrow of Ne Win's government, there was little consensus on what kind of government should replace it.

University students in Rangoon, Mandalay and Moulmein took to the streets on several occasions between 1962 and the late 1970s. Inspired by the role students had played in leading resistance protests against the colonial regime, and also because they were young and generally free of financial responsibilities, they saw themselves as having a moral duty to speak out. Most students were motivated by anger at the injustices they witnessed around them.

Once a demonstration started, the military feared, it could spread quickly. Thus, the military and riot police usually responded immediately to isolate and arrest the protesters. In the 1960s and 1970s, each spate of demonstrations was easily contained but, not long after, another crop of students volunteered to put themselves at risk again.

In 1969, a riot broke out at the South-East Asian Peninsular Games, held at a university campus in Rangoon. Students who couldn't get tickets to see the boxing matches pushed their way in. Soldiers shot into the crowd to disperse them, leading to more protests and university closures. In 1970, some university students organized a fiftieth anniversary commemoration of the founding of Rangoon University. The regime ordered teachers to prevent students from politicizing the event, but a history of the July 1962 killings was distributed and students at some other universities also handed out anti-government pamphlets. Students and teachers were punished, and universities around the country were shut for a month.[12]

In 1974, much larger demonstrations broke out in May and June, this time led by workers in state-owned factories. The authorities had recently cut rations in half, and the workers demanded more subsidized rice and better pay. When the number of workers taking to the streets increased, the military responded by firing into the crowds. The government reported twenty-two deaths, although other witnesses cited much higher figures. The military sentenced more than one hundred workers to lengthy imprisonment and immediately closed the universities, fearing escalating protests.

In December 1974, university student protests broke out over the government's handling of U Thant's funeral. This time the protesters' anger was clearly directed towards General Ne Win, and speech-makers called for his removal. General Ne Win had been jealous of U Thant, a Burmese diplomat who became secretary-general of the United Nations in the 1960s. While General Ne Win was leading his country into isolation and economic ruin, U Thant was receiving international accolades for his level-headed handling of numerous crises during the escalating cold war period. After U Thant died in New York, his body was flown back to Rangoon, but General Ne Win ordered that no state official should meet the body, and he would be buried like any other ordinary person. But when his body was unceremoniously laid out at Kyaikkasan grounds, the old racetrack, thousands of Burmese came to place wreaths and pay their last respects.[13]

Incensed at the regime's disregard for the senior statesman, a group of university students decided to take matters into their own hands. Amassing a large number of students from various campuses in Rangoon, they marched to Kyaikkasan grounds on 5 December. Once there, they persuaded the officiating monks to give them the body, which they took on a decorated truck to Rangoon University and then placed on a platform in the Convocation Hall.

One participant, Thein San, explained what happened next. The students began building a mausoleum for U Thant on the site of the old student union. Supporters outside the university donated money and food packets to the students inside, and thousands of people, including monks, came into the university compound in the evenings to pay their respects and to listen to the students' speeches. Many of the speeches dealt with the economic crisis, while others had a more explicit anti-government theme. Thein San said: 'I don't know whether it was out of love and respect for U Thant or to do anything against Ne Win and the way things were, but ordinary people were just taking off their pieces of gold jewellery and donating them.' The value of the donations was estimated to be as high as $42,000.[14]

Meanwhile, the military brought in troops to prepare for an assault on the university. The government announced the closure of all universities and ordered all students from outside Rangoon to return home. As the numbers of people on campus diminished, troops cordoned off the area and, in the middle of the night, soldiers and riot police stormed the campus. They arrested almost three thousand people, including a number of monks, who were forced to take off their outer robes and sit like criminals before being taken to the interrogation centre. The regime reported that eighteen people were killed, but student estimates were as high as one hundred.[15] Outrage at way the monks in particular were treated led to riots in Rangoon, with people targeting police stations, BSPP offices and especially the hated Ministry of Cooperatives. The regime was able to put a stop to this in a day, but had to declare martial law and nightly curfews to restore order.

Then in June 1975, students and workers held a joint demonstration marking the anniversary of the 1974 workers' strike. As they marched down a main thoroughfare in Rangoon, more and more people began to join in. The authorities quickly crushed the protest and shut the universities again.

In March 1976, students in Rangoon, Mandalay, Taunggyi, Moulmein and Bassein honoured the centenary of Thakin Kodaw Hmaing's birth. Thakin Kodaw Hmaing was a famous writer, nationalist and key supporter of the 1963 peace talks between the government and armed resistance groups. The commemoration turned into a demonstration and the universities were closed, with over one hundred students in Rangoon alone arrested and sentenced from five to fifteen years' imprisonment. Tin Maung Oo, a prominent student leader of Chin ethnicity, was hanged.

One student group tried to launch a '7-7-77 movement' to begin on 7 July 1977. Besides being a lucky number, 7/7/77 was also the anniversary of the military crackdown on the 1962 student demonstrations. Students handed out pamphlets in Rangoon, but the campaign did not take off and the organizers were arrested. There were more arrests at the

Rangoon Institute of Technology in August and September 1978 after students were caught distributing an underground history of the student movement in Burma.

Despite all these protests, the activists did not succeed in creating an organization or leadership that could maintain momentum. While the military intelligence could not prevent small protests from breaking out, they were adept at identifying emergent student leaders and getting them quickly into prison. Even in the planning stages, activists found it difficult to link up with each other because of fears that intelligence agents had penetrated their circles. Once activists were released from prison, they were always under surveillance, making it nearly impossible for them to resume political organizing. Thus, individuals became known for their heroic speeches or actions during strikes, but they were never able to translate these into sustainable movements.

The BSPP regime tried to stamp out resistance by increasing surveillance and limiting contact between students. First, professors were held responsible for the political activities of their students. Thus, professors could not just look the other way but, in order to protect their jobs, had to try to stop students from engaging in anti-government activities. Second, it increased the number of MI among the students. And third, in the mid-1970s, the regime sought to separate university students by setting up regional colleges. University students from rural areas would spend their first two years at a regional college and come to campuses in Rangoon or Mandalay only for their final two years, when they were thinking more about their future careers and were less likely to be politically active. Political ideology classes were also made required subjects for all majors, and students were encouraged to join the BSPP.

The often spontaneous and uncoordinated actions of students, monks and workers can be compared with those of General Ne Win, who was in a position to implement long-range plans for maintaining power. One story that circulated among the writers' community at the time was that Ne Win, who loved horse-racing and gambling, once bought a horse and sent it to the best trainer. At every race, he told the jockey to hold the horse back, so that no one would think it had much potential. One day, he bet his entire fortune on that horse, and to everyone else's utter amazement, it beat all the other horses. Even in horse-racing, the story concluded, General Ne Win planned for the long run.

More worrying to General Ne Win than the student- and monk-led protests was the uncovering of a coup plot by some junior officers in 1976. Within the military, some officers were also dissatisfied with the regime's failed economic policies and the increasing corruption among party members, and a small group sought to remove General Ne Win from power. Lieutenant General Tin Oo (sometimes spelled Tin U), who later became a senior leader in the National League for Democracy, was serving as General Ne Win's chief of staff at the time, and he was widely respected for having urged restraint in dealing with the demonstrators in 1974 and 1975. The junior officers plotting the coup were reportedly considering asking Lieutenant General Tin Oo to take over. When their plot was uncovered, both they and Lieutenant General Tin Oo were imprisoned, although there was no evidence that he had prior knowledge of the plot. Nevertheless, many of Lieutenant General Tin Oo's supporters were questioned and a number of the better-educated army officers were transferred or retired. General Ne Win also sought to reconsolidate his hold over the BSPP by dismissing more than 50,000 party members.

Outside the 'legal fold'

Besides occasional political challenges in urban areas, General Ne Win and his regime also had to contend with the armed groups headquartered in the mountainous areas ringing the plains. In Burma, armed groups who fight against the government are referred to as living outside the legal fold. When these groups or their members surrender, they are said to have returned to the legal fold or 're-entered the light'. In the Revolutionary Council and BSPP periods, the Communist Party of Burma (CPB) was the largest ideologically oriented organization outside the legal fold.

Some students who became politicized through campus protests, prison experiences or rough treatment from the authorities, and wanted to continue their political work, headed for the Communist Party. Many of them did not have a firm grasp of communist theory, but they believed that the communists were committed to a struggle for justice. As Aung Zeya, who grew up in Rangoon and joined the CPB at their headquarters on the China border in the mid-1970s, put it: 'What sent me to the border was not an admiration of communist ideology but the inspiration I got from communists who sacrificed for the country.'

In some intellectual circles, capitalism and democracy had been thoroughly discredited by the colonial experience and the actions of certain pro-West politicians in the 1950s who were seen as manipulative and self-serving. Aung Zeya, who now supports the democracy movement, says: 'We believed that democrats were traitors. There was only one way to sacrifice for the people, and the way was to become a communist.' As in other colonized countries in Asia, communism had been popular with

Burmese intellectuals. General Aung San had even helped to found the Communist Party in Burma, although he later moved away from it. After independence, communism continued to have an appeal, in part because of communist-led victories against the West in countries like Vietnam and the apparent relevance of Mao Zedong's theories about protracted guerrilla warfare in peasant-based societies.

In the late 1940s, members of the two armed branches of the Communist Party occupied territory in lower and central Burma, but by 1975 the *tatmadaw* had driven them out of these areas. The CPB regained strength, however, after establishing its headquarters in a mountainous region on the Chinese border. It was able to recruit thousands of local Was and other minority peoples as soldiers, and until the mid-1980s it received support in the form of money, advisers, soldiers, weapons and other equipment from the Chinese government.[16] The *tatmadaw* lost thousands of soldiers fighting the CPB and blamed the communists for every political protest that broke out in central Burma. In fact, the Communist Party devoted little energy to the political struggles in the cities and was unable to rally support in the lowland rural areas. While it continued to hold its ground in northern Burma, it could not reoccupy territory in the heartland of the country. Eventually, the Chinese government realized that the CPB was never going to capture Rangoon. It stopped supplying the CPB and gradually improved its relations with General Ne Win. Ultimately the Chinese leadership was not so concerned about whether the government of Burma was communist as long as it was willing to cooperate with Beijing.

In the 1970s, there were also pro-democracy supporters who turned to armed resistance. After U Nu was released from prison in 1966, he realized that he could do little to change the country from within. In 1969, he agreed to join with Edward Law Yone, a former newspaper editor who had also been imprisoned, and four members of the Thirty Comrades, in setting up the Parliamentary Democracy Party (later renamed the People's Patriotic Party), based on the Thai–Burma border. Their plan was to launch joint attacks into Burma with the KNU and the New Mon State Party's army, while also encouraging monks to lead demonstrations inside the country. Although the force was openly tolerated by the Thai government and had some early successes, it was unable to maintain its momentum. Besides financial problems, the leaders had difficulties working closely with the Karens because of continued differences of opinion over the political rights of the ethnic nationalities in a post-Ne Win Burma.[17]

In addition to the Burman-led opposition forces, numerous ethnic armies seeking autonomy were continuing to battle against the regime during this period. The largest groups were the Karen National Union (KNU), the Kachin Independence Organization (KIO), the New Mon State Party (NMSP) and the Shan State Army (SSA), each with armies of several thousand members. Led by a mix of university-educated men and soldiers who had fought with the British, they were able to support themselves by logging, mining and maintaining toll-gates along Burma's borders. With a constant stream of black-market traders going to and from neighbouring countries, those who controlled the toll-gates reaped huge profits. Some of the armies operating in the hills of northern Burma, including the CPB, also raised money through taxing the opium and heroin trade.

Most of the larger ethnic nationalist armies were anti-communist, but some of the smaller multi-ethnic groups, such as the Karenni State Nationalities People's Liberation Front (KNPLF) and the Shan State Nationalities People's Liberation Organization (SNPLO), trained with the CPB and adopted a communist-inspired organizational structure. Some factions in the KNU and the NMSP were also more left-leaning. At the same time, small armed groups of Muslims were operating in Arakan State, and Pa'o and Palaung forces were fighting for autonomy within Shan State.

Much of the mountainous territory controlled by the ethnic armies had never been under direct Burman rule, and the villagers considered Burman troops to be foreign invaders. The larger ethnic nationalist armies set up administrative structures as well as clinics and schools, where students were taught in their native tongues with Burmese and English introduced as second and third languages. The ethnic nationalist armies largely adopted defensive postures, trying to prevent *tatmadaw* troops from entering their areas but not organizing strikes deep into central Burma.

While most recruits came from villages in the ethnic areas affected by the civil war, young people of various ethnicities continued to make their way out from the plains to join these armies. Reasons included sympathy for members of their ethnic group, frustration with government policies, and the desire to live what they perceived as the heroic life of a guerrilla fighter.

Although alliances were formed between the various anti-government armies, many were in name only. Most of the ethnic nationalist armies distrusted the Burman-dominated groups, and their relations with other ethnic armies were also strained. Neighbouring ethnic armies sometimes fought each other over territory, and differences in ideologies also kept them apart. Thus each army generally fought on its own, neither making any headway nor being forced to surrender.

Civil war was the normal state of affairs for many areas in northern and eastern Burma. The war affected not only the soldiers on both sides, but also all the civilians who lived in the military operation areas. Starting in the mid-1960s, the military regime ruthlessly implemented a policy known as the Four Cuts. The objective was to eliminate all forms of support to resistance forces by cutting their access to food, money, intelligence and recruits. Many villagers were forced to leave their villages and were often brutally treated and even killed, whether they had anything to do with the opposition forces or not. As Martin Smith has written in *Burma: Insurgency and the Politics of Ethnicity*: 'For the *tatmadaw* in the Four Cuts campaign, there is no such thing as an innocent or neutral villager. Every community must fight, flee, or join the *tatmadaw*.'[18] As a result of *tatmadaw* campaigns in the Karen, Kachin and other areas, tens of thousands of people lost family members, their land and their homes.

Civilians in towns controlled by the government were also affected, because they could be rounded up as porters for military campaigns at any time. Young men were grabbed coming out of cinema halls or getting off ferries, and sent off to the front lines with no guarantee they would ever return.

Given the BSPP government's lack of interest in resolving the country's political problems through dialogue, it is not surprising that some Burmans and ethnic minorities joined armed resistance movements in an attempt to achieve their objectives by force. With none of these armies appearing to be making much headway, however, most Burmese became cynical about their abilities to effect change. Farmers continued farming, suffering arrests when they could not fulfil their paddy quotas. Smugglers continued smuggling, as legal imports continued to be restricted and domestic industry languished. And civil servants kept working for the government, whether they believed in it or not.

3 | Breaking the silence, 1988–90

If somebody is against the government, we have to follow. We have
to show that we also don't like this way. (Son of a military engineer)

In 1987, the United Nations designated Burma a 'Least Developed Country', grouping it together with the poorest African nations. The public stayed quiet, but a few students and intellectuals, gathering in tea shops and friends' houses, hatched plans and wrote articles intended to shake people out of their passivity.

One person involved in underground organizing since the mid-1980s was Moe Thee Zun. He had purposely failed his third-year university exams so that he could stay on campus longer. Like many other activists, he believed that the best place to cultivate anti-government activities was in the university, where there were a large number of single people more willing to take risks.

When the military regime announced the demonetization of 25-, 35- and 75-kyat notes on Friday, 5 September 1987, Moe Thee Zun and his colleagues thought their chance had finally come. Many people's savings were wiped out in an instant, and the activists believed people would surely take to the streets. But after a small protest organized by university students, the regime announced the closure of the universities. As a result, nothing could be done on campus, and no protests coalesced on the streets. Families stayed quiet, hoping the government would eventually offer partial reimbursement, as it had after two previous demonetizations.

The universities reopened two months later, and exams were held immediately. Moe Thee Zun and some of his friends tried to stir up activity, but other students expressed no interest. Moe Thee Zun graduated, but he continued to frequent tea shops near campus, meeting with friends to discuss why Russia was transforming and the Philippines had already changed but Burma hadn't. They shared books and formed study groups while continuing to recruit new members for their underground student union. Then, in March 1988, they got another chance.

A tea-shop brawl broke out between university students and local youths on 12 March. Because the young man who started the brawl was the son of a BSPP official, he was quickly released. Students gathered in front of the police station to protest, and riot police stormed them, killing a student named Phone Maw. Phone Maw's fellow students were outraged. They demanded that the government announce the truth about the incident in the government-controlled media. Instead, the regime's spokesmen blamed the students for inciting unrest.

The next day demonstrations broke out at Rangoon Institute of Technology and Rangoon University. Students gave impromptu speeches about the need for a student union to represent their interests. Soon they also began demanding the end of one-party rule. On 16 March, students from Rangoon University decided to march towards the Institute of Technology campus a couple of miles away. When they reached Inya Lake on Prome Road, they found themselves squeezed between soldiers in front of them and riot police behind them. To their left were large homes surrounded by high walls. To their right was the lake.

Min Ko Naing, a student activist who later became famous, tried to convince the soldiers to let the students pass. But the riot police attacked from behind, the soldiers followed suit, and the students were trapped in between. Some fleeing students made it down alleys and over walls into people's yards. Others ran into the lake with soldiers following them. Some students drowned because they couldn't swim or because they were beaten unconscious by soldiers. Witnesses recalled being horrified to hear the soldiers shouting 'Don't let them escape!' and 'Kill them!' as they beat the unarmed students. Several students were arrested and taken away. Forty-one suffocated to death in an overcrowded prison van. Later, word got out that some of the arrested female students were gang-raped. People were shocked. The event came to be known as the Red Bridge incident, because the site of the attack was a bridge that was splattered with blood.[1]

The next day, further demonstrations occurred at Rangoon University, where students gathered for Phone Maw's funeral. His body had already been secretly cremated by the military, but students gave fiery speeches throughout the day, while military men surrounded the area and cut the electricity and water. No one could enter or pass food in, although students were allowed to escape through a small back gate.

Ye Min, a medical student from a rural town who had never witnessed a demonstration before, came with a few friends to see what was happening. By the afternoon, he was hungry and thirsty and felt worn down by the military pressure outside the gates. He was preparing to slip out the back when he saw a female student going up on to the makeshift stage. He decided that if she had enough courage to make a speech in these

47

conditions, he shouldn't leave. Later he was arrested with others and questioned at length, because the military was worried that the protests which had started in two universities the day before now appeared to be spreading to the medical institutes. Approximately one thousand students were arrested that evening, while others were beaten and left, because there were not enough prison vans to take everyone.

The next day, a huge demonstration of over ten thousand people took place in central Rangoon, and many more were arrested. The regime closed the universities for two months. When they reopened on 1 June, Ye Min and three others learned they were to be expelled for attending the March demonstrations. That sparked a movement within the medical institutes to boycott classes until the four students were reinstated.

At Rangoon University, political organizing was also continuing, and Moe Thee Zun prepared to make his first public speech. Like Min Ko Naing (Conqueror of Kings), Moe Thee Zun was not his real name; to protect themselves from identification and arrest, and in imitation of the Thirty Comrades, many student leaders took on 'noms de guerre'. Moe Thee means 'hailstorm', a pen name he had used for his poetry in underground publications. He added Zun, Burmese for 'June'.

Moe Thee Zun recalled that, the night before, he wrote a goodbye letter to his parents, gave his younger brother a final hug, telling him they would meet again 'when victory had been won', and headed for the door. To his chagrin, his mother had suspected that he was up to something, so she had padlocked all the doors. He remembered, laughing: 'She thought she had caught the fish, so she was satisfied and went to sleep. But there was a big tamarind tree, and one branch went to the second-floor window. My mother forgot that!' He climbed down the tree, hopped on the back of his friend's bicycle, and they pedalled off into the night.

The next day, he gave his speech. After explaining the history of the students' movement since 1962, he stressed his belief that students should fight for all the people, not just for students' rights. Specifically he urged the audience to denounce the demonetization and demand reimbursement. He insisted that because one-party rule was responsible for the country's decline, students should demand that multiparty democracy be reinstated.

Then another group of students went up on to the stage and accused Moe Thee Zun and his colleagues of being too political. This group felt that the students should concern themselves only with student affairs, such as the release of arrested students, the construction of a memorial to students who had been killed, and the right to form a student union.

Finally, the students decided to vote on which policy they liked better after holding a debate. Moe Thee Zun emerged the winner, insisting that the students should fight for the overthrow of one-party rule, and there was no time to lose. He told the audience: 'The opportunity will never come twice.' That afternoon, the authorities arrived at Moe Thee Zun's house to arrest him, but he had known better than to go home.

The following day, 21 June, thousands of students marched towards central Rangoon. They were stopped by riot police at Myenigone junction and showered with tear-gas. Some riot police shot bullets at the students as they shot handmade darts back at them. Eighty civilians and twenty riot police were killed.[2]

The rest of the country was still quiet, but the government was nervous and closed the universities again. A night-time curfew was imposed and public gatherings banned, but some students set up a strike centre at the Shwedagon Pagoda. On 23 June, demonstrations broke out in Pegu, an hour's drive from Rangoon, and resulted in seventy deaths. Meanwhile, students studying in Rangoon went back to their home towns, bringing with them news of the military's brutality. The more active students visited many towns, trying to interest others in preparing for future protests.

Hoping to defuse the tension, the government announced on 7 July that all of the students who had been arrested would be released. But the next day, Min Ko Naing and his colleagues issued a statement urging the students to continue the struggle. The statement bore the seal of the All Burma Federation of Students' Unions (ABFSU), the first time this name had appeared since the student union was destroyed in 1962. The ABFSU then put out four more statements asking various professional groups to consider how they had suffered under BSPP rule. By doing so, the ABFSU hoped to expand the protests to the general public.

Also circulating at the time were retired Brigadier Aung Gyi's letters. Brigadier Aung Gyi, who had worked closely with General Ne Win in the late 1950s and early 1960s, had written an open letter to General Ne Win in July 1987 warning him that if he did not deal with the economic crisis, violent protests were likely. Aung Gyi had recently travelled abroad for the first time in over twenty-five years. He was stunned by the level of economic progress in other South-East Asian countries. In May and June 1988 he wrote two more open letters to General Ne Win and also sent a forty-page analysis of how the BSPP had misruled the country and brought about economic ruin. These letters were copied and distributed widely, and the public was amazed that a senior public figure was daring to speak out so openly.[3]

Meanwhile, in the towns of Prome and Taunggyi, communal violence between Buddhists and Muslims broke out. Many suspected the disturbances were started by the military authorities, who were trying to divert attention from political issues.[4]

Then the BSPP held an extraordinary conference starting on 23 July, and General Ne Win announced his resignation. He admitted that the people's demonstrations reflected a lack of support for his regime, suggested holding a referendum on whether to maintain one-party rule or change to a multiparty system, and declared that he was stepping down. People were astounded but questioned his sincerity. Indeed, even though General Ne Win resigned, the idea of holding a referendum on whether to institute multiparty rule was shelved, and before the conference ended, General Sein Lwin, who had only four years of education, was selected as General Ne Win's successor. General Sein Lwin was the head of the riot police and the orchestrator of the 16 March slaughter at Inya Lake. He was hardly a moderate choice.

Most parents doubted that change was imminent and tried to keep their children out of trouble. Some even sent their sons to monasteries so they would not be drawn into further political activities. Min Zaw was one of them. A student at Rangoon University in 1988, he and his close friends had become involved in literature circles and political discussions, and in June they wrote and distributed a couple of political pamphlets, mostly in the university bathrooms. After Min Zaw participated in the June 1988 demonstrations, the military intelligence tried to arrest him. His mother sent him to a monastery well outside the city. Although he did not want to become a monk, he felt that he could not refuse his mother and the abbot. Frustrated by his isolation at the monastery, every evening he walked for twenty minutes to a village where he could listen to the British Broadcasting Corporation's evening news programme. During that period, more people than usual were tuning into BBC radio broadcasts (in Burmese and English) because it was one of the few ways to get news about what was happening in the rest of the country.

Towards the end of July, the BBC broadcast an interview with a student by Christopher Gunness, a correspondent visiting Rangoon. The student called for a nationwide demonstration on the numerologically significant date of 8 August 1988 (8888). Even people in the countryside started getting excited. Min Zaw remembers the abbot giving a religious speech to the community in which he told people that if they needed to do something, they should go ahead and do it. Min Zaw said it was his way of encouraging the people to organize. The abbot also gave Min Zaw a *gahta*, or incantation, telling him, 'You have to practise saying it. It will protect you from arrest.'

When some local teachers organized a rally in early August, Min Zaw insisted on attending. A layman who had come to know Min Zaw at the temple and often gave him extra meals encouraged him to give a speech. After shouting nervously at the audience, 'Do you think I am a monk?', Min Zaw told them that he was actually a student from Rangoon University and explained everything he had witnessed during the demonstrations in March and June. The community had planned a protest for the next day, and Min Zaw decided he could no longer be a monk.[5] The next morning, he changed into street clothes, and walked out of the monastery. When the abbot saw him, he smiled and said nothing.

Six weeks of nationwide protests

In Rangoon, following the walkout of the dock workers at 8.08 a.m. on 8 August, thousands of people took to the streets. Surprisingly, the soldiers just watched. Late that night, however, the killing began. Violence incited more anger, and people continued to come out on to the streets over the next few days. With the fearlessness of youth, high-school students led numerous demonstrations in their school uniforms. Many provocatively bared their chests in front of the troops, daring the soldiers to shoot or bayonet them. Although a number of soldiers refused, others obeyed orders to kill the young students. Many soldiers had been brought into the city from remote areas, having been told that the students were communists bent on destroying the country. Between 8 and 12 August, several hundred people were killed in Rangoon alone.[6]

In Rangoon students played the central role in organizing demonstrations. In Mandalay students and monks led together. Kyaw Tint, a student activist in Mandalay, remembers:

We started on the morning of 8/8/88, but the monks had to eat their morning meal, so they asked us to please wait until after eleven. But some students couldn't wait so they started. At that time one youth was shot and died. At eleven thirty the monks' group started marching. And the next day, we started the boycott camps in monasteries and pagodas and some schools.

In medical student Ye Min's township in the delta, students began their demonstration at the local high school. As they marched, they called for the release of two locally arrested students as well as for the end of one-party rule. As in many rural areas where there were no soldiers, only

51

local police, the atmosphere was not as frightening as it was in Rangoon or Mandalay. When the crowds poured into the police station, the police had no choice but to release the two students. In the following days, the students organized a strike committee camp at one of the monasteries with the full support of the monks. They formed a township student union including high-school and university students, and encouraged teachers to become involved. Later, teachers' unions, workers' unions, a health workers' union and a lawyers' union were also set up. Then the various unions joined together to select a township general strike committee. Other towns followed a similar pattern, with professional groups organizing themselves into impromptu unions and their leaders forming strike committees to coordinate demonstrations and later administrative affairs.

Back in Rangoon, Moe Thee Zun had become one of the leading speakers and strategists. He urged students to move their demonstrations out of the universities and into the markets and other centres of activity. Wherever the students began speaking, the troops attacked. Unable to tell who was a student and who a bystander, the soldiers beat everyone, and sometimes shot people. As a result, everyone automatically became involved. Moe Thee Zun also encouraged activists to hold demonstrations in the evenings, when people were on their way home. Such protests didn't interrupt their work, and the protesters could more easily escape in the dark if soldiers came after them.

In every demonstration, students carried fighting-peacock student union flags, banned since 1962, and portraits of General Aung San. By doing so, they sought to convey that they represented General Aung San's true legacy. Moreover, the protesters sought to remind the army that General Aung San's vision had been of an army that defended the people's interests, not one that killed its fellow citizens.

Nevertheless, during the demonstrations, as many as three thousand people in Rangoon and other towns were killed, most shot by the military while marching.[7] There were also incidents when civilians surrounded and killed suspected military intelligence personnel and others. Some civilians also came out with swords, daggers and sharpened bicycle and umbrella spokes. After years of feeling frustrated and powerless, the desire for revenge was overwhelming.

The ABFSU in Rangoon set up a security department early on to manage the crowds during demonstrations. Ko Doe, a serious-looking young man who was a member of the security department, remembers how difficult it was to stop some of the violence, which included beheadings.

Those who carried out the beheadings didn't have proof that the person was an intelligence agent, he said. 'They just suspected or hated that person, so they killed him.' Sometimes Ko Doe and his team received telephone calls telling them to rush to a scene where violence was breaking out, but by the time they arrived, it was too late. Ko Doe said: 'We students didn't want this kind of thing.'

Ko Doe explained that he and other student activists suspected two kinds of people were behind the killings: ordinary people who were angry and lost control and military people in plain clothes trying to create a chaotic situation so that the military would have a justification for clamping down. Although the students understood these problems, Ko Doe said they were too inexperienced to know how to prevent them.

Ko Doe came from a military family, so his primary duty was to collect information about the military's activities. Through sympathetic military people, he learned what kind of guns and other equipment they had and, on some occasions, whether or not the soldiers had been given orders to shoot. Some of the military people told him they had to shoot because they were ordered to, but they didn't want to. He said: 'They felt really confused and found it difficult to understand. So they gave us all the information.'

Not only in Rangoon, but also in some rural towns and villages, there were soldiers, though rarely intelligence officers or higher-ranking army officers, who helped the demonstrators. One long-time activist, Myat Hla, who was in a town in central Burma at the time, said: 'Some of the local army men defected to the demonstrators and even told me they would give training to the villagers when the time came.'

Myat Hla was helping villagers establish local strike committees, but he said that the situation in his area was chaotic. Mobs of villagers captured weapons from police stations, and it was very close to armed struggle. Although he urged the villagers to use non-violent methods, they laughed at him and said he was naive. Myat Hla said: 'Ordinary people do not believe in non-violent methods. They were surprised that they shouldn't do anything when the soldiers shot at them. At least they wanted to use swords.' In Myat Hla's area, local authorities apparently tried to stir up trouble by provoking clashes between Muslims and Burmese and allowing soldiers to steal rice and take all the money out of the local bank.

With demonstrations taking place all over the country, on 12 August 1988 General Sein Lwin was removed as president. On 19 August, Dr Maung Maung, a legal scholar with a senior position in the BSPP government, was appointed as Sein Lwin's successor. Five days later, troops were called back to their bases and the shooting stopped.

No longer afraid of being killed, numerous people who had originally hesitated to come out now took to the streets. Even in the ethnic states, the demonstrations drew huge crowds. Residents of Hsipaw, a market town in northern Shan State, reported that tens of thousands of villagers poured into their town to find out what was going on and to express their feelings. These villagers had suffered more under military rule than farmers in the plains. Shan nationalist armies operated in the region, and villagers were frequently forced to accompany the *tatmadaw* during their anti-insurgent operations, carrying their ammunition and supplies. Many had also experienced other forms of forced labour or had their property confiscated, and they were eager to see political change.

In Pa-an, the sleepy capital of Karen State, Karens, Burmans and others also came in from miles away to march around the central area for days. Like villagers in Shan State, they had been the victims of military campaigns and faced far greater difficulties than people living near or in the urban centres of Rangoon and Mandalay.

Civil society re-emerges

During this chaotic, often violent but also exciting time, independent organizations sprang up in the towns and cities. Artists, actors, civil servants and housewives organized unions and marched in the streets. Large groups of people resigned from the BSPP and other military-controlled organizations, holding 'burn-ins' where membership cards were thrown into fires in front of local BSPP offices. Several dozen newspapers, magazines and pamphlets appeared overnight.[8] The budding free press provided information about what was going on as well as fresh ideas, while comedians critiqued the dictatorship in the streets. Zarganar, a dentist and comedian, became a famous regular at Rangoon demonstrations, using mime and satire to ridicule General Ne Win's rule.

As more and more professionals joined the movement, even the foreign service members began organizing. Many had found representing Burma's policies abroad humiliating. Maung Maung Nyo, a Canberra-based senior diplomat who eventually defected, talked about how he had usually taken what he called a 'minimalist approach' to dealing with foreign journalists and critics. He tried to avoid them, but if he absolutely had to meet with them, he would answer all their sensitive questions with 'no comment'. In August, the staff at the Canberra embassy became consumed with discussions about what to do. They busily cabled back and forth to other

Burmese embassies to find out what steps they were taking. One staff member who had witnessed the killings in Rangoon insisted that they should do something, but others said that it would be better to minimize the risk to themselves by letting others take the lead.

Then, on 30 August, Foreign Ministry personnel in Rangoon put out a statement saying that the BSPP policy had 'tarnished Burma's pride and prestige in international fora. We've lost face implementing policies which lack essence.' They also called for free and fair elections under a multiparty system. Following this statement, letters of support were issued by staff members at many Burmese embassies, including the embassy in Canberra.

Not surprisingly, given the lack of respect for the law under the BSPP regime, lawyers were also active. The Bar Council drafted a statement critiquing the BSPP's disastrous monetary policies and abuse of the legal system. Selected lawyers simultaneously read out the statement all over the country.

While citizens were enjoying the freedom to organize into groups, maintaining law and order became a serious concern. The student unions had called for a nationwide strike on 26 August but, in what appears to have been an effort to disrupt the strike, the authorities opened most of the country's prisons that morning. Mi Mi, a lawyer living in a town in the delta, remembered how terrified people were that anarchy would break out. Her township strike committee was able to resolve the problem by convincing the prisoners to stay in prison under the protection of Buddhist monks. Each prisoner's case would be reviewed by the town's lawyers and anyone who had been unjustly imprisoned or convicted of a minor crime would be released. Both the prisoners and the townspeople accepted the arrangement.

In Rangoon, the YMCA took care of young people who had been released from juvenile prison. They also joined with other religious leaders to set up an interfaith council of Buddhists, Christians, Hindus and Muslims which provided rice to some of the most needy people in the city.

In other areas, though, tensions began to rise because of the food shortages and widespread looting of government property. The strikes had caused a total breakdown in the transportation infrastructure, all work stopped, and getting food became increasingly difficult for many people. Many families feared that the mobs would not stop at the government warehouses but would raid their shops and houses too.

In most towns, local committees were set up to handle daily affairs; in particular, security and food distribution. These committees were usually run by teachers, lawyers, doctors and intellectuals, but in many places monks played the leading role. They provided shelter at their monasteries for those who could not return home, they restrained protesters who wanted to kill captured military men, and they settled disputes.

In parts of Mandalay and many surrounding villages, local people asked the monks to take charge until peace was restored. Several groups of monks did so. At night, young monks in some towns armed themselves with sticks and patrolled the streets, watching not only for soldiers but also for criminals hoping to take advantage of the breakdown of order.

While the monks often tried to prevent killings, in many places they encouraged people to demonstrate their disapproval of BSPP rule. Linking the struggle against the regime to a need for spiritual purification, in Mandalay a group of monks led Burmese residents in evening rituals usually reserved for the last day of the new year celebrations. Gathering on street corners, monks asked the crowds three times, 'Do you want evil spirits, who make people suffer in all kinds of ways, to stay around here?' The people responded, 'No, we don't want that!', as they beat gongs and pots and pans to drive the bad spirits away. In this case, they were referring not to ghosts of the deceased but to living members of the regime.

Monks also indirectly supported popular participation by giving demonstrators protective charms and tattoos. As in the days of the Saya San rebellion in the 1930s, many people still believed such charms could protect them and thus were emboldened to take to the streets. The deaths of those who had such protections were explained by the assumption that they must have broken one of the rules that must be followed for the charm to work. Some monks were believed to have supernatural powers which allowed them to see the future and travel from place to place invisibly. Many demonstrators drew strength from the presence of the monks in the demonstrations.

The need for leadership

In the early days of the demonstrations, General Aung San's daughter, Aung San Suu Kyi, played no role. Her father had died when she was two, and she had lived outside Burma since she was a teenager. Her mother was appointed ambassador to India, so the family moved to Delhi. Then she attended university in England and married Michael Aris, a British scholar of Tibet. Although she often returned to Burma for visits, she was settled in England, where she and her husband were raising their two sons. She had written to Michael Aris before their marriage saying that if her country ever needed her, she would have to go, but such a scenario had appeared unlikely.

In 1988, Aung San Suu Kyi happened to be in Rangoon taking care of her ailing mother when the demonstrations broke out. At first she stayed at home but, at the urging of others, she put out a statement calling for the establishment of an independent committee to oversee multiparty elections. Then she decided to make a speech on the field beneath Shwedagon Pagoda on 26 August, the day student organizers had called for a nationwide strike. That morning, the area filled with over half a million people, curious to see the daughter of their beloved national leader. Her eloquence and poise captivated the audience as she urged people not to turn on the army but to seek democracy in a peaceful and unified way.[9] She immediately became a key figure in the movement, although she was not affiliated with any particular group.

While the demonstrations drew widespread participation, the lack of a unified leadership became a problem. Block, neighbourhood and village organizations emerged to handle local affairs, but there was still no recognized national organization. Student groups took the lead in organizing demonstrations, but they were not capable of establishing a new administration. Veteran politicians and retired military leaders were out making speeches but none had total support. In early September, rumours started to spread that the army was going to stage a coup. Pressure was increasing on the leading activists and politicians to try to establish an interim government.

On 9 September, former prime minister U Nu, who had returned to Burma under amnesty in 1980, released a press statement announcing that he had formed a government himself. Most people had lost faith in him and were dismayed by his cabinet appointees, many of whom were old cronies or his relatives.

Two days later, BSPP leaders announced that they would hold an election for a new multiparty parliament. Although they had dropped their original plan to first hold a referendum on one-party versus multiparty rule, many people still doubted whether the BSPP could be trusted to hold multiparty elections. As a result, the demonstrations continued.

Meanwhile, student representatives and veteran politicians went to a number of embassies to enquire whether they would support an interim government. After receiving positive feedback from a few of the embassies, they held meetings on 13 and 14 September. Aung San Suu Kyi, U Nu, Bo Yan Naing (one of the Thirty Comrades), Tin Oo (the army chief of staff sacked in 1976) and Brigadier Aung Gyi (who had written the open letters to General Ne Win) participated. Moe Thee Zun was selected to represent the 100 leading student activists who attended, and he urged the five politicians to agree with the students' plan to form an interim government within forty-eight hours.

The meeting was held inside Medical Institute No. 1 in Rangoon, and loudspeakers had been set up on the street so that the thousands of people outside could listen. Moe Thee Zun remembered: 'We told the politicians, "Please forget your problems and form the interim government."' But U Nu insisted that everyone should support his government, and the others were unwilling to do so. The meeting ended without any agreement on how to proceed.

There were still many unresolved differences of opinion between the politicians, and some of the senior leaders felt that it was better to wait and see whether the BSPP would follow through on its election promise. Meanwhile, student activists continued to try to build support for an interim government, meeting with representatives of the various professional unions and compiling a list of nominees, including Aung San Suu Kyi. But on 18 September the military staged a coup, and their opportunity had gone.

The afternoon of the coup, troops appeared on the streets all over the country and began clearing out strike centres and breaking down the protective barriers that residents had erected at many crossroads. Those who resisted were shot. After two days and several hundred killings, especially of young students, the military re-established control.

Why didn't the 1988 demonstrations succeed? First, the demonstrations had broken out spontaneously, and while there was a fair amount of quick coordinating at the local level, there was no national leadership that could unite the strike committees. As the strikes continued, food shortages worsened, public services stopped and people grew tired, giving the military an opportunity to retake control.

Another factor was the marked lack of participation of the armed ethnic organizations. None of their armies came into the towns, although small groups ventured in to see what was happening and handed over a few weapons to individual contacts. The KNU and NMSP were actually fighting each other over contested territory at the time. While many of the ethnic minorities living in the cities and towns in the heartland of Burma participated, the leaders of the armed ethnic organizations felt this was not their struggle. They saw it as a battle between Burmans, so they remained on the sidelines. As General Mya, the head of the KNU at the time, was quoted as saying in *Asiaweek*: 'The recent uprisings were good for the people, but we cannot yet say it will be directly beneficial to the revolutionaries.'[10]

Another group that did not send its army into the cities was the Communist Party of Burma.[11] As Myat Hla, who had contacts in the CPB, put it, 'Many slogans were introduced by the CPB's underground movement members, but sometimes these UGs [underground operatives] did not consult the party. The SLORC scapegoated them, but they played only a limited role. Even one of the senior leaders in the CPB admitted that.'

Most importantly, the regime was able to regain control because the generals could command the obedience of enough of their officers and soldiers. Although some soldiers did join the movement, or refused to shoot, there were plenty who did not desert but stayed to pull the trigger as they were told. Still, the movement had a profound psychological effect on its participants. Before 1988, the police and intelligence agents had been widely disliked, but after the troops' killings of students and monks, the military itself became hated. People who had grown up assuming authoritarian rule would continue indefinitely now believed that the country's politics could be different. Activists from different generations had been able to link up and present a new vision for the country. As a result, people's hopes were raised that democracy would be restored, and the coup organizers were compelled to offer the promise of change.

General Ne Win's name did not appear in the new ruling junta, which called itself the State Law and Order Restoration Council (SLORC). But General Saw Maung, the chairman, and the other top leaders in the SLORC were known to be loyal to him. Meanwhile, General Ne Win was widely believed to be calling the shots from behind the scenes.

At that time, rumours began circulating of guns and ammunition at the Thai–Burma border. Students who were determined to continue the fight, and felt that armed struggle was their only alternative, streamed out of the cities. Others left to escape arrest. Moe Thee Zun recalled that he and some other students who still believed in the need for a continued mass movement inside the country urged students not to leave, insisting, 'This is not a Rambo movie.' Nevertheless, as many as 10,000 students made their way to the Thai, Chinese, Indian and Bangladesh borders. While it was a frightening journey for the students, who had never been in the jungle, not many were chased by *tatmadaw* troops. The military regime was eager for the students to move out of the cities, recognizing that as successful as the students had been in organizing people in urban areas, they were no match for the battle-hardened *tatmadaw* troops in the jungle.

The election campaign

Just days after the coup, General Saw Maung announced that political parties could begin registering. The National League for Democracy (NLD), led by Aung San Suu Kyi, Tin Oo and Aung Gyi, was one of the first to do so, on 27 September 1988. The day before, the National Unity Party (NUP) announced its formation. Former military men and BSPP loyalists made up the bulk of the NUP, which was quickly characterized as representing a continuation of the old order. The party had a distinct financial advantage because it was able to take over many of the BSPP offices and its equipment for free. It soon became clear that the regime hoped to engineer the election so that the NUP would win an outright victory or at least become the leading member of a coalition government.

How did the SLORC think the NUP could win when so many citizens had been in the streets demanding change? First, the regime, like most authoritarian governments, tended to see and hear only what it wanted to believe. Thus, it overestimated its support, particularly among soldiers and former active BSPP members. Second, it encouraged the formation of a plethora of parties which would divide pro-democracy voters. Third, as the campaign went on, it tried to weaken the other parties by arresting particularly popular and capable challengers. And fourth, it severely limited campaigning opportunities in direct and indirect ways.

Political parties were allowed to open offices and given telephone lines and extra rations of petrol at the subsidized government price. Most people believe that at least one of the reasons the SLORC provided these incentives was so that a large number of parties would register, people would feel utterly confused, and the vote would be split in a thousand directions. Indeed, over two hundred parties were established in all, set up by former politicians, intellectuals, ethnic minority representatives and students. Some of these so-called parties, however, were nothing more than groups of friends who wanted a place to meet and access to the perks that were being offered. Others were formed by students who did not want to compete in the elections but needed a cover for continuing their political activities.

Before the SLORC's coup, both Aung San Suu Kyi and Tin Oo had called for the formation of an interim government. After the coup, they had asked civil servants to continue to stay home, but people were hungry and in desperate need of money. The junta ordered civil servants to go back to work by 3 October or lose their jobs. The offer was sweetened by the promise that they would receive back pay for September, when no one had gone to work. On 3 October almost everyone showed up at their offices.[12] As a result, Aung San Suu Kyi and other NLD leaders decided the best course was to go ahead with election campaigning, hoping to bring about change through the ballot box.

Student activists initially continued to press for an interim government that would write a new constitution and take responsibility for holding elections. To carry out their work, ABFSU members in Rangoon organized the Democratic Party for a New Society (DPNS), which held political education sessions at its offices and investigated and publicized the problems of farmers and relocated urban residents. Similarly, in Mandalay, many high-school and university students continued their activities under the auspices of a political party called the Organization of Students and Youth for National Politics.

During this period, as many as sixteen student fronts appeared, including groups led by ethnic minority students. While they tried to unite, differences in ideology, mistrust between rural people and city people, and tensions between ethnic minorities and Burmans made it difficult for them to work together. Also, some of the larger student groups could not easily accept that they did not have the right to speak for everyone.

Senior politicians also often broke with each other over personal differences and contentious power dynamics. The difficulties that many of the political organizations faced with factionalism related to the fact that most were organized in the pattern of patron–client relations. When conflicts emerged, leaders were reluctant to compromise, and many thought the better option was to leave and form a new group.

Ethnic minorities that supported participation in the elections faced difficult decisions of their own. Some thought it was best to join the NLD, because the NLD had a chance of winning the election and effecting change through legislation. Others chose to support ethnic-based parties that might succeed only in minority regions, but offered more space for voicing demands for ethnic cultural and political rights.

The NLD was the most successful in bringing diverse people together under a common platform, but it too had to struggle to maintain internal unity. It was composed of two different groups: ex-military men on the one hand, and intellectuals and students on the other. Nevertheless, the NLD quickly attracted widespread support, primarily because the public was so taken with Aung San Suu Kyi. Almost three million people joined the party and large crowds attended her rallies. She and Tin Oo campaigned extensively, including in the ethnic minority states. Wherever she arrived, excited crowds waited to greet her. The ethnic nationalities were particularly touched by Aung San Suu Kyi's visits to their areas, which echoed her father's visits four decades earlier. Many hoped that she too would be sympathetic to their concerns.

Aung San Suu Kyi and her party members stood out because whenever they appeared in public they wore traditional clothes and often *kamauk*, the wide-brimmed farmers' hats which became the symbol of the party. Many men in the NLD wore dark-coloured Kachin *longyis*, which had been favoured by student demonstrators in 1988. Aung San Suu Kyi donned the clothes of the various ethnic groups in each region and, like Burmese women in the past, always pinned a sprig of flowers in her hair.

Aung San Suu Kyi's words also resonated with the feelings of the people. Drawing on both Western democratic practice and Buddhist ideology, she articulated what was wrong with authoritarian rule. She often talked about the ten ethical rules for kings, which are based on Buddhist concepts of loving kindness, tolerance and self-control.[13] Derived from Buddhist scriptures, the rules were widely applied to pre-colonial kings in Burma. It was believed that kings who strayed would see their kingdoms disintegrate, and they themselves would lose the right to hold power.

The SLORC realized that, despite the proliferation of parties, Aung San Suu Kyi had the power to unite people and posed a serious challenge to their own party. Something had to be done. First the authorities threatened supporters with serious consequences if they attended her rallies, but people still came. The regime's propaganda wing circulated vulgar cartoon images of her and repeatedly argued that her long years abroad and marriage to a Westerner made her unfit to be a leader.[14] Because of lingering memories of foreigners taking Burmese wives in the colonial period, this did bother some citizens, but her status as the daughter of a great national hero carried more weight.

In April 1989, when she arrived in the town of Danubyu in the Irrawaddy Delta and was about to address the crowd, an army captain gave six soldiers the order to shoot her. Just before they did, a major stepped forward and stopped the soldiers.[15] Aung San Suu Kyi continued walking towards the stage, but the pressure had clearly escalated.

Although Aung San Suu Kyi and the NLD focused on the election campaign rather than resuscitating a mass movement, they joined with student groups in commemorating the anniversaries of significant days from the 1988 demonstrations. The regime saw such events as provocative and sent troops. At a commemoration Aung San Suu Kyi attended for students killed at Myenigone the year before, soldiers shot and killed one of the student participants. Aung San Suu Kyi herself was briefly arrested.[16]

What really upset the military top brass, however, was that Aung San Suu Kyi dared to criticize General Ne Win by name. Furthermore, she urged the army to be loyal to the country and the people rather than to General Ne Win. The government-controlled press attacked her for sowing discord between the *tatmadaw* and the people, and within the *tatmadaw* itself.[17]

On 19 July, Aung San Suu Kyi had planned to march with thousands of students to the tomb of her father to honour Martyr's Day, the day that General Aung San and his cabinet were assassinated in 1947. The SLORC responded by filling the streets with troops. Fearing that the military would storm the marchers, she called off the march at the last minute.[18] Rumours were already spreading that she would be arrested. It happened the next day. The military surrounded her compound on 20 July 1989 and put her under house arrest while sending thirty supporters who were there off to prison. On the same day, Tin Oo was arrested at his house, although neither he nor Aung San Suu Kyi was formally charged.[19]

The military intelligence had no legal justification for arresting Aung San Suu Kyi, but they searched her compound thoroughly for anything that could be used against her. They had found out that General Kyaw Zaw, a leading member of the CPB and one of General Aung San's close associates in the Thirty Comrades, had sent a letter for Aung San Suu Kyi through his daughter. Although the CPB had collapsed in April 1989 and the letter was apparently of a personal nature, the military intelligence hoped to use it to show a connection between the NLD and the outlawed CPB.[20]

San Kyaw Zaw, General Kyaw Zaw's daughter, was arrested. She had been a lecturer at Rangoon Institute of Economics but was never promoted to full professor because her father and other family members had joined the CPB. She insisted that she had not been able to meet with Aung San Suu Kyi and had destroyed the letter, but she was still ordered to sign a confession saying that she had delivered it. She refused. She was held at an interrogation centre for forty-five days, during which she was at first denied the right to sleep or bathe. Suffering from gynaecological problems, she was taken to a military hospital at one point, but not allowed to stay for treatment. Instead she was taken back to the interrogation centre where she says a drunk captain tried to rape her.

When they were not intimidating her, San Kyaw Zaw's interrogators sought to break her resolve through flattery. They told her that she was much better than Aung San Suu Kyi, because she had never left the country or married a foreigner. Still she held firm. When she started a hunger strike, they finally released her without having obtained the false confession. Nevertheless, the regime justified its arrest of Aung San Suu Kyi with the charge that she was being manipulated by the CPB while also involved in a rightist conspiracy involving Burmese exiles and foreign embassies. The faulty logic implicit in the contradictory accusations did not seem to bother the SLORC, and they never produced any hard evidence.[21]

Numerous NLD members throughout the country were also arrested in July, and Aung San Suu Kyi and Tin Oo were both later disqualified from running in the election. U Nu was arrested in December 1989 for refusing to withdraw his claim that his party represented a parallel government. Some other active parties were banned for their supposed CPB connections. Arrests of leading student activists had begun even earlier. The students' commemorations of the bloody days of one year before were drawing large crowds. To prevent them from spreading any further, the SLORC decided to quash the organizers.

Min Ko Naing was taken in March 1989, and when the Democratic Party for a New Society held its first conference in Rangoon, several central executive committee members were arrested and imprisoned. Moe Thee Zun managed to escape to the Thai–Burma border, where he joined the All Burma Students' Democratic Front (ABSDF), which had formed in late 1988.

In addition, the SLORC imposed numerous restrictions that limited the parties' ability to campaign. First, martial law was still in effect and anyone who said anything considered to be an attempt to split or defame the *tatmadaw* could be arrested. Moreover, meetings of more than five people were prohibited. Parties could not distribute party literature unless it had been cleared by the Home Ministry. The regime controlled all forms of media, and often used the media to attack the NLD and student organizations. Parties were promised the right to hold rallies and to have access to media airtime only during the last three months of the election campaign, but the election was not until May 1990, giving the regime over a year to try to manipulate the situation in its favour. Perhaps most worrying, when the election rules came out, there was no mention of how or when a new constitution would be written or when power would actually be transferred.

Despite the political arrests, which totalled an estimated six thousand by November 1989, members of the NLD continued to campaign throughout the country.[22] University students who had joined the NLD's youth wing were particularly active campaigners, finding the work both challenging and exhilarating. Even those who were not NLD members began to campaign for the NLD, realizing that only by uniting behind one party could they achieve a decisive election victory.

In the villages, those campaigning for the NLD often came into conflict with NUP organizers. Village heads who supported or were afraid of local military authorities sometimes let the NUP give public speeches, but not the NLD. To get around this obstacle, student activists sometimes pretended they were visiting friends and went quietly from house to house promoting the NLD. In some cases, the monks stood up for the NLD campaigners, giving them a chance to campaign more freely. But villagers were often afraid to be seen talking to NLD party members and publicly feigned indifference. They worried that if the NLD lost, they would be punished by the authorities and their livelihoods would be affected.

Another problem for the campaigners was that they often could not obtain the support of an entire village because of pre-existing social divisions. For instance, if there were two monasteries in the village, each abbot would have his own supporters. If one abbot came out in favour of the NLD, his supporters would follow suit. But the other abbot might refuse to support the NLD as a result. The same could happen if there were influential families in the village with long-standing rivalries.

Much of the campaigners' time was spent instructing illiterate villagers about how to mark the ballot properly and how to recognize the parties' symbols. The campaigners also explained what they thought democracy would mean for the villagers. Economic issues were a key concern, and Dr Tint Swe, an NLD candidate, often emphasized in his speeches how Burma had once been the richest country in South-East Asia, but was now one of the poorest. Putting it in terms the villagers could understand, he said that 5-ton trucks full of gold had disappeared because of General Ne Win's rule. Some campaigners told farmers that if the NLD won, they would be able to grow whatever they wanted without government interference, and they would no longer be locked in stocks in front of the police station if they could not meet their rice quotas.

Despite the authorities' harassment of political parties during the campaigning, the voting on election day itself was relatively free. Out of the 20.8 million people who had the right to vote, 72.5 per cent cast ballots.[23] Party representatives were allowed to be present at the polling stations, and the vote counting appears to have been fair. In the rural areas there were reports of intimidation, and some villagers could not reach polling stations because they were over a day's walk from their villages. Rangoon residents who had been moved to satellite towns because of their vigorous support for the pro-democracy demonstrations in 1988 also could not vote.[24] These problems, though, were relatively minor. It seems that the regime believed that with the top NLD leaders under arrest and many of the leading student activists in prison or exile, the NUP could pull off an election victory.

When the results came out, both the military and the people were astonished by the NLD's overwhelming victory. Most significantly, the NLD won seats in military-dominated districts in Rangoon and elsewhere, indicating that a number of the NLD candidates' votes came from army personnel. Although Aung San Suu Kyi was still under house arrest at the time of the election, the votes that the NLD received were largely because people strongly desired a return to democracy and had faith in her ability to lead. In some districts the NLD candidates were not inspiring leaders, and some did almost no campaigning, but they were voted into office on the strength of the people's conviction that the NLD needed a decisive victory.

Out of the 234 registered parties, ninety-three ended up fielding candidates and there were eighty-eight independent candidates. The NLD won 392 of the 485 parliamentary seats, including all fifty-nine seats in Rangoon Division. The military-backed National Unity Party won only ten seats. Twenty-five other parties, nineteen of which were ethnic minority parties, and six independents captured the remaining eighty-three seats.[25] Out of those, the Shan Nationalities League for Democracy won twenty-three seats, and the Arakan League for Democracy took eleven seats.

Post-election struggles

Before the election, the military had not mentioned when power would be handed over to the winning party, and General Saw Maung had said only that the winners would be able to form a provisional government and write a constitution. Once the regime realized it had lost, and badly, the generals began announcing delaying tactics. By early September, General Saw Maung was saying that first a National Convention would have to be convened to draw up the ground rules for the new constitution. Then, the elected representatives could meet to write the constitution, which would have to be approved by the people in a referendum. In the meantime, military rule would continue.[26]

After the 1988 coup, the SLORC had tried to distance itself from the BSPP regime. This was symbolically represented by the Burmanization of place names, which was intended to instil pride in being Burmese. The long-used colonial transliterations were discarded and Rangoon became 'Yangon' and Burma, 'Myanmar'. The most significant change, however, was the decision to open up the country to foreign investment. Many people had participated in the 1988 demonstrations as much for economic reasons as for political rights. Although the regime was stalling, Burmese citizens were at least left with the hope that the new economic policies might bring some measure of prosperity to the country.

Meanwhile, the NLD began planning how to transform their election victory into an actual transfer of power. NLD officials organized a party meeting at Gandhi Hall from 27 to 29 July to come to a consensus about how to proceed. Some members advocated negotiating with the regime, not wanting to do anything that might result in the disqualification of the party. Other members and many in the crowds outside the hall believed that the NLD should simply announce the formation of a new government then and there. The meeting ended up calling for the convening of the parliament by 30 September, a move that was seen as too assertive by some and not assertive enough by others.

In the following weeks, some MPs-elect held a number of secret meetings to discuss the formation of a parallel government if the regime did not transfer power. After the SLORC generals found out about the plans, they tried to arrest all involved, including Dr Sein Win, Aung San Suu Kyi's cousin. He and some of his colleagues, however, escaped to the KNU's headquarters on the Thai–Burma border. There he and eleven other elected members of parliament in exile formed the National Coalition Government of the Union of Burma (NCGUB), an organization that could take the democracy movement's case to the international community.

Inside the country, monks and students, particularly in Mandalay, engaged in various forms of civil disobedience to put pressure on the regime. The monks in Mandalay had been active throughout the election campaign, often openly supporting the NLD and using religious rituals to express their discontent with the junta. On 8 August 1990, student activists organized a commemoration of the second anniversary of the 1988 uprising. Monks gathered on 84th Street, and Mandalay residents brought alms in remembrance of those who had died. The student unions also came with their flags coloured black as a sign of mourning. The situation turned ugly after the military insisted that the students lower the flag, and a high-school student leader talked back to them. When soldiers started beating him in front of the crowd, a monk came forward to plead for a peaceful resolution of the problem. Then the soldiers started beating monks, and people began throwing rocks at the soldiers. The soldiers shot into the crowd, reportedly killing two monks and injuring many others. Several people were arrested.

In the meantime, the monks in Mandalay were so upset about the killings and arrests that they decided to start a religious boycott (*patta ni kozana kan*) against the regime. The organizers contacted monks in the towns of Sagaing, Monywa, Pegu and elsewhere, encouraging them to join the boycott. Thus, starting on 27 August 1990, participating monks rejected alms from soldiers and their families. Monks also refused to attend merit-making ceremonies at the houses of army families. Many army members and their families were visibly upset. Merit-making was an essential part of their lives. If monks were not present at funerals, for instance, it was believed that merit could not be made for the dead, and they would become ghosts rather than moving on to a higher form of existence.

Tensions also increased between the inhabitants of the monasteries and the soldiers camped out near or beside many of the larger monasteries in Mandalay. Many student activists were still based in the monasteries and traded insults with the soldiers. Finally, anger on both sides erupted into, of all things, slingshot battles. Apparently, the soldiers had been ordered not to fire their guns, but slingshots were permitted. In general, the soldiers fared much better in the battles at various monasteries than the untrained students and young monks. The soldiers knew how to coordinate their attacks and their ammunition was better. On one occasion the students beat a hasty retreat after it began raining. Their clay balls dissolved, while the military continued shooting steel balls.

Although it might seem strange that monks were participating in such violent activities, many people supported them, feeling that only the monks could continue the struggle for democracy. Older monks stayed away from the slingshot fights but did not punish the teenaged monks for breaking the monastic code of conduct.

After the religious boycott had continued for almost two months, spreading to other cities, without showing any signs of abating, the regime ordered it stopped. On 20 October 1990, military authorities in Mandalay were told to arrest and disrobe recalcitrant monks and to disband Buddhist organizations participating in anti-government activities. A few days later, the military raided over one hundred monasteries in Mandalay.[27] The boycott ended, and the remaining monks began accepting alms again. By forcing the monks into submission and chasing down and arresting elected members of parliament, the regime made it clear that protecting its own interests was its primary concern. A transfer of power appeared increasingly unlikely.

Although the elected MPs were unable to assume power, the NLD's election victory greatly enhanced the legitimacy of the pro-democracy movement both domestically and abroad. Clearly, the majority of the people in Burma favoured a democratic government under the leadership of Aung San Suu Kyi and her party. The pro-democracy movement had also benefited from being able to set up a nationwide organizational structure which reached into nearly every district and township. In the following years, members of the pro-democracy movement tried to keep the political focus on honouring the election results while the military regime sought to delegitimize the results and dismantle the NLD and other political organizations outside its control.

4 | Military rule continues, 1990–2000

> People might have had strong determination about '88, but in reality, the stomach also plays an important part. So, many people retreated. (NLD member from Upper Burma)

In the years following the 1990 election, Burma's leading generals focused on four objectives. First, they sought to expand the size of the armed forces in order to be in a stronger position against their armed and unarmed opponents. As a result, the number of soldiers was increased from 180,000 in 1988 to approximately 300,000 by the late 1990s, and new military compounds and bases were constructed throughout the country.[1] If mass protests were to break out again, there would be troops near by ready to take action. The number of military intelligence agents was also increased in order to infiltrate opposition organizations and monitor soldiers as well.

Second, the ruling generals worked to break up the organizational structure of the pro-democracy movement, and particularly the NLD. By keeping Aung San Suu Kyi under house arrest and the top party strategists in prison, they ensured that the party leadership was in disarray. Meanwhile local authorities used a variety of methods to put pressure on NLD members to resign.

Third, the regime attempted to neutralize the ethnic armed resistance movements by making ceasefire agreements with many of the armed groups. While some of the regime's early ceasefire deals gave de facto autonomy to the ceasefire groups, in other cases the ceasefires resulted in a weakening of the strength of the armed ethnic organizations and greater *tatmadaw* access into ethnic nationality areas. Whereas in the 1970s and 1980s the *tatmadaw* was facing numerous armed opponents along most of its northern and eastern borders, by 2000 only pockets of resistance remained.

Fourth, the SLORC tried to improve the economy by opening up the country to trade and foreign investment. The regime had no expertise in economic planning, however, and the generals were unwilling to delegate responsibility to trained economists. After an initial growth spurt in the early 1990s, the country suffered from declining investment, a severe depletion of foreign reserves and rampant inflation.

Military ascendancy

The period following the May 1990 elections until Aung San Suu Kyi's release from house arrest in July 1995 was one of ascendancy for the military regime. The high energy of the 1988 demonstrations and 1989/90 campaign period had dissipated. Non-violent means of bringing about change seemed to have proved unsuccessful. The international community had not intervened. People felt demoralized.

With Aung San Suu Kyi under house arrest and other prominent politicians and student activists in prison, in hiding or in the jungle, the democratic movement's momentum collapsed. Those who were still free had no clear plan of action for how to continue the struggle, and the military regime was taking steps systematically to eliminate its opposition.

Over the next two years, the military weeded out civil servants and military personnel who had been active in the 1988 demonstrations or showed clear anti-military attitudes. One way they determined who posed a threat was by administering a questionnaire to all civil servants in 1991. This questionnaire had two functions: first, to identify those openly disloyal to the regime and, second, to intimidate others into submission. Those who answered 'yes' to the question 'Is it appropriate to elect as the Head of State somebody who is married to a foreigner?' were likely to find themselves out of a job or transferred to a remote or inactive post. The question clearly referred to Aung San Suu Kyi. Other questions included: 'How should the military, which is shouldering the country's welfare, regard those who view it as their enemy?' and 'As the government has already instructed civil servants to be free from party politics, do you know that disciplinary actions will be taken in case of violating these instructions?'

In the meantime, there was no constitution in effect, and the SLORC ruled by decree, citing whichever laws from previous political eras proved useful. The SLORC initially appeared to follow through on its pledge to open the economy, however. Many people consoled themselves with the hope that at least their standard of living might improve and perhaps gradual political changes would result.

The SLORC legalized private enterprise and welcomed foreign investment, particularly in joint ventures with military-owned companies. A number of foreign businesses came into the country to invest in oil, gas, lumber and mining, to set up labour-intensive manufacturing industries and to import consumer goods. New jobs became available to Burmese working with these foreign companies and in the service sectors that supported them. With the regime's promotion of tourism, several new hotels were constructed in Rangoon, Mandalay and Pagan, also providing employment. Opportunities for trade grew, and some Burmese were able to travel out of the country for business or pleasure.

To facilitate economic development, the SLORC initiated infrastructure projects such as roads, bridges and irrigation canals throughout Burma. Although such projects are part of the normal work of any modern government, the generals in power since 1988 have taken great pride in their achievements in this area. As a headline in the *New Light of Myanmar* put it: 'Progress Made in Nation-building Projects at Present Many Times Greater than in Periods when the Country Received Foreign Assistance'.[2] In fact, many of the projects were carried out by forced labourers working under duress.

At the same time, the military regime was scoring victories in its long-standing battles with armed groups. In 1989, the Communist Party of Burma collapsed. The ethnic minority factions within the CPB broke off and agreed to ceasefires with the regime in return for minimal *tatmadaw* interference in their internal affairs. In practice, this meant that the newly formed United Wa State Army and the Kokang-led Myanmar National Democratic Alliance Army could produce and traffic drugs with impunity. Between 1989 and 1991, twenty-three new heroin refineries opened in Kokang territory in the hills of northern Burma.[3] At the local level, Burmese military officers profited from the drug business through taxing the farmers, the owners of heroin refineries and the traffickers.[4] Moreover, a number of the country's major investments in infrastructure projects and hotels were made by drug kingpins permitted to launder their money and establish legal businesses, often in the form of joint ventures with military-owned holding companies.[5]

In the early and mid-1990s, the SLORC was also successful in splitting the Democratic Alliance of Burma, an alliance of many of the ethnic nationalist armies who had previously refused to negotiate separately. The Pa'o National Organization was the first to break with its allies and made a ceasefire deal with the SLORC in March 1991. Others, including the powerful Kachin Independence Organization, soon followed, leaving only a few diehard groups to battle on by themselves. Most of the groups felt that they could not compete with the increasingly powerful *tatmadaw*, and they were better off making a deal that would give them continued control over some territory as well as the chance to bring development to the civilians in their areas.

In 1996, Khun Sa, an armed opposition leader and drug warlord long wanted in the United States on heroin-trafficking charges, gave up his armed struggle and moved to Rangoon. The regime refused to extradite him despite the US government's offer of a $2 million reward. Instead, he was allowed to make property and transportation investments, and to build two casinos near the Thai border.[6]

With the military firmly in control and taking steps to open up the economy, many of the people who had participated so actively in the 1988 demonstrations and election campaign decided to forget about politics for a while. Instead they focused on finding good jobs and taking advantage of the new opportunities.

One former student activist, Zaw Zaw Oo, talked about how his feelings changed over the years. After the regime suppressed the NLD following the 1990 elections, he said: 'The NLD became less and less active, so I had to find something else.' He finished his university education and found a job with a foreign investment firm with interests in Burma. His job gave him not only a good salary but also a chance to travel and to meet with high-powered foreign businessmen and senior government officials. Zaw Zaw Oo said democracy was still a priority, but not his top priority. He believed that developing the country was more important. He saw his change in ideas as very much related to his experiences in the business world, in which, he said, 'you look for possible things, not ideal things'. Particularly in the early and mid-1990s when the economy seemed to be turning around, many people agreed with Zaw Zaw Oo.

For student activists committed to continuing the struggle for democracy, it was a depressing period. At least three female students, including Tin Tin Nyo, a prominent activist in 1988, committed suicide after being released from prison in the mid-1990s, in part because they felt so alienated from their relatives and peers, who had seemingly forsaken their ideals.

At the same time, the regime's new policies also made it more difficult for students to congregate. Because of the backlog of students who had graduated from high school but not been able to proceed on to the universities, when universities were finally reopened, one-year courses were reduced to three or four months. Thus, students had little chance to get to know each other before they found themselves taking exams and sent home on vacation again.

There were a few small protests, but these led only to more arrests. In December 1991, when Aung San Suu Kyi was awarded the Nobel Peace Prize, there was a brief resurgence of hope and calls for her release by university students in Rangoon and Mandalay. The regime responded by closing the universities for several months. In February 1995, when

73

former prime minister U Nu died, some students daringly unfurled party banners and sang pro-democracy songs as they marched in his funeral procession. Those who did not manage to run away in time were arrested and sent to prison.

Some student activists sought to keep the struggle alive through writing political pamphlets and articles and trying to maintain and expand their networks. A few, such as Min Zin, spent several years in hiding, moving from place to place to stay one step ahead of the intelligence agents. Others took on new identities in faraway towns and villages. This type of student was by far the exception, but they continued to hope for another spark to set off a mass movement like that of 1988, despite people's still-vivid memories of the widespread killings and destruction.

The National Convention

In 1992, the junta sacked General Saw Maung. The SLORC was now headed by Senior General Than Shwe, with Lieutenant General Khin Nyunt and General Maung Aye playing leading roles in policy-making, and General Ne Win still possibly exerting influence behind the scenes. Lieutenant General Khin Nyunt, known as Secretary-1 of the SLORC and the head of Directorate of Defence Services Intelligence, made his career in military intelligence. General Maung Aye, the vice-chairman of the SLORC and the commander-in-chief of the army, rose through battle-field command positions. In general, the field commanders in Burma look down on the intelligence personnel, because they do not risk their lives for their country, but General Ne Win always nurtured the leading intelligence men in order to check the power of the field commanders. The intelligence officers gathered as much information on the commanders as they did on political dissidents.

Despite some tension between the two branches, the leading generals seem to have agreed that holding the National Convention to write a new constitution would help them all stay in power. Besides ensuring their own key role in the country's political life, the generals hoped to use the National Convention to marginalize the 1990 election winners and resolve the ethnic nationalities' demands without giving much ground. The first meeting was convened in January 1993. Of the 702 delegates whom the regime invited, only ninety-nine were elected members of parliament, out of which eighty-one were from the NLD. The other 603 delegates were all appointed by the SLORC. Some came from ceasefire groups, with a few being suspected drug traffickers.[7]

With the announcement of the National Convention, the NLD had to decide whether it should participate or not. Some members believed it was important to keep the party legal, and by attending the convention they could have a forum for voicing their views. Others thought the NLD should boycott the National Convention because it was a sham and the entire process delegitimized the 1990 election results. Finally, the NLD decided to attend.

Representatives of ethnic minority political parties that had won seats in the election also participated. Some were initially optimistic that the drafting process would allow them to push for a political structure that would provide for greater ethnic autonomy. Once the convention began, however, their hopes were dashed. While many outsiders hoped that the convention would provide a viable arena for resolving Burma's political future, in fact the delegates never had a chance. Daniel Aung, a delegate who later fled the country, explained how the convention actually worked.

An elected Lahu representative from the Lahu National Progressive Party, Daniel Aung was impressed with his invitation to participate in the National Convention. The letter stated that, because he was a political leader, he was responsible for drafting the constitution. He remembered: 'I thought they really meant it.' He had previously worked as an editor in the foreign department of the government-controlled Burma News Agency, but he had resigned in 1988 and run for election in 1990. Still eager to participate in the political process, he looked forward to the convention.

When he attended the first session, he was surprised when the meeting lasted only two days. Some delegates from distant towns hadn't even arrived, but that didn't seem to matter to the generals in charge. Lieutenant General Myo Nyunt, the chairman of the National Convention Convening Committee, gave the opening speech. Daniel Aung recalled that most of the speech consisted of praise for the military. Lieutenant General Myo Nyunt informed the delegates that the Burmese military was different from militaries in other countries. Because the Burmese military had saved the country from collapse so many times, it must take the leading role in political affairs.

Daniel Aung and the other delegates soon found out that the six main objectives of the constitution had already been written by the SLORC. Although no one had any arguments with the first five, the sixth objective stated that 25 per cent of the parliament's seats must be held by military members chosen by the commander in chief of the armed forces.

When the convention next convened, the delegates were divided into eight groups and ordered to come up with points to be included in the constitution. The SLORC had provided the delegates with a list of points drawn from other countries' constitutions, with many calling for military involvement in political affairs. Still, the delegates were told they could draft their own suggestions, and they were given access to a library with many constitutional books.

The working groups were told that they could discuss freely, but each group was assigned government clerks to take notes. The clerks became nervous when the delegates spoke against the institutionalization of the military's role in politics. Daniel Aung remembers a clerk passing him a note asking him to tell one of the delegates to stop talking. As the chairman of his working group, Daniel Aung wrote back, 'You are not responsible, I am,' and allowed the man to continue. Daniel Aung said that some of the clerks privately asked the delegates to forgive them, but they had to intervene in the meetings because of their bosses' orders.

Although the delegates were allowed to write their own suggestions, the SLORC took no notice of them. The delegates were not even allowed to read their drafts in front of the entire assembly. The authorities would rewrite their papers first and insist that the delegates read the corrected versions, without adding as much as a word. Daniel Aung remembers the authorities who handed them the revised papers saying, 'Feel pity on us and read it.' In one instance, a representative from the Shan State prefaced his paper by reminding the delegates how important it was that they should not leave the country with a shameful legacy. At once, a general stood up and shouted to the chairman to silence him.

The authorities also maintained surveillance over the delegates in the barracks where they had to stay. Although the delegates were treated well by the various military people assigned to assist them, their primary function was to keep an eye on the delegates. If three or four delegates sat together talking, military agents would approach, turn their backs and listen intently. The regime also tried to prevent delegates from the political parties from developing close relations with the non-elected delegates by housing them separately and assigning them separate tables in the dining hall. If the elected delegates tried to engage the appointed delegates in conversation, the appointed delegates became nervous. Among the appointed delegates were several of Daniel Aung's old friends and classmates, but they did not dare to talk to him.

Like many of the other ethnic minority representatives, Daniel Aung was frustrated in his attempts to obtain political rights for his people. He hoped to create an autonomous region for the Lahus, most of whom live in four townships in Shan State. The regime rejected his proposal, however, saying that the Lahu population did not constitute a majority in all four of the townships. Moreover, the regime was opposed to the word 'autonomy'. Only 'national area' was allowed, a term that did not convey any power or rights. The Wa representatives were also upset because no significant political rights were being accorded to them, although the United Wa State Army controlled a large part of Shan State. But some of the other appointed ethnic representatives said little. They could not speak Burmese well, and there were no official translators.

Eventually, Daniel Aung and others realized that the principles they were supposedly drafting were already written. But still they had to participate in the charade. Attendance at the general assembly sessions was required. Many delegates simply read books or slept. Even Lieutenant General Myo Nyunt could often be found dozing. Daniel Aung and some other delegates spent a fair amount of time in the bathroom, the only place where they could talk freely.

When the military came out with the final draft of 104 basic principles, it bore little resemblance to what the committees had put together. What bothered Daniel Aung the most was that the generals thanked the delegates for doing such a good job. He told Aung Shwe, the head of the NLD delegation, 'We have to protest.' Another delegate said that since the delegates were forced to attend, they didn't bear any responsibility for the constitution, but Daniel Aung insisted, 'We'll be blacklisted in history.'

U Aung Shwe suggested that each of the six elected parties attending write their own protest letters to Lieutenant General Myo Nyunt. The letters all requested the military authorities to reconsider what they had done. Although Daniel Aung said he encouraged some of the non-elected delegates to join them in protesting, they were too afraid. For writing letters of protest, the NLD and the SNLD leaders were called in by Lieutenant General Myo Nyunt and scolded for their insolence. Daniel Aung decided he had had enough. During the next break, he and his family went back to their home town in the north, rode motorbikes into the mountains and continued on foot for four days to the Thai border. They have been living in exile ever since.

With the subsequent walkout of the NLD and the serious disgruntlement of some of the ethnic representatives, convention meetings ceased for eight years, although the generals sitting on the Convening Committee continued to meet periodically. The fact that the process was still ongoing provided a convenient justification for why power could not yet be transferred.

The release of Aung San Suu Kyi, 1995

Aung San Suu Kyi's release came as a surprise to almost everyone. On 10 July 1995 she was informed that her period of house arrest had ended. She did not rush out of her compound, and no announcement was made in the official media, but as the rumour of her release spread, people ventured near her house to find out whether it was true. Soon she appeared from behind her gate, standing on a table, assuring her well-wishers that she was indeed free and in good health. That week she went to her gate every afternoon to greet the groups of people who continued to gather there. Finally she announced that she would come to the gate only on weekends because she had to get back to the party's political work, as if the almost six years of house arrest had been nothing more than a brief irritation.

Stories began emerging about the hardships she had faced during her house arrest. She had run out of money and refused donations of food from the military authorities. When her poor diet led to illness, she finally agreed to sell her furniture to the regime to obtain cash. On a few occasions her husband and sons had been permitted to visit, but most of her time was spent alone, reading, listening to the radio and meditating. Military intelligence lived just inside her front gate, preventing all except a few relatives from entering or leaving. Although she tried to befriend the intelligence agents, the personnel were changed regularly to prevent warm relations from developing.

Upon her release, foreign journalists poured into the country to interview her. When they expressed sympathy with her plight she insisted that others had suffered much more than she had. Two other senior party members, Tin Oo and Kyi Maung, for instance, had been sent to Insein prison. But they had recently been freed and, when they learned of Aung San Suu Kyi's release, they headed to her compound and agreed to work with her to rebuild the party.

It seems that the SLORC let Aung San Suu Kyi go in order to improve relations with Japan. Japan was promising to resume full-scale development aid if the regime restored greater political and economic openness in Burma.[8] The SLORC felt confident that with the economy picking up, people would soon lose interest in Aung San Suu Kyi, and she would fade from the political scene. Moreover, Aung San Suu Kyi's party was a shambles, and she and Tin Oo had been removed from their positions on the Central Executive Committee in 1991 to keep the party legal. Many NLD members were still in prison or had given up political work.

Aung San Suu Kyi didn't appear to be much of a threat, but the regime underestimated her power to revitalize the party and to draw international attention. Foreign journalists were captivated, NLD party members from the various townships and divisions came to Rangoon for instructions, and the NLD Central Executive Committee started holding daily meetings, with Aung San Suu Kyi and Tin Oo reinstated in their former positions. Although a posse of military intelligence officers continued to live just inside the compound, registering everyone who entered, at first they did not hinder anyone. Soon the compound was in full swing, with meetings, study groups and press conferences taking place. The National Convention was still holding sessions, but the NLD members who had attended the convention felt as frustrated as Daniel Aung did. When the convention reconvened at the end of November 1995, the NLD delegates decided to walk out, saying they would not return until a real political dialogue began. The SLORC dismissed their demand and announced their expulsion from the convention a few days later.

Meanwhile, a new political centre emerged at Aung San Suu Kyi's compound, with foreign governments, ethnic political leaders and the domestic population carefully watching her every move. Many hoped that a dialogue between the NLD and the regime could take place, but the generals thought it was unnecessary. They believed they could limit Aung San Suu Kyi's influence and maintain control without having to make any concessions.

With the regime seemingly unwilling to talk, the NLD felt compelled to raise its public profile. In January 1996, the NLD held an Independence Day celebration at Aung San Suu Kyi's compound and invited a famous troupe of comedians and dancers from Mandalay to perform. Exhilarated by the NLD's resurgence, Par Par Lay and Lu Zaw used mime to parody the regime indirectly. In one skit, one of the comedians sat on a chair beaming. There was only a single chair, so when the second man came on to the stage, he gestured that he would like a turn. The first comedian refused to yield to him, despite his pleas for fairness and attempts at persuasion. Watching this, the audience was doubled over in laughter, for the chair obviously represented the government, the person sitting on the chair was the military regime, and the person asking politely for his turn symbolized the elected MPs.[9]

Because they dared to make these kinds of jokes, the two comedians were arrested. Aung San Suu Kyi and several other members tried to go to Mandalay to attend the trial, but when they arrived at the train station in Rangoon, they were informed that their assigned carriage happened to have mechanical problems, so they wouldn't be able to travel. Meanwhile, the comedians were sentenced to seven years' imprisonment.[10] They were sent to a hard labour camp in Kachin State, where they were originally set to work breaking rocks. The health of both declined rapidly, and they were later moved to a prison in Myitkyina, the capital of Kachin State.

Still, the NLD went on to hold large meetings in May 1996 to commemorate the 1990 election victory and in September 1996 to mark the eighth anniversary of the party's founding. Each time, military intelligence prevented large numbers of invitees from leaving their home towns, or put them under detention in military barracks until the meetings were over. In one case, delegates who made it to Aung San Suu Kyi's street were simply put into a truck and driven to a rural area several miles out of Rangoon, where they were dumped and had to make their own way back. By the time they reached the city, the meeting was over.

In the meantime, Aung San Suu Kyi had been giving public talks from her gate every weekend. On Saturdays, she would speak for an hour, and on Sundays, she, Tin Oo and Kyi Maung would each speak for twenty minutes. These talks, which came to be known as 'People's Forums', were an attempt by the NLD leadership to communicate their ideas to the people and to inspire them to take part in the political movement. Aung San Suu Kyi had a mailbox attached to the front of her gate so that people could drop off questions during the week. Her staff selected the most pressing questions for her to address. The reading and answering of the letters gave the talks a give-and-take feeling, and the audience frequently chimed in with laughter and applause.

Two hours before the talk was scheduled to begin, people would begin arriving in front of her house, bringing pieces of newspaper to sit on and umbrellas to block the sun or rain. Soon hawkers would arrive peddling betel nut, cold water and snacks. Friends gathered at appointed locations, chatting happily in the festive atmosphere. By 3 p.m., the area in front of her gate and across the street would be packed with people. At 3.45, the crowd would begin chanting, 'Long live Daw Aung San Suu Kyi! Long live U Kyi Maung! Long live U Tin Oo!' By 3.55, the chanting would have reached fever pitch, and when the NLD leaders arrived at the gate, everyone would leap up, shouting and clapping ecstatically.

On the several occasions that I attended, I found all kinds of people in the crowd, including students, retired businessmen, young couples, market vendors and monks. Once I made the mistake of sitting next to a wizened old man, long past seventy and missing most of his teeth. When Aung San Suu Kyi appeared, he was so eager to signal his joy that he jumped to his feet and proceeded to twirl his umbrella over his head faster and faster, endangering the lives of all sitting around him. He had to be gently restrained by the students behind him.

Each week, Aung San Suu Kyi urged her listeners to consider ways in which they could participate in the movement. Despite many people's hopes that she would effect political change for them, she realized that she and the remaining NLD members could do little without popular participation. On 16 March 1996, she urged her audience to recognize the power that they had but were not tapping into. She read out a question that had been sent to her. 'Why don't we have democracy yet in our country? Why is it delayed?' She answered,

> Some people [the generals] don't really want to give democracy. And people aren't really working for it. Democracy activists need to put in more effort ... The reason for the delay in getting democracy is that we Burmese people lack confidence in ourselves. People think they are not able to do it.

She then brought up Vaclav Havel's essay, 'The power of the powerless'. Written about Czechoslovakia under Soviet rule, Havel's words had relevance for the struggle in Burma as well. She said, 'We need to understand that people who are not in power have their own power. Don't think you don't have any power just because you are not part of the power structure.' She talked about how the regime made great efforts to demonstrate they had the support of the people, for instance by staging pro-government rallies which people were forced to attend. The regime, she said, was using the power of the people to prop up their own power structure. If people didn't have power, the regime would not bother with them. She declared, 'That is why we rely on the people. Because you have power. For that reason, we are openly requesting people-power from the people.'

On Sundays, Tin Oo talked mostly about legal issues and the application of Buddhist principles. After being expelled from the military and imprisoned in the mid-1970s, he studied law and also spent a period of time as a monk. On 18 February 1996, he related the words of the Buddha to the current political situation, explaining how the Buddha had said that you must do exactly as you say and you must be honest in reporting what you have done. The regime, he said, was always talking about restoring democracy but was doing nothing to make it happen.

Kyi Maung, also a former senior military officer who had retired in the 1960s, often used the format of his young grandson asking him simple questions. On 5 May 1996, he said that his grandson had asked him what kind of newspaper he wanted to see in Burma. Because all the newspapers in the country were under state control and the regime sought to turn public opinion against the NLD through scathing editorials, freedom of expression was naturally an important issue for the NLD. Kyi Maung said that he told his grandson he wanted a newspaper that was 'not slanted, not weighted to one side, not expressing a personal point of view as if it's everyone's view'. He concluded by pointing out that in democratic countries there are no government-controlled newspapers.

The celebratory feeling at the talks was infectious. Here were people announcing over loudspeakers what other people only dared to whisper. Still, the talks never attracted more than 10,000 people, and usually only around 3,000 or so. The SLORC assumed people would soon become bored, but the crowds, while not growing, held steady. So the regime began intimidating the audience by having military intelligence personnel walk slowly through the crowds videotaping each and every face. This brought the size of the audiences down somewhat, but didn't eliminate them. Some people resorted to driving slowly back and forth in front of the house or taking the bus that passed the compound so that they could get a taste of the event without being identified. Others listened to the audio tapes or even watched videotapes of the talks, made and copied by pro-democracy supporters. The video and audio tapes found their way to Mandalay and other towns around the country, where NLD members set up free lending libraries. The authorities began arresting people caught distributing these tapes outside Rangoon.[11]

The battle was also played out in the entertainment industry. The military-sponsored TV station ran a programme mocking Aung San Suu Kyi. A dishevelled old hag missing her front teeth stood behind a rickety gate haranguing a group of sorry-looking children. Some people stoned the house of the actress who played Aung San Suu Kyi. Around the same time, Lay Phyu, a popular rock singer, released a cassette entitled *Power 54*. At first the censorship board passed it, but they later recalled all the cassettes when they realized that the 54 intentionally referred to, or could be interpreted as referring to, Aung San Suu Kyi's home address, 54 University Avenue. Lay Phyu was forced to change the title to *Power*.

Unwilling to tolerate continued public challenges to their authority, the generals decided to end the talks once and for all. Starting in late September 1996, the military simply placed barbed-wire barricades at either end of the block every weekend and refused to allow people through. Aung San Suu Kyi and Tin Oo managed to get around the barricades to meet the crowds at another junction a few times, but on one occasion in November they were attacked by a mob of 200 people who pelted their car with stones and smashed it with iron bars. Aung San Suu Kyi was not hurt, although Tin Oo suffered minor injuries. Witnesses reported seeing the young attackers arriving on military trucks, and the attack took place in the lane in front of Kyi Maung's house, where ordinary people had no access because it was cordoned off by government security personnel. Still, the regime denied its involvement and in a commentary in the government-controlled *New Light of Myanmar* wrote that Aung San Suu Kyi was 'trying to destroy all prospects for stability of the state with her fangs' and that many kinds of people were opposed to her.[12]

During this period, the regime tried to split the NLD by focusing its attacks on Aung San Suu Kyi and stressing her links to the West. Newspaper editorials often referred to her as 'Suu Kyi', dropping the first part of her name, which links her to her father, the national hero. Alternatively, they called her 'Mrs Michael Aris', using her husband's name, which emphasized her marriage to a foreigner. This goes against Burmese norms in which women keep their own name after marriage and are not referred to by their husbands' names.

In the meantime, Aung San Suu Kyi's political activities in 1995 and 1996 had spurred some old and new activists to take action. Many former student activists who had had little contact since 1988 found each other again at Aung San Suu Kyi's compound. And as in the mid-1980s, a new generation of student activists began looking for activities they could undertake to spark a movement.

Student demonstrations, 1996

To politicize university students, young activists began marking the anniversary of the March 1988 death of the student Phone Maw. In 1996, numbers of university students came to classes dressed in black. Some of the male students were particularly happy to see fashionable female models wearing black hats and black jean shirts with red roses attached, because the modelling industry had become extremely popular after the country had begun to allow foreign investment. Young activists also found inspiration in the Free Burma groups that began forming in the United States and elsewhere. The Free Burma Coalition was particularly active on American university campuses, where students began boycotting Pepsi because of its investment in Burma. Some students quietly took up the Pepsi boycott in Rangoon as well. Although the students' activities were limited, they tried to work in parallel to Aung San Suu Kyi and the NLD by raising people's awareness and encouraging them to participate in simple acts of political defiance.

Student activism spread after a brawl in October 1996 similar to the March 1988 incident. Some students from Rangoon Institute of Technology got into an altercation at a restaurant with a few auxiliary police, who beat them up. The students were detained, and the news quickly spread around campus. Students organized an on-campus demonstration protesting against police brutality and calling for the punishment of the auxiliary policemen and an accurate news report of the event in the official media. The beaten students were quickly released, but students involved in organizing the demonstration were later detained, prompting more demonstrations in early December. This time, the students took the demonstrations into the city centre. On the night of 2 December, students marched from the busy Hledan junction past the Shwedagon Pagoda and on to the American embassy. Then on the night of 6 December, they held another demonstration at Hledan junction, which I happened to witness.

When a friend and I arrived at around 7 p.m., the junction was blocked off by military barricades in all five directions. We could hear people making speeches and the audience shouting its approval as we made our way through the wide circle of perhaps two thousand standing people. In the centre about a thousand students were seated on the ground surrounding a student holding a fighting-peacock flag on a makeshift bamboo pole. Other students held framed photographs of General Aung San, and some had handmade posters with slogans in Burmese and English. Students took turns coming to the flagpole to give short speeches. One shouted: 'University courses are supposed to last a year, but we get only a few months. How can we learn anything like this?' Another countered: 'It will be OK if all of us are uneducated. The degree is not useful. So we have to sacrifice here to form the student union.'

Soon the speeches became more heated, with speakers calling on the audience to remember the country's long history of student activism. Whenever there was a lull in the speech-making, the students sang revolutionary songs and shouted in a call-and-response form: 'Do we have unity? Yes, we do!' and 'To set up student unions: our cause!'

I and the other dozen Westerners present were approached by students eager to tell us why they were protesting. Many also wanted to inform us about the situation in their home towns. One student told me that he was from an island where his family and others' boats were routinely requisitioned by the military authorities, and they had recently been pressed into forced labour to build a bridge to another island. Another complained that all the houses in his village, including his own, had been torn down without compensation to make way for a new jail. A third announced how fed up he was with the FOC system. When I asked what FOC meant, he said, '"Free of charge", the military just takes everything it wants without paying.'

A group of students circulated around the area distributing water and sweets donated by local shopkeepers, while others picked up rubbish. As students from different universities arrived and announced their presence, cheers broke out. But as the night wore on, and armed soldiers and riot police began moving closer, the atmosphere changed. Many students and onlookers became afraid and silently slipped away. Professors sent by the military came several times to ask the students to disperse, but they refused to leave until Lieutenant General Khin Nyunt, Secretary-1 of the SLORC and also the chairman of the Myanmar Education Committee, came to meet with them. He did not. Instead, the troops and riot police began inching towards the students, clearly hoping to intimidate them into leaving without having to use force.

By 2 a.m., there were only 100 students left, sitting in a tight triangle, praying as they faced the Shwedagon Pagoda. On the pavement, there were about 150 students and locals armed with chair legs, determined to fight back even while the students in the centre had called for non-violent resistance. The remaining onlookers, including myself and the other Westerners, had moved up to balconies overlooking the junction. After giving a final warning, the troops trained water-cannons on the silent students and stormed the area. Everywhere shattering glass, screams and wails could be heard as people were injured and arrested. We made our way into people's apartments, where we sat out the rest of the night in utter silence and darkness, though some of the Burmese girls in the room could barely stifle their sobs. In the early morning hours, we were able to slip out, although the apartment owners were later interrogated and the leaders of the demonstration imprisoned.

Over the next week, several smaller 'lightning' demonstrations occurred in front of various universities in Rangoon and other towns, but the universities were soon closed down and barricades erected on all the main thoroughfares, making it impossible for the students to network. The demonstrations ceased, but the military was clearly troubled to see that many Rangoon residents had been quick to provide food and money for the students, even if they had not joined in themselves. Moreover, the demonstrators had included a number of ethnic minority students from the different ethnic states.

From December 1996 until mid-1998, the main universities in Rangoon and Mandalay were closed. Universities in Rangoon were briefly reopened in August 1998 so that registered students could take exams. Protests broke out, however, and the universities were shut again. One of the students involved in organizing the protests, Thet Win Aung, was sentenced to fifty-three years in prison, with the sentence later increased to fifty-nine years. Other student activists were also given long sentences in what was clearly an attempt by the regime to deter students from participating in political activities.

The regime eventually reopened some of the smaller institutes and colleges, but they moved most of the student body out of the central campuses in Rangoon and Mandalay. Rangoon Institute of Technology and Mandalay Institute of Technology were folded into a new government technical college system with thirty small campuses around the country. The level of education offered at these colleges was lower than at the former institutes of technology, with six-year programmes being reduced to four years. When some of the new government technical college campuses opened in mid-December 1999, students protested because of the poor facilities and the downgrading of the educational level. Many students gave up on obtaining a university degree and enrolled in short-term diploma courses or went abroad as migrant workers.

Regular university courses reopened in 2000, but most were no longer held on their former campuses in Rangoon. Instead, new campuses had been built in satellite towns outside the city. Most importantly, from a political point of view, students could not easily organize demonstrations any more, because the campuses were scattered and the access roads into Rangoon could be easily blocked. At the same time, students were frustrated by the long commute time, the poor quality of the facilities and the general uselessness of a university education.

The regime changes its name

The regime faced challenges in the mid- and late 1990s, as it struggled with a weakening economy and pressure from domestic political groups and foreign organizations and governments. Foreign investment began declining in the mid-1990s owing to poor economic management and constantly changing regulations. The Asian economic crisis in 1997 and Aung San Suu Kyi's repeated calls for foreign businesses to stay out also resulted in reduced investment. Throughout the late 1990s, inflation was running in double-digit numbers, eroding the value of fixed salaries and leading hundreds of thousands of Burmese to seek work outside the country.

In November 1997, the SLORC renamed itself the State Peace and Development Council (SPDC). The switch was meant to project a softer image, because the regime had been ridiculed for years for calling itself by such a monstrous-sounding name. At the same time, some of the most blatantly corrupt SLORC members, such as Lieutenant Generals Tun Kyi, the minister of trade, Myint Aung, the minister of agriculture, and Kyaw Ba, the minister of tourism, were removed. All three had been prominent regional commanders in the past and were viewed as potential rivals to other senior SLORC members. Lieutenant General Khin Nyunt and General Maung Aye used the occasion to strengthen their own positions by promoting younger, more loyal men to second-line leadership positions.

At the time of the name change, rumours were rife about possible splits in the military and whether these might not possibly lead to one side negotiating with the NLD. The differences appear to have been over tactics rather than goals, however. Lieutenant General Khin Nyunt was trying to destroy the NLD by having local authorities intimidate party members, harass their families and incarcerate those who refused to resign. The intention was to isolate Aung San Suu Kyi and reduce her party's legitimacy. Some of the field commanders, on the other hand, apparently favoured more heavy-handed tactics such as mob attacks against her.

There was a similar divergence in tactics used to weaken the ethnic resistance movements. While Lieutenant General Khin Nyunt tried to break up and buy off armed ethnic nationalist groups with promises of lucrative economic concessions, troops under General Maung Aye's command undertook military offensives and massive depopulations of the areas where the ethnic nationalist armies operated. In fact, the mixed tactics succeeded in making many of the ethnic armies decide they were better off negotiating.

Nevertheless, as an intelligence officer with no support base among the infantry, Lieutenant General Khin Nyunt's position within the regime was contingent on General Ne Win's support. In an effort to make himself indispensable, Khin Nyunt asserted his personal authority over many aspects of national policy. In the late 1990s, he led the Directorate of Defence Services Intelligence, and was also the chairman of over a dozen policy-making committees, including the Office of Strategic Studies, the Information Policy Committee, the Association of South-East Asian Nations (ASEAN) steering committee, the National Health Committee, the Myanmar Education Committee, the Work Committee for the Development of Border Areas and National Races, and the Leading Committee for Perpetual All-round Renovation of Shwedagon Pagoda.

Meanwhile, the regime's chairman, Senior General Than Shwe, tried to woo the masses and secure his own base of support through the establishment of the Union Solidarity and Development Association (USDA). Although purportedly a social organization, the USDA was often used to defend the interests of the regime.[13] Membership in the USDA, founded in 1993, quickly rose to several million people. In rural areas, many farmers joined because they were informed that USDA members would be exempted from forced labour projects. Others became members so that they could travel without police harassment and receive other perks. The USDA also held occasional courses in computing, English and other subjects for its members.

Less-educated people in particular were drawn to the USDA, believing it was really working for the country. In several districts, however, people's names were simply added to membership lists without their ever being consulted. In some schools, teachers of eighth-standard students (age fourteen) and up were ordered to give the names of their students to the USDA for automatic membership. And it was virtually impossible to become a civil servant without first joining the USDA.

Beginning in 1996, the regime sought to turn the USDA into a counter-force against the NLD and student activists. This was reflected in many of the USDA leaders' speeches. As reported in the state-controlled press, Than Shwe himself told senior USDA leaders in November 1996:

> It is the duty of the entire people including USDA members to resolutely crush destructive elements inside and outside the country as the common enemy who are disrupting all the development endeavours with the sole aim of gaining power.[14]

The authorities also gave military training to some USDA youth and used them to intimidate and attack Aung San Suu Kyi and her supporters. The aim was to make it appear that the people, and not just the regime, were opposed to her and the NLD. Periodically, the USDA organized mass rallies throughout the country to demonstrate support for military rule and to denounce the NLD. As in the pre-1988 period, respected individuals were handed speeches which they were ordered to read with sufficient passion. While few people enjoyed attending these rallies, except in cases when they were happy for a break from work, almost nobody refused to go. Names were checked at the gate and those who did not turn up were threatened with fines and other unpleasant consequences.

Frustrated that the regime was refusing to engage in a political dialogue with Aung San Suu Kyi, the NLD began taking more aggressive steps. After the party congress held on 27 May 1998, the NLD urged the regime to recognize the 1990 election results and convene the parliament within sixty days. In August, the NLD announced that if the regime refused to convene the parliament, the NLD would do so itself. The regime responded by arresting hundreds of NLD members to prevent them from meeting. In September 1998, the NLD formed a Committee Representing the People's Parliament (CRPP), consisting of NLD and other ethnic political party members.

Determined to crush the NLD, the regime stepped up its efforts to shut down remaining party offices and force not only elected MPs but also party members to resign. In late 1998 and 1999, almost every day the state-controlled newspapers featured articles about the latest mass resignations from the NLD in various townships. Not reported in the newspapers was the fact that USDA members in some districts were going house to house threatening NLD members that, if they did not resign, they would suffer serious consequences. Afraid of losing their jobs or having their businesses closed down, many members did resign. In some cases, USDA members came by a few days later telling them they should now join the USDA.

One statement issued by the CRPP in February 1999 indicates the range of techniques the regime used to intimidate NLD members into resigning. According to the statement, the wife of an NLD MP-elect from Mandalay Division was called to the township chairman's office where she was told:

> The NLD would inevitably be destroyed; that family members would be removed from public service and the children would be expelled from school; that every means would be used to cause loss in any business undertaking; that ... future bank loans would be refused; that the NLD is an organization that is in opposition to the government; and that these measures formed part of a special campaign.[15]

According to the CRPP statement, the family of another NLD MP-elect from the same township was told the same thing, and the next day both men were taken into custody and pressured to resign, but they refused. They were released after about nine hours but, soon after, the secretary of the local USDA chapter went house to house copying the names of all the people on the household registrations and asking the head of each household to sign. These names were then put into petitions which stated that the signatories and their families had no confidence in the NLD MPs-elect, and the petition results were reported in the government-controlled media. By October 1999, only 183 of the original 485 representatives who were elected in 1990 remained valid, with many of the MPs-elect having resigned, been arrested or had their elections declared invalid.[16]

The regime sought to break down the NLD in other ways as well. The most talented thinkers in the party, such as Win Tin, an intellectual, and Win Htein, a former military officer, were kept in prison along with many other committed party members. Because of the poor living conditions and lack of adequate medical care, many became ill and a few died. Meanwhile, party members unhappy with some of Aung San Suu Kyi's policies were cultivated by the regime, and their views were given prominence in the government's publications.

Communications between NLD party offices were limited, because the NLD was not legally permitted to print or reproduce party literature or to use a fax machine. The party had minimal funds for travel and communication expenses anyway, so keeping everyone informed of the central committee's policies was difficult. Whenever Aung San Suu Kyi tried to travel outside Rangoon to meet party members, she was stopped and ordered to return home. In distant districts, NLD members usually learned about what was going on at the party headquarters through foreign radio broadcasts or informally from the occasional member who made a trip to Rangoon.

At the same time, the regime tried to destroy Aung San Suu Kyi's morale by forcing her to choose between her family and her political activities. When her husband, Michael Aris, was dying in England in early 1999, the regime refused to give him a visa to come to Burma. The state-controlled media insisted that since she was the healthy one, she should be visiting him. She made the painful decision not to leave, knowing that the regime would never allow her back in. But the generals punished her by cutting the line on every phone conversation she tried to have with her husband in the days before his death.[17] Michael Aris died on 27 March 1999, Burma's Resistance Day, and his fifty-third birthday.

Some of the remaining Thirty Comrades, particularly Bohmu Aung, repeatedly called for the military regime to engage in a dialogue with Aung San Suu Kyi, but the regime ignored them. The regime also tried to prevent the formation of links between the NLD and the ethnic nationalities' organizations. The NLD members inside the country could not correspond directly with the armed ethnic groups, because the party could be declared illegal for having contact with insurgent organizations. But NLD members who fled to the border areas tried to develop good working relations with the leaders of the armed ethnic groups, as did students who went out to the ethnic-controlled areas in 1988.

On several occasions, the leaders of armed ethnic organizations wrote individual and joint statements declaring their support for Aung San Suu Kyi and the democratic struggle. In January 1997, a number of ethnic minority leaders met in Mae Tha Raw Hta on the Thai–Burma border and signed an agreement calling for tripartite dialogue (the military regime, pro-democracy forces and ethnic leaders), a federal union and a democratic political system. The agreement stated: 'We agree also to join hands with the pro-democracy forces led by Daw Aung San Suu Kyi, and act unitedly and simultaneously for the achievement of rights of the nationalities as well as democratic rights.' While many of the attendees represented small organizations, the generals were upset that representatives of the United Wa State Army and the New Mon State Party (NMSP), two large ceasefire groups, also signed. The regime later punished the NMSP for its attendance by cutting its monthly logging quota.

A number of ceasefire groups subsequently issued joint statements supporting the Committee Representing the People's Parliament and calling for a tripartite dialogue. However, the SPDC ordered them to rescind their statements and urged other ceasefire groups to make statements against the CRPP.[18]

Inside the country, NLD members tried to build more cohesive relations with the ethnic political parties. In the period just after the 1990 election, the NLD and the UNLD, the alliance of ethnic minority political parties affiliated with the NLD, met regularly to discuss federalism and other issues. Together they came up with the Bo Aung Gyaw Street Agreement No. 1, which stated the need to build a real democratic union of Burma, with the understanding that 'real democratic' meant more autonomy for the ethnic states. At the National Convention, the elected ethnic and NLD party members were housed in the same barracks and had a chance to deepen their relationships.

In the late 1990s, the NLD tried to arrange meetings and informal get-togethers with ethnic political leaders, although the regime often blocked such efforts. Even Aung San Suu Kyi's attempts to attend Karen new year celebrations in Insein township, just outside Rangoon, were thwarted.

Despite the NLD's efforts to develop closer relations with ethnic nationality leaders, the regime continued to drive wedges between them. The armed ethnic groups were often reluctant to do anything that might

jeopardize their ceasefire agreements. While the ceasefires had not resulted in the granting of ethnic rights and political autonomy, they did
mean the end of decades-long civil wars and far less suffering for the civilian population. Thus, as long as the *tatmadaw* was in control, most of the
leaders of the armed ethnic organizations felt it necessary to cooperate
with the regime. At the same time, some of the ethnic leaders, particularly
in the remote areas, wondered whether any Burman-dominated government would accede to their demands for political autonomy. And indeed,
many Burmans, including some in the pro-democracy movement, continued to harbour serious doubts about federalism.

Fifty years after independence, Burma was still struggling to resolve
its political and economic problems. The regime continued to cling
to the idea of a unitary state with centralized powers, while the ethnic
nationalities continued to insist on greater political freedoms. The military regime managed to severely damage the organizational capacity of
the pro-democracy movement, but it was not able to build a prosperous
nation. While military generals' families and their friends managed to
amass fortunes through virtual monopolies over many of the most lucrative businesses, ordinary Burmese businessmen found that without the
necessary bribes and connections, they were not able to participate much
in the new market economy.

Because the regime devoted so much of the country's resources to
repressing its citizens, everyone suffered. Water and electricity shortages
became acute in the late 1990s, with frequent blackouts in Rangoon,
and some rural towns receiving electricity only once every three to five
days. One joke circulating in Rangoon was: it's fortunate that the military
government only takes responsibility for water and electricity, not air.
Thus, Burma entered the twenty-first century lagging far behind many
other countries in the region, with the generals still in power and the
majority of the people feeling unable to do anything about it.

5 | The Than Shwe years, 2000 and beyond

What the Myanmar government calls a process of democratization is in fact a process of consolidation of an authoritarian regime.[1] (Paulo Sergio Pinheiro, former UN Special Rapporteur on Human Rights in Myanmar)

In the first several years of the twenty-first century, the ruling generals maintained their grip on power by suppressing potential domestic threats and engaging with the international community only to the extent that they felt absolutely necessary. The regime continued to project an image of confidence in its right to rule, despite internal and external calls for change and an increasing flow of migrants out of the country. The 2007 monks' demonstrations and Cyclone Nargis posed unexpected challenges for a regime that was used to dictating events, but neither led to a dislodgement of the top generals.

The Depayin Massacre

In 2000, Aung San Suu Kyi was put under house arrest again after she and members of her party tried to take a train from Rangoon to Mandalay. The NLD had recently stated they would write their own constitution and Aung San Suu Kyi was trying to defy the travel restrictions the regime had put on her. Although this was a setback for her and her party, over the next two years she engaged in secret talks with the military intelligence. UN Special Envoy Razali Ismail made several trips to Burma during this period, and in part because of his efforts, she was released from house arrest, with no restrictions on her movements, in 2002. At the time, there was some optimism that the regime might be ready to engage in policy discussions with her.

To reconnect with NLD party members and ordinary people, Aung San Suu Kyi began touring parts of the country by car. Stopping in towns along the way, she gave informal talks and reopened local NLD offices. In the ethnic states as well as in the central divisions, people poured into the streets to catch a glimpse of her or hear her speeches. It became clear that she still had a great deal of popular support. Although she had official permission for the trips, she and NLD party members faced increasing harassment from USDA members and some local authorities.

On 30 May 2003, her travels ended when her convoy of cars was attacked by a mob of people in darkness not far from Depayin town. The regime stated that four people died, but witnesses claim that many more were killed, as men armed with bamboo clubs and iron bars beat NLD members and supporters until they collapsed.[2] With up to five thousand attackers gathered at this out-of-the-way spot and police and military stationed at points down the road, it was clear that the assault was premeditated.[3]

Aung San Suu Kyi's driver managed to manoeuvre the car out of the mêlée but they were stopped farther down the road. She was then taken away and held in a small house in the Insein Prison compound and then at an army camp.[4] She underwent surgery at a hospital in September 2003, and following that she was taken back to her house, where she was put back under indefinite house arrest. Tin Oo, another senior member in the NLD, was beaten on the head during the attack and then taken to a prison in north-western Burma, where he spent several months. He was brought home in February 2004 and was also put under indefinite house arrest. None of the perpetrators of the attack was arrested, but more than 150 NLD members and supporters were incarcerated instead.[5] This incident came to be known as the Depayin Massacre, and it sparked outrage around the world.

The Seven Point Road Map

In an effort to deflect attention away from the Depayin Massacre, General Khin Nyunt announced a Seven Point Road Map to political reform in August 2003.

1 Reconvene the National Convention (to finish drafting the basic principles for the constitution)
2 Implement 'the process necessary for the emergence of a genuine and disciplined democratic system'
3 Draft the new constitution
4 Adopt the constitution through a national referendum
5 Hold elections
6 Convene the new parliament
7 Build 'a modern, developed, and democratic nation'.[6]

No time frame was provided, giving the regime the opportunity to speed up or draw out any steps of the process as they wished.

While Aung San Suu Kyi and many other leading NLD members remained under detention, the regime proceeded to implement the road map. The National Convention had not met since March 1996, but it was reconvened in May 2004. The NLD was invited to attend, but boycotted after the regime refused to release Aung San Suu Kyi and Tin Oo from house arrest. The Shan Nationalities League for Democracy and most of the other ethnic political parties that won seats in the 1990 election boycotted as well, because the regime would not change the way the convention operated or remove the principle that the military must play the leading role in politics.[7] The regime tried to enhance the legitimacy of the National Convention by inviting a number of new members to attend, particularly from the ethnic ceasefire groups. When the ceasefire groups called for more powers to be given to the ethnic states, however, they were ignored. The delegates met for two months and then were sent home.

In early February 2005, a group of leaders from the Shan Nationalities League for Democracy and the Shan ceasefire groups, as well as some other Shan and Burmese representatives, held a meeting to discuss the future of Shan State and what role the ceasefire groups should play in the National Convention.[8] The regime responded by arresting the Shan leaders who had participated and sentencing each of them to seventy-five years or more in prison. Hkun Htun Oo, the chairman of the SNLD, was given ninety-three years.

When the National Convention met again from mid-February until the end of March 2005, the Shan ceasefire group representatives boycotted because of the arrest of the other Shan leaders. The National Convention held another session from early December 2005 to 31 January 2006. From this session on, the New Mon State Party sent only observers, as it was frustrated with the regime's unwillingness to discuss the political rights of the ethnic minority groups.[9]

Meanwhile, the regime continued to tell the international community to give it time as it worked on the principles for the new constitution. But given the long breaks between sessions, it was clear that the top generals were in no hurry to finish the convention.

Khin Nyunt sacked

In the mid- and late 1990s power seemed to be shared between Generals Than Shwe, Maung Aye and Khin Nyunt, but by the early 2000s it was clear that Than Shwe was in command. Tensions were often reported between the three, with Than Shwe worried that Maung Aye or Khin Nyunt might try to unseat him. In addition, Maung Aye, who was a pure military man, didn't like the way that Khin Nyunt, an intelligence officer, had expanded the intelligence's role into so many spheres. In October 2004, Than Shwe decided that Khin Nyunt had become too powerful, and had him sacked from his positions of prime minister and head of military intelligence (see Chapter 8). After Khin Nyunt was removed, tensions were noted between Generals Than Shwe and Maung Aye regarding who would succeed Than Shwe, who was already in his seventies, and whose trusted men would receive which appointments during the annual reshuffles.[10]

Meanwhile, the military intelligence service was disbanded, and a new intelligence agency, called Military Affairs Security, was set up with much narrower jurisdiction. In addition, the national intelligence bureau, which had previously coordinated all intelligence-gathering, was dissolved. To dilute the power of the intelligence services, each branch of intelligence now reports to different government agencies.

The 88 Generation Students Group

In 2006, a number of former student activists formed the 88 Generation Students Group. Leaders of the network included Min Ko Naing, who had spent sixteen years in solitary confinement, and other former long-term political prisoners such as Ko Ko Gyi, Pyone Cho, Min Zeya and Htay Kywe. Focused on developing a grassroots movement, they sought to involve the general public in politics through the initiation of relatively low-risk activities.

In October 2006, they travelled all over the country dressed in white asking citizens to sign a petition calling for the release of all political prisoners and the beginning of a process of national reconciliation. They reportedly received over 500,000 signatures.[11] The next month, they initiated a multi-religious week of prayer, with tens of thousands of people heeding the call. Buddhists, Christians, Muslims and Hindus held candlelit vigils or prayed in their own ways for the release of political prisoners and national reconciliation, as well as relief for the victims of floods that had hit many parts of the country.[12] This campaign reflected the broad-mindedness of the organizers as they reached beyond the Buddhist majority to citizens of all faiths. Moreover, it encouraged participation from people who were normally too afraid to engage in political activities.

In January 2007, the 88 Generation Students Group launched the Open Heart Campaign. Citizens were asked to write letters expressing their social and political grievances. The group would then send the letters to General Than Shwe. A month later, Min Ko Naing told *The Irrawaddy* that his group had received over eight thousand letters from monks, retired civil servants, students and others.[13] The letter writers complained about political repression, corruption, problems in the educational system, poor healthcare and *tatmadaw* abuses in rural areas.

In March 2007, the group initiated the 'White Sunday' campaign. They would go and visit the families of political prisoners on Sundays to give them moral support, but they were often harassed by local authorities.

These campaigns awakened people's hopes at a time when the NLD seemed to be able to offer no guidance. The elderly NLD leaders insisted on sticking to a strategy of refraining from provocative actions in order to keep the party legal. Many of the NLD's youth members were frustrated with the party leadership's approach, feeling that it was far more important to try to build a grassroots movement for change. The combination of military pressure on NLD members and differences of opinion within the party led to a weakening of the party. Some NLD youths formed links with the 88 Students Generation Group while other young activists joined new groups such as the Human Rights Defenders and Promoters, which focused on educating people about human rights.

The 'royal abode'

Senior General Than Shwe's national funding priorities were revealed when in November 2005 he moved the capital to a formerly undeveloped area in central Burma. According to Sean Turnell, an expert on the Burmese economy, the cost of building the new capital was approximately four to five billion US dollars.[14] Meanwhile, in 2004/05, the regime spent only 458 kyat per person on healthcare, which works out at less than half a dollar per person.[15] Concerns about a potential US invasion were cited as one of the likely reasons for the move. US ships could easily reach the port-city of Rangoon, but the regime could better protect itself by moving to an area surrounded by mountains in which underground tunnels could be dug. Nevertheless, the likelihood of a US attack seemed hard to imagine in the first years of the twenty-first century, when the USA was embroiled in conflicts in Iraq and Afghanistan.

Other reasons have also been suggested. By moving away from Rangoon, any further demonstrations there would not directly threaten the regime's security. Than Shwe may also have wanted to create a legacy for himself by establishing a new capital in the part of the country where Burmese kings had traditionally reigned. He had the new capital named Naypyidaw (also spelled Nay Pyi Taw), which means 'royal abode'.

While the move was probably due to a combination of factors, the impact was to further isolate the regime from the civilian population and from foreign governments. When the regime first moved, diplomats in Rangoon were told that if they needed something, they could get in touch with the Foreign Ministry not in person or by phone but by fax. In 2007, embassies and UN agencies were informed that land had been allocated for them to build new missions in Naypyidaw starting in 2008, but none immediately accepted.[16] With Rangoon remaining the country's centre for business, culture and development work, most diplomats preferred to stay put.

The vast majority of the civil servants and military officers who were ordered to move to Naypyidaw would also have preferred to remain in Rangoon, but they were given no choice. Most left their families in Rangoon and tried to get back when they could. When they wanted to call home, they had to do so from a public phone, as there is purposely no cell-phone coverage in Naypyidaw, and few apartments are allowed to have private landlines.[17] Although the top generals depend on lower-ranking officers and bureaucrats to provide security and implement government policies, they apparently do not completely trust them.

In July 2006, Than Shwe threw a lavish wedding party for his youngest daughter, Thandar Shwe, who married an army major named Zaw Phyo Win. Dripping in jewels, she was reportedly presented with $50 million worth of gifts, including jewellery, cars and even houses.[18] A leaked ten-minute clip of a video taken during the wedding reception appeared three months later. Posted on YouTube, copies were also secretly distributed inside the country. Those who saw the footage were outraged by the carefree extravagance of the participants when so many people in Burma were living in abject poverty.

Economic policy, business and corruption

Unwilling to give away any power, the top generals have insisted on dictating economic policy as they see fit rather than relying on civilian experts. By being able to grant and take away lucrative business permits, the top generals can ensure the cooperation of leading businessmen. The generals tend to work out business deals on the basis of understandings between individuals, which can be altered at any time.

Small and large business owners alike face numerous constraints in running their businesses. Regulations regarding imports and exports are frequently changed, making the import–export business itself quite difficult, while companies that need imported goods can't be sure of their availability or price. The transportation infrastructure is also still extremely underdeveloped. According to one businessman, businesses that use trucks to transport goods long distances face problems because of the bad roads, which increase transport times, and the trucks require more frequent repairs. Because the import of spare parts for cars and trucks is highly restricted, such parts are expensive and sometimes difficult to find. Since electricity is provided for only five or six hours a day even in Rangoon, businesses must run their own generators in order to keep the lights on and factories running. Meanwhile uncertainties about regulations and the lack of impartial courts that could enforce contracts make investing large amounts of capital a big risk. All of these factors make it difficult for business people to operate successful enterprises, as do economic sanctions for those companies that seek to export goods.

Some entrepreneurs have made handsome profits, but others have not been so lucky. Those without the right connections can run into serious trouble. In 1996, a car importer learned this the hard way. He wasn't very well connected to the senior generals, but he was managing to bring in small shipments of cars without any serious problems, so he decided to expand. When he went to collect his latest shipment of cars at the port, he learned that all 140 had been confiscated. The reason given was that some of the models had been updated and weren't exactly the same as those listed on the original permission request. All his appeals to the customs department were in vain. He was told that military intelligence had taken over the case. Later he found out that the cars had all been sold at low prices to senior military officers, for their personal use or resale at their actual price.

Distraught, the importer wrote a letter to Lieutenant General Khin Nyunt, suggesting that if the military routinely confiscated legitimate companies' goods, no one would want to do business in Burma any more. The military intelligence accused him of writing the letter at the request of anti-regime politicians. In fact, he had had no contact with the pro-democracy movement and was interested only in making money, but his safety was in jeopardy, so he decided he had to leave the country.

Another problem business people face is that their companies may be taken over by the regime or by relatives of top generals. Win Win Nu, a businesswoman who ran Mandalay Brewery as a joint venture with the Ministry of Industry, had this experience. After she was able to dramatically increase the profits of the brewery, the regime decided they didn't want to split the money with her any more. One day in November 1998, a lieutenant colonel and sixty soldiers stormed into her office and told her to get out. Following that, the business was nationalized.[19] All her attempts to obtain justice were futile.

Companies with close ties to particular generals have more opportunities to expand, but they also must continually curry favour. For instance, the wives of the businessmen must regularly go and pay their respects and give gifts to the wives of the generals their husbands work with. According to one businessman, as rich as some of the businessmen may be, the top generals do not hesitate to order them around. If they want to continue to run their business activities smoothly, they are expected to do the generals' bidding.

It is also true that if a general loses power, the business people close to that person may suffer as well. After Khin Nyunt was sacked, the deputy chief executive officer of the *Myanmar Times*, Sonny Swe, was sentenced to fourteen years in prison for supposedly violating the censorship laws.[20] The newspaper had had a good relationship with the intelligence branch, and Sonny's father, Brigadier General Thein Swe, had worked closely with Khin Nyunt. Sonny's father was sentenced to 152 years in prison.

Meanwhile, in the agricultural sector, while the authorities have tried to introduce some improvements, they have also made life difficult for many farmers by issuing orders to grow certain crops. Since mid-2006, farmers all over Burma have been ordered to grow *kyet su* plants or physic nuts (also called jatropha). Each farmer was required to buy the seeds from the authorities and plant 200 seeds around the edge of their fields.[21] Once the trees grew, the nuts were supposed to be processed into biofuel. Two years after the project began, however, the regime still had no facilities for refining the nuts into fuel that could actually be used. It is likely that the project was the product of an ill-conceived order from above which lower officials were afraid to question. Nevertheless, some people wondered whether there wasn't a second motive: namely, a desire to contain Aung San Suu Kyi's power by using *yadaya*, a magical technique. *Kyet su* sounds similar to Suu Kyi backwards, so by blanketing the country in *kyet su* trees, the generals were perhaps trying to negate Aung San Suu Kyi's influence.

In other parts of the energy sector, the regime began reaping profits, with the promise of far larger amounts to come. A number of Asian companies signed joint ventures to explore and extract oil and natural gas and to build hydropower plants. Still, throughout the early 2000s, the regime had to rely on printing money to cover its expenditures, leading to high rates of inflation. In 2002, the inflation rate exceeded 55 per cent, and in 2005, it was estimated at just over 20 per cent.[22] By the end of 2007, it had jumped again to at least 35 per cent.[23] Young people from both urban and rural areas poured out of Burma looking for jobs in other more dynamic economies so that they could support themselves and their families. This was facilitated by the authorities' loosening of restrictions on applying for passports, as the generals recognized that remittances could inject much-needed money into the economy.

As many as 1.5 million Burmese workers (legal and illegal) were in Thailand in 2008, with large numbers in India, Malaysia and Singapore as well.[24] While most travelled back home rarely, they could transfer money to their families whenever they wanted through an informal banking system run by agents in Burma and abroad.

For the poor in both urban and rural areas, the government provided few direct support services. As a result, some activists and other individuals turned to social work. In the Rangoon area, small groups started rice distribution programmes, provided treatment and support for people living with AIDS – often in conjunction with sympathetic monks – and ran orphanages. Monks in Rangoon Division and other parts of the country established primary schools and boarding houses to serve poor children, many of whom were not orphans, but their parents could not provide for them. The Sitagu Monastery in Sagaing even opened a hospital and an eye clinic with services free of charge for people of all religions, and Christian, Muslim and secular organizations have also run free clinics.

The UN, international NGOs and Burmese organizations have also provided services directly to communities in various parts of the country, although they are often hampered by changing restrictions and limitations on where they can work. Relief and development workers frequently have to operate on the basis of understandings with the authorities, but without necessarily having authorization on paper. As a result, they are never certain whether or not their projects might suddenly be halted or even whether they themselves might face trouble. As one community worker put it, 'We feel like gophers. We pop our heads up, look around, do something, and go back down into our holes.'

Monks take to the streets

In mid-August 2007, the regime unexpectedly announced a large price hike for diesel and compressed natural gas. Transportation and food costs skyrocketed, with a devastating effect on the poor. Almost immediately, the 88 Generation Students Group began their own small protest marches in Rangoon and called for the regime to rescind the price increases. Worried that the number of marchers would grow, the authorities quickly arrested most of the leaders of the 88 Generation Students Group, although a few were able to escape arrest for a period of time.

Specially trained USDA units and members of the more recently formed *Swan Arr Shin* (Masters of Force) paramilitary organization patrolled the streets in the following weeks, ready to beat up anyone who dared to continue the protests. *Swan Arr Shin* members included local thugs and day labourers from poorer quarters and satellite towns. People were afraid and kept quiet.

Following that, a small network of politically educated monks decided to continue the demonstrations in their own way: by calmly proceeding through the streets chanting the *metta sutta* of loving kindness. The objective was to awaken the regime to the suffering its policies were causing ordinary people and to encourage them to make changes.

On 5 September, hundreds of monks appeared in the streets of Pakkoku carrying signs denouncing the price hike. They were cheered on by thousands of clapping residents, but the authorities reacted angrily and tied up and beat some of the monks. News of this shocking act of disrespect spread around the country by exile radio and word of mouth, sparking mass indignation.

Five days later, the All Burma Monks' Alliance (ABMA) announced its formation and issued a statement calling on the regime to apologize to the monks, reduce the prices of fuel and other basic commodities, release all political prisoners, and begin a dialogue with the democratic movement for national reconciliation.[25] The statement also threatened that if the regime did not comply by 17 September, the monks would initiate a religious boycott, refusing to receive offerings from the military and their families or to perform religious rites for them. The regime ignored their demands, expecting that few monks would dare to participate. But many monks were so upset about the regime's callousness towards monks and the people that they decided to participate, with or without the permission of their abbots.

Starting on 18 September, monks in Rangoon, Mandalay, Sittwe and other towns gathered at famous temples or city centres and then proceeded to walk through the streets, often for hours at a time in the pouring rain, chanting the *metta sutta* and waving their religious flags.[26] Some of the monks carried overturned alms bowls to symbolize the monks' refusal to accept alms from the authorities. Because of the saffron colour of some of the monks' robes, the movement was dubbed 'the Saffron Revolution' by outsiders, although most monks in Burma actually wear maroon-coloured robes.

Many ordinary people were moved to tears by the monks' efforts on their behalf. A number felt guilty that the monks were marching and they weren't, so they tried to join in. During the first few days, the monks did not allow lay people to participate. By keeping it a religious movement, they hoped, the authorities would not react with violence. Many young people urged the monks to let them join, however, while some of the leading monks thought broadening the movement would make it more effective. Thus, lay people were allowed to form a human chain on either side of the marching monks.

Although the vast majority of the monks who joined were young and had no political experience, some of the ABMA leaders had taken part in the 1988 demonstrations or the 1990 monks' boycott and had been imprisoned with student activists. Since their release, some had become respected lecturers and administrators in the larger temples in Rangoon. The 88 Generation Students Group leaders had re-established contact with them and some NLD members patronized their temples. Some of the leading monks who emerged in 2007 had been children in 1988 but had later received some political training through democracy activists in exile or other channels. On 21 September, the ABMA, together with other democracy activists, issued a statement urging the people to join the monks in order to 'banish the evil regime'.[27]

On 22 September, one group of marching monks turned down University Avenue towards Aung San Suu Kyi's house. They were stopped at the barriers by the police, but then allowed to proceed, apparently because the police weren't sure what to do. Aung San Suu Kyi briefly appeared at her gate with tears in her eyes before the monks moved on. News of this moment was spread through the international and Burmese exile media, electrifying the population and leading yet more people to join.

Starting on 24 September, Zarganar, the famous comedian, Kyaw Thu, a famous actor, and Aung Way, a well-known poet, gave offerings to the gathered monks at Shwedagon Pagoda before they set off on their daily procession. The monks in Rangoon also allowed the NLD and other democracy activists to walk in the middle of their processions holding their flags but strictly forbade anyone from carrying weapons.

As many as 100,000 people were on the streets in Rangoon. The second-largest congregation of demonstrators was in Sittwe, the capital of Arakan State. There, tens of thousands of people congregated near the statue of U Ottama, the famous Arakanese monk who had led anti-colonial demonstrations many decades before. Thousands were on the streets of Mandalay and smaller numbers came out in more than twenty other towns as well.

While the NLD leadership had originally been reluctant to join in the demonstrations in Rangoon, in the townships outside the capital, many NLD organizers and youths played an active role in urging people to participate. One NLD youth organizer from a small town in Arakan State said that in places in Arakan State where there were no big monasteries, NLD members took the lead, organizing short demonstrations in which people shouted slogans such as 'Reduce the prices' and 'Free Aung San Suu Kyi'.

The regime was shocked by the speed with which the demonstrations were gaining momentum and, at first, not sure how to proceed. Using violence against the monks in Pakkoku had backfired, but it looked as if the demonstrations were not going to fizzle out on their own. Once the demonstrations became clearly political, General Than Shwe gave the order to crush them. Apparently, the general never considered responding to any of the protesters' demands.

On 24 September, the regime had the state-controlled monastic council issue a warning to monks to stay out of secular affairs. Then, on the 25th, the authorities in Rangoon and Mandalay declared a night-time curfew and ordered the monks to get off the streets. The next morning, the *tatmadaw* soldiers and riot police poured into the streets of Rangoon ready to take action.

In front of the Shwedagon Pagoda, U Kosita, one of the monks who had emerged as a leader, used his megaphone to ask the riot police to stop and think. He told them, 'We're doing this for everybody, including you.' But a riot policeman replied curtly: 'If you [monks] don't get on the trucks, we'll have to shoot you.' The monks knew that getting on the trucks meant being taken into custody, so U Kosita replied, 'Well, we can't get on. If you want to shoot, shoot. We'll die in front of Shwedagon Pagoda.' Then the riot police began beating the monks and others with iron rods.

That day and the following days, the soldiers and riot police used tear-gas and rubber and live bullets as well to inflict injuries and sometimes death and to scare the crowds into dispersing. Because they did not want any images of the violence to get out, the security forces especially targeted people with cameras and video cameras. Kenji Nagai, a Japanese journalist, was shot dead as he was running with his camera. *Swan Arr Shin* militia members participated in beating people, while the security forces also arrested anyone they could grab, including some ill-fated onlookers in tea shops.

That night and the next, soldiers and riot police raided the monasteries from which many of the leading monks had come. Neighbours remained in anguished silence in their houses as they heard monks being beaten and taken away.

Over the next few days, defiant crowds of mostly young people continued to gather in front of the raided temples and near former demonstration sites. In two instances, people were shot and killed. After that, the demonstrations dissipated as there were troops, USDA and *Swan Arr Shin* members everywhere, and the leadership was gone. Many more temples were raided in the following days, and monks from the teaching monasteries were ordered to go back to their home towns. Some of the leading monks and participants were able to make their way to neighbouring countries.

No images came out from Sittwe, Mandalay, Pakkoku or other smaller towns where demonstrations took place, as demonstrators in those towns had little or no access to cell phones and the Internet. But in Rangoon, numbers of lay citizens and monks took it upon themselves to become on-the-spot reporters and send out eyewitness accounts, photographs and videos by phone and Internet. Exile media groups also worked hard to get the news out – and back into Burma. As the people on the streets hoped, governments and leading figures around the world urged the regime to handle the peaceful demonstrators with restraint, although China and India asserted that it was Burma's internal affair. Nevertheless, General Than Shwe was unfazed by the international community's pleas. He authorized the use of force, and the soldiers acted accordingly, despite the fact that many in the military apparently did not want to harm the monks.

Afterwards, the regime stated that only fifteen people had been killed, including the Japanese reporter. Human rights groups, however, believed the number was much higher. As many as four thousand people were detained in hastily prepared detention centres, where monks were disrobed and detainees were interrogated to determine the extent of their participation.

Two years later, approximately one thousand people remained behind bars because of their participation in the August and September demonstrations. Several leading members of the 88 Generation Students Group were sentenced to sixty-five years in prison, and Nay Phone Latt, one of the main bloggers who got news out about the demonstrations, was sentenced to twenty and a half years. The regime clearly wanted to send a strong message that no one should consider organizing such protests again. Even some monks came to the conclusion that only violence could remove such a brutal regime.

Why weren't the protests successful? As Aung Way, the poet, said, 'We underestimated the SPDC. We didn't expect they would be that ruthless with the monks.' He and others also noted that the activists who had been playing a strategic role behind the scenes hadn't planned well enough how to organize and continue the movement. Another analyst noted they had also not thought about how to try to persuade the authorities to negotiate. Meanwhile, the regime knew it could count on China and India for a certain degree of diplomatic cover, while the generals felt confident that other members of the international community wouldn't directly intervene.

Preparing for the referendum

The generals knew how deeply angry Burmese citizens felt and decided that they had to offer some immediate hope for a better future. The regime moved quickly ahead with its road map. The closing ceremony of the National Convention had already been held in early September. Next, the regime set up a committee to write the constitution, which it finalized in February 2008. Then the regime announced that it would hold a referendum on the constitution in May 2008 and used all its propaganda machinery to urge a yes vote. Billboards were erected stating: 'To approve the state Constitution is a national duty of the entire people today. Let us all cast a "yes" vote in the national interest.' Vote-yes cartoons, editorials and slogans appeared in the state media. The authorities made almost no effort to educate people about the contents of the constitution, however. Copies had to be bought, and they were hard to find, especially outside Rangoon. Few people thought there was any point in reading it anyway, because they knew it would pass.

Anyone campaigning for people to vote no could be sentenced to three years' imprisonment, and the domestic media were not allowed to cover the vote-no campaign. Still, the NLD urged people to vote no, as did the 88 Generation Students Group, the ABMA and other pro-democracy groups in exile. Some people in Rangoon and Mandalay dared to wear T-shirts that simply said 'no', but most people were afraid to show their feelings.

The constitution allows a degree of civilian participation in politics, as there will be an elected national parliament and state/regional legislatures. The seven divisions of central Burma are renamed regions and will have legislatures, just as the seven ethnic states will. Twenty-five per cent of the seats in each legislative body are reserved for the military, however, and the president of the country must have a military background.

Even more important, the *tatmadaw* will have the right to manage military affairs without any civilian interference, and the military can take power if they believe that national security is threatened. Moreover, Chapter VII, Article 4 states: 'The Tatmadaw must play a leading role in safeguarding the Union of Myanmar against all internal and external dangers.'

All the security laws that have been used to arrest political activists in the past will remain valid, and all citizens have a duty to uphold the three national causes: namely, non-disintegration of the union, non-disintegration of national solidarity, and perpetuation of sovereignty.

Many of the ethnic nationalist leaders were strongly dissatisfied with the constitution because no significant powers were devolved to the ethnic states. Although there are separate lists for the legislative powers of the union and the states, states generally only carry out the maintenance work on infrastructure and other projects approved by the union. Burma's constitution is likely the first in the world in which the state legislatures are specifically assigned responsibility for the prevention and control of agricultural pests and teaching people how to use chemical fertilizers properly.[28]

To appease some of the smaller ethnic groups and reduce the power of the Shan, one self-administered division for the Wa and four smaller self-administered zones for the Danu, Pa-O, Palaung and Kokang peoples are to be set up. The Naga in Sagaing Division will also have a self-administered zone. Yet the local governments in these areas will also have *tatmadaw* representation and will lack any real independent power.

In the ethnic states, the ceasefire groups came under pressure to support the referendum and begin preparing to set up political parties to run in the 2010 election. For some of the ceasefire groups, deciding what to do was not easy. They had not gained any rights but they were also not in a strong position to fight the *tatmadaw* again. Some ethnic leaders felt resigned and tried to console themselves with the hope that there would be some space to make changes in the parliament. It is highly unlikely, however, that they will be able to change much as all amendments to the constitution must be passed by more than 75 per cent of the MPs.

Cyclone Nargis

On 2 and 3 May 2008, Cyclone Nargis slammed into Burma's low-lying Irrawaddy Delta and Rangoon Division with 160kph winds and pouring rain. The accompanying storm surge, a huge wave caused by the cyclone, was estimated to be 3.5 metres high. Villagers clung on to roofs, house posts and trees in an attempt to secure themselves, but tens of thousands of people were dragged out to sea, never to return again. Many survivors reported watching their family members pulled away by the retreating wall of water and being unable to save them. They are haunted by the horror, guilt and pain of the losses they suffered.

According to the military regime's statistics, over 130,000 people were confirmed dead or could not be accounted for. Whole villages were erased from the landscape, bridges and roads were washed out, and human and animal corpses were piled up in stagnant water. Fields were inundated with salty water, and fishing boats smashed. More than two million people were badly affected by the cyclone and were desperate for food, clothing, clean water and shelter. Reaching all the affected people, many of whom could only be accessed by boat or helicopter, and helping them rebuild their lives, would be a daunting task for any government.

While foreign governments and relief organizations were eager to help, the regime was determined to handle the relief and recovery work on its own terms. Despite lacking the capacity to respond effectively to a disaster of such magnitude, the regime initially denied visas to foreign relief workers and refused the assistance of US and French naval ships, which were prepared to bring large amounts of aid directly to the delta area. In the first week after the cyclone, General Than Shwe did not answer UN Secretary-General Ban Ki-moon's phone calls.[29] He only made his first visit to a cyclone-affected area two weeks after the cyclone hit.[30]

Meanwhile, the French foreign minister, Bernard Kouchner, was so perplexed by the regime's intransigence that he asked the UN Security Council to consider using the 'Responsibility to Protect' mandate – originally meant for the protection of civilians in civil wars. The Security Council could, for instance, pass a resolution ordering Burma to accept foreign assistance and foreign aid workers, and if it didn't comply, perhaps authorize air drops of relief supplies.[31] Several countries on the UN Security Council opposed this idea, but the regime was unnerved by the proposal. Than Shwe finally allowed Ban Ki-moon to make a visit and agreed to permit large numbers of foreign aid workers to enter the country. ASEAN played a role in persuading the regime to open up and, together with the UN and the authorities, coordinated the initial international relief efforts.

Why was the regime so recalcitrant? It viewed the pouring in of hundreds of foreign relief workers from numerous different countries and organizations as a potential security threat. The relief workers might use the cyclone relief and rehabilitation effort as a way to get into Burma so they could engage in other activities. The top generals also did not want to be seen as doing less than foreigners, and particularly Western countries, to help Burmese citizens. Indeed, in the days immediately after the cyclone, the generals sought to take credit for the relief supplies by having stickers with their names plastered on to some of the boxes of goods donated by other countries.[32]

In addition, the regime is used to controlling all major activities and didn't like the idea of any large organizations operating independently on its territory. Yet the generals were also not prepared to take full financial responsibility, nor did they have enough staff or vehicles available to manage the distribution of the aid. This was partly because their top priority at the time was carrying out the referendum on the new constitution, not helping the cyclone victims. The regime's solution was to order the heads of large businesses to take on much of the aid distribution, with each company assigned to a specific region in the delta and ordered to work together with local authorities.[33] The companies were told that they would be compensated by the regime later.

Just a few days after the cyclone, CDs with images of the devastation and suffering were being sold on the streets of Rangoon. After viewing the images and hearing the reports of starving villagers lining the roads begging for food, many Burmese citizens decided they had to do something. Some Rangoon residents simply bought as much as food they could, loaded up their cars, and drove out of the city to hand over their donations to whomever they found along the way. Others organized into groups to pool resources and move greater quantities of food, clothing and other basic supplies into areas reachable only by boat. Monks and churches from various parts of the country collected donations and provided assistance through their religious networks.

The authorities were somewhat wary of the voluntary networks that took on cyclone relief work. As with the international organizations, they worried that such independent organizing might lead to more politically motivated activities in the future, and they felt that it made the government look bad if it couldn't handle the work itself. The voluntary groups did not always have official permission to carry out their activities, and some groups faced difficulties at checkpoints set up along the roads. Authorities were reluctant to let them pass for fear of punishment from above, although the presentation of 'gifts' often helped smooth the way. Despite these difficulties, ordinary people joined in, because they felt such sympathy for their fellow citizens.

After a few weeks, the regime announced that it was time for all the refugees in monasteries and temporary shelters to return home and start rebuilding their houses and planting their fields. The problem was that many survivors had no materials with which to rebuild their houses, there was often little or no food or clean water in the villages, and their fields were still inundated with salt water.

Although foreign aid workers now had access to the delta, it was difficult to move goods out to the scattered villages, a number of which could be reached only by long rides in small boats. Many of the foreign aid workers were also struck by how little infrastructure had been in place previously. Outside the towns, there were no phones, no electricity and almost no healthcare centres. Nevertheless, over the course of a year, international organizations were able to provide much-needed humanitarian assistance and help reconstruct infrastructure.

While the authorities and government-connected organizations did provide relief and reconstruction supplies too, they approached the situation differently from international relief organizations and Burmese voluntary organizations. According to Burmese workers involved in non-governmental relief work, there were a couple of reasons for this.

First, the regime perceived the needs of the cyclone survivors and the responsibility of the government to assist them as far more limited than the relief organizations did. Even though a large percentage of cylone survivors had lost all their food stocks and their seed reserves, the generals originally thought of providing food assistance only in the short term, not for a period of several months or a year. In addition, the generals did not think about the need for specialized care for those suffering from psychological trauma, and particularly for the children who had lost their parents.

Second, the higher-level authorities in general were less concerned about monitoring the distribution of the relief supplies than the relief organizations were. As a result, some lower- and middle-level authorities sold relief goods rather than giving them for free, favoured relatives and friends in the distribution of aid, or did not check to see that religious leaders and headmen in charge of village-level distribution discharged their responsibilities fairly.

The referendum

The referendum went ahead on 10 May for most of the country, and was held on 24 May in forty-seven townships in Rangoon and Irrawaddy Divisions, which had been hit hard by the cyclone. The referendum was conducted in an atmosphere of intimidation and harassment and plenty of vote-rigging. Many people did not vote either out of apathy or in protest, so in some places the authorities simply voted for them.

Some defiant voters, particularly in the cities and the ethnic states, voted no, but their votes were easily cancelled out. There were plenty of voters who decided to vote yes because they feared punishment if they voted no. Voters had to write their addresses and ID numbers on the ballot, so the authorities would be able to trace how individuals had voted. Others voted yes because they figured that having a partially elected legislature and a constitution might lead to a somewhat better situation than the current one in which the military ruled by decree.

In some government offices and state enterprises, employees had to vote in advance, in front of their bosses. Meanwhile, the authorities used a variety of other techniques to ensure that there were sufficient yes votes. Methods varied from place to place but included being handed pre-marked ballots, having local authorities, USDA officials or *Swan Arr Shin* members closely watching voters, moving the ballot box for no votes to an area surrounded by military officials, and having voters fill out only their addresses and ID numbers and the authorities mark the ballot for them.[34] Journalists were not allowed into the polling areas. When the results were announced, citizens were told that 99 per cent of the eligible voters had voted and, of those, 92.4 per cent voted yes.[35] Everyone knew that these numbers had little to do with reality, but protesting seemed pointless.

Soon after, the state media announced that the 1990 election results were no longer valid. Whether the NLD would be allowed to participate in the elections, which were scheduled for 2010, was unclear. The USDA began preparing to set up proxy parties to run in the 2010 elections, however, and cultivating businessmen who would be willing to run as candidates. If the elections go ahead as scheduled, pro-regime parties are likely to take a share of the vote, and with the *tatmadaw* representatives holding 25 per cent of the seats, it will be difficult for other parties to have much influence. The implementation of the constitution will lead to a division of power at the top, however, with the president appointing the commander-in-chief of the defence services. Whether Than Shwe will take the job of president or finally retire is unclear.

Meanwhile, Aung San Suu Kyi continued to be held under house arrest without ever being charged with committing a crime. According to the regime's laws, a person can be held for five years without being charged. In Aung San Suu Kyi's case, 30 May 2008 marked the fifth anniversary of her detention, but she was not released. When Ibrahim Gambari, the UN

Special Envoy, visited Burma for the fourth time in two years in August 2008, Aung San Suu Kyi refused to meet with him, apparently out of frustration with the lack of any political progress.

The regime wanted to keep Aung San Suu Kyi under detention during the planned 2010 election in order to prevent the re-emergence of a dynamic and united opposition movement. In May 2009, they found a pretext for doing so. On 3 May 2009, a fifty-three-year-old American man named John Yettaw secretly swam across Inya Lake to her house with the hope of talking with her. He had made a previous attempt in late 2008, but Aung San Suu Kyi refused to meet with him. She later asked her doctor to inform the authorities about the incident. When John Yettaw arrived the second time, Aung San Suu Kyi again asked him to leave, but he begged for some food and time to rest, saying he was exhausted. He was arrested on his swim back across the lake early on the morning of 5 May.

On 11 May 2009, the authorities charged Aung San Suu Kyi with violating the terms of her house arrest, as foreigners are not allowed to visit her compound. She was moved to Insein Prison, and informed that she could be imprisoned for up to five years for her 'crime'. Despite the international outcry, the trial proceeded in a closed courtroom at the prison. Her lawyers argued that she was innocent, as Yettaw was an intruder, not an invited guest. Yettaw claimed in court that he had felt compelled to journey to her compound because he believed she was going to be assassinated and needed to warn her. When this book was finished, she had not yet been sentenced and the authorities had not accepted responsibility for failing to provide adequate security around her compound.

In conclusion, the regime seemed to be fully in control, although not because it had any legitimacy in the eyes of its people. Those who witnessed the brutal crackdown on the September 2007 demonstrations were seething inside, while increasing access to the Internet and outside media, and increasing travel abroad, had made many people realize that few governments in the world were as cruel and incompetent as theirs. Many people sought a better life abroad while others tried to do what they could to make the country a better place.

1 Farmers transplanting rice in Rangoon Division, 1996

2 A procession of boys who are about to be ordained as novice monks and their relatives, Thaton, Mon State, 2000

3 A Karenni mass in a refugee camp on the Thai–Burma
border, 2007

4 Novice monks studying in a monastery near Mandalay, 1996

5 Aung San Suu Kyi speaking from her gate, 1996

6 Armed Forces Day parade in Naypyidaw, 2007

7 A young Burmese soldier at a train station in Kachin State, 1998

8 A policeman watching monks walk by in Nyaung Shwe, Shan State, 2005

6 | Families: fostering conformity

We're always acting, saying what we think the authorities want to hear. It's so exhausting. (A pastor)

Individuals in Burma often talk and act in seemingly contradictory ways. When they sense that the political atmosphere is more relaxed, they complain openly about the regime or voice their support for Aung San Suu Kyi and the pro-democracy movement. During periods of greater repression, however, they tend to stay silent or even criticize democracy activists as ineffective. At moments when the democracy struggle seems to have no chance of success, some people even dismiss its validity, as they seek to make peace with their lives under military rule.

Similarly, the public may enjoy reading critiques of the regime or watching movies that indirectly parody military rule, but when family members or neighbours are the ones acting against the government, they may find they have little support. This is because the authorities have been known to harass and arrest the family members and close friends of activists, even if they have done nothing against the regime themselves. By punishing those who surround activists, the authorities can isolate them and discourage activism from spreading. Thus, as much as relatives and neighbours might admire those who are courageous enough to act for change, they can be reluctant to offer any direct support.

The following chapters look more closely at how families, communities and professional groups are torn between protecting themselves and standing up for what they believe. Under military rule in Burma, it seems that doing what is right is often directly opposed to doing what is necessary to survive. As the military's influence has seeped into virtually every aspect of people's lives, resistance becomes difficult to imagine. Yet, there are dynamic individuals who have tried to reclaim certain activities, such as education, social work, art and religious practice, from military control or to fend off military involvement.

Collective amnesia

Despite their own dislike of the military regime, most parents raise their children to conform with military domination, and even to become part of the system. When they were younger, a number of parents themselves participated in anti-government rallies, but as they aged and nothing changed, many began to see resistance as futile. Like parents everywhere, Burmese parents want their children to be successful and financially secure. They don't want them to become politically active and end up in prison.

In order to protect their children, many parents discourage them from critically examining military rule. One man, who was a university student in 1988, talked about his mother's reaction to his realization that the government's policies were not benefiting the people. After the March 1988 demonstrations, his university was closed and he came back to his home town, where he struck up conversations with local businessmen and people around the market. One day he said to his mother, 'I have some weird feelings which I've never had before. There is something wrong with this system.' She told him, 'Don't take it seriously. This is life.'

As Aung Myat, a sweet-faced young man in his twenties, put it in 2008, no one he knew in his generation was interested in politics in the years before the 2007 monks' demonstrations. His parents never talked about politics, so he didn't think about it either. He said, 'We only knew that other countries were rich, and we wanted to be rich too.' He didn't like some of the restrictions he faced, but like others, he just thought about how to get around them. For instance, if he needed official authorization to do something, he would pay a bribe. He didn't think about whether this was right or wrong, and he certainly didn't think about his rights. He said that, since he didn't know the meaning of freedom, he just stayed quiet.

In Burma, most families are close knit, and parents are very involved in their children's decisions about education and work. Not surprisingly, those who can afford their children's university fees strongly encourage them to major in subjects leading to secure and high-paying jobs after they graduate. Entering the Defence Services Academy, a university-level programme that trains military officers, is one option that many parents favour. Other prized careers include becoming doctors, engineers or administrators in the civil service. Although their salaries may be low, those who enter these professions will have a guaranteed job and will be provided with perks such as housing and the opportunity to make money on the side, often through corruption.

But with the civilian ministries generally headed by military men, nonconformists are quickly weeded out. To enter any of these professions, a high-school or university graduate must have no history of anti-government political activities. Thus the need to foster conformity begins early. Parents encourage their children to join government-sponsored organizations, because those who don't are viewed with suspicion. Since the formation of the Union Solidarity and Development Association (USDA) in 1993, high-school and university students are expected to become members. Teachers, who themselves must be USDA members, pressure students to join, sometimes by threatening lower grades or even expulsion if they don't. Some students find their names added to the rolls without ever being asked. Others willingly join so they can take advantage of special classes, which are offered only to USDA members.

Under the BSPP, outstanding students were honoured by the ruling party. Today, outstanding students who score highly in school exams are recognized by the USDA. The USDA also presents awards to outstanding members of organizations closely affiliated with the military regime, such as the Myanmar Red Cross and the fire brigades.

With many middle- and upper-class mothers so involved in their children's education that they regularly go through their school work with them, the greatest pride for parents is to have their child selected as an outstanding student. No matter how smart their children are, however, if they are caught writing anti-government pamphlets or drawing political cartoons, they will not be honoured for their academic achievements.

Students who are arrested for participation in a local demonstration or for the distribution of political pamphlets are marked for life. They might not be able to finish their schooling, they will find it difficult to obtain a job in the civil service or a company, and even finding a marriage partner becomes complicated, as parents worry that former political activists will bring nothing but trouble to their families. Thus, in order to ensure their children's well-being, most parents encourage them to go along with the regime, or at the very least to keep any negative thoughts to themselves.

Moe Thee Zun, the student leader, explained the attitude of parents when he was growing up in Rangoon in the 1970s and 1980s. He said:

> One type of parent strongly supported the BSPP and thought the BSPP could develop the country. Some parents hated the BSPP but said to their children, 'Don't play with fire. If you want to do anything against the government, pack your bags.' They really thought it was useless. Even my parents said, 'Son, don't make any problem. Get your education. Make your life better. You can go abroad.'

The relatives of Ma Pyu, a university student who campaigned for the NLD in the 1990 election, expressed similar sentiments. They told Ma

115

Pyu's parents: 'Ma Pyu doesn't know anything. Why are you letting her do this political work, fighting the government? Our government is very big and your daughter is so small and has no knowledge. It's useless.'

The attitude of Ma Pyu's relatives is exactly what successive military regimes have tried to cultivate. The relatives took it for granted that the people in power knew everything and ordinary people did not have the capacity to change the situation, so they should stay quiet. Not only did her relatives see themselves as powerless, but they sought to disempower Ma Pyu as well.

Despite the tremendous value placed on education in Burma, most parents have done little to make up for the regime's silence on much of the country's recent history. In particular, parents do not bring up past incidents of resistance, or they use the failure of such incidents as cautionary tales for why their children should remain politically passive. Parents know that the authorities are either not teaching these events in school or are distorting them, but they generally refrain from discussing such subjects at home. Some parents' silence can be attributed in part to a belief that it is not their duty to explain politics, but often it is due to a feeling that it is better if their children don't know. Other parents discuss only the negative consequences of past events, such as the numbers killed during the 1988 demonstrations and the regime's ability to reassert control. This is used as evidence of the futility of protesting. Few young people in the early 2000s knew the names of the leaders of the 1988 demonstrations, or any details about which groups in society participated. Some parents even discourage their children from reading serious books for fear this will lead them into politics. Thus, children in Burma grow up thinking that there is no reason to question the situation in their country. They and their family might be suffering as a result of government policies, but these problems are taken as unavoidable. No one has given the youth a frame of reference for critiquing their country's current situation.

When children obtain positions in government, their parents are relieved. One diplomat with several dissident uncles but conformist parents told me that he had joined the foreign service to please his parents. Initially, he unquestioningly accepted the government's line that human rights should be considered only after there was economic progress. Without having ever studied how political rights were understood in other countries, he bought the 'Asian Values' argument that collective security was more important than individual rights. It wasn't until he had lived abroad that he began to see things differently. Finally, his ideas changed so radically that he ended up defecting.

The children of military officers in particular grow up believing that it is right for the military to run the country. Military officers' families are given special privileges such as access to better-equipped hospitals, sports facilities and housing. They are taught that they deserve these benefits because they are the ones who are sacrificing for the country. Few question this logic unless they spend time abroad. For instance, Kyaw Kyaw, a young man whose father was a high-ranking officer, has lived in a Western country since the late 1980s, and his views have been completely reshaped by his experiences outside the sheltered environment in which he grew up. He said when he was young, he appreciated that his family's status was higher than that of ordinary people. Knowing that he would immediately be released whenever he was stopped by the police, he would brazenly drive over the speed limit and commit other traffic violations.

Kyaw Kyaw explained that he understood the inequities that existed in Burma only after experiencing an open society. He was surprised that, in the West, even top political leaders' sons had to obey the law and work for success. Now, he says, he is ashamed of his past. He thinks people should have to earn their cars and their houses, rather than receive them as gifts because of who their fathers are. Going back to Burma after ten years, he was shocked by the lives of some of his former friends from military families, who thought nothing of spending more money than an ordinary worker made in many months in just one day on food, drink and women. He found them to be totally unconcerned with the problems that ordinary people were facing. After he had expressed his dismay to his family, his parents became worried that he might air his views publicly. They urged him to continue to live abroad.

Having gone through the crackdown on the pro-democracy uprising in 1988, the regime's refusal to honour the 1990 election results, and the crushing of the 2007 monks' demonstrations, few people outside the military talk about the current regime with enthusiasm, but they also have no idea about how to effect a change. While parents might reminisce about the past when their salaries went farther and goods were cheaper, they rarely link their complaints to a political programme of action. As much as Aung San Suu Kyi has called on people to resist unreasonable demands by the authorities, such as the extortion of supplementary school fees, parents tend to feel that they can best serve their children by going along with the regime. While they may believe that ultimately their children would be better off under a democratic government, they see that anyone who works for change is soon arrested.

117

As Ne Myo, a farmer and part-time carpenter from Mon State, explained, even if the government-imposed rice quota is too onerous, farmers cannot protest because they have to think about their families' survival. He said:

> Let's say I get arrested and go to prison because the farmers gathered at my house and demonstrated. My family will starve. Since I'm afraid my family will starve if I go to prison, I won't dare to participate in demonstrations. Since I don't have food to eat and I'm struggling for food, I have to be afraid of everyone and I have to keep my head low, whether they are doing the right thing or not.

The rural population of Burma is affected by military rule more than the urban population because, in many areas, villagers must perform forced labour on infrastructure projects and act as porters on military operations, unless they can pay bribes. Few have enough money to do so regularly. In addition, farmers who cannot provide the annual rice quota, which must be sold to the government at a price well below the market rate, must buy rice at the market price and sell it back to the authorities at the government price. As a result, farmers often have trouble providing for their families, and family members have increasingly migrated to neighbouring countries so that they can earn money to send home.

Unable to afford their children's school fees, Ne Myo and his wife joined several hundred thousand illegal Burmese migrant workers in Thailand, leaving their four young children with their maternal grandparents. Although their salaries at a garment factory were far below the Thai minimum wage and police raids left them without a penny some months, they managed to send money home regularly for school fees, food and clothing. Ne Myo explained: 'Now that I'm working in Thailand, I can send my children at least four outfits each a year. I can tell my parents to buy good-quality rice. They can eat good curries. I am happy.'

Ne Myo's own father was able to pass on only his carpentry skills to Ne Myo, but Ne Myo wants to do more for his children. He thinks that if his children are well educated, they will live an easier life than he has. But the price he and his wife have had to pay is high. In order to provide for their children, they cannot live with them. When he sees Thai children on their way to school, he is reminded of his own children. 'I become really sad and tears well up in my eyes,' he said. 'I miss them very much.'

Ne Myo and his wife are admirable parents, doing all they can to take care of their children. Moreover, the grandparents don't have to suffer unduly because they now have enough money to pay off the military men who come to the house to extort fees for porters and forced labour. But by feeding money into the system that has put them in this untenable position, they are inadvertently helping to prop it up. I say this not to criticize families trying their best to survive but to demonstrate how a military regime becomes self-sustaining even when most of its citizens are opposed to it. The collective effect of almost every family protecting its own members is that challenges to military rule are generally not promoted or valorized except in rare situations, such as in 1988, when it looks as if real change is imminent.

Meanwhile, more and more middle-class parents have urged their children to seek careers abroad, even selling their property to finance the move. Once the children are established and begin families of their own, their parents often join them to take care of the grandchildren.

Among families who remain in Burma, many encourage other family members to engage in corruption. Because civil servants' salaries are insufficient, officials demand bribes for routine assistance, and military men of all ranks steal petrol meant for military use and sell it on the black market. Such behaviour has become acceptable in most families, because parents have responsibilities to provide for their families, and they certainly can't do so on a government salary alone. Those who are honest and refuse to engage in corrupt activities may be perceived as stupid or irresponsible if they cannot properly take care of their families.

Insufficient salaries have also meant that people are so busy hustling to survive that they have no time for politics. More important, because so many soldiers and civil servants have engaged in corruption and illegal activities, they are also implicated in the evil that the system has produced. The whole notion of legality has been turned upside down, because many activities that would be perfectly acceptable under other forms of government are treated as illegal, while other activities that most would agree are wrong have been openly tolerated.

Activist families

Nevertheless, there are some devoted activists who do raise their children to shun corruption and to be aware of the country's political problems. These parents try to live outside the government's reach, and often consign their families to poverty as a result. Such parents don't allow their children to attend government-organized activities, which is often hard on their children when they see all their friends participating. As they get older, though, many of these children follow in their parents' footsteps. Here I want to tell the story of two such families in detail, because it is easier to understand why people go along with the regime after looking at the experiences of those who don't.

Than Dai grew up with a father who was strongly determined to have the family live their lives untainted by involvement with the military regime. Total avoidance was impossible, because the children had to attend government-run schools. But Than Dai's father made tremendous efforts to ensure that his children were instilled with the moral and political ideas that he considered important. When Than Dai was young, however, he found it difficult to understand his father's extreme behaviour.

Than Dai's father had participated in anti-military demonstrations after General Ne Win seized power in 1962. A university student at the time, he was arrested and kept in custody at the police station. There he tutored the daughter of one of the policemen, and she later became his wife. Than Dai's father went on to become a private schoolteacher, but when his school was nationalized in the mid-1960s he automatically became a government schoolteacher. He loved teaching, and his students and their parents loved him, but, from the authorities' perspective, this was a problem. He had a political record and could easily organize students, so, to keep bonds of attachment from forming, he was transferred again and again. Finally, he decided to leave the government service and start a private tuition class in his home. Than Dai's father was known by everyone in the town and respected for his intellect and moral convictions.

Than Dai's father was not appreciated, however, by his wife's family. Than Dai's grandmother was ashamed to see Than Dai and his siblings dressed in old clothes, while her other children had prospered by co-operating with the authorities. Than Dai too found it difficult to put up with his family's poverty. Once he suggested that his father start an illegal side business with some of his friends, who were government officers. He said: 'We cannot go on like this. Why don't you do some work for us?' His father was outraged. He threw everything off the table and shouted at Than Dai to leave the house. 'When I think about it now,' Than Dai said, 'my words were insulting to him, because all the time he restrained himself and kept his dignity. He could stand by himself without being involved in any government service.'

Than Dai's father refused to attend government-sponsored activities and celebrations, and would not allow his children to attend either. Than Dai and his siblings were often in trouble at school, because they could not participate in school-organized 'voluntary labour' activities or commemorations of Independence Day and Union Day. Than Dai's house was very near the town hall, so whenever the party officials held meetings or celebrations, Than Dai's father locked the gate to their house and denied entrance to any BSPP members. 'At that time,' Than Dai said,

> most people in Burma had to join the BSPP, even if they didn't like it. Cadres had a lot of opportunities. Some of those township cadres were my father's pupils and his friends. They could come to our home any time to visit or pay their respects to my parents, but whenever there was a celebration and they came to attend, he would never allow them to come in his house.

During the summer holidays, however, Than Dai's house was filled with dissident teachers and former political prisoners. Most were also poor, but as they sipped tea and snacked on tea-leaf salad, they found pleasure in each other's company.

When Than Dai was fourteen, he competed in the 'Outstanding Student' contest. He was chosen as the second best in his school, so his teachers prepared him to enter the next level of competition. Than Dai remembers his father telling him to go ahead and try, but said he wouldn't be chosen because of Than Dai's father's political history. 'He was right,' Than Dai said. 'I could answer the questions, but I didn't get it. Since that time I never competed in that competition again. But I was always first or second in my class.' I asked Than Dai whether he had felt angry with his father at that time. But he said no, because by then he could appreciate what his father had done. 'In school sometimes some people would say, "He is from the rebel family." They said this with admiration. We were very proud. Sons of a rebel.'

When Than Dai's younger brother passed the high-school matriculation exam, he wanted to apply to the Defence Services Academy. Before 1988, many boys dreamed of becoming military officers, not only because of the material benefits but also because in school they were taught that military officers were heroes. Than Dai remarked that despite his brother's unusual upbringing, he still 'lost the way' because of the schooling system and the prevailing social environment. When Than Dai's brother asked his father whether he could attend the Defence Services Academy, his father said grimly, 'You can go, but you cannot come home.' Finally the brother decided not to apply.

After Than Dai started university classes, his father insisted that Than Dai continue to study English with him. Than Dai's friends were incredulous that, on top of his course work, he had to do homework for his father. Than Dai himself was embarrassed about it. Every weekend, he had to return home to tutor his younger brother and sister and go over his homework. This was hard on Than Dai, who wanted to have time to go out with his friends. He often complained, but his father said, 'One day you will understand me. If you want to do things for other people, you have to be educated. So you have to do it even if you don't like it, because you are my son.' Than Dai said that although he didn't dare object, he secretly requested his mother to tell his father to ease up on him.

Than Dai's father even came to stay with him in his university dormitory from time to time. At night, he would ask Than Dai to read to him, because his eyesight was failing and the wattage of the dormitory lights was so weak. Than Dai protested, saying, 'I never saw any other parents come and sleep with their sons or ask their sons to read loudly in the room.' But his father said, 'It doesn't matter. We are not disturbing others.' Than Dai's friends came by to see what was going on and were amused by the scene. Than Dai was embarrassed. Only later did Than Dai come to believe that his father was right.

In June 1988, Than Dai's elder brother participated in the student movement in Rangoon. Some of his friends came to Than Dai's house to tell his parents that, unlike the other students, Than Dai's brother had not worn a bandana across his face to disguise himself. More than that, he publicly announced his name and the names of everyone in the family when everyone else was trying to hide their identities. Soon after, military intelligence agents brought Than Dai's brother back to his home town and put him in custody. Than Dai's grandmother was furious. She berated Than Dai's parents for not preventing her eldest grandson from getting involved in politics.

When the demonstrations were about to start in Than Dai's home town in August 1988, Than Dai told his father he was going to participate. His father did not forbid him, but that night he had Than Dai look at several books about past political movements in Burma and elsewhere. He also showed Than Dai photographs of people who had been tortured, and asked him, 'If you want to do politics, you may face this one day. Do you dare to do so?'

The next day Than Dai decided he did. He and his friends led the first demonstration in their town, and his mother and older brother both gave speeches to the gathered crowd. Than Dai's father stayed home. When the marchers passed Than Dai's house shouting slogans, Than Dai's father came out smiling. The crowd asked Than Dai's father to join in, but he replied jokingly, 'It's not necessary for me to come. All of my family has joined with you. I am the eldest, so I have to give a chance to them.' Than Dai said everyone understood, because Than Dai's father was living under watch and everyone knew it. 'In the blacklist in our town,' Than Dai said, 'my father was first.'

Two or three days after the first demonstration, the town activists formed a strike committee and asked Than Dai's father to become a member. He did, but when the SLORC staged a coup on 18 September, he and Than Dai knew they were likely to be arrested. They and some others hid in rural villages, moving from place to place. Finally, the authorities tracked them down. Than Dai was sleeping under some toddy trees when he was awakened by an armed soldier kicking him. He was tied up, as was his father, who had been sleeping in the monastery. When the soldiers searched their bags, they confiscated a book that discussed how soldiers should treat civilians. Than Dai complained, saying, 'This book says that soldiers must pay respect to civilians.' The soldiers responded by beating him with a stick. Then father and son were tied together and taken back into town, where they had to sign an agreement saying they would not participate in politics again. They signed but, soon after, Than Dai's father and older brother were arrested together with the rest of the strike committee.

Than Dai didn't know what to do. He thought about going to the jungle to take up arms. His mother told him he could leave if he wanted to, but that he should consider carefully, because his life would never be the same if he did. She also told him that if he left, he should not come home again until the struggle was successful. She was displeased with students who had come back from the border and condemned the student movement in interviews with the state-controlled press.

Within a couple of months, Than Dai's father and brother were released on bail, and Than Dai and his brother decided to join up with the student army on the border. Their parents supported them. The day they were to leave, everyone in the family was overcome with sadness. They did not know when they would see each other again. Than Dai said:

> Some friends came by that day, but we dared not reveal our plan. We had to be cautious, but we kept looking at each other. The visitors were talking. My mother was cooking. We prepared some money and clothes. We had to wait for the visitors to leave and we ate lunch together, the last lunch for us. Just before we left our home, we paid respect to our parents. My parents sat on the bed inside the room, because outside some more visitors had arrived so we dared not talk loudly. My mother was not

crying, but my father was. Tears ran down his glasses. My brother asked him, 'Why are you crying?' My father replied, 'I'm crying because I'm proud. Because my two sons will continue the revolution which I cannot afford to do at my age.'

Than Dai and his brother managed to make their way to the border and have been working with resistance groups ever since. Although they know they have the love and support of their parents, they have had to sacrifice their family connections. More than ten years later, they still had no contact with their parents and didn't know if they would ever be reunited.

Still, Than Dai is grateful for the way he was raised. He said:

My father was a good example. Now I thank him very much. If we didn't have him, we could have gone the wrong way. And I thank my mother because she never complained about his political views and his guidance in education. And then I thank both of them because they always taught us not to exploit others, to sympathize with the poor and oppressed. Sometimes we are human beings, so we lose our focus, but at those times, I remember my parents. They faced a lot of difficulties, especially with money, but they never knelt down or betrayed their beliefs, so I love them.

While it is clear from Than Dai's story that some of the other town residents admired his family, no one else he knew chose to live in the same way. Trying to live outside the regime's influence takes tremendous effort, particularly when everyone else is going along with the authorities. The family became fully integrated into the community only during the 1988 demonstrations, when it seemed as if democracy was within reach.

Than Dai lived in a small town in Upper Burma. Lin Htet, another young man who grew up in a political family, lived in Rangoon. Like Than Dai, Lin Htet went through difficult years as a teenager, when he still couldn't fully appreciate his father's commitment to living by different rules. Lin Htet's father was also a former student activist who had become a private tuition teacher. And Lin Htet's family was always struggling for money, too, because his father charged less than the going rate so that poorer students would have a chance to attend his classes. Like Than Dai, Lin Htet sometimes resented his father's moral uprightness, because their family could not afford the nice clothes that some other kids proudly wore.

Every summer vacation, Lin Htet's parents took him and his siblings to a rural village so that they would understand the hardships of the poor. 'My father hated privileged people exploiting peasants,' Lin Htet said. 'And he didn't want us to be rich people but to be educated people.' In the village that Lin Htet and his family regularly visited, there was no school, hospital or electricity. There were no cars, only cows. Lin Htet's father encouraged his children to ride the cows and roll around in the dust with the village children. Once Lin Htet and his siblings settled in, they enjoyed themselves, but when it came time to head for the village the next year, they resisted again. Particularly once they were teenagers, they wanted to spend their holidays hanging out with friends in the city, but Lin Htet's father insisted they return to the village so that they would understand the suffering of others.

Like Than Dai's father, Lin Htet's father did not allow the family to participate in government-sponsored activities. Lin Htet talked about how, when he was young, he wanted to go to the Armed Forces Day celebration to see the fireworks and other amusements, but his father refused to let the family go. As a teenager, Lin Htet remembers secretly fantasizing about becoming a military doctor. He thought to himself, 'I would get a lot of respect. Girls would like me. I'd look really smart.' But he knew he could never do it because of his father and his father's dissident friends. Lin Htet said they always told him and his brothers that if someone asked them what they wanted to be when they grew up, they should answer 'a revolutionary'. Such talk terrified Lin Htet's mother's relatives.

Even though Lin Htet grew up in a family that promoted resistance to military rule, his parents found it difficult to accept Lin Htet's decision to take up politics at the tender age of fifteen. After the March 1988 demonstrations broke out, Lin Htet skipped school one day to attend a secret meeting at the zoo. As some students were break-dancing to music on their tape player, others quietly conferred with an older female student, who explained to them how they could work together with the university student activists by distributing pamphlets. Many of the eager young high-school students, including Lin Htet, took up the cause.

When Lin Htet arrived home, his mother asked him where he had been. Afraid she might become angry, he lied and said he had come back from school. But his mother replied that Lin Htet's teacher had already come by and told her that he hadn't attended school that day. Lin Htet remembered, 'She took a broomstick and asked me again, "Where did you go?" At first she was worried I'd been smoking. So I told her I'd attended the high-school student meeting.' This only made matters worse. She scolded him angrily, reminding him that his eldest

125

brother and sisters were already in prison for their participation in the demonstrations, and that was upsetting her terribly. He ought to think of her feelings. And besides, he was far too young. She started beating him with the broomstick.

At this point, Lin Htet's father came into the room and told his wife to stop. He said, 'I know he's young, but we should give him the facts and let him think for himself. It's up to him whether he wants to get involved or not. But first we should explain to him in more detail about political life and family life.' Lin Htet remembers that his mother was weeping, and he felt very sorry because he missed his arrested siblings too. Every night, his mother put their photographs under her pillow and recited prayers for them. She had even gone to a fortune-teller to enquire what magical actions (*yadaya*) she could take to improve their chances of release. And now Lin Htet had become another burden for her.

His father, though, insisted on discussing the situation with Lin Htet. He told his son how harsh a political life could be and said that he didn't think Lin Htet was old enough to make an informed decision. He asked Lin Htet to think about the family, and in particular his mother and his grandmother, who had also come into the room and started crying. But given his political upbringing and the mood in his high-school class, Lin Htet felt compelled to act. Throughout the 1988 demonstrations and the election campaign period, he participated in student politics. When military intelligence imprisoned Min Ko Naing and other student activists in mid-1989, Lin Htet realized he too might be arrested. One evening he came home in the rain, and his mother greeted him at the door with the words, 'Go! Go!' Military intelligence agents had been there looking for him and were still lurking around the neighbourhood awaiting his return. He fled into the night and has not been able to return home since.

Lin Htet's mother's reaction was typical of many Burmese families who find out their children have become politically active. But the way she and her husband and Than Dai's parents raised their children was quite unusual. Most families try to insulate their children from political realities and urge them to conform. Parents worry about their children's safety, but many also depend on their children to take on some of the family's responsibilities. With a deteriorating economy and high inflation, many older children are expected to help pay for their younger siblings' educations. Moreover, grown children in poor families are expected to provide financial support for their ageing parents. If children are in and out of prison, on the run and unable to get jobs because of their political activities, how can they support their family?

The demands of the family and the democracy movement pull politically aware individuals in opposite directions. Some choose to stop their political activities so they can take care of their families, while others decide that they must work for their country despite their families' objections. By entering politics, activists realize they are also potentially putting their family members at risk, as parents and siblings are sometimes harassed or denied jobs because of their activities. Many activists find wrestling with these tensions extremely painful.

For young women, the decision to participate in political activities is particularly difficult. Single women are not supposed to go out alone or with male friends; they should be accompanied by parents, aunts or older brothers until they are married. They cannot easily stay out late at night to attend meetings or not come home to sleep. If they do go around with male colleagues or sleep elsewhere, they can be accused of being 'bad' girls. Such cultural norms make it even harder for young women than for young men to take up politics.

Shifting values

It was not until 1988, when large numbers of people joined the pro-democracy demonstrations, that ideas about activists changed. In the early stages, only university and high-school students and other long-time but often socially marginalized political activists joined in. Yet when the soldiers retreated to their barracks and the government seemingly collapsed, more and more of the parents who had raised their children to go along with the system joined their sons and daughters on the streets. Mothers took an active role, cooking for hungry protesters and joining in the marches.

During this brief six-week period, values changed. When the pro-democracy forces appeared to be winning, those who were most active in organizing the strike committees gained prestige and respect in their communities. Often shunned in earlier days, older activists like Than Dai's father found themselves the centre of attention during those heady days of freedom. At the same time, hatred of the military grew dramatically as many people witnessed soldiers brutally firing on unarmed demonstrators, including children. Thus, some military men were shocked when they were suddenly ostracized even by those closest to them.

One soldier named Maung Maung, who returned to his home town in Karen State shortly after the coup, discussed the cold treatment he received from his friends and family. Ten years had passed by the time I interviewed him, but he still clearly felt upset. He remembered:

'Before the '88 demonstrations, when I took leave and met my friends and classmates, they warmly welcomed me. They were proud of my being a soldier. But after the '88 affair, when I took leave and went home, they didn't even want to speak with me.' Even his parents were unhappy with him.

Maung Maung was a member of Light Infantry Division 22, the division most responsible for the 1988 killings. But during the shootings he had been in a remote border camp, only vaguely aware of what was happening in the urban areas. When he arrived home, his father asked him accusingly, 'Do you know what Division 22 did in Rangoon?' Maung Maung said that he explained to everyone that he wasn't involved in those shootings, and that he would never shoot students even if he were ordered to. But his friends clearly didn't believe him. 'At that time I felt very sad,' Maung Maung said. 'It really affected me.'

Maung Maung maintained that he had originally joined the military because he was impressed with the *tatmadaw*'s image. But after the shootings, the military no longer had any dignity in the eyes of the people. He said: 'Previously people loved us and looked on us as people they could rely on. But now they look at us with disgust. Also in their eyes, now I see fear. I can't deal with that. That's why I didn't stay for my whole leave time. I had ten days, but after seven days I went back to my battalion.'

When the military refused to transfer power after the 1990 election, family attitudes changed again. Soldiers had lost much of the respect they had once had, but parents again began thinking that officers in the military had the best chance of a secure career. Sons were again encouraged to seek entrance into the Defence Services Academy. Moreover, the authorities' technique of making life difficult not just for activists but also for their families turned many people against their activist relatives.

Kyi Kyi, a young woman who was sentenced to four years in prison for continuing underground political activities after the 1990 election, explained how her mother's treatment of her changed over time. When she first joined the movement in 1988, her mother was worried. Her husband had died several years before, so she had had to raise her children alone. But Kyi Kyi's mother gradually became more supportive, because, Kyi Kyi says, she herself had suffered so much.

While Kyi Kyi was in prison, her mother regularly brought her food, but her relatives had all turned against her. Many served in the military. When Kyi Kyi was released, none of her relatives would talk to her, even when she visited their houses. Kyi Kyi tried to resume a normal life and sought work to support her mother and siblings. Yet whenever she managed to secure a job, a military intelligence agent would show up and inform her employers about her political background. After that, the employers would be scared to keep her on and would fire her. In one instance, the cleaning girl at a company where she worked admitted to Kyi Kyi that even she had been ordered to keep a watch on her.

The military intelligence officer also often came to Kyi Kyi's home to question her or order her to come to his office. Kyi Kyi refused to go with him, but her family was scared and implored her to go. He used crude language with her and demanded that she tell him where she had been, whom she had met and what they talked about. This was hard enough on Kyi Kyi, but what was worse was that even her mother and her younger siblings started to blame her. She said, 'They asked me what I had done. Of course I said, "Nothing." My family thought I must be up to something to be treated this way. I became a sort of black sheep in my family.' Finally, Kyi Kyi could no longer stand the pressure and left home.

Some children have faced even more extreme forms of disapproval from their parents. One woman I interviewed who had participated in anti-government activities in the mid-1990s was publicly disowned by her parents in a newspaper announcement. Although her family got word to her beforehand that they were doing it only because of military pressure, it was still emotionally upsetting for her.

Although the military's actions are meant to break up resistance among the civilian population, military families are also affected by their policies. The SPDC Secretary-1, Lieutenant General Khin Nyunt, felt compelled to disown publicly one of his sons, Dr Ye Naing Win, when he married a Singaporean woman.[1] After all the regime's rhetoric against Aung San Suu Kyi for marrying a foreigner, Khin Nyunt's son's marriage was highly embarrassing.

Split families

While there are families that are purely anti-government or pro-military, many families have relatives in both the military and the democracy struggle. Thus, in past demonstrations, there have been instances where some relatives were taking part in the protests while other relatives were attacking the demonstrators. Older siblings who had gone into the military officer corps, and had been appreciated for regularly sending money home, became pariahs. Younger siblings who had looked up to their older brothers with admiration now viewed them with repugnance. The realization that the enemy was part of their own family was too much for some to bear.

A soft-spoken former student activist named Zaw Lwin, who comes from a town in central Burma, explained how he was raised with the idea that he would become an officer; his three male cousins were all in the army or police, and his mother had encouraged him to follow the same path. But in 1988, he joined the student demonstrations. The political climate had changed, and so did his mother's perspective. For more than two years, she fed and supported him and his colleagues as they moved from the demonstrations to election campaign work.

Zaw Lwin's aunt in Rangoon was a teacher, and her son was an army officer. In 1988, she told her son that if he shot any students, he should not return home. She said the students were her pupils and she loved them. Zaw Lwin said that his cousin was so frustrated that he cried. He had graduated from the university and knew what was right and wrong, but he was thinking of his family's survival. He was already married and didn't dare challenge his superiors' orders.

Later that year, Zaw Lwin ran into this cousin at Aung San Suu Kyi's compound, just after the death of her mother, Khin Kyi, in December 1988. He was shocked to see his cousin in plain clothes, wearing an NLD pin and acting like an NLD sympathizer. The cousin had been sent to the compound to see who was there and report back to military intelligence. Zaw Lwin refrained from greeting his cousin, but when his cousin caught his eye, he held up his hand, signalling him not to approach. Another military informer saw their exchange and assumed Zaw Lwin was also an intelligence agent. As Zaw Lwin was sitting at a table, the agent leaned over and whispered, 'What does the black ribbon mean?' Zaw Lwin told him it meant mourning for Khin Kyi. The man was writing notes in the margins of a magazine, and Zaw Lwin sensed he was in a dangerous situation. If the real NLD people realized that his cousin and the other man were intelligence agents, they might think he was too. He decided his only option was to leave immediately.

When he returned to his home town, Zaw Lwin told all his relatives about seeing the cousin spying on the NLD. Later, his cousin came to Zaw Lwin's home to try to make amends. The cousin had transferred from the military to the police, and arrived at Zaw Lwin's house on a new motorcycle, smoking a cigar. Zaw Lwin recalled that his family was put off by his manner, but because of his age and rank they treated him respectfully and offered him food and tea. The cousin talked openly about his frustration with the military but said he had a family to feed. He also warned Zaw Lwin to stop his involvement in the democracy movement, for his own safety. Zaw Lwin said that his mother lost her temper and told her nephew that if he didn't have the courage to resign and do what her son was doing, he need not come to visit again.

Other families, however, have tried to smooth over their political differences and maintain close family relations. When siblings end up in opposing camps, the parents try to keep politics out of family discussions and focus on keeping the family together. Siblings are often torn by their own conflicting feelings.

Such was the case with a middle-aged man named Tint Moe, who was involved in a demonstration in the mid-1970s. He continued to hold anti-government views, while one of his older brothers rose in a career in the foreign service. Tint Moe vividly recalled that after he was released from prison, his brother wrote to him, saying, 'You are at an age when you are very idealistic, but remember that all these things will pass and remember what you owe to your parents.'

Despite their political differences, his brother continued to send him gifts from his various postings. This made it difficult for Tint Moe to hate his brother, even though he resented the suggestion that he stop his political activities. But when the brothers met up at their parents' house in Rangoon after several years, the discussion quickly became heated. As they got on to politics, Tint Moe demanded, 'Should I talk to you as a brother or should I talk to you as someone who works for the Foreign Ministry?'

Even at home, Tint Moe's brother refused to let down his guard or admit any negative feelings towards the regime. Tint Moe's father would sometimes ask whether various rumours about the government were true or not, but Tint Moe's brother would not answer. As Tint Moe put it, 'He had just one face. The private face and the public face were the same.'

Yet when I asked Tint Moe if he felt that the military regime was to blame for the tensions in his relationship with his brother, he replied, 'You could say that, but I don't feel any personal animosity towards my brother. Whatever decisions he and I have made have been influenced by the stars we were born with.'

Ethnic minority families

Non-Burman families face the same challenges that Burman families face, but also some additional ones. Because successive regimes have stressed Burman culture, Burman history and Buddhism as central to Burmese nationalism, people of other ethnic and religious backgrounds often feel marginalized. Ethnic minority languages are only rarely permitted to be taught in government schools, and non-Burmans often find it hard to rise in government careers. While ethnic minority parents tend to be forthcoming with their children about the implications of their status as minorities, like Burman parents, their intention is to raise their children for success within the pre-existing political structure.

Because minorities in Burma are often discriminated against, they feel that they have to work extra hard to gain their rightful place. Many Indian and Chinese children, as well as the children of Rohingya Muslims in Northern Arakan State, have been denied full citizenship and cannot legally travel out of their districts without official permission.[2] Although they were born in Burma, as were most of their parents, and often even grandparents, they are not granted automatic citizenship. Instead, they are issued with Foreign Resident Certificates, which disqualify them from entering medical and engineering schools. Thus, parents must prepare their children for the fact that, no matter how smart they are, many careers will be closed to them. Many gravitate to business or seek their fortunes abroad. Parents rarely suggest fighting against these discriminatory policies, but try to help their children adapt instead.

Among the indigenous ethnic nationalities, parents also push their children to conform. A young Mon named Nai Panna told me how his parents had their children speak Mon at home but did not encourage involvement in other Mon cultural activities. He said that, in his area, few parents wanted their children to join in Mon activities, because after learning more about Mon history and the regime's repression of their culture, they were likely to volunteer for the New Mon State Party's liberation army and end up being killed by the *tatmadaw*. When Nai Panna moved to Rangoon, he joined the Mon Literature and Culture group and quickly appreciated that without achieving greater political freedom, a renaissance of Mon culture was also not possible. In 1988, he did exactly what his parents had not wanted him to do: he joined the New Mon State Party.

With the emergence of ethnic-based political parties and student fronts between 1988 and 1990, many ethnic minority families also split over which groups they should join. Some of the disputes revolved around the value placed on loyalty to one's race versus a belief in the more universal ideology of democracy. In some cases it was less a disagreement over where one's loyalties lay than an issue of idealism versus pragmatism. Some believed that only by working with a united front could they ever be successful, while others were so distrustful of ethnic Burmans that they insisted separate paths must be taken.

Among siblings, there were conflicts when one joined an ethnic-based organization and another joined a broader organization. Nai Panna talked about how upset he was in 1988 when his brother joined the ABSDF instead of the New Mon State Party. Nai Panna's brother had come to the border with a Burman friend and felt that the best way forward was to work for democracy first. More than ten years later, they still did not see eye to eye.

Thus, many families in Burma have felt the effects of military rule on relations within the family. As various members have chosen different ways of responding to the ongoing political crisis, families have often been pulled apart. And whenever there is a dramatic change in the political situation, family relations are invariably shaken up as well.

Even in cases where the parents have maintained private support for the democracy movement, young activists have sometimes felt irritated at their parents for not doing more. Some activists have tried to use this frustration to urge this generation of youth to take action. As a former ABSDF leader, Dr Naing Aung, put it, 'Our parents didn't do it, so we have to take this responsibility. If we don't do it, the next generation will face the same problem.' This has been Aung San Suu Kyi's argument. People must join together and participate now, so that everybody can live in peace and security in the future. But remembering the farmer-carpenter who is worried about getting the next meal on the table for his family, it is easy to understand why people hesitate.

The fact that parents of all backgrounds tend to promote conformity with the regime reflects an interesting twist on the 'Asian Values' argument, which prioritizes collective well-being over individual rights. Because Burmese parents, like parents everywhere, try to protect themselves and their children from harm, there is no collective well-being but only continued fear and insecurity for everybody.

7 | Communities: going with the flow

In Burmese we have an expression *ye laik, nga laik*, which means 'where the water flows, the fish must go'. In other words, we must go with the flow. (Daw Sabei)

Communities have been damaged in many ways by continued military rule, in which surveillance, intimidation and arrest are used to keep people in line. The regime has also exploited traditions of respect for authority to exercise its control over communities. In the civil war areas, communities have been uprooted and destroyed because of the *tatmadaw*'s counter-insurgency techniques, which focus on removing civilian support for resistance armies. Nevertheless, in all parts of the country, the number of community organizations has grown significantly in recent years as people seek to address issues largely ignored by the authorities. While many of these organizations have faced harassment and interference, some have found ways to survive and make contributions that have benefited society.

Obedience is a habit

When people in Burma meet each other for the first time, they immediately try to determine whether the other person is above or below them in status. This is primarily determined by age, but also by other factors, such as wealth and type of employment. Recognition of one's own and others' relative position in society is constantly reaffirmed through the use of prefixes in front of names and different pronouns to signify 'I' and 'you'. Thus, a man or a woman would address men their father's age as *U*, or 'uncle', and women their mother's age as *Daw* or 'aunt'. Similarly, in the army, younger men are encouraged to call their senior officers *ah bah*, or father/grandfather, and to call those just above them in rank *ko gyi*, or big brother. As a result, everyone knows his place and acts accordingly. This linguistic practice creates a positive feeling of social cohesiveness, because people relate to each other as if they were all part of one big family. But at the same time, individuals must generally defer to those above them, regardless of whether they are right or wrong.

Related to the use of status markers is the concept of *ah nah*, which often connotes a desire not to impose on others. The objective is to maintain smooth relations by considering others' feelings and speaking and acting accordingly. For instance, one should refrain from saying or doing anything that might be upsetting to a superior, including making what might be perceived as excessive demands. At the same time, a person may feel *ah nah* if he or she has promised to do something but then cannot do it.

In a social context, friendly relations can be easily developed, as each side tries to demonstrate goodwill towards the other. The junior-ranking person in the exchange will be particularly hesitant to bring up troubling issues, instead trying to say things that will make the superior feel pleased or happy. In a political context, feelings of *ah nah* can be used to justify silence and inaction. Thus, lower-level authorities are hesitant to report bad news to those above them. Moreover, when military officers make demands on individuals and communities, they know that most people will not dare to talk back. Although fear is the main reason people stay quiet, they may tell others that they felt it wasn't their place to object. When people do speak up, military authorities often react with shock and anger, telling them to remember to whom they are talking. The regime plays on a tradition of respect for elders to insist on unquestioning obedience from both lower-ranking soldiers and civilians.

Some activists have argued that the military has habituated people to silently obeying as part of a strategy of disempowerment. Control through humiliation is often used by the authorities. Sanda explained that to impress a government minister who would be passing their town on a train, the local authorities ordered all those living on both sides of the track to repaint their houses. 'Those who didn't do it,' she said, 'had to pay fifty kyat. Those who couldn't pay were sent out on to the train track to jump like frogs.' In order to avoid such humiliations, people try to comply with the authorities' demands, whether they consider them justified or not.

Po Khin, a farmer who became a labour organizer, talked about how the military has made regular, and sometimes arbitrary, demands on citizens, so that eventually people don't even think about protesting. He gave an example of how some villagers were toyed with in Sagaing Division. The military officers said they were going to repair the road that linked the towns of Kalaymyo and Tamu. They ordered the villagers to collect stones and firewood, clear a site, and make tar. After the villagers had complied, the battalion withdrew. The tar spoiled, and all their work had been in vain. Later, the military officers came again and said this time they really were going to repair the road and made the villagers collect everything again, without any payment. The villagers were told to pile all the supplies on one side of the road. When the officers reappeared later, they ordered the villagers to move everything to the other side of the road, and then again to the first side. The villagers had to do as they were told, no matter how capricious the command.

Demands for money are also common. For instance, businessmen are often compelled to buy tickets for military-sponsored functions or to make donations to military-sponsored charities, because if they don't, they may find their business activities hindered in all kinds of ways. Po Khin concluded that, with time, 'When a man in an army uniform stands in front of your house and says you have to pay this amount of money, the house-owner has no thought of complaining or asking, "For what?" He just gives it.' Po Khin said that when he and his colleagues told villagers, 'You have the right to refuse. You have the right to question,' they answered, 'Oh, they are from the government, how can I?'

Po Khin's colleague, Tun Shein, added, 'To refuse a government order, we need a gathering. If only I refuse, I will be punished, it is sure.' With no independent workers' unions or independent village administrative committees, individuals often feel overwhelmed by their helplessness in the face of the powerful military organization.

The authorities have also implemented divide-and-rule policies. Individuals may be criticized for trying to represent their communities or even their neighbours, making people feel separated and weak. Po Khin explained: 'If I say to the soldiers, "Sir, Tun Shein is handicapped, so I think he cannot work, so just forget him," they will say, "Who are you? Are you a politician? If you want to speak, speak for yourself. If Tun Shein cannot work, he will say it himself."'

So many people in Burma talk of living in silence and talking in whispers. As one writer put it, 'We have no mouths, only ears.' This should be understood in the active sense. It is an effort to keep thoughts to yourself and to stop words from spilling out. Nevertheless, without meaning to, people serve as instruments of the regime when they decide not to talk.

Yet while the authorities may not let one citizen speak for another, the regime asserts the right of its members, and its mass organization, the USDA, to speak on behalf of all citizens. The division of Burmese society into the military who issue orders and the people who obey them is reflected in the distortion of an old military slogan. When General Aung San was still alive, he and the military leaders of the day promoted the slogan 'The people are our mother, the people are our father'. Under the

136

SLORC and the SPDC, this has been changed to 'The *tatmadaw* is our mother, the *tatmadaw* is our father'.[1]

Likewise, whenever senior generals visit agricultural development projects, industrial enterprises or schools, they always give the managers and workers 'necessary instructions', even if they have no expertise in that area. The regime has trivialized the country's citizens by treating them as if they have no important ideas of their own. People are treated like children who must obey their elders.

This is reflected in the regime's handling of the thousands of Cyclone Nargis survivors who sought shelter at temples and temporary relief camps. A few weeks after the storm, when dead bodies were still floating in the rivers, the authorities announced that the relief phase was over and that everyone would have to return to their villages to begin reconstruction.[2] They did not bother to consult with the villagers to see whether they were ready or able to return, but simply decided for them.

Since 1988 the military has encouraged people to greet them with a prayerful gesture of respect formerly reserved for kings and monks. A return of the gesture would signal mutual respect, but the gesture is not returned.

A climate of fear

Community life in central Burma has been warped by concerns about monitoring and surveillance. Under the household registration system, all households must possess an official form listing the residents of the house. When anyone comes to spend the night, even if the person is an aunt or grandson, the family must report this to the ward authorities. If the guest is not reported, both the guest and the house-owner can be punished. While registering guests may be little more than a nuisance for apolitical families, it reflects the regime's desire to be able to monitor activities at the household level.

Travel, particularly to areas outside the central plains, is slow and sometimes nerve-racking because of the numerous checkpoints along the way. Soldiers at the checkpoints are looking not only for armed anti-government soldiers but also non-violent activists trying to network with people in other parts of the country. Young people who might be student activists are particularly singled out for close scrutiny, unless they can show USDA membership cards. After the 2007 monks' demonstrations, travelling monks often faced lengthy questioning as well. But members of armed groups that have made ceasefire agreements with the regime, even if they are believed to be involved in drug trafficking, are given special permits that allow them to sail through checkpoints without their passengers or vehicles being checked. This arrangement has made some Burmese citizens resentful of the ceasefire groups.

In urban areas, monitoring is undertaken by both trained officers and local informers. According to Thiha, an experienced former military intelligence officer who left Burma after Khin Nyunt's arrest in 2004, surveillance worked as follows: in Rangoon and Mandalay, each township was overseen by a middle-ranking intelligence officer, with one lower-ranking intelligence agent assigned to each ward. These agents then recruited five informers from each ward, with the job of the fifth informer being to monitor the other four informers. The ward peace and development council also monitored citizens through local informers, with one informer per street. Military intelligence agents consulted with the head of the ward development council to see whether the information both sides were getting matched.

Informers come from various backgrounds. Some are nationalists who can be persuaded to see dissidents as people who are being used by foreigners to destroy the country, while others provide information because they are intimidated or they need money.

Thiha also explained how he and other intelligence agents cleverly worked their way into sensitive locations such as mosques and even generals' houses. By spending weeks pretending to be a garbage collector or a street vendor in a particular area, an agent could become a routine part of the scene and could befriend members of households or gain access to religious centres without drawing attention to himself. He could then plant listening devices without anyone knowing.

Since the fall of Khin Nyunt, the Military Affairs Service, the Special Branch of the police and a unit within the USDA have all been assigned to monitor the country's citizens. While the new intelligence units have been perceived as less effective than the former military intelligence service thus far, those who dare to engage in politics have to assume they are under watch.

Burmese love to go to tea shops and have long discussions with friends. These discussions often hit on political topics, but when the conversation becomes heated, the participants often catch themselves and change the subject, because they don't know who might be listening in.

As the number of restaurants, nightclubs and shopping malls has expanded in Rangoon, there seems to be more freedom to meet and talk. But for activists who want to have long discussions with colleagues, there still seem to be very few places where they can meet undetected. Likewise, everyone knows that government agents, who look and act just like everyone else, have been planted in communities with a history of political activism, such as university campuses and certain monasteries.

A number of activists have had the painful experience of finding out that people they once trusted or closely associated with were in fact reporting on them behind their backs. In some cases, the informers may not have wanted to do so but felt they had no choice. Htway Win, a student activist in 1988, told how one of his fellow student union members switched sides after the failed demonstrations. His family was poor, and he needed a job, so he joined the military and was assigned to intelligence work. Meanwhile, Htway Win continued to be involved in underground student organizing into the 1990s. At first his friend warned him and his colleagues that some intelligence agents were shadowing them; later, he identified Htway Win to other authorities who had Htway Win's name but didn't know what he looked like. Htway Win was taken to one of the military intelligence's interrogation centres, where he suffered brutal torture. At one point, his former friend brought him fried noodles and apologized. Htway Win said he was very angry at the time but, after spending many months meditating in prison, he was able to forgive him.

Htway Win himself came under suspicion, however, when he was released much earlier than the three colleagues arrested with him. The parents of the other three assumed that Htway Win must have become an informer or an intelligence agent, otherwise he wouldn't have been let out before the others. According to Htway Win and other former political prisoners, this was one of the regime's tactics. The authorities tried to sow doubts among groups that were formerly cohesive, so that they would no longer want to work together. Distrust is also created by some activists and ordinary individuals who label their rivals as intelligence agents or informers in order to reduce their popularity.

For those who involve themselves in politics, suspicion has thus become one of the primary lenses through which others are viewed. Such a climate makes political organizing extremely difficult. Not knowing who can or cannot be trusted, activists find it hard to expand their networks beyond a small group of close friends. But even non-activists have to worry. With such a system in place, informers and agents can make trouble for people against whom they have personal grudges.

Viewing the world as a hostile place also relates to long-held spiritual beliefs. The continued worship of *nats*, capricious spirits demanding appeasement for often unintentional slights, still colours the worldview of many Burmese today. One person I talked to compared the military

139

intelligence to *nats*, always keeping you under their surveillance. He said that you have to respect, fear and appease them, because otherwise they may just show up and make life very uncomfortable for you.

Still, there are many instances of solidarity between local authorities and citizens. Some activists told of ward authorities who would warn them in advance about house searches, giving them time to hide any incriminating books or documents. Others believe they were able to escape arrest because local authorities, who were also their friends, did not search for them as thoroughly as they might have. One person even told of the local police secretly releasing a political prisoner for a few hours so that he could celebrate a holiday with his family. To some extent the regime must rely on these local authorities, who tend to be much more sympathetic to their neighbours' activities. But as the regime continues to increase the size of its army, it can replace more of the local civilian authorities with military men assigned to districts far from their homes. Such soldiers can usually be counted on to enforce policies more strictly.

In many areas, particularly outside the bigger cities, communities also participate in sanctioning people who dare to rock the boat, because they are seen as possibly endangering the rest of the community. The authorities may interpret neighbours' contact with activists and their families as indicating that they are also against the state. At the same time, activists' actions threaten the rationalizations to which the rest of the community clings. To use a phrase of Czech playwright and politician Vaclav Havel, they force others to confront the fact that they are 'living within a lie'. Most people tell themselves that resistance is impossible and useless, while certain individuals insist that resistance is a moral necessity. This challenges people's sense of integrity, despite the fact that they may feel they are doing the best they can for their families by keeping their heads down. Thus, during times of greater repression, communities tend to push away those who are targeted by the state, although there are usually some people who will take risks to help them.

Khin Khin Yi told of her experience after her husband, a member of the group of NLD parliamentarians who wanted to set up a parallel government, fled in 1991. She was routinely interrogated by a group of men at odd times, and two military intelligence agents were posted near her house. The MI tried to isolate her family by going to her friends' houses and telling them not to visit her.

A few months after her husband's escape, she was arrested. Unable to come up with a charge against her, the intelligence agents accused her of stealing a bicycle and imprisoned her. After two months of late-night interrogations she was released and returned home. Then some officials glued a poster with photographs of her husband and another NLD MP-elect on the house and in public places. The posters claimed the men were wanted criminals who had run away.

Shortly thereafter, the authorities informed her that she could no longer stay in her house, unless she could pay a large sum for it through a friend. She decided to move with her children to a larger town in the district, but she found it difficult to secure accommodation because people were nervous about associating with her. Finally, an old man who supported the democracy movement agreed to rent to her on the condition that she take sole responsibility if there were any trouble. Every week she had to sign in with the ward authorities confirming that she wouldn't leave town. Although she said that the local authorities treated her decently, she had to sign in for three years.

Her children also faced difficulties at school. While most of the teachers and students rallied around her daughter and sons, some were afraid. All students had to sign a form stating that they would participate in USDA functions, but her children refused. Fortunately, some teachers tried to protect them by concealing this information. On Armed Forces Day and Independence Day, the authorities demanded that her daughter give garlands to army personnel, but she wouldn't do it. At last, her children were overcome with frustration, and her daughter sank into a deep depression.

Many of her former friends avoided the family. Khin Khin Yi recalls, 'They wouldn't even meet my eyes in the street.' But there were others who helped and encouraged her, even though the SLORC threatened them. Ironically, it was the strangers who were her cell-mates during the two months she was incarcerated who really reached out to her. When she was first thrown into the room of female prisoners, most of whom were sex workers, they suspected she was a brothel owner. She explained that actually she was a housewife, but her husband was an NLD parliamentarian who had had to flee. As they got to know her better, they sympathized with her, shared their food with her, and helped her in other ways. For one week, the guards forced her to sleep in the dankest corner of the cell, where ants and mosquitoes made their homes. She was given no mat or blanket. Her cell-mates eased her discomfort by crushing up tobacco leaves and spreading them on the ground to keep the insects away. Her children didn't know where she was, so her fellow prisoners asked their relatives to send news to them.

There were people in the community who tried to help Khin Khin Yi's family, but many others, worried about endangering their own families, stayed away. For those who are attempting to break through the lies, it is not the repression by the authorities which is so painful, for that is expected; it is the lack of support from neighbours, friends and sometimes even family members which makes it so difficult for activists to maintain their morale.

Min Zin, a student activist who spent several years in hiding in the 1990s, talked about the strain of living in other people's houses, where inevitably some members of the household felt that the family was taking an undue risk by sheltering him. He wanted to stay in Rangoon to continue to network with other activists, but, he said, 'politics is not twenty-four hours. Twenty-four hours is social relations.' The stress was constant.

Unable to go out, he would spend almost all his time upstairs, listening to foreign radio broadcasts, reading and writing. To get exercise, he would walk diagonally back and forth in his cramped room. When relatives or other guests came to stay, as they often did, Min Zin had to be especially careful. Family members would secretly bring him his food, and they would leave him with a chamber pot, since he could not go to the bathroom.

During the rare occasions when Min Zin's friends took him out, he said he would stay out almost the whole night, sitting on a bench by Inya Lake and sometimes crying. He said that judging from the government TV broadcasts, people seemed to be happy to go to SLORC-sponsored merit-making ceremonies, boat races and trade fairs. He said he believed that people only appeared to be happy with the SLORC, but that he couldn't bear it.

Sometimes a friend would come in the middle of the night, saying that someone who knew where Min Zin was had been arrested. He would have to move immediately. 'I couldn't expect anything,' Min Zin said. 'Life felt so meaningless.'

Later, Min Zin spent periods of time in meditation centres, where no one knew his identity. Moreover, he could find peace in his religious practice. Finally, in 1997, a friend of his was arrested and admitted his whereabouts, and the intelligence agents were close on his heels. He decided that his only choice was to leave the country.

Amazingly, there continue to be committed individuals like Min Zin who refuse to give up their political activities despite their fear and the lack of full support from the community. Most eventually end up either in prison or in exile. They realize that they cannot make a change happen unless there is widespread participation. Likewise, the regime recognizes that it can forestall broader engagement by isolating those who dare to act from the rest of the community.

The impact of forced labour on communities

Soldiers appear on the streets in cities only during periods of political tension, but in many towns and rural areas in the ethnic states, they are a constant presence. Wherever there are soldiers in rural areas, there are always demands for forced labour, with adverse impacts for families and communities.

The *tatmadaw* sends orders to the village headman stating how many people are required for what kind of work, when and where. Types of work include road, bridge, railway and dam construction, the construction and maintenance of army camps, cooking and cleaning at army camps, and work for military-owned commercial businesses.[3] Villagers may be asked to work for a day or several days at a time, they must bring their own food and tools, and they are not paid. Sometimes they must sleep on the worksite without proper shelter. There is no medicine if they contract malaria or dysentery or if they are hurt. Moreover, for families barely making ends meet, to lose a labourer for a week at a time has a huge impact on their incomes. For this reason, wives often go, or parents may send older children.

The authorities' use of forced labour increased significantly under the SLORC and SPDC. The generals sought to upgrade the country's infrastructure and expand the military's access throughout the ethnic states, but often did not provide sufficient funding for the projects.

In 1997, some colleagues and I interviewed a number of Burmese about the situation in Chin State and Sagaing Division, where the use of forced labour was common. Zaw Htun told us about his experience working on the Thazi dam in north-western Burma.[4] He and his brother took turns doing forced labour on the dam over a period of four or five months in early 1995. Zaw Htun said,

> Soldiers were guarding us. They scolded the people and even beat them. On the worksite, the soldiers were always drunk. They always tried to fool around with the girls. The people were so angry with the soldiers but they couldn't do anything. There were also several work accidents on the construction site, but no compensation was paid.

Another form of forced labour is portering. Whenever soldiers are travelling through the jungle, they use local villagers, people they have

Communities

rounded up in other locations or criminal prisoners to carry their ammunition and supplies. Porters tend to be poorly fed and often beaten. Some are killed or left to die if they cannot keep up with the troops.

The exact number of people who engage in forced labour each year is difficult to pinpoint, but the International Confederation of Free Trade Unions estimated it at 800,000 in 1999, out of a population of just under fifty million.[5] A commission of inquiry working for the International Labour Organization (ILO) concluded that the regime was inflicting 'a contemporary form of slavery' on its citizens.[6] As a result, the ILO took the unprecedented step of banning the military regime from attending its meetings or receiving funding until it stopped using forced labour. Lieutenant General Khin Nyunt reacted angrily, insisting that in Burma villagers were happy to work for the military or to speed up development projects.[7] While some of the development projects have had benefits for the local people, rural communities are treated as a free labour pool to be exploited by the military as needed.

In response to growing international pressure, the regime issued orders in 1999 and 2000 which banned most forms of forced labour and imposed criminal penalties on those who requisitioned forced labour. The ILO was finally permitted to open an office in Burma in 2002 to monitor the use of forced labour and to work with the regime to end the practice. Since then, less forced labour has been used in central Burma, where companies may be contracted to carry out the work, machinery is used, and labourers are paid, but according to numerous human rights groups, *tatmadaw* units have continued to routinely use forced labour in the ethnic states.[8]

Many communities have disintegrated, because of onerous demands for forced labour combined with the weak domestic economy. In numerous villages and towns within striking distance of the Thai and Indian borders, only old people and small children remain. As one young Chin migrant worker sadly told us, 'Our village [in Chin State] used to have twenty-eight houses, but now only five houses remain. All the youth fled to [India] because we could not work in our fields due to portering and heavy forced labour.'

Intra-community tensions are also exacerbated by the authorities' demands for forced labour, various taxes and new recruits for the army. Some people can pay off the authorities and escape forced labour while others cannot and must go in their place. When the *tatmadaw* demands army recruits and there are not enough volunteers, the village headman either has to force people to go or he has to tax the villagers to pay someone to go. In some areas, headmen also have to collect monthly taxes for porter fees. Even if a headman tries to be perfectly fair, inequities are inevitable.

The most terrifying form of forced labour is having to work as a human minesweeper. In areas where the civil war continues, both sides use mines, but the *tatmadaw* tries to protect its own soldiers from stepping on them by having villagers walk in front of the troops. Rather than protecting the people, then, the soldiers use the people to protect themselves.

Cho Zin, who lived near the Thai–Burma border, explained that throughout 1996 people from his village had to 'clear the route with their legs'. On the day that Cho Zin was forced to go with the *tatmadaw*, he and another villager stepped on mines laid by the KNU. The other villager died on the spot. Cho Zin was lucky. Fellow villagers got him to a hospital in Thailand, his lower leg was amputated, and he survived. The *tatmadaw* offered him no compensation or assistance.

After Cho Zin was well enough to get around on crutches, he staged a one-man protest against the ongoing civil war on the Thai side of the Thai–Burmese 'Friendship Bridge', which links the two countries. Thai officials at the bridge, nervous that his actions would upset their Burmese counterparts, said they sympathized with him but he would have to stop his protest.

According to Cho Zin, in the four or five villages near his own, there were over a hundred amputees. 'If you count those who died,' he said, 'there will be about three or four hundred.' Although KNU troops had laid many of the mines, Cho Zin did not want to lay the blame specifically on either side. He said, 'We think of this as due to the civil war. If there's peace, there is no need for the mines to be there any more.'

The dismemberment of communities in conflict areas

The weight of military rule has fallen most heavily on those living in areas of armed resistance. As part of the Four Cuts policy, the *tatmadaw* depopulates its operational areas so that the ethnic nationalist armies have no one to provide them with food, information, new recruits or financial support. The human and social costs are incalculable. Some villagers living in distant hamlets have been forcibly relocated to strategic villages along roads, usually with a battalion of *tatmadaw* soldiers based near by. They are given no compensation and often no new land to farm. In the most extreme cases, they are put into fenced relocation sites, which are more like concentration camps. Food is insufficient, water often unclean, and medicine completely lacking. In the Shadaw relocation

Communities

camp in Karenni State in 1996, Amnesty International reported that out of an initial population of 4,000, between 200 and 300 died from disease and malnutrition in the first year.[9]

Along with conflict-related displacement, the *tatmadaw* has also removed populations from areas in the ethnic states and Tenasserim Division for large-scale development projects such as gas pipelines and hydropower dams. One of the strongest resistance armies in the late 1990s was the Shan State Army (South). Finding it difficult to flush the Shan troops out of the mountainous area where they operated, and eager to construct a large dam in the area, between 1996 and 1998 the *tatmadaw* ordered over 300,000 people from 1,400 villages to leave their homes.[10] Anyone caught returning to his or her village or field would be assumed to be contacting the Shan resistance and immediately shot. The human population was literally erased from the landscape, with villagers dispersed in all directions. Lacking jobs and food, many villagers hid in the forests or slept on the outskirts of towns, but secretly returned to their land to recover stored rice. On several occasions, *tatmadaw* soldiers massacred groups of villagers found hunting for food near their old homes.[11] As many as 150,000 of the displaced Shan eventually ended up in Thailand with many of the able-bodied adults seeking to support their families as labourers on farms, orange plantations or construction sites.[12]

The Thailand Burma Border Consortium, which has worked closely with local relief and development groups, found that between 1996 and 2007, more than 3,200 villages in eastern Burma were destroyed, forcibly relocated or abandoned because of threats from the *tatmadaw*.[13] While the regime routinely dismisses critical reports as made up or exaggerated, this information has been corroborated by high-resolution commercial satellite imagery.[14]

Since the late 1990s, there have been three armies operating in Karen State: the *tatmadaw*, the Karen National Union's Liberation Army (KNLA) and the Democratic Karen Buddhist Army (DKBA). The DKBA consists of soldiers who left the KNLA and allied themselves with the *tatmadaw*. For the villagers, managing all the armies' demands and staying on good terms with them is a nearly impossible task. Cho Zin, who lost his leg as a human minesweeper, explained, 'If one side comes, we have to be afraid of them. If the other side comes, we have to be afraid of them. We don't love them or hate them. We are only afraid of them.'

When the *tatmadaw* soldiers suspect someone is giving information to the resistance armies, they often use threats, torture and murder to extract the information and intimidate other villagers. Whole villages may be punished if one or a few people are believed to have assisted the ethnic resistance armies. *Tatmadaw* officers and soldiers have also raped girls and women in civil war areas with impunity.[15] Torture and rape cases demoralize families and communities and instil bitterness that will not easily be forgotten. Moreover, for the girls and women who are raped, the trauma of the experience is often compounded by the stigma they face if people know.[16] As a result, women who have been raped may not inform others about what has happened to them, or if it is known, they may leave their communities.

There have also been instances of rape and other forms of abuse by soldiers from the ethnic nationalist armies, although there is virtually no documentation of this.[17] Soldiers from the resistance armies are generally more careful about how they treat civilians, and in at least some of the armies they are more likely to face punishment.

In conflict areas, older women have often been compelled to take on the position of village head. Because the *tatmadaw* is more likely to perceive male villagers as active enemy supporters and the headman's job involves dealing with all the armies that come through, few men are willing to take on the job. While the villagers may expect that older women can use their position as mothers in society to persuade younger soldiers to reduce certain demands, there are also numerous instances of female village heads having been beaten, tortured or raped.[18] In some areas, the position rotates among different women, as no one wants to take on the burden for long.

Because of the systematic and widespread nature of the abuses committed by *tatmadaw* soldiers in conflict areas, Amnesty International has accused the *tatmadaw* of committing crimes against humanity.[19] Clearly, the destructive impact of the violations on communities has been profound and, rather than building unity, the *tatmadaw*'s practices have engendered mistrust and hatred.

In areas where ceasefires have been negotiated, the use of physical violence against civilians is much rarer, although *tatmadaw* units may still confiscate land and demand forced labour in areas where they have access.[20] In most ceasefire areas, civilians have been able to rebuild their lives and begin new business ventures. Even after the New Mon State Party agreed to a ceasefire, however, thousands of displaced villagers were afraid to return to their original village sites because of the proximity of *tatmadaw* army camps.

Pitting communities against each other

Military commanders and other state authorities have implemented additional policies which have created a legacy of increased racial hatred in some areas. Policies include confiscating land which is then either given or sold to people of other ethnic groups, encouraging Burmans to move into the ethnic states, and rewarding Burman soldiers who marry non-Burmans. The intention of all these policies is to dilute the concentration of non-Burman, non-Buddhist populations and delegitimize ethnic groups' demands for autonomy. While these policies have not been practised in all areas at all times, there are several examples.

In Northern Arakan State, the authorities have moved Rohingya populations out of many villages, and resettled Arakanese and Burman Buddhists in their place.[21] In many cases, Arakanese Buddhists have supported this policy as they do not want the population of Rohingya Muslims in their state to increase. Meanwhile, with the agreement of the SPDC, between 1999 and 2001 the United Wa State Army moved between 50,000 and 126,000 Wa hill farmers from north-eastern Shan State to an area close to the Thai border.[22] Forty-eight thousand Shan, Lahu and Akha villagers, who lived in an area where the Shan State Army (South) was active, were forcibly displaced to make room for the Wa settlers.[23] The relocation programme was carried out because the UWSA wanted to expand its area of control while the SPDC wanted to remove support for the Shan State Army (South) and mix up the population in the area. In Northern Shan State, recent Chinese immigrants have been able to buy up land from indebted farmers, fuelling resentment at the growing Chinese presence.[24] Groups such as the Shan, who found comfort in their dominant numbers locally, now risk becoming minorities even in their own districts and states.

A piecemeal process of Burmanization in the ethnic states is also taking place, as new bases are built, land is confiscated, and *tatmadaw* soldiers resettle their families around the bases. Over the past twenty years, there have been periodic reports of Burman soldiers in the *tatmadaw* being rewarded with money or a promotion if they marry Chin, Karen or Shan girls in the ethnic states.[25] By mixing the blood of ethnic minority populations, future generations are likely to become Burmanized and adopt Burman-style Buddhism. The impact of these policies is to shift the balance in the composition of local populations and to create the conditions for communal strife in the future.

The threat of independent groups

Successive military regimes have fostered state-controlled organizations at the expense of independent organizations. In the 1970s and 1980s, citizens were strongly encouraged to join the BSPP, while since 1993, young people and adults have been pushed to join the USDA. In addition, there are a number of government-organized non-governmental organizations (GONGOs) which have been used by the authorities to promote government policies. These include the Myanmar Red Cross Society, the Fire Brigades, the Myanmar Women's Affairs Federation, the Myanmar Maternal and Child Welfare Association, as well as a number of professional organizations. Many people join the local chapters of the Myanmar Red Cross or the Maternal Child and Welfare Association out of a genuine desire to help their communities. The leaders of the GONGOs tend, however, to have close links to the authorities and frequently speak out on behalf of the regime at mass meetings.[26]

While the GONGOs take prominence in the state media, a number of religious associations of all faiths and social and cultural clubs have quietly managed to establish themselves or continue their activities throughout military rule. Community-based organizations working on social welfare issues have been tolerated; independent farmers' or workers' unions, however, have not been allowed.

Since the early 1990s, the number of both NGOs and smaller community-based organizations has increased markedly.[27] This has come about in part because of official permission for some international NGOs to begin working in Burma and for UN agencies to expand their programming. International NGOs and UN agencies have often funded or partnered with local organizations, and in some cases have provided training to their staff. At the same time, there is a sense among many Burmese that the needs for social welfare assistance have increased and that they must try to do something about it. Some political activists have also turned to social welfare work as a more immediate and less risky way to help their fellow citizens. Furthermore, with more foreigners travelling into Burma and more Burmese travelling abroad for conferences, study tours and training programmes, there is now a greater awareness of what community organizations are doing in other countries and how to operate and fund community organizations in Burma.

When an organization is founded, the members must decide whether or not to register with the government and to what degree they will cooperate with the authorities. While some have preferred to operate completely independently, others have found that when they could win over local authorities, they could work far more easily. Groups that become prominent or include former political activists, however, can come under pressure to reorganize as a GONGO or to cease their activities altogether.

One group that was turned into a GONGO was the Myanmar Women's Entrepreneurial Association (MWEA). Founded in 1995 by a group of Burmese businesswomen, the association was allowed to register with the Home Ministry only after its members had all signed pledges that they would not become involved in political activities. The association became quite active in the business community, and even planned to erect a new office building in central Rangoon. A few days before holding a celebration to mark its first anniversary, one of Lieutenant General Khin Nyunt's staff called the association and demanded tickets for several SLORC officials. He also informed them that they must allow Lieutenant General Khin Nyunt to give the keynote address. Following the event, Lieutenant General Khin Nyunt's speech was quoted at length in the newspapers.

The USDA also went after the association, demanding that MWEA members join the USDA and give contributions. A conflict erupted in the women's organization. Some argued that members should be able to decide individually whether or not they would join the USDA rather than having the whole association sucked in. But others thought it would be better for the MWEA to cooperate with the USDA in order to avoid trouble. In the end, the MWEA was compelled to work more closely with the regime. In the words of one observer, the MWEA was 'SLORCed'.

In another instance in the mid-1990s, a former 1988 activist named Ye Naing worked together with some friends to start a social welfare association in a town in central Burma. Although he had grown up in a rough area and started using drugs when he was thirteen, he gave up drinking and drugs a few years later in 1988, when he joined the democracy movement. In the mid-1990s, he started trying to reform other young alcoholics and drug addicts in his area by applying positive peer pressure.

After being praised by some of the neighbourhood elders for his good work, he went on to organize other students to help repair the local monastery. Although he was a Muslim, he decided that, as a Burmese citizen, he should be willing to do anything that would be good for his society.

At the same time, he formed a small organization to assist with funerals and other social events, especially for the needy. Usually people have to hire coffin bearers and buy them alcohol, because the task is considered a distasteful one. But poor people cannot afford this, so Ye Naing's group offered to carry coffins for no charge. If a couple eloped and needed money for their wedding ceremony, Ye Naing's group would give them a small interest-free loan.

According to Ye Naing, 'The ward authorities and the local USDA chapter felt insulted when we got involved in these kinds of cases, because they felt we were doing their job.' Also, he said, the authorities were suspicious of his group because of the recognition it was gaining in the community and because he was a former student activist. In 1996, when student demonstrations broke out in Rangoon and threatened to spread to other towns, Ye Naing learned that the authorities were planning to use the occasion to arrest his group. They all ran away, but Ye Naing said that some missed home and went back. They were imprisoned.

Nevertheless, there are many other more positive stories of organizations that have survived and managed to provide basic assistance or promote local development. The Metta Development Foundation is a good example. It was established in 1998 by Seng Raw, a Kachin woman who wanted to support post-ceasefire reconstruction in Kachin State. The foundation has been able to set up farmer field schools and sustainable agriculture training courses which have helped to improve the livelihoods of thousands of farmers in Kachin State as well as in other ethnic states.

Similarly, as tragic as the devastation wrought by Cyclone Nargis was, one positive outcome was that many new groups emerged or temporarily shifted their focus to provide humanitarian assistance. Yadana, a modest but self-assured woman from Rangoon, talked about how she and a few others put together a group of about thirty-five people from their neighbourhood to assist cyclone victims. The group included merchants, private teachers, street vendors and day labourers, who could help load and unload relief supplies. Each time they assembled a large enough stockpile of donations, members of the group would take a day off work to take the supplies out to villages in the delta. While they were irritated by the fact that the authorities often made it difficult for them to operate independently, Yadana said they found great pleasure in providing assistance to people who really needed it. The members of the group quickly became very close, even though they hadn't known each other well before. As Yadana put it, 'we have the same heartbeat'.

In the ethnic resistance areas and along Burma's borders, members of various ethnic communities have also set up independent organizations. Some, like organizations in government-controlled areas, focus on relief and development work, healthcare and education. Others, however, have focused on human rights documentation and awareness raising and the promotion of women's and children's rights. The Karen Women's Organization, for instance, transformed itself from a social welfare organization into an organization that provides a much more diverse range of services. Operating along the Thai–Burma border and in KNU-controlled territory, it has written reports on the rape of Karen women by *tatmadaw* soldiers, co-produced a video on gender-based violence for Karen audiences, provided human rights and democracy training, and established women's leadership courses. It is also an active member of the Women's League of Burma, which brings together women's groups from a variety of ethnicities and advocates for women's rights and democracy in Burma.

The growing number of NGOs and community organizations inside Burma and along its borders offers hope that Burma's future will be brighter. At the very least, the people who work or volunteer for such organizations are becoming part of an active community of people who insist on addressing community problems despite the challenges imposed by the authorities. As such organizations expand and become more confident, perhaps the authorities will no longer find it so easy to divide communities and pit people against each other.

8 | The military: a life sentence

Prisoners get released, but for us soldiers, there is no hope ...
We will be forced to work until the day we die. (Ex-sergeant
Maung Maung)

While the *tatmadaw* was respected as an honourable institution by many
Burmese in the past, after the brutal killing of civilians in the cities in
1988, its reputation was severely tarnished. The military's violent crackdown on monks in 2007 further tainted its image, affecting the morale of
soldiers within the military as well. Enlisting ordinary soldiers has become
much more difficult owing to low pay and poor treatment. Although there
are still young men who join voluntarily because of family problems and
a lack of other opportunities, the *tatmadaw* has had to resort to forced
recruitment to fill its ranks. Nevertheless, ambitious young men are still
attracted to joining the military at the officer level because of the material
benefits and power that can be accrued.

The *tatmadaw* leaders indoctrinate new recruits to believe in the need
for *tatmadaw* leadership in politics and the essential role of the *tatmadaw*
in protecting the country, while also insisting on absolute obedience.
Loyalty is valued far more than good behaviour, and the often inhuman
treatment of villagers in conflict areas is broadly tolerated or promoted
by higher-ranking officers. Similarly, corruption permeates all levels of
the military, given the low salaries and a culture of impunity. Meanwhile,
at the top level, concerns about internal coups and struggles for power
lead higher-ranking generals to try to shore up their power bases even
though such behaviour can raise suspicions about their motives and
ultimately bring about their downfall.

From the regime's perspective, expanding the *tatmadaw* is essential
to maintaining its authority. According to one inside source, the SLORC
calculated that since there were 50,000 insurgents, the *tatmadaw* should
have ten times as many troops, 500,000, in order to have the upper hand
in negotiations. In other words, might, rather than right, will be used to
decide the political situation. Military analyst Andrew Selth has written
that the regime wants to have a permanent military presence throughout
the country so that if there is trouble anywhere, there are troops on hand
to immediately take action.[1] Professionalism is not as important as sheer

numbers, since the soldiers are primarily used to intimidate and terrorize the civilian population into submission.

Reasons for joining

In government textbooks and the popular media, the greatest heroes in Burma's history are almost all military men. Most venerated are the imperialist kings who made Burmese kingdoms some of the most powerful in South-East Asia. In modern history, General Aung San and the Thirty Comrades are revered for their daring in slipping off to Japan for military training and then fighting for Burma's independence. Young men from rural and urban areas alike are drawn to these images, particularly if they have not personally witnessed instances of *tatmadaw* brutality.

Foot soldiers generally join the *tatmadaw* because they have few other economic opportunities. Poorly educated, generally from impoverished rural families, and often escaping from problems at home, they see the army as their only refuge. Kyaw Win, who joined the army when he was fifteen, is typical. His parents had sent him to stay in town with his grandparents so he could attend school for a few years, but when they ordered him to return home to work on the farm, he ran away. He said, 'I joined the army because I didn't have a place to stay. There were forty people in my group. All of them had fought with their parents or fought with their brothers or sisters or uncles. I didn't meet anyone who admired the army. Not in my group.'

In practical terms, it is much better to be a military man than a civilian. It is humiliating to have to live in silence and fear; by becoming soldiers, men can, to a certain extent, empower themselves. As one Burmese put it, 'After training, they have a gun and they have some authority. They like that.' Nevertheless, in recent years, bad conditions in the *tatmadaw* and the high demand for cheap labour in neighbouring countries have led many young men from farming families to seek their fortunes as migrant workers rather than soldiers. As a result, the *tatmadaw* has had difficulties recruiting and keeping soldiers. Migrant labourers who were arrested in Thailand and sent back to the Burma border in the late 1990s were sometimes held by Burmese authorities and told to choose between becoming a soldier or a porter. While both were potential death sentences, most decided that they were better off with a gun in their hands.

The *tatmadaw* has also resorted to not letting enlisted men resign and setting recruitment quotas for villages and army units. Human Rights Watch has documented how large numbers of young men and even children have been compelled to join against their will.[2]

Orphaned boys are particularly desired by the *tatmadaw*, because they belong to no one and have no other allegiances.[3] The army is their only family and the barracks their only home. The military has set up special schools to train these children; once they are teenagers, they are sent into the army.

I met one such boy, only about six years old, on a train in Shan State in 1996. His parents had died and he was being taken by a group of soldiers back to their battalion headquarters. They had shaved his head and put him in an army uniform that was several sizes too big, but for the moment he was happy to be receiving so much attention.

Until at least 2000, boys from ethnic minority areas were also brought into the armed forces through *Ye Nyunt* (Greatest Bravery) schools, where children receive room and board and a free education. These junior high schools are usually located on battalion bases. The students do chores around the base, and are given basic military training as well as regular classes. Parents from mountain villages often do not realize that their sons will be expected to become soldiers afterwards, wanting only for them to have a chance to learn Burmese and obtain an education. After a couple of years of schooling, the students usually have little choice but to join the military.[4]

It is easier to find recruits for officer training. Many parents view getting their children into the officer class as the best way for them to succeed and for the family to be protected. They believe that as long as the regime is in firm control, it is better to work with it than against it. Moreover, military officers are considered eligible marriage prospects, because, as one young man put it, 'They can spend a lot of money. Their status is really different from ordinary people.'

People do not necessarily associate a military career with fully fledged support for the regime. The *tatmadaw* makes great efforts to indoctrinate officer trainees, however, because if the officers are not loyal they could organize a coup against the top leaders. Through their training, officer recruits largely come to believe in the need for continued military rule and their own important role in perpetuating it. Those who don't agree or try to challenge what they are taught are expelled. All new recruits go through careful interviews and intensive background checks to ensure they have no connections to anti-government groups. Later on, officers who aren't completely trusted – for instance, because they are ethnic minorities – are assigned to jobs where security is not at stake, such as accounting, administrative work, teaching or research.

Thiha, who later became an intelligence agent, explained how he came to believe in the *tatmadaw* even though he had joined the Defence Services Academy only because his parents had pushed him to do so. He hated the first year because of the terrible hazing and bullying, but by the second year he had started thinking about staying so he could get revenge by doing the same to the younger students. By the third year, his military teachers' indoctrination started taking effect. The students were repeatedly told that they were different from ordinary civilians, because they would be leading the country and, without them, the country could collapse. They were taught about the links between politics and the economy and the military's role in nation-building. Thiha started feeling proud that he had acquired special knowledge which ordinary civilians didn't have access to, and he believed he would be a leader in the future. The students were also repeatedly told how Aung San Suu Kyi wanted to divide the military, and that democracy would only lead to political chaos as it had in the past. By his final year, he said he had even more confidence in the *tatmadaw*, because he had been persuaded that, unlike the *tatmadaw*, the ethnic insurgents were only working for their own ethnic groups, not for the good of the whole country. Furthermore, he was told, they were funded by the West. He was convinced that only the *tatmadaw* could hold the country together.

Military officers tend to be more committed to continued military rule than ordinary soldiers. Having been encouraged to believe that they have a higher status than ordinary people, many come to see themselves as deserving the special treatment they receive. Military officers benefit from much-sought-after privileges such as free healthcare at military hospitals and access to various money-making opportunities, whether through side businesses or corruption. Moreover, the higher ranks are afforded opportunities to obtain or purchase imported cars and cell phones at a reduced price. This matters because the regime strictly limits the number that can be imported each year and registration can be difficult and costly. As a result, in 2008, cell phones were selling for as much as $2,500 and Japanese sports utility vehicles for $250,000.[5]

Generals appear to be fully committed to continued military rule, if for no other reason than to preserve their privileges and to ensure they do not end up sentenced to prison or worse. According to one highly placed official, some of the higher-ranking officers realize that Burma's military rulers made mistakes in the past, but believe the *tatmadaw* deserves a chance to correct those mistakes. There are also current and retired officers who believe that military rule should continue, but the particular individuals leading the regime should be changed. Because of the generals' generally low levels of education and lack of exposure to other systems and ideas, many have difficulties imagining a system other than that which they have known.

The wives and grown children of many senior generals tend to be strong supporters of continued military rule, because of the privileged lives they live. The wives rarely have to buy things, because they are showered with presents from people who seek their husbands' favour. They keep the gifts they like and sell the rest. The wives of generals also expect the wives of lower-ranking officers to do their bidding, including accompanying them when they go out and assisting them at home. This happens not only in the capital but also on army bases.

A former military doctor related how a friend of his was the personal assistant to a regional commander. His wife worked as a schoolteacher, but when she came home at night, she had to go over to the regional commander's house to grind *thanaka* (traditional facial powder) for his wife, as if she were her personal servant.

Corruption and poor treatment

After General Ne Win's coup, many educated military men, particularly in the technical corps, retired or went abroad. As in the civilian sector, those who stayed were underpaid and saw their standard of living decline. Many increasingly resorted to theft and corruption. Usually this meant stealing military supplies and selling them outside the base. In other cases, it meant using soldiers for their own economic interests. Particularly in the rural areas, soldiers were forced to work on senior officers' plantations and for their various commercial ventures, including logging, brick-making and other labour-intensive enterprises. After 1988, such abuses increased, with some officers even stealing the rations meant for front-line soldiers and selling them on the black market.[6] In the late 1990s, the battalions were told that the central command would no longer be providing rations for them, and they would have to support themselves. In many cases this meant confiscating villagers' farmland or forcing villagers to bring them food.

Without sufficient rations or clothing, living conditions for ordinary soldiers stationed in the countryside are extremely difficult. Kyaw Win, who served in the Shan and Karen states from 1981 to 1989, recalled angrily:

We were not fed well. If we got to eat *ngapi* [fish paste], it was rotten. There was sand in the rice. The officers told us to get along with the villagers. But we had nothing to eat. And so we ate the vegetables that the villagers had planted. We didn't have the money to buy them. So if they didn't give them to us, we would go and steal them at night.

He also talked about how much the soldiers drank. Many were depressed and their salaries were insufficient to purchase anything of value, so they just bought alcohol. Members of soldiers' families also had to find paying jobs. According to a long-time resident in the Chinese border town of Ruili, a significant percentage of the many sex workers operating there in the 1990s were from Burmese army families who couldn't make ends meet.

Back at the battalion headquarters in town, the soldiers lived more comfortably, but they were often forced to work like servants for their officers' families. Many resented having to clean their superiors' houses, wash their clothes and do other chores, all of which were outside their official duties. Kyaw Win said some officers treated soldiers well at the front lines because they were scared, but back at the battalion headquarters they became arrogant and demanding.

In addition, permission for leave was rarely granted. According to Kyaw Win, in his battalion only fifteen to twenty people out of 800 were allowed leave during the one-month rest periods after six months at the front lines. Kyaw Win said that if you did not send a bribe along with your application for leave, you would be automatically rejected.

Moreover, it was almost impossible to resign. Like other soldiers I interviewed, Kyaw Win was unable to leave, even after ten years' service. He had joined when he was fifteen, but when he turned twenty-six and thought about resigning, his superior officers refused to consider it, arguing he could still serve for many more years. Kyaw Win said,

> If you submit your resignation letter often, you will be given a promotion. Then, since you have a bar [epaulette] on your shoulder, you will become proud and you won't [want to] leave any more. You can get another bar in six months. And so you carry out your duty. After having two bars, you will become fed up. It'll be harder for you to get a third bar. But if you submit your resignation quite often, they'll give you another bar. They won't let you leave. So when soldiers want to leave, what they have to do is to bribe people from the hospital to hospitalize them. They have to tell them, 'Help me quit. I've gone crazy. I can't see. I can't hear.'

Only if a specialist signs such a declaration can a youngish soldier retire.

For all these reasons, another military man, ex-sergeant Maung Maung, referred to life in the military as worse than a prison sentence. While actual prison inmates would surely disagree, he felt that he was treated terribly, even though he had done nothing wrong. He talked about how his unit had had to work for several days on the rubber plantation of his divisional commander's daughter. When the daughter married, the family sold the plantation for a large sum of money, but the soldiers were not even provided with extra food when doing this work, let alone given any monetary compensation. 'That's why we constantly said to each other that we had been charged with life imprisonment with hard labour,' he said. 'We have no days free from that.'

Interestingly, Maung Maung is Karen and grew up in Pa-an, the capital of Karen State. He said he joined the *tatmadaw* because he was inspired by what he read at school about the important role the armed forces had played during Burma's independence struggle. He said that although he was often distrusted and discriminated against in the army because he was Karen, this didn't bother him too much. What did upset him, though, was how the officers abused their power. 'In the military, there is great discrimination among the ranks,' he said. 'The officers treat us as having much less value than themselves. They eat good food. But when the soldiers get sick, they don't even check up on them. They have no sympathy.'

The danger of expressing an opinion

Even when senior officers do ask about the well-being of the lower ranks, it is better not to tell the truth. Maung Maung learned this the hard way. On one occasion when the chief tactical commander came through on an inspection, he asked the troops whether they had any complaints. Maung Maung said that they had water difficulties. The chief tactical commander promised to look into it but, after he left, Maung Maung's commanding officer summoned him and some of his men and angrily told them to solve the water problem themselves by digging a well. Maung Maung said, 'Later, when any senior officer asked us if there were any problems, we kept quiet. We realized that what "expressing your opinion" really means is you should keep your mouth shut.'

Maung Maung said he joined the army not to reach a certain rank or make a certain amount of money; fighting was what he was interested in. He wanted to be a good soldier on whom people could rely. 'But actually,' he said, 'now I'm not a good soldier for all the people, but only a good soldier for a handful of people. I cannot protect the people. I am only protecting my high-ranking officers.'

In his last post, Maung Maung's relationship with his Burmese company commander was not good. They were based in a Karen village, and the wife of the headman told Maung Maung that she was worried about her two teenaged daughters. The captain would often get drunk and stay late into the night at her house chatting up her daughters. She said her daughters had studying to do and the captain's behaviour was inappropriate in a socially conservative Karen village. She asked Maung Maung to tell his captain to stop visiting. Maung Maung explained to her that he couldn't say this to the captain because he was an officer and Maung Maung was only a sergeant. He suggested that she send her daughters to stay at another relative's house. So the next day, she sent them to stay with her niece.

That afternoon, the captain summoned Maung Maung and ordered him to get his platoon ready. Claiming there were enemy movements about forty-five minutes away, he told Maung Maung to march over there immediately and radio back about the situation. Maung Maung did as he was told, but when he arrived at the named location, there were no enemy troops to be found. Still, his captain ordered him to stay there overnight. Maung Maung felt it would not be safe, however. With only twenty-eight soldiers in the platoon, they could be easily overpowered by KNU troops. Maung Maung protested, but the captain told him to obey and turned off his radio.

Maung Maung didn't know what to do. To disobey an order was a serious offence, but to stay could mean risking their lives. He called his troops and informed them of what the company commander had said. Then he said that they would return to the base. 'Whether I get fired or punished, I don't care,' he said. 'I don't want you to all die here.'

After they had reached the camp, the company commander summoned him, grabbed him by the shirt and shouted, 'You didn't obey my order!' Soon after, Maung Maung found out that his captain had sent him on the mission to punish him for encouraging the headman's daughters to move.

That night, the captain got drunk and barged into the room where the headman's daughters were staying. The headman's wife ran to Maung Maung and asked him to help, but he had no authority to stop his superior. Still, he accompanied the headman's wife to her relative's house and heard the girls shouting fearfully to their mother. He pulled out his gun, put it on automatic fire and shot over the house. The captain burst out of the house and shot at Maung Maung three times with his pistol, but Maung Maung managed to escape without injury.

The captain followed him, drunk and swearing that he would take action against him the next morning. Maung Maung replied, 'If you take action against me, I will tell the senior officer that you, a captain, went into the girls' room.' This only made the captain angrier. Soon after, Maung Maung ran away to escape being imprisoned. At the time of our interview, he was a migrant worker in Thailand.[7]

Maung Maung explained that although there were only two officers per company, they were able to control the troops by relying on divide-and-rule tactics. If the sergeants united with the soldiers against the officers, the officers wouldn't be able to act so abusively, so the officers used rewards and punishments to split the lower ranks. Those who went against their commanders were sent off on dangerous missions, while those who were submissive were allowed to stay in safe locations. Maung Maung said that he explained to his soldiers how they were being manipulated, and they understood. But some wanted promotions badly enough that they went along with the officers' tactics anyway.

Maung Maung served in the army for eleven years. 'If the military were good,' he said, 'there wouldn't be any reason for me to come over to Thailand. I still haven't completely lost my desire to be a soldier. But it's not that I want to hold a gun without reason. I want to sacrifice for the country.' He decided that serving merely to support senior officers was pointless, particularly since the senior officers had so little concern for their soldiers. 'I feel that if I continued staying in the military, there would be no one left in the army who was as stupid as me,' Maung Maung said. 'If I were killed, it would be meaningless.'

Although it is impossible to know the number of soldiers who have run away like Maung Maung, desertion has become a serious problem for the army. The numbers would probably be greater if soldiers had a safe haven to which they could flee. Senior officers try to scare soldiers by telling them that if deserters are caught inside the country they will be sent to prison or executed, and if they try to escape across one of the borders, they will be killed by insurgents.[8] In 1997, a group of *tatmadaw* deserters who made their way to India and joined with the Burmese pro-democracy groups there were later deported back to Burma by the Indian government.[9] Deserters who make it to Thailand generally hide their identities and work as migrant labourers, but few migrant labourers have work permits, so they can be sent back to Burma at any time. Despite the risks, four members of Maung Maung's battalion fled to Thailand within seven months of his desertion.

A cycle of violence

According to all accounts, brutality within the military has increased since 1988. This is most likely because the economic situation has continued to decline and the current military regime has no real ideology beyond enforcing national unity. Moreover, officers are generally not punished for treating their soldiers or civilians badly; they are punished only for disloyalty to their higher-ups.

As a result, a cycle of violence has developed, particularly in the remote areas, with officers treating their soldiers harshly and military men taking out their aggression on civilians. While few soldiers will admit the more unsavoury things they have done, they will discuss the abuses committed by others in the army. Ex-sergeant Maung Maung talked about how so many civilian porters died because of ill-treatment by military officers. 'But', he said, 'we were given orders to march on, so I had to keep going ahead without looking back at them.' Reflecting on how upset he would feel if members of his own family were taken as porters, he said, 'Those officers didn't treat the porters even as cows or animals. If the porters died, they just left their bodies there. At the very least, they should cover the corpse with leaves.'

In conflict areas, *tatmadaw* soldiers tend to perceive ethnic minority villagers as supporters of the ethnic resistance armies even though the villagers present themselves as neutral. According to Moe Kyaw, a former *tatmadaw* captain who spent several years in Karen civil war areas, this is in part because the soldiers know that many of the villagers have relatives in the resistance armies and that some villagers work for them, but they don't know exactly who. In practice, this often leads to their treating all the villagers as the enemy.

Moe Kyaw said that *tatmadaw* officers may countenance the rape of villagers for various reasons. One reason is their anger at the villagers, whom they see as endangering their troops' security by supporting the resistance armies. Another reason is that they feel sorry for soldiers who must serve in the front lines for such long periods at a time. A third reason is that they don't want to lose current soldiers because recruiting new soldiers is so difficult. It is not only enlisted men who have committed rape, however. Human rights organizations have documented numerous cases of rape by officers and gang rape involving officers and soldiers as well.[10]

Other abuses include laying landmines in front of villagers' houses and torturing and murdering those suspected of providing information to the resistance armies, sometimes in front of other villagers. Many soldiers may not want to terrorize local populations but they are scared or feel compelled to obey orders. They may believe that their own security is dependent on such behaviour, or they take advantage of unarmed civilians to release their own pent-up anger.

Moe Kyaw said that in his officer training course, they were not given any practical training on how to handle local communities. As an officer, he said, his main priority was to protect his men. Thus, he never thought about the suffering his orders caused people who had to serve as porters or do other work for the military. He thought only about getting his job done and making sure his own soldiers didn't get hurt. He said he was never trained to analyse orders, only to obey them. It wasn't until he left the military that he began to see how the *tatmadaw* was not serving the people, even though this is one of the army's main principles. He took the bold step of writing letters about this to former colleagues in the military. He was later informed by a friend that a case had been filed against him in which he was accused of dividing the military, a very serious crime, so he decided he had to leave the country.

With no knowledge of how other countries have handled ethnic conflict and no training in critical thinking, it is not surprising that military officers have not challenged the military's strategy for dealing with the armed ethnic minority groups. Colonel Soe Thein, who resigned in 1993 and later joined an anti-government group based on the Thai–Burma border, said that previously he never thought that the regime should try to negotiate with the ethnic nationalists. 'We didn't think about a political solution to the problem, only fighting.' Moreover, he explained that at that time he and his colleagues thought federalism meant anarchy. 'Now', he said, 'I realize we must give autonomy to ethnic groups, but I don't agree with independent states.' Since most of the ethnic leaders are now calling for federalism rather than full independence, he has come to believe that a negotiated solution is possible.

While some soldiers are still swayed by the argument that the military is needed to unify the country and wipe out insurgents, others have been dismayed by the regime's respectful treatment of some of their former enemies who have been involved in drug production and trafficking. Khun Sa, for instance, was one of the world's top heroin traffickers in the 1980s and 1990s and the former head of the Mong Tai Army in Shan State. In the past, the government-controlled press always referred to him in derogatory terms, but after he cut a deal with the regime in 1996, he was officially called 'U Khun Sa' and given a home in Rangoon, where he lived comfortably until he died in 2007.

A former soldier related how he and some of the captains he knew were not satisfied with the regime's handling of Khun Sa. 'When Khun Sa was making opium,' he said, 'these captains had to go and fight Khun Sa. Now, since they announced on the front page of the newspaper, "May U Khun Sa live longer than a hundred years," the captains started to swear at the SPDC. They said, "When we had to fight Khun Sa, many of us died. They treat us like we're nothing."'

Dissenting soldiers

Throughout the period of military rule, there have been people in the military who have come to disagree with the system, but they have rarely spoken up. Colonel Soe Thein declared, 'I'm a pure soldier. I don't like the military playing in politics. Our main duty is to protect the country and the people.' He said that, even before 1988, many other officers shared his feelings, but out of fear, they pretended otherwise.

In 1988, a number of military personnel joined the demonstrators on the streets. Most came from the better-educated corps based in and near Rangoon. One who joined was a young Rakhine, Khaing Aung Soe, who had been working in the air force's supply department for three years. He and his friends were also enrolled in correspondence courses through the Workers' College and were sympathetic to the university students' demands. Starting in March 1988, they had begun secretly collecting money for anti-government activities at Rangoon University.

When the demonstrations started in August, they at first stayed in their barracks at Mingaladon outside Rangoon, but cheered on truckloads of people heading into the city. Then, on 9 September 1988, Khaing Aung Soe and a group of his friends left the barracks and joined the Rangoon University students. Khaing Aung Soe said, 'We went in full uniforms but with no guns. We arrived in the student compound and had a kind of press conference in the evening.' There were about 450 of them, including a female sergeant. The students arranged for them to stay at Thayet Daw monastery, where the monks were very supportive of the movement.

'During 1988,' Khaing Aung Soe said,

> we didn't think we'd win just by these demonstrations. We left some people in the main base to collect guns if necessary. We also made contacts with people in the navy and army. On the seventeenth, some students seized ammunition from the Trade Ministry and kept it in the monastery so they would be ready to fight the soldiers.

On the morning of 19 September, the day after the coup, the abbot of the monastery grew increasingly nervous and insisted that all the democracy soldiers leave that day.

Khaing Aung Soe recalled:

> We took the guns and hid in civilian houses. We moved every day, but after a couple of days, people were afraid and changed to civilian clothes, stored all the ammunition in monasteries and spread out. We didn't want to go back to the barracks without democracy, so six others and I made our way out to the border where we joined one of the pro-democracy armies.

He said that a number of the officers he knew also supported the democracy movement. Some went out on the streets in civilian clothes without informing their superiors, while others encouraged those who went out but were afraid to leave the bases themselves. Khaing Aung Soe remembers his commander telling him and others, 'I won't stop you or support you if you join the demonstrations. You have to decide by yourself. But we must try to get democracy.' Before the coup, he sent a message to the monastery where all the air force defectors were staying and asked them to come back to the base. Khaing Aung Soe said that friends of his who returned to the base were imprisoned for six months and expelled from the military. His commander was forced to resign.

Many more soldiers were loyal to the regime, and followed orders to shoot the civilian demonstrators. At least some troops from other battalions, however, were upset with their comrades. According to one soldier at the time, 'None of the battalions could stand the sight of Division 22,' the light infantry division that gunned down the most demonstrators in 1988. Still, it is likely that most of them would have done the same thing had they been sent to Rangoon.

During and after the election campaign period, the SLORC fired military personnel and civil servants who had actively supported the demonstrations. The regime tried to weaken support for Aung San Suu Kyi by calling her a traitor to the Burman race for marrying a Westerner. In newspaper editorials and in propaganda speeches she was termed a prostitute and other shockingly derogatory epithets. Whipping up nationalist fervour, the regime achieved a measure of success with these attacks, particularly in the military. After thinking it through, though, some later changed their minds.

Maung Maung recalled that, after the coup, Brigadier General Tin Hla gave a speech to his battalion. He said, 'Aung San Suu Kyi is the wife of a foreigner. Do you want to be ruled by a woman who is the wife of a foreigner?' At first, Maung Maung said, he and others agreed that they definitely did not. Later, he reconsidered and discussed the issue with the soldiers under him. 'In Burma's history,' Maung Maung told them,

> King Thibaw was taken to India by the British. At that time, King Thibaw's relatives got married to whoever was close to them [Indians]. It's the same for the daughter of General Aung San. After the assassination of General Aung San, U Ne Win sent her abroad and she grew up abroad. Who else could she marry besides a foreigner? She didn't do anything wrong.

While *tatmadaw* leaders and instructors at the officer training schools told the soldiers that Aung San Suu Kyi and the NLD wanted to break up the army, those who had a chance to hear Aung San Suu Kyi speak in person began to doubt their superiors' claims. Another former sergeant, Nyi Nyi, who worked at the army's weapons production factory in Rangoon in the 1980s, attended one of Aung San Suu Kyi's campaign speeches in 1989. He remembers her explaining that the *tatmadaw* was founded by her father and that she herself was born in the military and grew up among soldiers. She said that she would never divide the military and the people. Nyi Nyi said, 'Some soldiers – I met four or five – cried when she said that. It really affected them.'

Nyi Nyi said he realized that his superiors were worried that the soldiers might vote for the NLD in the 1990 election, so they were trying to create a rift between the military personnel and Aung San Suu Kyi. Both sergeants claimed that they represented many of their peers in the army when they said that they supported Aung San Suu Kyi and wanted the military to return to the barracks. But they didn't want to join the NLD themselves. Instead, they were hoping for the emergence of a visionary leader within the military whom they could follow. Nyi Nyi considered soldiers demonstrating within the military unimaginable, but he thought some might break away if there were someone or some organization that could provide support and capable leadership. He said, however, 'If there is no leader who sides with the people, it is impossible for people in the military to break away even though they wish to do so.'

Given the fact that Maung Maung and Nyi Nyi had to flee and are now living outside Burma, they may be overstating the support of soldiers inside Burma for democracy. But they still love the army and see themselves as army men, so they are perhaps not too far off the mark.

The large number of military votes for the NLD in the 1990 election confirmed a significant degree of dissatisfaction with military rule at that time. The SLORC leaders were apparently nervous enough about their troops' loyalty that they had them moved around, the composition of battalions rearranged, and counter-intelligence personnel sent to the units to monitor their activities.[11]

According to Thiha, an intelligence agent in the 1990s, intelligence officers were even used to spy on senior generals to find out whether they had any intention of trying to overthrow General Than Shwe and take power for themselves.

The *tatmadaw* has also attempted to strengthen the loyalty of its forces by recruiting family members of current military personnel. With parents, brothers or uncles in the military service, a soldier would be reluctant to engage in anti-government activities, both because of family pressure and worries that his relatives would be adversely affected.

Nevertheless, the regime has done little to improve morale or working conditions in the *tatmadaw*. In the years since 1990, the regime has invested large sums in upgrading the *tatmadaw*'s weapons and equipment, but it has continued to pay insufficient salaries to its officers and soldiers. Moreover, officers' positions are never certain and, like ordinary soldiers, they must curry favour with their superiors in order to ensure promotion. The imperious behaviour of the senior generals, their inability to improve the economy and their orders to shoot monks in 2007 have further soured many soldiers' and officers' feelings about the regime.

The danger of falling

While the rewards of reaching the top echelons of the military have remained high, the dangers of falling are also very real for generals, their families and their supporters. Successive leaders have maintained their control by rewarding talented and loyal officers with promotions, until they become potential threats to the leader's own power. At that point, they are often sidelined, retired early or charged with corruption or other offences. The most senior generals have used various military intelligence units to gather information on the weaknesses of other generals, so that they could be blackmailed into loyalty or sacked if necessary.

The insecurity of the top leaders is exemplified by the case of General Ne Win, who had ruled Burma for over twenty years and nurtured the generation of leaders who replaced him. In March 2002, he was put under house arrest after one of his sons-in-law and three of his grandsons were charged with treason. The grandsons were the sons of his favourite daughter, Sandar Win, and they were notorious for their wild behaviour on the streets and in the nightclubs of Rangoon. They were also involved in various commercial ventures, and may have been frustrated that lucrative contracts were increasingly going to other generals' children and friends. The grandsons and their father were accused of plotting a coup attempt with some military officers. While they may have raised the issue with a few lower-ranking military officers, it doesn't seem to have gone farther than that.[12] Nevertheless, they were sentenced to death by hanging. The sentence was not carried out, but they have remained in Insein Prison ever since.

That this would be their fate seemed unimaginable not only to them but also to others in Burma, who had viewed them as untouchable. But successive generals have proved time and again that they will act ruthlessly against anyone they perceive as posing a potential threat to their continued rule. General Ne Win, who was already in his nineties and was not accused of involvement in the coup plot, was kept under house arrest until he died in December 2002. The senior generals did not accord him a state funeral and only a few dozen family members and friends attended the simple ceremony.

Similarly, in October 2004, Lieutenant General Khin Nyunt, who was the head of military intelligence and the prime minister at the time, was suddenly sacked. Soon thereafter, he was accused of insubordination and responsibility for corruption scandals involving military intelligence officers under his supervision. The real problem was that Khin Nyunt and his military intelligence service had become too powerful.

Many military intelligence officers were operating lucrative illegal businesses or taking bribes. They tended to have a much better standard of living than other military officers. Some had opportunities to go abroad for training or as spies, and they rarely had to risk their lives. Intelligence agents tended to think highly of themselves and to treat other military officers with little respect.[13] At the same time, military intelligence had been gathering information on the illegal activities of military officers and sometimes used this against them.[14] For all these reasons, tensions between the two groups often ran high.

Meanwhile, under Khin Nyunt, the Directorate of Defence Services Intelligence had been busily expanding its scope of operations. Khin Nyunt set up the Office of Strategic Studies in 1994, and it soon began to engage in developing domestic and foreign policies, writing speeches for the junta's spokesmen, and even overseeing archaeological digs.[15] In an effort to boost national pride and his own stature, Khin Nyunt had one of his staff lead an expedition to uncover positive proof that there were 40-million-year-old primate fossils in Burma. Khin Nyunt claimed that this would mean that humans might have originated in Burma (a claim later asserted as fact in the state media although debated by international scientists).[16]

After successfully negotiating ceasefire agreements with many of the armed ethnic groups, Khin Nyunt had confidence in his ability to handle the country's politics. He had also been praised in the foreign press as a reformer and someone the international community could work with. Than Shwe is likely to have had doubts about Khin Nyunt's ultimate intentions. Khin Nyunt was given a forty-four-year suspended sentence, and along with his wife and two sons, has been kept under house arrest ever since. Three hundred military intelligence officers were also arrested in 2004, with convicted officers receiving prison sentences ranging from twenty to a hundred years.

The punishment of whole families and groups of officials might seem extreme to outsiders, but such practices have a long history in Burma. In the pre-colonial period, there was no fixed system for determining the king's successor, and because kings generally had many wives, there were many princes to choose from. Claimants to the throne sometimes resorted to killing all their potential rivals in order to secure their rule. For instance, after Thibaw became king in 1878, his wife, Queen Supayalat, and his chief minister ordered the execution of no fewer than forty of Thibaw's half-brothers and half-sisters.[17] A number of court officials and military officers of doubtful loyalty were put to death as well.

Similarly, since the commencement of military rule in 1962, no clear mechanism has been established for determining the top general's successor. As a result, ambitious generals have jockeyed for the highest position. Lower-ranking officers have sought to improve their own fortunes by allying themselves with powerful military patrons, but they also run the risk of being punished if their patron falls. Some officers seek to maintain a more neutral stance or cultivate relations with all the leading generals in order to protect themselves.

The personalization of power and the lack of well-defined systems for decision-making have other consequences as well. Many officers are afraid to make any decisions by themselves for fear their decision will displease a higher-ranking officer. As a result, they pass even small matters up to a higher level or ignore the problem and hope it will disappear by itself. This creates great inefficiencies in governance and reinforces feelings of indispensability among those top generals who do dare to make decisions.

Those in power continue to enjoy an opulent lifestyle and public demonstrations of respect, whether heartfelt or not. Although it seems clear that there is plenty of disaffection within the military, such feelings will not easily translate into insurrection. Officers and soldiers doubt their ability to succeed at such an effort and fear severe punishment. Others worry that if there were political reform, they would face retribution for the abuses they committed in the past. As a result, military rule continues, even though those with the guns are not all in favour of it.

9 | Prison: 'life university'

Many people in Burma avoid politics because of their well-founded fear of being tortured and sent to prison. Torture is carried out both to extract information and to destroy the morale of activists, and includes intense physical pain, intimidation and humiliation. Conditions in Burmese prisons are extremely difficult, with insufficient food, medicine and bathing water frequently leading to debilitating health conditions and the premature deaths of many. Prison sentences can range anywhere from a few years to one hundred years, and prisoners can continue to be held even after they have completed their sentences.

Still, prison is a place where people have a chance to think and analyse issues deeply and intimate bonds are formed. While the entire country, and even the military itself, has been compared to a prison, for some, experiences in Burma's actual prison system can be mentally liberating. Despite the miserable living conditions, in some prisons activists endeavour to find ways to engage in political debates and to learn from each other. This chapter explores how political prisoners try to create a community, maintain their morale and improve themselves, and looks at what happens to them after they are released.

Arrest and sentencing

Political activists are usually arrested without a warrant in the middle of the night and taken away with a hood over their heads. Before they are charged in court, they are tortured to extract information and to punish them. As one intelligence officer told an activist, 'You will be squeezed to the last drop like sugar cane in a juice press.' This is usually the most terrifying period for a political prisoner and can last from a few days to a few months.[1] Until late 2004, interrogation and torture during the detention period were carried out by military intelligence agents generally at interrogation centres. Since then, the newly established Military Affairs Security or the Special Branch of the police have carried out this function.

The Human Rights Yearbook for 1997/98, compiled by the Human Rights Documentation Unit of the exiled National Coalition Government of the Union of Burma, describes the techniques used in interrogation centres as including:

> beatings rigorous enough to cause permanent injury; shackling of the legs or arms; burning victims with cigarettes; applying electric shocks to the victims' genitals, finger tips, toes, ear lobes, and elsewhere; suffocation; stabbing; rubbing of salt and chemicals in open wounds; forcing victims to stand in unusual and uncomfortable positions for extended periods of time, including 'riding the motorcycle,' which entails standing with arms outstretched and legs bent, and the 'helicopter,' in which the victim is suspended by the wrists or feet from a ceiling fixture and then spun around; deprivation of light and sleep; denial of medicine, food, exercise, and water for washing; employing the 'iron rod' in which iron or bamboo rods are rolled up and down the shins until the skin is lacerated; ordering solitary confinement with extremely small and unsanitary cells for prolonged periods, and using psychological torture including threats of death and rape.[2]

During this period, family members are not informed where their loved one is being held, increasing the mental stress for both the person detained and his or her family.

After the interrogation period is over, activists are charged. Trials are often perfunctory affairs, sometimes lasting less than fifteen minutes.[3] Many defendants are not allowed to have a lawyer represent them or must accept a lawyer appointed by the authorities.[4] The accused generally cannot produce their own witnesses or speak in their own defence. Many trials are held in a closed court at Insein Prison, with the judge simply reading out the sentence from a piece of paper.

Since the mid-1990s, sentences for political activists accused of even the most trivial offences have typically ranged from seven to fifteen years. On 7 June 1996, the military regime announced Decree 5/96, 'The Protection of the Stable, Peaceful, and Systematic Transfer of State Responsibility and the Successful Implementation of National Convention Tasks, Free from Disruption and Opposition'. According to this decree, anyone caught publicly airing views or issuing statements critical of the regime can be sentenced to up to twenty years in prison.[5]

NLD members have been sentenced for violating this decree and other acts in an effort to gradually eliminate the party. In 1998, when the NLD called for the 1990 parliament to be convened within sixty days, 700 NLD members were detained, including 194 elected members of parliament.[6]

Those who organize protests or create links between opposition groups receive even longer prison terms. Thet Win Aung, for instance, was sentenced to fifty-nine years in prison for helping to organize peaceful demonstrations calling for student rights and the release of political prisoners and for having contacts with exile organizations. He had previously been imprisoned in 1991 and, after his release, he spent some time in Thailand before deciding to return to Burma to continue his activism. He died in Mandalay Prison in 2006 at the age of thirty-four.[7]

In 2005, Hkun Htun Oo, the chairman of the Shan National League for Democracy, who kept in regular contact with Shan ceasefire armies, was sentenced to ninety-three years in prison for attempting to form a Shan umbrella group. The regime was also unhappy with his closeness to the NLD and his party's support for NLD policies.

From 1990 until 2007, Burmese prisons held over one thousand political prisoners at any given time, as released prisoners were replaced by newly arrested activists and political party members.[8] After the arrests of participants in the 2007 monks' demonstrations, the political prisoner population increased by several hundred to over 2,100 in late 2008.[9]

As of 2006, there were forty-two prisons and ninety-one labour camps in Burma.[10] Most political prisoners end up at one of the dozen larger prisons, and are frequently incarcerated in the same rooms as criminals. Political prisoners arrested in the Rangoon area are sent to Insein Prison, on the outskirts of the city. Many are later transferred to prisons up-country, however, which makes it difficult for family members to visit. This causes great hardship because prisoners are dependent on their families for supplemental food and medicine. The very poor quality of the prison food and the lack of access to proper medical care take a great physical toll on many prisoners. HIV has also spread in Burma's prisons, in part, say former prisoners, because hospital needles are reused without being sterilized.[11] According to the political prisoners I interviewed, drug

173

addicts are often allowed to work in the hospitals, giving injections to themselves and other prisoners.

Although criminals are more likely to be sent to the front lines as porters and to labour camps to work in quarries and build roads, a few political prisoners have also faced these punishments.[12] According to Amnesty International, hundreds of labour camp prisoners have died from untreated injuries and illnesses, malnutrition and ill-treatment.[13]

A group of former political prisoners who formed the Assistance Association for Political Prisoners (AAPP) in Thailand have documented the deaths of 137 political prisoners between 1988 and late 2008.[14] This includes people who died during interrogation, in prisons and labour camps, and within a short time after being released.

Nevertheless, perhaps the hardest thing for many political prisoners to accept is that they are considered criminals. From their perspective, they are exemplary citizens who are struggling against injustice for the good of their country. To have to wear a prison uniform, squat and bow their heads when prison authorities approach, and often to have to share cells with real criminals, is highly insulting.

While political activists are in prison, the military intelligence and prison authorities try to destroy their morale, so that after they are released they will not participate in resistance activities again. In Myingyan Prison, for instance, one group of political prisoners was ordered to spend hours catching flies, shining the iron cell doors, and 'polishing' the bare ground in their cells with the base of a small bottle. Those who are particularly charismatic or dare to lead strikes inside prison are left in solitary confinement for months or, in the case of student activist Min Ko Naing, years at a time. If political prisoners do not literally go mad or become numb from being repeatedly degraded in various ways, they may resort to informing on their comrades in return for special privileges that make life in prison bearable. For those who are trying to maintain their commitment, it is disheartening to see fellow prisoners deteriorate psychologically or give up their political ideals for material comforts.

Torture and maintaining morale

U Hla Aye, a poet who was imprisoned in the BSPP period for anti-government activities, found the mental tortures at the interrogation centre as painful as the physical tortures. When he was interrogated in the heat of the summer, he was stripped naked, covered in salt and beaten. He and other colleagues were also forced to stand barefoot on heated iron sheets to burn the soles of their feet. Most horrible were the electric shocks. He explained, 'They did it to our genitals so that we became disfigured.'

Besides the pain, the authorities used humiliation. U Hla Aye said: 'The authorities were acting under the belief that there are no political prisoners. Everyone is a criminal. That's the simplest form of torture in prison.' In the interrogation room, he and others were forced to pretend they were riding aeroplanes and motorcycles, making all the accompanying noises as if they were small children. Intelligence operatives also tried to depress him and other political prisoners by telling them their wives had taken other lovers or that their mothers were about to die.

Once he had passed through the interrogation centre, he was sent for trial. Rather than being held in a courtroom, the trial was conducted at the entrance of the prison, with the judge reading out his sentence according to the instructions given by military intelligence personnel. Then he was taken into the prison, where, he says, the military intelligence 'instructed the prison wardens to break our spirits'.

While U Hla Aye was held at Insein Prison, he was frequently summoned for further interrogations. In order to make them talk, they would be left naked for several days in a tiny cell full of faeces and maggots. U Hla Aye managed to keep himself together during his experiences in this cell, but some of his colleagues suffered mental breakdowns.

U Hla Aye and some other inmates were later moved to Thayawaddy Prison, a three-hour drive from Rangoon. At first many of the prisoners' families didn't know where they had been sent. Even after they found out, it was hard for them to travel there. U Hla Aye recalled: 'It was just to create more difficulties for living and eating. It is a form of torture intended to make groups of political prisoners become fed up with politics.'

Although family members were allowed to send food parcels to political prisoners, part of the food was usually taken by the prison authorities. U Hla Aye remembers that some of his cell-mates who had been in prison before didn't even try to fight the situation. They simply told their families to divide the food into separate packages, with half for the prison wardens and half for themselves. Some prison wardens even went to prisoners' cells just after visitors had left. U Hla Aye said: 'They came with their dinner plate to ask for food. If you gave it to them willingly, you could have a quick extra cup [of water] on top of the five that you were allowed for bathing.'

The desire for communication is so strong that prisoners are willing to risk punishment in order to create a connection with other prisoners. U Hla Aye recalled that even if prisoners were put in solitary confinement, they would try to communicate with those in neighbouring cells by knocking on the walls. At the very least, they tried to learn each other's names and why they were there, even though they knew they would be severely beaten if they were caught.

Obtaining news from outside is also important to political prisoners, who are eager to keep abreast of current events. U Hla Aye said families and friends were sometimes able to send information in by wrapping food in pieces of newspaper. If someone was taken to the court, he would try to get news from his family there. Upon returning to his cell, he would pass on what he had learned to other prisoners.

When I asked how people maintained their political convictions under these circumstances, U Hla Aye said, 'Each person has his own way of doing it. Some say to themselves, "I will never betray my work and my beliefs. I will never become a traitor."' Others, he said, relied on their loyalty to their colleagues, turned to religion, or focused on their hobbies. U Hla Aye tried to comfort himself by composing poems.

After U Hla Aye was released, he was eager to convey the bitterness of his prison experience and the thirst he had felt for freedom in his poetry, but he could not publish such poems in Burma. Poets and writers with anti-government backgrounds find that their work on even the most innocent subjects comes under intense scrutiny by the censorship board.

Life university

Tun Way had just graduated from high school when he was imprisoned in 1975. For him, prison really was his university, and he treated it as such. He had been a good student who often contributed articles to the school bulletin board, but after witnessing the military's repression of the workers' strike in Rangoon in 1974, he became politicized. The following year, he made posters and banners for the one-year anniversary demonstration. On 11 June 1975, he was arrested along with many others at Shwedagon Pagoda, where the strike committee had set up its headquarters. He was taken to an interrogation centre, and the torture began.

Tun Way said that the interrogators often alternated styles, treating him nicely and using persuasion and then beating him up without asking him anything particularly important. 'Even if we sincerely did not know the answer,' Tun Way said, 'the authorities thought we were lying and used more brutal methods of torture.' Fighting the exhaustion was also difficult. Tun Way remembered, 'When the interrogators went out of the room, we tried to lean against the wall and take a nap because we were so sleepy after two or three days of non-stop interrogation. When they came back into the room and saw that we were leaning against the wall and sleeping, they kicked us all over with their military boots.'

After ten days, Tun Way and about fifty other prisoners were sent to a building in the Criminal Investigation Department's compound near Insein Prison. A military officer told them they were in a military tribunal and read out the charges against them, including threatening the state, violating the Insurgency Act, misusing public property and stealing.

During the demonstrations, students had burned coffins with the names of Ne Win and San Yu, a senior military general at the time, written on the side. Tun Way remembered: 'We had requested the coffins from one man as a donation, but he was called as a witness during our trial. The officer asked him whether the students had taken the coffins by force. He said yes, so we were charged with robbing coffins from that man.'

Tun Way tried to come to terms with his imprisonment by telling himself that change never comes without sacrifice. While in prison he could do little to bring about change, but at least he could study. Despite constant bouts of skin diseases and other ailments, he and his university student cell-mates held frequent discussions on the political history of the country and why resistance was necessary.

For much of the time, Tun Way was held in a large cell with fifty other people, including politicians and lawyers. Although they were not allowed to read or write, some of the prisoners secretly managed to obtain articles from foreign magazines. In Tun Way's cell, one of the older prisoners translated articles on foreign politics from *Time* magazine and explained them to the other inmates. Another gave a contextual analysis of the events presented in the articles. 'Then free discussion followed,' said Tun Way. 'All had the right to speak, discuss and give different opinions.'

Tun Way was exposed to a variety of views through these discussions and revelled in the diversity. He also began to study English and modern Burmese poetry and to develop his talents as a poet. As time went on, he and his fellow inmates began to put together magazines in their cells. With no pens or pencils permitted, Tun Way and his friends had their visitors hide ink refills in food packages. They created makeshift pens by encasing the refills in two thin strips from their sleeping mats, held together with a rubber band. Tun Way became a member of the editorial group and collected articles from other inmates. Because they could write only at night, when they were not being watched, it took over a month to finish producing one issue. Once the publication was complete, prisoners would take turns reading it, secretly passing it from cell to cell.

Tun Way and his cell-mates also organized ceremonies to mark the anniversaries of political strikes. Sometimes they held a hunger strike and spent the day in silence. On other occasions they sang political songs. Around the new year, they chanted *thangyat*, anti-government songs written for the occasion.

Tun Way found prison a good place to develop his intellect and create deep bonds of friendship. Having to share food, blankets and secrets for four or five years, he and some of his cell-mates became closer than siblings. But, he said, some prisoners could not endure the difficulties of prison life and resorted to informing on fellow inmates in return for a blanket or some small privilege. 'The privilege would be quite small,' he said, 'but these people were happy to have it under such harsh living conditions.'

For Tun Way, family visits were especially emotional. He was overjoyed when a family member visited, because he could get food and obtain news about the rest of his family and friends. Prison visits were always on Sundays, so on Saturday night everyone would be happy and excited. On Sunday mornings, prisoners were called out in small groups for the brief visits. When his parents appeared for the first visit, they didn't recognize him. He looked so different because of the torture he had undergone, the inadequate food and the fact that he was dressed in a prison uniform. 'My mother started crying,' he said. 'Within the very short five-minute meeting, she could not speak a word; she just kept crying.' Later, the prison authorities allowed the prisoners to wear civilian clothes during the visits. Tun Way, like other prisoners, borrowed a shirt, *longyi* and slippers from other prisoners. When he returned to his cell, he passed the set of nice clothes to someone else to wear. He said: 'We wanted to make ourselves look as good as possible. Some even wore a jacket to look better.'

Being thrown in prison at such a young age, Tun Way matured quickly. He recalled: 'Prison was like a university of life. In real universities, you have to spend four academic years to be a graduate. But for me I spent four years at life university.' Tun Way realized that he needed to develop his knowledge while in prison, because after his release he would not be allowed to enrol in a formal educational institution. Moreover, he would not be treated like an ordinary person. He said: 'People who are just released from prison are always one step behind and different from normal people. So it is important to study and learn, as well as to be confident.'

After his release, Tun Way became a poet, and in 1988 he joined the pro-democracy demonstrations. Now he is living outside Burma, and his poems are often featured on Burmese-language radio broadcasts from abroad.

Feelings of guilt

Many prisoners feel guilty about the trouble they have caused their families by taking up politics. Often they are the primary wage-earners. If they are students, they may have dashed their families' hopes for their futures and even negatively affected their parents' and siblings' job opportunities. Once a member of the household is arrested, the whole family comes under increased surveillance and sometimes harassment. Some political prisoners feel so guilty that they encourage their wives or girlfriends to break up with them so that their lives will not also be destroyed. One political prisoner who felt this way wrote a song about it and sang it for me when I interviewed him several years later.

Released Maiden
A miserable wild night in a storm,
without a chance to meet a sunbeam.
There is still turbulent, heavy rain everywhere.
It is time for us to part.
Take this white scarf, darling,
as my gift to keep you company.
And tie up your loose hair with it.
Please try to comprehend
the meaning of my gift, a white scarf.
And encourage yourself
to pass through the sea of life.
Don't worry for me.
My white scarf will help you
to tie up your loose hair.
Feel free and leave tenderly from my shore.
Feel free darling,
Feel free darling,
Leave tenderly from my shore.[15]

During his many years in prison, this man's girlfriend did end up going her own way. Although he is now free, everyone who gets close to him knows they may be putting themselves at risk.

Female prisoners

In the 1990s, there were more female political prisoners than ever before, as many young women took active roles in the 1988 demonstrations and the election campaign and then continued underground, organizing activities despite their parents' objections. Particularly difficult for younger female prisoners is the humiliation of being told by their interrogators that they are loose girls who are surely sleeping around with male colleagues.

One young woman, Kyi Kyi, had been a university student in 1988 and had participated enthusiastically in the 1990 election campaign. She spent a year in a rural area going from door to door explaining to villagers and townspeople what the BSPP had done wrong and what the NLD planned to do for the country. She returned to Rangoon at the time of the elections, but, after the junta ignored the election results, she continued working with a student group that was writing and distributing pamphlets about the political situation. In 1991, she was arrested. When she told me her story in 1998, her eyes were still bright, but there was a weariness about her that reflected what she had been through.

After her arrest, she was taken to an interrogation centre. She was not beaten, but the intelligence personnel taunted her and suggested she had had affairs with her male colleagues. She said: 'For example, if I had gone to a meeting with a group of male friends, they would say something like, "You have the audacity to go with all these men when you're the only girl? Your pluck is very commendable."' Her interrogators referred to her as *kaung ma*, a derogatory term for a woman. They said, 'Hey, *kaung ma*, we're asking you nicely because we don't want to get physical. So you better just answer. You want us to beat you, don't you? That's the only way you would talk. You're so cunning. You think so highly of yourself. Who do you think you are?'

When they asked her, blindfolded, whether she would continue to be involved in politics if they let her go, Kyi Kyi said she wasn't doing politics. She was involved in the students' movement and would continue to be. With that, a heavy object was slammed down next to her. She was asked, 'What do you think that was? That was a gun. I can kill you right now if I want to.'

Letting her rest only for brief intervals between long periods of interrogation, the intelligence agents also tried to play her against other detainees. Kyi Kyi remembered: 'They would say, "That *kaung ma* is revealing everything about you. Why do you keep covering for her?" And they would say the same thing about me to another person.'

Although Kyi Kyi says she did not reveal the names of her colleagues or their activities, in most cases prisoners cannot resist the torture inflicted on them and do confess. After they have been broken, prisoners are sometimes brought into a room with sacks over their heads and made to confess everything again, without knowing that their colleagues are sitting in front of them. The political prisoners were depressed by such confessions, and some had difficulty keeping up their morale. But once in prison, fellow inmates tried to encourage each other so that they could survive.

When Kyi Kyi first arrived in prison, she said she was so afraid that she did not have the courage to look around. Exhausted from the days of interrogation, she slept almost constantly. Finally, other inmates urged her to get up and eat or her health would deteriorate. Sleeping on the cold cement floor, she, like others, soon developed high blood pressure. She had trouble eating the prison food, but other prisoners shared their food from home with her, helping her to keep her spirits up.

For Kyi Kyi, developing empathy and warmth towards other prisoners, political and criminal, was an important part of her prison experience. She explained how she became close to other prisoners after talking to them about their lives. 'Those charged with murder told me why they felt they had to kill and the injustice done to them,' she said.

> The prostitutes too described their experiences to me. Their lives were absolutely pitiful. When we asked them why they decided to become prostitutes, the main reason was that they didn't know how to make a living any other way. For some, their lives were destroyed. They didn't have any money and their parents too were helpless. They were un-educated. They said to us: 'How else could we make a living? We don't know how to do anything.'

Kyi Kyi said that the sex workers and some of the other female criminal prisoners hoped that one day the activists could bring about changes that would make their lives better. For that reason, they sometimes helped the political prisoners.

Still, Kyi Kyi found it hard to overcome the physical difficulties of prison life. At one point, she was housed in a building that was divided into ten cells, all of which were infested with mice and rats. At night, the inmates would awaken to rats biting their hands and feet, and, even when they were eating, the mice would sometimes steal their food. Finally the author-ities agreed to renovate the building because of the threat of plague. The prisoners were moved to another building, where they met up with other political prisoners and began doing physical exercises together. Accusing the women of engaging in military training, the prison authorities sent them back to their former cells before the walls were dry. The overwhelm-ing chemical vapours caused many of the prisoners to become ill.

Kyi Kyi and her cell-mates were allowed to walk outside for only fifteen minutes a day, and they could use only two or three cups of water per day for showering. Kyi Kyi recalled: 'As for washing clothes, we [political prisoners] had to use second-hand water already used by those who had given bribes. This was a kind of torture. They didn't severely limit water because it was expensive. It was done on purpose.' Like the male prisoners, female prisoners were not allowed any pens, pencils or books, even about religion. But Kyi Kyi crafted writing implements to write poetry, and she and her cell-mates often sang at night to pass the time. On the anniversaries of important days, the female political prisoners would wear white, make little wreaths out of twigs and flowers, and float them in the prison drainage ditch. Although the prisoners had to do this surreptitiously, Kyi Kyi said, they experienced a feeling of gratification at being able to make the secret gesture.

A couple of times a month, the female prisoners gathered together to share their food, discuss politics and analyse each other's behaviour. During Kyi Kyi's first two years of imprisonment, she was housed with about fifty female political prisoners in one common area, and they would break into groups of seven or eight for the sessions. Later, when there were fewer political prisoners, Kyi Kyi said they held the discussions more often. Although the female political prisoners generally tried to live within the prison rules, some criminal prisoners invented complaints and reported on them to the authorities. Their numbers reduced, the political prisoners were less able to stand up to abusive guards. Thus, Kyi Kyi recalled, 'people were becoming increasingly depressed and tensions were building. So these discussions were necessary as a means to boost morale and encourage each other.'

As time went on, Kyi Kyi herself struggled with the emotional difficulties of prison life. She began to smoke and isolated herself from others. She was disillusioned by some of the other political prisoners, who had turned on their comrades, and she began to lose faith in the movement. But when she stared out of the window and saw the child prostitutes lined up for their meals, she said her determination to continue the struggle returned. She recalled: 'The girls were only about thirteen or fourteen years old and wearing little skirts. I felt the utmost pity for them.' She also observed hunched-over old women who had been arrested for selling snacks on the street without a permit. Seeing such people imprisoned made her angry, an emotion that helped her maintain her commitment during the last three years of her imprisonment.

After Kyi Kyi's release, as described in Chapter 6, she continued to be hounded by military intelligence and even her family became increasingly suspicious of her.

Covert assistance

Moe Aye was arrested in 1990. Like Kyi Kyi, he had been involved in the 1990 election campaign and continued to work with politically active student groups when the election results were not honoured. After being tortured in an interrogation centre for two months, he was sent to Insein Prison. There he and his colleagues, with the secret help of some prison authorities, were able to set up elaborate systems for studying.[16]

At first, he said, the political activists were divided by their ideologies, but eventually they were able to overcome these differences and accept that, regardless of which organization they originally came from, they now belonged to only one category, that of political prisoners. Incarcerated with Buddhist monks as well as Protestant pastors who had been part of a failed Karen insurrection in the Irrawaddy Delta in 1991, the student prisoners had a chance to study Buddhism and Christianity. Drawing on their collective talents, the prisoners also set up study groups for English, Burmese history and even Japanese. All the studying had to be done covertly, for if they were caught, they would be severely punished and sometimes put in isolation cells. But the prisoners were not deterred. They created sheets out of plastic bags used to deliver food and wrote on those with pointed implements. By holding the piece of plastic up to the light, the scratches could be read.

Moe Aye lived in a row of cell blocks with four political prisoners in each cell. During bathing time, one person would forfeit his bath to hurry to the cell of an older political prisoner, who would write out five or ten English vocabulary words with translations in Burmese. After a couple of months, the student prisoners moved on to grammar. If they didn't understand what was written, the next day one would use his bathing time to get an explanation. Then the lessons would be sent on to the next cell. Moe Aye recalled: 'For over one year, we studied by plastic. After that, we knew how to approach the warden.'

Moe Aye and several of the other inmates came up with a plan to sell the coffee mix and milk powder their families gave them in return for study materials. They started off by asking the warden to bring them an issue of *Time* magazine, which could be purchased on Pansodan Road in central Rangoon. The prisoners offered to pay the warden five times the actual price for smuggling the magazine in. The warden agreed and secretly carried in a few folded-up pages at a time. It took twenty days to get the whole magazine.

Moe Aye wanted to translate the articles into Burmese for others to read, but it was too difficult to do so on plastic. So he and his friends

183

collected more coffee and milk powder and again paid the warden the equivalent of five times the actual price for bringing in a notebook, page by page, and a pencil. Then Moe Aye began translating, selecting particular articles about regional politics as well as essays and opinion pieces. Although Moe Aye knew more English than his cell-mates, he was not fluent. Thus, they decided they needed a dictionary and began saving their milk powder for that as well. Moe Aye recalled: 'All students were trying very hard to study English. If the SLORC gave the right to study, it would be very good. But as you know, they never gave that right. They sent us to prison because they wanted to close our eyes and our ears.'[17]

In 1992, Moe Aye and his friends managed to get information about the American presidential election from a recently released friend, who obtained newsletters and election materials from the American embassy. They were eager to learn about the American election system, and although they weren't sure how Democrats and Republicans differed, Moe Aye said they were hopeful that whoever won would support the democratic movement in Burma.

Moe Aye and his friends also developed a knocking system for communicating from cell to cell during times when the prisoners were ordered to remain silent. Because the Burmese alphabet has many more letters and vowels than English, they decided to use English. One tap equalled A, two taps equalled B, and so on. To decode a sentence from the next cell, one person would count the number of taps while another would translate the numbers into letters and words. The usefulness of this communication system only increased the prisoners' desire to study English.

Moe Aye explained how during one less restrictive period, political discussions were held almost every night in his block of cells. To come up with the discussion topic, one person per cell would forgo his bath to consult with the inmates in the other cells. By the time all of the cells had been let out in turn for their baths, the inmates would have agreed on a specific topic. In the afternoons, cell-mates would quietly discuss the topic in their cells. Late at night, after the guards had retired, one spokesman per cell would state his cell-mates' views on the topic. Each cell would take a turn. If intelligence personnel showed up to carry out a surprise check, a code would be knocked from wall to wall, and everyone would fall silent. The prisoners knew that if the authorities found out about such talks, the instigators would be punished and transferred to another part of the prison.

During these dialogues, older politicians would sometimes challenge the younger inmates' interpretations of historical events. The younger inmates had gained their knowledge from books written by the government and did not know what had really happened, for instance, during the 1974/75 workers' strikes. Some of the prisoners were old communists, and the younger prisoners would ask them to tell of their experiences with the Communist Party in the jungle. On those nights, everyone would listen quietly as one of the elder men shared his recollections.

Moe Aye said that during the less tense periods he and his friends were so busy studying English and politics that they were almost happy. 'Sometimes', he said, 'we forgot our mothers and our family.' But whenever there was a crackdown and no one could talk or study, it was not so easy. Moe Aye said: 'On those nights we asked each other, "Hey, don't you miss your mother?" And others would answer wistfully, "Yes, I miss my mother."'

Moe Aye explained that some of the prison authorities shared the students' frustrations with military rule but, like others in Burma, they did not dare to openly express their discontent for fear of losing their jobs. As a half-measure, a few tried to help the political prisoners in small ways.

In one case, the prisoners banded together to demand the right to read the newspaper, threatening a hunger strike if their demand was not granted. One of the senior prison authorities became worried and called some of the prisoners to his office. He said: 'Please understand my situation. I can do nothing. I understand you, because my son and daughter are students. If you want the newspaper, please request it of the MI office.' But the intelligence personnel refused the request, telling the prisoners that if they initiated a hunger strike, they would be beaten.

Later, that senior prison officer often walked by the student prisoners' cells chewing betel nut. The first time he offered betel nut to them, they didn't know what to say, because it was not allowed in prison. But then Moe Aye thought he was trying to convey something, so he accepted the offer. When the prison officer handed over the betel nut, it was wrapped in a page of newspaper. Similarly, when Aung San Suu Kyi was released from house arrest in 1995, a sympathetic prison warden gleefully brought the news to Moe Aye and his cell-mates. In other instances, some of the usually tight-lipped wardens came to the political prisoners' cells when they were drunk to complain about the military regime.

Most of the prison authorities were not particularly interested in human rights, but some were angry with the regime because they had been passed over for promotion. Like other civil servants, they resented having to serve under retired military officers who were less educated than themselves. Moe Aye said he and his colleagues tried to convince such wardens that their situation would not improve until democracy was achieved.

Improvements and setbacks

In 1999, the International Committee of the Red Cross (ICRC) negotiated an agreement with the regime, granting it access to all of Burma's prisons. Besides meeting with prisoners and investigating prison conditions, the ICRC also gave money to needy political prisoners' families so they could make prison visits. The ICRC regularly met with Burmese authorities and sought to improve prison conditions. As a result, the cement floors of jail cells were covered with wood and prisoners were granted longer periods of time out of their cells. The ICRC also provided assistance for improving the water supply at some prisons and donated good-quality medicine for prisoners with serious medical conditions.[18] Former prisoners claim, however, that much of this medicine never made it into the prisoners' hands, or that they had to pay money to the prison authorities to obtain it.[19]

According to the Burmese Jail Manual, prisoners have the right to read books and to write letters to their families once every two weeks, but these rights were denied for many years. Since the early 2000s, prisoners have been allowed to read religious books and some news publications, and they can write letters home once every two weeks if their families cannot visit them. Families can also send money orders, allowing prisoners to buy food from prison commissaries. These rights have been gained owing to a combination of factors, including prisoners' repeated demands, the ICRC's discussions with the authorities, the UN Special Rapporteur's attention to prison conditions, and greater reporting on the situation in prisons by AAPP, Burmese media in exile and international human rights organizations.[20] UN human rights bodies and several foreign governments also raised the issue of political prisoners and prison conditions repeatedly.

There have been serious setbacks as well, however. In late 2003, the regime banned Paulo Sergio Pinheiro, the UN Special Rapporteur on Human Rights, from visiting Burma after he found a listening device in the room where he was interviewing political prisoners and spoke out angrily about it. He was not allowed back into the country until 2007. In 2005, the regime insisted that ICRC staff be accompanied by USDA members when making prison visits. Such accompaniment violates ICRC principles, so as of December 2005, the ICRC stopped making prison visits. Since then, prisoners have continued to suffer from a lack of access to proper medical examinations and treatment. Beatings and other forms of torture are still used in prisons, and conditions in the labour camps remain particularly harsh. Criminal prisoners whose families can provide money can use bribes to ease their conditions, but those who are poor suffer terribly.

Release

Once political prisoners are released, their lives are never the same. They and their family members are followed, treated with suspicion and hassled. In some cases, former political prisoners' families even turn against them. Although they have been freed from physical confinement, they often find themselves socially isolated.

Moe Aye talked about how lonely he felt after his release. As the only person from his village to have served a long prison sentence, he was the subject of intense gossip. He had to report to the MI regularly, and he couldn't meet his old friends because he was under surveillance. Although his family said to him in private that they were proud of him, in public they told everyone that he was bad and they couldn't control him.

Moe Aye recalled how difficult it was to reintegrate into his family. His first night home, his mother was so happy about his return that she had made many kinds of curry to celebrate. But he said he couldn't eat. 'I at once remembered my friends in prison, and I wanted to pack up the food and send it to them. For over one month I couldn't eat very well.'

The local military intelligence agents warned Moe Aye to stay away from all political groups, and especially from the township NLD. He agreed to comply, but the agents had their informers checking on him constantly. This worried his mother. When he went to a hospital in another town for medical treatment, an intelligence agent there approached him and demanded to know why he had come without reporting to the MI officer in his township first. Moe Aye told him that he had been ordered only to stay away from the NLD and going to the hospital had nothing to do with politics. The intelligence officer let him go, but Moe Aye found the experience upsetting. The tension increased during the December 1996 student demonstrations in Rangoon. Three policemen were posted outside his house and kept a constant watch on him. Although the policemen were friends of his, Moe Aye realized he could be rearrested at any time, and the stress was taking a toll on his mother.

Min Thein, another student who spent four years in prison in the early 1990s, faced similar problems. After his release, his friends were reluctant to sit and talk to him in a tea shop, and some even tried to persuade him to give up politics. When he visited his friends' houses, their parents treated him coldly. They were worried that Min Thein might try to recruit their children for anti-government activities.

Some former political prisoners wash their hands of politics and look for jobs in the private sector. Others try to contribute to society through teaching or writing. To avoid rearrest or relieve pressure on their families, a number of former political prisoners go into exile. Moe Aye, for instance, ended up in Norway, working for the Democratic Voice of Burma. Some other former political prisoners, such as several of the leaders of the 88 Students Generation Group, return to activism. Although they know the risks involved, and many indeed end up back in prison, they are unwilling to live their lives in any other way.

In conclusion, then, prison in Burma remains a grim place, where people are broken down physically and mentally. Yet some political prisoners manage to keep their spirits free and, once released, refuse to live in silence.

10 | Education: floating books and bathroom tracts

Education gives you confidence in yourself and strength to make decisions. The more people are uneducated, the more you can keep them down. (A Burmese educator)

In the late 1940s and 1950s, Burma boasted one of the highest literacy rates in Asia and an expanding educational system. It has been devastating for educated parents to see their children growing up far less knowledgeable than they. The military regime has placed a low priority on education for several reasons. First, they fear that the more people are educated, the more likely they are to mount serious challenges to military rule. Second, the top generals are not highly educated themselves, and often resent better-educated people. And third, with limited funds at hand, they have funnelled resources into expanding and equipping the army rather than the schools. Since the 1990s, government spending on education has declined as a percentage of GDP, despite the fact that it was already extremely low compared to other countries.[1]

While the number of schools and primary teachers has increased, schools are generally run down and lacking even the most basic equipment. There are a few showcase schools in the cities with computers and other technology, but these are by far the exception. In most areas, so little money is provided that many schools levy an annual tax on students, along with various other fees throughout the year (such as table, water pot and maintenance fees), to keep the school running.[2] There are rarely enough textbooks available, so students who do not receive books in the classroom must buy photocopied versions, at a much higher price, on the black market. On top of this, parents must purchase uniforms for their children. Many families cannot afford all these expenses, and their children end up spending little or no time in school.

Starting in the 1990s, monks began trying to address this problem by opening up free primary schools at their monasteries. They hire teachers to teach the government curriculum as well as Buddhism, and the schools are supported by donations to the temple. In 2007, as many as 180,000 children were attending monastery schools, but the authorities have been very reluctant to allow the monasteries to expand beyond the primary level.[3]

According to UNICEF, in 2008, of the 80 per cent of children who enrol in primary school, less than 55 per cent actually finish.[4] Particularly in rural areas, parents often need their children to help them with farm work and household chores, including taking care of younger siblings. Many parents feel that a few years of education will not help their children get a job anyway. Indeed, the primary education curriculum focuses on memorizing facts and preparing for secondary school rather than giving children life skills and the ability to think.[5]

For those who do attend school, poverty and malnutrition also affect their performance. A primary school teacher in Karen State in the 1970s and 1980s talked about how the parents of one of his students told him to punish their son if he did not behave in class. In fact, the child had a hard time concentrating, because, as the teacher found out, his parents were unable to feed him before he came to school in the morning. The child was too hungry to pay attention. This remains a problem today, as indicated by UNICEF figures, which state that one-third of children under five are moderately or severely stunted and underweight because of malnutrition.[6]

The curriculum

Every government uses its education system to try to inculcate certain attitudes in the minds of the country's youth. In Burma, successive military regimes have asserted central control over the development of the curriculum to promote loyalty to the regime. Government textbooks, reinforcing the regime's propaganda in the state-controlled media, stress the honour of the military and the necessity of continued military rule to maintain the country's political stability.

In primary and secondary education, teachers and even headmasters have no input in curriculum development and cannot deviate from the textbooks in their teaching. As one former headmaster explained, designing the curriculum was a top-down process, with teachers not allowed to make criticisms or give suggestions. The instructors merely had to follow it.

In the mid-1960s, General Ne Win ordered that English no longer be used as a medium of instruction. English was linked to colonial rule, and true nationalists were supposed to speak in Burmese only. Many educated parents, who spoke beautiful English from their days in school, were anguished by this policy. They realized that fluency in English was essential to integrating with the global economy and keeping up with outside ideological currents. Nevertheless, some high-school and university students absorbed the government's propaganda and mocked friends who used English words in conversation. It was not until 1979, when General Ne Win's daughter failed her entrance exam into a British medical school because of her poor English, that teaching in English was reinstated.[7] Still, English teaching in Burma today tends to be inferior to what it was in the past, because so few fluent teachers remain.

Rewriting history has been a key project for the regime. Since Aung San Suu Kyi's rise in political importance in 1988, for instance, the military people in charge of textbook production have downplayed the role of General Aung San and focused instead on the need for military leadership to hold the country together. General Aung San was a military leader, but he later resigned in order to enter democratic politics as a civilian. In the past, the regime emphasized General Aung San's role as founder of the army, but Aung San Suu Kyi has argued that General Aung San never intended for the army to oppress the Burmese people. In the past, schools hung pictures of General Aung San as an inspiration to students, but with Than Shwe's rise to power, schools have been required to hang his picture instead (or in addition to Aung San's). In 2008, a speech by General Aung San was removed from the high-school history curriculum, as were writings by Thakin Kodaw Hmaing, a revered literary figure and a strong advocate of peace and national reconciliation.[8] The regime is more interested in promoting the history of Burmese warrior kings, as evidenced by the construction in Naypyidaw of towering statues of the three great imperializing kings from the past.

Kyaw Moe, a former high-school teacher, worries about the implications of the government's educational policies on students. He realizes that they will grow up thinking that their teachers have taught them 'the facts', when in fact they are being given large doses of propaganda. He found teaching history and economics the most difficult, because the gap between the textbooks and reality was so wide.

Another teacher agreed but said he did not have any ideas about how to change the educational system. 'We had only one system that we knew,' he said. 'If we had had a chance to see books about other systems, about which education system is good, we could have compared. But we had no books.'

Since the regime acceded to the UN's Convention on Child Rights in 1991, the generals have been required to report periodically to the convention's monitoring committee. The rights include the right to a free education, the right not to have to perform any type of labour that would be dangerous or disrupt children's schooling, and the right to social welfare assistance. Countries that agree to follow the convention are also supposed to make the rights in the convention known to their citizens. To show they are working to implement the rights in the convention, the authorities agreed to UNICEF's suggestion that information about child rights be put in the national curriculum. While children now have a chance to learn something about child rights, the authorities have done little else to ensure that children's rights are respected.

One thing the regime is willing to spend money on is government-run courses for teachers. Under the SLORC and SPDC regimes, as well as in the BSPP days, teachers attending teacher training and refresher courses have been taught military drills, techniques for monitoring students, and political ideology. Such courses are used to weed out or dampen the spirits of independent-minded teachers and to instruct them in how to inculcate the regime's propaganda.[9]

Kyaw Moe attended such a three-month course in the early 1970s before becoming a high-school teacher. He said the instructors taught them how to control and indoctrinate their students. His group was told: 'Your students' ideology only depends on you, the teachers. If your students get bad ideas, it is because of you, so you must think of the students as clean toys which you can form as you like.'

When I asked Kyaw Moe how he felt about this, he said, 'There was a great storm in my heart and in my mind. But what could I do at that time? I had a family.' But several years later, during the election period, he joined the NLD and offered an alternative education to certain students who were also NLD members. He says that in his private classes, he and his students spent far more time discussing politics than lessons. But in school he didn't dare to deviate from the curriculum. If he were arrested, he feared his family would not be able to make ends meet.

Even primary-school teachers, it seems, must be on guard and engage in political indoctrination efforts. At the closing ceremony of a refresher course for primary-school teachers in 2006, then Secretary-1 and Chairman of the Myanmar Education Committee, Lieutenant General Thein Sein, asserted:

> The saboteurs who oppose national development are trying to destroy national unity and peace and stability. They are systematically hatching plots to revive racism, and ideological and sectarian differences. Teachers will have to organize the people to clearly see the perpetration of the saboteurs and to ward it off with Union Spirit.[10]

In the government's school system, learning consists of rote memorization, and exams call for the exact repetition of the teachers' or textbooks' words, with no room for critical thinking. This teaching method is regarded as normal and parallels a common learning style for young students in the monasteries, where monks order small boys to memorize Buddhist texts.[11] Rote memorization has been the usual teaching method throughout Asia, although this is beginning to change. In Burma the effect can be damaging, because it reinforces submission to all authority, a message students are getting in virtually every dimension of their lives.

Kyaw Moe, who now lives abroad, said: 'It is very hard for Westerners to understand, but in Burma, there is no retort to elders or teachers. They must obey everything in front of the teacher or their parents.' Even if the teacher makes a mistake, the student has no right to correct the teacher. While students may grumble behind their elders' backs, they do not learn how to make logical arguments or how to understand the complicated nature of many issues for which there is no single right answer.

Kyaw Moe thought that, in theory, the Educational Ministry could shift to a more open teaching style, because some Burmese educators have been abroad to study other educational techniques. But he said it was not in the regime's interest. If students and teachers are permitted to discuss issues freely, the students will be far less likely to accept the regime's propaganda.

Ethnic nationality education systems

For many citizens whose native language is not Burmese, maintaining their own languages and histories is of great importance because this constitutes a major part of their identity. Successive regimes have, however, tried to gradually assimilate non-Burman ethnic groups in part through compelling students to study in Burmese and to learn a Burman nationalist version of the country's history. Some ethnic minorities learn to read and write their languages in their churches or monasteries, but many only learn to speak their languages.

Although ethnic minority languages are theoretically allowed to be taught at the early primary-school level, implementation of the policy has been fraught with obstacles. According to a Karen headmaster who promoted the Karen curriculum, the Karen textbooks were submitted for approval in 1967, but they were not actually printed until the 1980s. Whenever he asked about the delays, he was told there was not enough paper. After the textbooks were finally printed, no new teachers were provided to teach Karen. If the teachers on staff could not read and write Karen already, they were unable to instruct their students. Such policies are perhaps not surprising, because it is in the regime's interest that fluency in other languages be gradually eliminated and minority populations become assimilated into the Burman majority population. In this way, there will be less basis for minority claims against the state's unifying projects.

In areas controlled by the armed ethnic organizations, they have developed their own curriculums in their native languages. While they usually simply translate the maths and science textbooks into their own languages, they take great pains to use their own history books. Maintaining the right to run their own schools was one of the most important issues for the New Mon State Party when it made a ceasefire agreement with the regime in 1995. The regime conceded on this, but tried to induce the NMSP to give up this policy by saying it would only pay the salaries of teachers using the state curriculum. The NMSP has struggled to maintain its educational system as it has limited funds. It has, however, been able to obtain some foreign funding, while villagers also generally support local teachers, who are paid almost nothing. In 2006, the NMSP's education department was running 186 schools of its own and contracted Mon teachers to teach Mon language as an extra subject in 189 state-run schools.[12] Mon teachers periodically face harassment from various local-level army officers and authorities, but so far the system as a whole has survived.

Mon monks and other interested individuals also organize Mon literacy courses at monasteries during the summer holidays. Tens of thousands of Mon students attending government schools have participated in these courses.

Similarly, the Karen National Union's Education Department uses its own curriculum, which is taught in the most widely used Karen dialect, Sgaw Karen. This curriculum is also used in Karen refugee camps in Thailand, with Burmese given little emphasis as it is treated as the enemy's language. English is introduced in primary school and used as the medium of instruction at the high-school level.

In government-controlled areas, ethnic minority teachers have had to teach a curriculum that almost completely excludes their histories and cultures. Divergent perspectives on pre-colonial Burman kings' history of conquest are not incorporated, giving the impression that ethnic tensions in Burma resulted only from British colonial policies.

In areas controlled by the ethnic resistance armies, their former warriors, kings and intellectuals are valorized, and the Burman conquerors are described as villains. Foreign and Burmese education-focused NGOs have worked with a number of the ethnic resistance organizations' education departments to introduce student-centred learning techniques and critical thinking skills. Nevertheless, history tends to be taught in the same way as in the regime's education system. Only one side of the story is presented.

Buying good grades

Corruption has been another factor which has lessened the value of the in-school educational experience. Teachers' salaries are so low that they must look for supplemental sources of income to make ends meet. Some run small businesses, such as selling snacks to students, but many survive by offering private tuition. They do not teach the full lessons during regular school hours so students must attend the extra classes after school. Although this is illegal, the authorities generally turn a blind eye, because they understand that the teachers cannot survive otherwise. In other cases, school authorities sell goods at inflated prices to students during school hours, which students often feel obliged to buy.

In 1995, a twelve-year-old student described such a situation in a letter to his aunt, who lived outside the country. His headmaster, Ba Pe, was trying to make some quick money before retiring. Nwe Nwe, his sister, could not resist the pressure, although the letter-writer, Moe Aung, did.

Dear Auntie,

How are you? I am praying that you are well. This evening I feel like writing, so I'm writing you ...

U Ba Pe is not good. He is forcing students to buy calendars worth about 20 kyat for 45 kyat. Nwe Nwe is scared of her teacher so she bought one. But I didn't buy it because it is not worth it. My class teacher loves me, so he didn't say anything about my not buying one.

They are also selling shoulder bags at inflated prices. They take a profit of about 75 kyat per bag. There are 5,000 total. The teachers had to go sell the bags in Rangoon. It's pitiful, isn't it. The truth is that the teachers have a duty to make the students excel in their education and to improve their morality. They are being ordered to do things which have nothing to do with teaching activities.

I can't say that U Ba Pe is a bad person. He is about to retire, so it's his last chance to take advantage of his position. He'll easily get at least 300,000 kyat.

I'm going to go to sleep. Good-bye.

Moe Aung

Another way for high-school teachers to make money is on the grading of the matriculation exam, the defining moment in a student's life. Entrance to college is decided solely by a student's score in the exam. In many instances, matriculation exams are marked up for students whose parents have given large cash donations to the teachers responsible for doing the marking. One former tutor who checked exams told of the examiners putting blue ink fillers into red pens so that they could change the answers on certain students' exam papers. Then they would use another red pen to mark the score.

Big money can also be made by selling the exam questions in advance. The result is not only the degradation of the education system, but also the introduction of greater inequalities in opportunities for further education. Poorer students are much less likely to make it into the universities, because they can afford neither all the private tuition classes nor the bribes for higher scores.

Since 1991, the same has been true at university level. Many lecturers do their real teaching in private tuition classes and sell their exam questions for large sums of money. Even medical students must attend tuition classes. As one university professor in the mid-1990s explained, the fee for the car that took her daughters to and from school was almost as high as her monthly salary, so she had to teach tuition classes to survive.

Many university students come from elite families and can afford tutoring charges and bribes to get their exam scores raised, but others cannot. Taking a cynical view, student activist Moe Thee Zun explained how he and his friends tried to equalize the differences in the mid-1980s. They encouraged poor students to copy during the examinations.

In the 1990s, university lecturers were reportedly being encouraged to put easy questions on the exams and even sometimes overlook copying in order to appease students whose frustrations with the educational system and economic problems could otherwise be channelled into political protests.[13] Needless to say, the idea of actually learning something in the classroom has been largely lost in all of this.

University life

Under successive military regimes, the primary focus in the development of the university system has been the containment of student activism rather than the improvement of the quality of education. The demonstrations that sparked the nationwide protests in 1988 originated on university campuses in Rangoon, where students from different universities could easily link up and mobilize the local population. Since 1988, the military regime has tried to prevent this from happening again by moving students from campuses in central Rangoon to sparsely populated areas outside the city and by expanding the number of regional colleges.

The expansion of regional colleges is theoretically positive in that it should mean wider access to higher education and lower costs, because more students could live at home while attending classes. The problem is that the regional colleges tend to be underfunded and under-equipped, so the quality of education tends not to be very good.

The regime also encourages students to enrol in distance education programmes, in which they come to the campus only once or twice a week or just for ten days before exams. This is convenient for students who need to work to support themselves, and are interested only in getting a degree. The quality of education is not as high as on the regular courses, but from the regime's perspective, there is a benefit. Distance education students do not have much of an opportunity to develop friendships and associations that could lead them into political activity.

Even those students who study full time on campuses generally get little out of the formal teaching. University curriculums must be approved by military censors, limiting the fields of enquiry, particularly in the humanities and social sciences. Moreover, many of the best teachers have gone abroad, where they can earn a decent income and teach more freely. In 2003, there were more than five hundred Burmese professors and lecturers working at universities in Thailand and hundreds more teaching in other countries.[14]

Since 1964, students have been assigned their courses according to the scores on their matriculation exams, regardless of whether or not they have any interest in the subject.[15] They can choose a subject that is ranked lower, but not one that is ranked higher. The regime decides how many students should enter each subject, but despite the fact that there are almost no jobs in certain fields, students continue to be assigned to subjects like physics and zoology. As a result, many families feel that a university education is useless unless their children are accepted on to courses that guarantee jobs, such as medicine and engineering.

Even at university level, students are not taught to develop analytical skills. A university graduate explained: 'It is just rote memorization. You either get the information from the textbook or go to class and get it from the teacher, but there is no need to go to class.' In his four years at Rangoon University, he never once went into the library. Even those who do visit the library may not be allowed to take out books unrelated to their subject.

Students who try to be conscientious about their studies often find it pointless. Aung Zin, a medical student, talked about his experience in preventive and social medicine in the mid-1980s. The class had to carry out health education programmes in nearby communities, and Aung Zin was sent to Mingaladon village, near the airport. He was expected to take care of three or four households, giving health education and treating minor illnesses. The idea was that after recommendations had been made, particularly about diet and sanitation, the families' health would improve. The students were expected to make follow-up visits to ensure this happened, but Aung Zin says he was the only one in the class who actually visited the villagers again. Everyone else made up their reports.

Aung Zin wanted to help the families. He found that in one of his assigned houses, the ventilation was poor, the latrine was not very clean, and there were two TB patients. He suggested that the TB patients get treatment at a hospital, but they could not afford it. Since Aung Zin was given no medicine by his department, he could do little for them. Soon he realized that his visits were making the family feel embarrassed and uncomfortable. According to Burmese tradition, when a visitor comes, the host must offer some coffee, tea or snacks. Since the family had little money, they could not afford to give Aung Zin anything, and they also couldn't show him any improvement. 'Later,' Aung Zin said, 'I gave up and made up reports like everyone else.'

Professors and lecturers are also assigned to watch for students engaging in political activities. In the mid-1990s, most professors had to patrol three times a week, and on anniversary days of political events, professors were compelled to skip their classes if they conflicted with their patrol duty.

One woman, Nway Nway, who taught at Rangoon University in the mid-1990s, explained how each professor had to take responsibility for the behaviour of several assigned students. Nway Nway told her students to stay out of politics, because, she said, 'If you get involved, we'll both be in trouble.' She said she didn't feel good about saying this, because, as an educator, her real duty was supposed to be teaching, not policing. But the authorities hoped to take advantage of the students' respect for their teachers to keep them in line. Nevertheless, Nway Nway and many of her friends refused to follow through on the regulation that their assigned students sign in at their offices every morning. She gave the students the sign-in sheets and told them to handle it by themselves.

The extent of the authorities' nervousness is apparent in another example. A university professor in Rangoon who had to teach English to a class of several hundred students in the early 1990s was ordered to hold on to the microphone at all times, even when writing on the chalk board. The authorities were concerned that a student might jump on stage and use the microphone to make a political speech.

Control is the primary concern for the military regime. At some university campuses, only those with current student or staff identification cards are allowed to enter, meaning they are off limits to the general public. The main reason is to prevent alumni and other activists from stirring up the students. Surveillance is carried out by intelligence agents and informers, with student activists claiming they often take the guise of gardeners, cleaners and other university employees.

Over the years, successive military regimes have not hesitated to close down the universities for extended periods whenever political unrest broke out. Between 1962 and 1999, universities were shut down thirteen times, from periods of a month up to more than three years.[16] Between 1988 and 2000, the universities were open for only thirty-six months. Classes were cancelled from June 1988 to May 1991, from December 1991 to May 1992, and from December 1996 to July 2000. Besides the military institutes, only some of the master's degree programmes in Rangoon and the smaller technical colleges, generally located far from Rangoon, continued classes during this period. When the main universities were reopened in 1991, one-year courses were shortened to four months in order to get the students out as quickly as possible.

Although the regime understands that the country will not be competitive without an educated workforce, its first priority is to prevent anti-government demonstrations from erupting. For that reason, some student activists argue, drug and alcohol use on campus has been widely tolerated. Alcoholic and drugged students have little interest in politics. While students engaged in even minor anti-government activities are quickly ferreted out, some students I interviewed complained that heroin was being sold out of dormitory rooms on campus.

In recent years some university-age students have decided taking diploma courses can be a better investment of time and money than attending a university. As one young man in his twenties put it, 'we felt that we could get a job with a Microsoft course certificate but a university degree is pretty useless'. Accounting, computer, business and English courses have all become popular.

In the meantime, the regime has put its energy into upgrading the educational qualifications of its own people. After 1988, the military established separate military medical and technology institutes, which never shut down. With more resources going to the military institutes, the regime is in effect creating a two-tier system where the best-quality education is available only to those who work for the military.

The military has also sent students abroad for higher studies, with the understanding that they would come back and work for the regime. Between 2001 and 2006, the authorities sent 1,500 carefully selected students to Russia, with many studying nuclear and computer technology.[17] Burma has been working with Russia on plans to build a nuclear research reactor, which the regime insists will be for purely peaceful purposes.

Many of the generals and other elites send their children to private international high schools in Rangoon and then abroad for a university education. Singapore is a particularly favoured destination. The generals are seeking to raise the educational achievements of the officer corps and their offspring while holding the civilian population's education hostage to political quiescence.

Study groups and floating books

Unable to rework the existing education system, some students have taken their education into their own hands. Students have sought out private tutors and created secret study groups as they have searched for an understanding of what is wrong with their country and how to go about changing it.

The idea of developing an alternative education in Burma has its roots in the colonial period. During the 1920 student strike against the Rangoon University Act, older students tutored younger students at the strike centres, and this led to the formation of National Schools, where the primary language of instruction was Burmese rather than English, and Burmese subjects were emphasized. Later, the young Aung San and other friends set up a communist study group to read political literature and make plans about how to achieve independence. Many other students and intellectuals in the colonial period also looked to foreign literature for clues as to how to overthrow colonial rule. Since General Ne Win's takeover in 1962, a small number of students have turned to private libraries, study groups and private teachers in order to study political developments in other countries and to learn more about resistance movements in Burma's past.

Some anti-government intellectuals and former political prisoners have set up private tuition classes or initiated informal study and discussion sessions at their homes. From time to time, they select students who demonstrate intelligence and an interest in politics and try to develop both their understanding of political history and their sense of responsibility to the community.

Mi Mi, a plucky female student who walked out alone to argue with the authorities during a tense student demonstration in the late 1990s, had studied with such a private teacher when the universities were closed between 1988 and 1991. Her teacher had been a student activist in 1974, and he believed in the importance of discipline as well as intellectual rigour. Mi Mi and his other students had to go for morning runs at four o'clock, with lessons beginning at nine. They spent the whole day reading and listening to his lectures about the history of Burma.

Htun Htun, a reflective young man, studied with another charismatic dissident in the early 1980s. A former communist, the tutor invited interested high-school-age students to his house, where he would lend them leftist-inspired novels and books on history and social analysis. Htun Htun started visiting the teacher when he was about fifteen and often spent the whole day there, cooking, eating and talking with his teacher and other students. The teacher sought to correct the students' understanding of their country's past as they had learned it in their school textbooks. He talked often about the independence struggle, emphasizing that it was not just the army, as the textbooks claimed, which had made independence possible. Political organizations and ordinary civilians had also played essential roles. By portraying the people as essentially passive, the regime was trying to make people believe that it was natural that the army should lead and the people should follow.

The tutor also insisted that his students spend a significant amount of their time doing social work, especially at the local monastery. Every holy day, his students were expected to circle the town with gongs, alms bowls and a Buddha image, collecting contributions for the monastery. Although the authorities knew this teacher was a dissident, he was also well respected in the community for his promotion of religious and social welfare activities.

After Htun Htun was arrested briefly in March 1988, he said, 'My teacher was so happy I was arrested that he was jumping up and down.' This teacher hoped his chosen students would become activists, and indeed Htun Htun did. Meanwhile, during the 1988 pro-democracy uprising and the election campaign, Htun Htun's teacher became so involved that he sold virtually all his possessions to support the movement. Later he ended up in prison, leaving his family penniless.

Forming student-led study groups is another way inquisitive high-school and university students have sought to expand their knowledge and challenge their intellects. While ordinary Burmese readers find pleasure in romance novels and translated bestsellers, politically inspired students seek out the literature of oppression and resistance, political theory and the biographies of freedom fighters such as Nelson Mandela.

Some intellectuals have private libraries in their homes, which are the sources of books for young readers. When Moe Thee Zun, the student activist, was in junior high school, he began visiting a house in his neighbourhood where a Rangoon University lecturer lived. During school holidays, he would spend the entire day reading at her house. On the weekends, many people visited this house, including former political prisoners, teachers and songwriters. As the adults sat together discussing books and politics, Moe Thee Zun would quietly listen.

Around 1980, Moe Thee Zun formed a study group with some older students, and he began leading a Tuesday and Saturday literature discussion in his ward. 'The group's purpose', he said, 'was to use literature to educate people about the political situation and motivate them to consider taking action.' The study groups provided students with an opportunity to question and discuss rather than merely listen and repeat. Much of what they read consisted of translations of great works by Tolstoy, Chekhov, Dostoyevsky, Camus, Sartre, Hemingway and Steinbeck. Because it was difficult to find these books, they took turns reading them. They also tried to obtain copies of *Time* and *Newsweek*, assigning one person to obtain back issues from the embassies. One member of the group would translate the articles into Burmese because most members were not fluent in English.

In 1986, the literature discussion groups expanded to several towns, and they were able to collect a number of books. The way the system worked was that no one could own a book permanently. Once a person had read it, he or she would write a short comment and the name of his or her home town in the back and pass it on to another member. In this way, books travelled all over Burma. Sometimes a book would return to the original owner six months or a year later. Moe Thee Zun remembers the excitement he felt when one of the books he had sent off months before was returned to him. 'My book was running through Burma,' he said, 'floating through our network.' For those who had developed political ideas, knowing they had similarly minded peers in other parts of the country was very important. They often felt isolated among their own schoolmates, most of whom thought it pointless to question military control.

Moreover, most parents did not want their children to become politicized, and teenagers who did begin independent political studies usually had to hide their activities from their parents. Aung Zin, for instance, had been a model high-school student who had written award-winning essays extolling the virtues of BSPP rule. His parents were thrilled when he was accepted at medical school and expected him to join the civil service as a doctor. Once he was at university, however, his interests changed. Rather than read his textbooks, he set himself a goal of reading one hundred key books in political science, literature and philosophy within a year. As a result of his reading, his ideas about his country's political situation shifted dramatically. He participated in the 1988 student demonstrations, escaped to the Thai–Burma border, and has worked for pro-democracy groups based there ever since.

Tea shops and bathrooms

Despite successive regimes' attempts to keep politics out of the classroom, daring students find ways to carry out underground political education activities in their schools and universities. Secret student groups write and distribute magazines on university campuses, with the goal of inspiring other students to recognize injustice. Such magazines contain fiction, poetry and other articles which have not been censored, and circulate among interested students.

Ethnic minority groups also organize government-recognized literature and culture committees on campus which produce annual magazines and calendars. While some members of these groups are interested only in social and cultural activities, the committees are also key recruiting grounds for ethnic minority political activists. Several ethnic minority university students who joined armed ethnic nationalist groups after the 1988 demonstrations had been active in university literature and culture committees, where they had become increasingly frustrated with the regime's restrictions on the teaching of their languages and histories.

Tea shops on and near university campuses are favourite gathering places for students, whether to discuss romance or politics. Min Zaw, the university student whose mother made him become a monk in 1988, told me that for two years he never went to the classroom. 'My classroom was the tea shop,' he said. 'We read poems and talked about what we should do, because at that time, we were all upset with the government.'

More politically aware students take it upon themselves to educate less aware friends through their discussions in tea shops and dormitory rooms.

Bathrooms have also been the site of alternative education, and even of minor political action. Many former students talked about learning of the destruction of the student union building in 1962 from pamphlets posted in the university bathroom stalls. Such pamphlets have also called for students to mark the anniversary each July by wearing black, which a varying number of students continue to do each year.

Bathrooms were a much-used site for political activity in schools in 1988, because they afforded anonymity to those who wanted to promote political messages. One former high-school student remembers that during the weeks before the nationwide demonstrations in August 1988, the bathroom at his school was full of political posters and cartoons. At lunchtime, he recalls, the teachers would be waiting at the entrance to the bathrooms, but they hesitated to go in, because everyone inside was shouting. Locking themselves in the stalls, where no one could see them, the boys shouted slogans to their classmates outside. Those students who really had to use the toilets were out of luck.

Teachers warned their students to stop their political activities, but most did not record the perpetrators' names as they were ordered to. According to several high-school student organizers, teachers were often torn between support for what the students were doing, worries about their students, and fear that they would get fired if they allowed the students to continue. One Rangoon high-school student who often wrote political slogans on the blackboard before the teacher arrived said his teacher begged her class not to do such things. She said, 'You should pity me. I'll lose my job.' But he said that when he went to his teachers privately to ask for money for the movement, many contributed. Some teachers did eventually join the demonstrations or at least clap in support of student speeches.

Another way in which young activists in Rangoon tried to educate students in the early 1990s was by handing out pamphlets to them on their way to school in the morning. Students caught with pamphlets were, however, sometimes arrested and severely interrogated until they revealed who had given them the pamphlets. Student activist Lin Htet and his colleagues devised a method to protect both the distributors and the recipients. Folding five pamphlets very tightly together, they stapled an instruction sheet on top saying: 'You can pass this on, you can use these slogans for demonstrations at your school, or you can stick this on a wall.'

University students would hand packets to the school students, telling them to give the packet to another classmate. The recipient would look for a name on the top, see the instructions and then start opening it, but because of the tight packaging, by the time it was open, the distributor would be gone. The recipient would not have had time to notice the distributor's face, so even if the recipient were arrested, he or she would hopefully not be severely punished, because the package had been unwittingly received.

'But then', Lin Htet said, 'the SLORC announced a new regulation that it was illegal to receive notes on the way to school. So the activists had to adapt. They used pretty university girls to do the distribution. The high-school guys couldn't resist.'

Male students sometimes had the opposite problem when giving pamphlets to female students. One male activist remembered: 'The female students were very shy and afraid it was a love letter.' Many boys in Burma declare their love by putting a letter in a girl's book-bag on her way home from school, so the activists had to reassure the girls that they weren't giving them love letters but pamphlets which they could read and pass on to friends.

Other techniques that students used to distribute pamphlets included leaving a stack on top of a bus, so that when it pulled out, the pamphlets would scatter in all directions and could be picked up by curious bystanders. Lin Htet and his friends also relied on what they called the 'Shelley method', named after the Romantic poet, Percy Bysshe Shelley. In the early 1800s, Shelley sent out pamphlets promoting atheism to academics and clerics around Oxford. Burmese students in Rangoon also sent pamphlets by post, selecting addresses from the telephone book, which Lin Htet referred to as 'the activist's best friend'. Sometimes military intelligence, who read the mail selectively, caught the pamphlets, but the students tried to ensure that at least some got through by using several different kinds of envelopes.

Lin Htet and his group also made pamphlets with questions about student issues, such as: 'Are you satisfied with the education system? Do you want to change it? Check the boxes "yes" or "no" and send [the pamphlet] back to this address.' The pamphlet-writers wanted the readers to take at least a small action in support of their beliefs. Following that, they sent out another questionnaire, saying, 'If you still support the NLD, check this box and send it to BBC, VOA and the NLD.'

Before 1988, most pamphlets and political literature were 'printed' individually, using a fluorescent tube. Although there were mimeograph machines in government offices at the time, students didn't dare use them for political pamphlets. Since the late 1990s, computer use has become more widespread and political literature can be far more easily printed and distributed through CDs and other means as well as on paper.

The students' political discussions at tea shops and the writing and distribution of pamphlets may seem like trivial activities in the face of a determined military regime, but because of the key role that students have played in political movements in the past, the authorities treat those distributing even the most rudimentary political literature harshly. The generals understand that if people do not have concrete ideas about how to change Burma and are lacking leaders and organizations to spearhead a movement, they will remain quiescent. If, however, a group of committed individuals can develop a vocabulary to describe the country's problems, propose alternatives and organize themselves into effective networks, they may be able to mobilize the general population. Many of the student leaders in the 1988 and 1996 demonstrations had previously been members of study groups or had worked with private tutors from dissident backgrounds, and some had been involved in writing and distributing political literature before the demonstrations broke out.

Although most students do not directly involve themselves in political activities, they are sometimes willing to help out their activist friends. Ma Aye Aye, who was a high-school student activist in the 1990s, explained: 'I have some friends who are interested in politics but they are not permitted to get involved by their parents. And some of them are totally uninterested in it. But they helped my work for the sake of friendship.' For instance, when she asked them to join her in wearing the *pinni*, a traditional cotton jacket regularly worn by NLD members, on National Day, they did so. When she wanted to stick anti-government stickers on a wall at school, her friends would help by watching to see whether there were any teachers near by. Sometimes her friends also let her hide pamphlets at their houses.

While politically active students are rare, when protests break out, other students often join in, whether out of loyalty to friends or a desire to participate in making history.

Radio, the Internet and other educational sources

Few people besides students and intellectuals read political books. A much broader audience, however, tunes into Burmese radio broadcasts from foreign-based stations. There are four stations that have Burmese broadcasts: the British Broadcasting Corporation (BBC), the Voice of America (VOA), Radio Free Asia (RFA) and the Democratic Voice of Burma (DVB), which was set up by pro-democracy activists in Norway. The radio broadcasts offer information about other countries' policies towards Burma as well as the perspectives of opposition leaders from both the democracy movement and the ethnic armed groups. Through the radio, Burmese have also found out about the successful political transition in South Africa, the collapse of Indonesian dictator Suharto's regime, and the democratic movement that overthrew Milosevic in Serbia. The BBC provides more international news and is popular for its English-language teaching, while RFA and DVB specialize more in Burmese news. The number of listeners for all the stations increases dramatically during periods of political activity, when people want to find out what really happened that day and what activists are planning for the days ahead.

The Democratic Voice of Burma and Radio Free Asia have also provided news, political education and cultural programmes in some of the other languages of Burma, such as Karen, Shan, Kachin and Mon. The ethnic nationalities appreciate these broadcasts, because they focus on local issues and their languages are never spoken on the state-controlled radio stations.

From time to time, the authorities have jammed the radio frequencies of the foreign stations, but threat of arrest is the main tactic used to deter people at least from listening in public. In December 1999, a seventy-year-old tea-shop owner in Kachin State was sentenced to two years' imprisonment with labour for tuning the tea shop's radio to a Voice of America broadcast. Thus, most people listen to foreign broadcasts only in the privacy of their own homes. Lower-ranking soldiers are not allowed to listen, although some of the top generals and intelligence agents certainly do.[18]

Other avenues for a political education include foreign news magazines, satellite TV, the Internet and study trips abroad. The Asia editions of *Time* and *Newsweek* magazines are allowed in Burma, although any articles relating to Burma or the trials of former dictators in other countries are ripped out. Restaurants and wealthier private homes in Rangoon and, to a lesser extent, other cities and towns often have satellite TV hook-ups, providing access to international news programmes along with foreign entertainment shows.

The Democratic Voice of Burma set up a TV station in 2005, providing, via satellite, the first alternative Burmese television programming. The station began with weekly broadcasts and later expanded to broadcasting every day. It was a major source of information for Burmese citizens during the monks' protests in 2007.

More and more young educated people in urban areas also use the

Internet, although, as elsewhere, they primarily use it to chat with friends, check out social networking sites and download music. The authorities block the political and news websites of Burmese exiles, but Burmese computer techies often delight in finding ways around these obstacles, either because it presents an exciting challenge or because they resent having their freedom curtailed. Thus, for those few people who seek to read other perspectives about their country or to communicate with friends in exile, there are computer experts who will help them. Students, monks and others made great use of the Internet during the 2007 Saffron Revolution, when they posted accounts of what they had witnessed and pictures of the brutality used against the demonstrators. Since then, the authorities have been more vigilant in monitoring Internet cafés to stop people from uploading images and accessing forbidden websites.[19]

Many book-lovers and people eager to learn English have turned to the American Center and the British Council in Rangoon. Both offer English courses and have libraries with books and magazines on a wide range of subjects, as well as English learning materials and computers with high-speed Internet connections. In 2006, the American Center boasted a membership of almost 16,000, indicating how eager so many Burmese are to pursue their own education.[20] Although many of the courses that have been offered at the American Center would hardly be considered subversive in a free country, the fact that they have promoted discussion and critical reflection make them so in Burma. In the years leading up to the Saffron Revolution, the American Center served as a refuge for some political activists, prompting strong condemnation in the state-controlled press. Nevertheless, most people who go there, and to the British Council, simply want to expand their knowledge and better themselves.

Study tours, short courses and higher-education programmes abroad have also provided opportunities for Burmese to broaden their education. Besides deepening their knowledge about the subjects they are being taught, they have an opportunity to observe social, economic and political life in another country. Burmese migrant workers are also made aware of other countries' greater levels of development and freedom (for citizens of the host country if not for migrant workers) through their experiences working abroad.

As we shall see in the next chapter, a number of Burmese film-makers, writers, musicians and artists have also tried to open the eyes of their fellow citizens and get them thinking.

9 Students leaving their high school near Mrauk U, Arakan
State, 2006

10 A tea shop with a sign urging discipline in the background,
Pa-an, Karen State, 1998

11 Villagers undertaking forced labour, Pegu Division, 2000

12 Insein Prison, where many political prisoners are held, just outside Rangoon, 2006

13 A man praying at Shwedagon Pagoda, Rangoon, 2006

14 A woman having her palm read, Rangoon, 2006

15 Organizing newspapers for delivery, Rangoon, 1996

16 Newly arrived refugees awaiting treatment for malaria and
tuberculosis, Thai–Burma border, 1992

11 | The artistic community: in the dark, every cat is black

We have no true pleasure because we cannot share our thoughts.
(A poet, Rangoon)

Writers, poets, film-makers, musicians and artists provide social commentary, express the deepest feelings of the people, and serve as creative forces that can inspire and motivate. Since the mid-1960s, however, their ability to communicate openly has been severely curtailed. Censorship boards operate in every field of public expression and impose harsh and often arbitrary judgements on the work submitted to them. Since 1988, successive military regimes have also used the carrot and the stick, bestowing awards and luxury goods on those who are loyal while threatening potential dissidents with oblivion. Most people in the artistic community try to walk a fine line between ensuring their ability to work and maintaining their integrity. Meanwhile, the authorities have sought to use the arts to project their own image of the country – as united and firmly rooted in Burman culture.

Writers pushing the boundaries

In August 1962, the Revolutionary Council promulgated the Printers' and Publishers' Registration Act, which stated that all printers and publishers must register with the Ministry of Information and provide copies of every published book, magazine and journal. This policy has remained in force ever since. The Press Scrutiny Board checks all publications, and this takes place not when they are in draft form, but after they have already been printed. In some cases entire books are banned and the whole print run has to be thrown away. In the past, magazine publishers were frequently ordered to delete certain paragraphs or even whole articles, so the publisher would have to go through every single issue inking over the section or ripping out the pertinent pages.[1] Magazine buyers would thus be aware of the hand of the censors when their magazine suddenly skipped from page 25 to 28, or when there was a silver square over a section of text. In the late 1990s, the regime decided to hide the work of the censors by requiring magazine editors to rewrite sections that were deemed inadmissible, so that the readers would never know that the magazine had tried to get across a more provocative point.

The effect of these practices is that authors and editors are under severe pressure to self-censor. Publishers don't want to risk financial loss by having their books printed and then rejected. Likewise, magazine editors try to avoid being subjected to extra scrutiny and delays because of articles that push the limits. Thus printers and publishers often prefer to work with writers who do not challenge the boundaries, although a number do try to push the boundaries when they think they can.

Writers who have previously been imprisoned for their work or for support for the democracy movement are often blacklisted for many years. Worries about being blacklisted hold many writers back from trying to push the limits or participating in political activities. Nevertheless, some writers still try to express what they believe is important, usually in hidden ways. Maung Tha Ya is one writer who refused to compromise. After 1988 he wrote short stories that alluded to the killings of pro-democracy demonstrators. As a result, his work has been banned ever since.[2]

In 2008, the well-known poet Saw Wei published a poem entitled 'February 14', about a man who is jilted by his lover. The poem seemed innocuous enough and easily passed the censors. But there was a hidden message: if the first letter of each line is read vertically, it says, 'Power-crazy Senior General Than Shwe'.[3] Once readers detected this and the news spread, Saw Wei was arrested and sent to prison.

Some writers give in and write only about non-controversial topics, some focus on doing translations, and some stop writing altogether. Still, there are writers who are committed to the idea that they should act as the moral conscience of the nation, and they try to convey their messages through the use of metaphors and symbols. As Anna Allott has described in *Inked Over, Ripped Out*, such writers are confronted with a dilemma: if their metaphors are too obvious, the censors will catch them; if they are too obscure, not only the censors but also the readers will miss the point.[4] Sometimes the opposite happens, and readers impute meanings to the text that the author did not intend, or at least that s/he publicly denies.

Since the mid-1990s, the number of magazines and journals has grown rapidly, and they cover a wide range of subjects, including economics, domestic and international news and literature, as well as sports, entertainment and the occult. News publications have to publish as weeklies or monthlies because of the onerous censorship process, leaving only state-controlled daily newspapers. While a much wider range of information can be printed, particularly in periodicals that have good connections to higher-ranking authorities, the censors do not allow anything that they think could make the regime look bad. All coverage of the monks' demonstrations in 2007 was banned, and in the weeks after Cyclone Nargis, journalists could not get approval for any stories about the problems that survivors and displaced people faced.[5] Such stories implied the government wasn't doing its job properly; only positive stories were allowed.

In addition, all publications must include the regime's propaganda slogans on the first page. Under the SLORC and SPDC regimes, this has meant the 'Three National Causes': namely, 'non-disintegration of the union, non-disintegration of national solidarity, and perpetuation of sovereignty'. Thus, even when reading a book or magazine in their own homes, people feel the presence of the state intruding. Moreover, magazine and journal editors are sometimes told to include commentaries by pro-regime writers which support the regime's policies. To refuse would be to risk having the publication shut down.

Some writers in the mid-1990s tried to have an impact on society by promoting self-improvement and a can-do attitude. Translations of American advice books such as *The Seven Habits of Highly Effective People* by Stephen R. Covey sold rapidly, while editors of serious journals featured 'overcome all odds' stories translated from *Reader's Digest*. One of the main proponents of this school of thought was a writer and public speaker named Aung Thinn. He advocated focusing on individual development, setting goals and using willpower to achieve results. Tapes of his motivational talks were extremely popular and sold well throughout the country.

Such ideas were criticized by more radical students, who saw them as a move away from broader political objectives and towards personal, and often materialistic, ends. Indeed, because the goals to which the self-help proponents were dedicated were not explicitly political, the regime allowed some of them to speak fairly openly.

Some proponents of the self-actualization school have argued that the restoration of democracy in Burma requires the development of a democratic culture, and a democratic culture depends on the widespread cultivation of management techniques, reasoning skills and self-reliance.

The regime, on the other hand, has promoted the idea that its leaders alone know what is best for society. Because the top authorities are sincerely working for the country, no one has the right to challenge their policies. This has led to a kind of numbness on the part of the general population. According to one writer who supports the self-actualization literature: 'We need to fight our passivity.' Many of the proponents of Western motivational techniques hope that by following concrete steps, people will gain confidence in their ability to think and act. As one well-educated woman put it: 'Fear has deprived a lot of people of their reasoning power.'

In the 1990s, some skilful writers such as Dr Tin Maung Than tried to get around the censors and also encourage people to refine their analytical skills by presenting a thorough discussion of an issue, and then have the readers do the work of comparing the current situation in Burma with that. For instance, he once wrote a long piece about the educational system under colonial rule. He wanted his readers to contrast that system with the current system and consider what changes needed to be made. Similarly, writers such as Kyaw Win have sought to introduce readers to current global trends and political theories in order to help them broaden their views and think about how to apply these ideas in Burma.

Writers have also tried to express themselves through public talks, or *haw pyaw bwe*. Writers typically travel around the country to give talks in the cold season. Talks are given in urban as well as rural areas and are much anticipated by audiences, who are eager to hear the writers' reflections on society and the issues of the day. Some talks contain implicit commentaries on the political situation, but they are also usually full of humour and wordplay, giving writers a chance to display their wit. At one such event in 1990, a well-known writer got the audience laughing when he recalled his reaction to a news item in one of the government-controlled newspapers which announced that the government's department of heavy industry had produced 300,000 spoons and forks. He asked, 'If the department of heavy industry produced 300,000 spoons and forks, what did the department of light industry produce?'[6]

In recent years, however, it has been difficult for writers not favoured by the authorities to get permission to speak. Township authorities say no either because they dislike such writers or they are afraid they will get in trouble. Writers giving public talks are severely warned not to make anti-government comments, and their talks are taped by intelligence agents.

The Writers and Journalists Association should provide a space for critical discussion and reflection, but it does not, because it is led by pro-regime writers. But in their informal get-togethers, writers can and do talk freely. Meeting frequently at certain tea shops or writers' houses, they can discuss literature and current events and privately circulate more political essays, poems and cartoons among their close colleagues.

With the advent of CDs, thumb-drives and the Internet, writers and poets have also been able to pass on censored work or pieces they know the censors would reject to other friends in Burma and in exile. In some cases, these pieces are posted on exile websites with a different pen-name. While the authorities cannot completely suppress such activity, it's also true that the most uncompromising writers tend to end up either in prison or in exile. Nevertheless, by attempting to circumvent the censors when possible and seeking solace and confirmation in the company of like-minded friends, many writers, poets and journalists in Burma attempt to contribute to society as best they can.

Film-makers and censorship

Like writers, film-makers are also subject to a thorough censorship process. First, a film-maker must submit approximately twenty pages detailing the storyline and scene descriptions to the censorship board. If its members see anything they perceive as possibly anti-regime, they demand an explanation or simply stop the project. U Sein, a well-known film-maker in the 1980s, explained: 'If there was a scene with a tree on a mountain, for instance, they might be suspicious about why the tree was situated on top of the mountain.' In addition, the Forestry Department representative would be called on to check that the forest was going to be properly depicted.

In the past, if the storyline was approved, the film-maker would then be issued permission to buy a certain amount of film. Because the film had to be imported, U Sein said, the regime rationed its distribution to limit the amount of foreign exchange leaving the country. Thus, film-makers were typically given only 25,000–30,000 feet of film to produce a 10,000-foot feature film, which was far less than the 100,000 feet they felt they needed. Because they could shoot only two or at most three cuts of a scene, the quality of the films was often uneven. Film-makers were also hampered by poor equipment. U Sein recalled: 'Most of the cameras I used were older than me, and I was forty at the time.'

By the time a film-maker received his film, as much as a year might have passed. U Sein said: 'At first, you feel very enthusiastic about your story, but after waiting a year, you lose the feeling, your mood is gone, and your ideas have changed. But you have to go through with it, or the financier will kill you.'

Starting in the 1990s, many film-makers moved to shooting and producing on video and then later to digital recording and DVDs. With access to better technology at lower prices and no restriction on the materials used, film-makers could improve the technical quality of their productions and increase the distribution. Actors and actresses make much of their money, however, from doing advertising, calendars and other work, so they do not give much time to the shooting and often don't put much effort into developing their characters. Moreover, their creativity is limited by all the rules they must follow regarding how they can dress and behave and what kinds of stories are acceptable.[7]

No matter how the movie is made, before it can be released, it must be presented to the censorship board. Censors can challenge the movie on any number of grounds. Moreover, the criticisms that are made by the censors are often considered arbitrary or even absurd by the film-makers. For decades, there has been a rule that film-makers should promote traditional culture whenever possible in their films. U Sein agreed with this rule, so in one film he included a scene with a mother singing a nursery rhyme to her newborn baby. He placed toys around the room, including a traditional set of small puppets, one of which was Zaw Gyi, a legendary alchemist-wizard. The censors rejected the scene; U Sein appealed, and they rejected it again, saying that since the regime was a socialist one, wizards were not allowed.

U Sein appealed yet again and pointed out that the Burmese national dance troupe routinely performed the Zaw Gyi dance around the world. He was told that the dance fell under the Culture Department while his film came under the Information Department, and their policies were not the same. Still, he was informed he could get a letter of recommendation from the Culture Department and resubmit his appeal. He did so, but this time he was accused of suggesting metaphorically that the regime was merely a set of puppets. After wasting six months on this, he gave up and cut the scene. As is so often the case, the problem was that none of the censors wanted to risk trouble with their superiors and therefore no one dared to stand up for him. U Sein was known to hold anti-government views, so his work came under greater scrutiny than that of other, less politicized film-makers, but still the unpredictability of the process was a burden on everyone.

In some cases, U Sein intentionally tried to produce movies that could be interpreted as imparting a political message. He made a film about a poor man who owes a debt of gratitude to a rich man. The rich friend invites the poor man and his family to come and live in his compound and pays for the poor man's son's education. Over time, he starts making greater and greater demands on the son, including that he marry a young relative who is pregnant out of wedlock. When the rich man makes yet another extreme demand, the young man and his family lose control and go after the rich man. A bloodbath ensues, and everyone dies, except for the young woman's newborn baby.

Soon after the film reached the censorship board, the authorities called U Sein in and demanded an explanation. They told him they suspected the rich man symbolized the military, the poor man and his family stood for the people, and the baby represented the students. The military may have saved the country during the independence period, but the demands it was now making on the people were unacceptable and were causing unnecessary tragedy and suffering. U Sein admitted that the film could be interpreted in that way, but said that it could also refer to the problems that arose when married couples or family members took advantage of debts of gratitude to make excessive demands.

Despite the fact that U Sein never mentioned the government in his film, he was almost arrested. In the end, he was allowed to distribute the film, but only after changing the title and the ending. In the revised conclusion, most of the characters survive, implying that the rich man's actions do not have widespread negative consequences.

Still, U Sein said, audiences easily grasped the real meaning of the film because they invariably related what they saw on the screen to their current suffering. Moreover, the scandal surrounding the film made it extremely popular, and elaborate descriptions of the real ending spread around the country. As U Sein recalled delightedly: 'The audiences had imaginations, so they participated in completing the film.'

In Burma, people grow up reading between the lines. This helps film-makers, writers and poets, who cannot criticize the regime directly. At the same time, film-makers may not always intend a political message, but the audience naturally relates the film's content to the national mood. As U Sein put it: 'The government was the common villain, so you couldn't avoid it.'

U Sein saw himself as particularly unlucky in this regard. He explained:

> Burmese believe that the position of the planets when you are born influences your fate. I have been born into a situation where people can easily read my hidden meanings. Sometimes I only have one or two messages, but people interpret it ten ways of their own. The military intelligence overhear these interpretations in tea shops, so it made it difficult for me.

Even if a movie has no anti-government overtones, the censors may try to find fault with it in order to extract bribes from the producer. Censorship board jobs are coveted because gifts of whisky and cash are virtually guaranteed in return for agreeing to sign off on a movie.

Film-makers have also had to contend with censors who come to think of themselves as art critics. One of U Sein's films was about a psychopath who killed six people. The censors decided the film would be even more thrilling if the psychopath killed nine people. U Sein was ordered to add three killings and even given more film, a rarity. U Sein felt that six killings were sufficient, but he had to do as they demanded. Commenting about the censors' intervention in his and others' work he said: 'They thought they had the right to decide this. These foolish things piled up, and we almost went crazy.'

From time to time, U Sein agreed to direct government propaganda films with storylines written by the regime. He said he didn't mind doing anti-drug and anti-smuggling films, and in return he was viewed with less suspicion by the authorities. Similarly, actors and actresses who agree to work in government propaganda films find their chances of winning Academy Awards vastly improved while those who decline are passed over. A well-known actor, Kyaw Thu, refused to participate in a propaganda film in 1993. In 1994, he made a film that received popular acclaim, and the film board wanted to give him the Academy Award. But, said a friend of his, the military interfered, so neither he nor the film was honoured. Later, he agreed to make one film with the government, and for that he received the Academy Award.

Much of the talk in the artistic community revolves around determining what level of cooperation with the regime is acceptable. Mo Mo Myint Aung, a famous actress who has won five Academy Awards, is seen as having gone too far by many of her peers. Besides appearing in government films, she wrote letters for the government newspapers declaring her support for soldiers on the front lines. Each time a well-known person agrees to a higher level of cooperation with the regime, the community's unwritten standards of acceptable behaviour are challenged. Because the regime ties the opportunity to work and receive public recognition to outward displays of support for military rule, however, most film-makers, writers and artists feel they must make some accommodations.

The power of music

Like film-makers and writers, musicians also face dilemmas over where to draw the line between being able to work creatively and having to do the regime's bidding. Not only do they have to deal with the censors but they can also be banned from performing in front of audiences if they challenge the rules. Having to dress and act conservatively are other difficulties for young singers trying to keep in step with modern trends, although the regime has relaxed its policies somewhat in this regard.

Mun Awng, a Kachin singer from northern Burma, remembered when the Beatles became famous and 'guitar fever' spread through Burma. The government distrusted the free-spirited nature of such music, and in state-controlled newspapers, cartoonists represented bad characters as men sporting long hair, belts with peace symbols and guitars in their laps. Mun Awng said the government called such musicians 'destroyers of tradition' and never gave them permission to perform in public venues.

Mun Awng and others resorted to playing their guitars outside girls' dormitories on university campuses. He often stayed up the whole night singing and playing music with friends, wooing female students at the same time. This custom developed out of the long tradition of village boys visiting girls' houses in the evening to chat, or strolling near their houses, singing or playing an instrument.

Mun Awng came from Myitkyina, the capital of Kachin State, where teenaged boys still spent their evenings hanging around in front of girls' houses, hoping for their attention. He had grown up singing in the church and dreaming of Rangoon, where there were recording studios, theatres and famous songwriters. In those days, Myitkyina bordered a war zone; the Kachin Independence Army and *tatmadaw* troops frequently engaged in shoot-outs just outside town. Mun Awng and his family waited out the gun battles in the trench behind their kitchen.

Although Mun Awng viewed Rangoon as the best place to develop his talents, once he began attending university there, he realized that only the campuses (at night) afforded the freedom to sing what he wanted. In his final year in university, Mun Awng deliberately failed his exams so he could enjoy one last year of relative independence. But he had just recorded an album with some friends, and soon after a producer agreed to distribute it. The album was an instant hit, and Mun Awng's life as a professional musician began.

In front of the girls' dormitories, Mun Awng could sing whatever he wanted, but his recorded albums were subject to strict controls. At that time, one out of every four songs had to be a 'constructive song'. Mun Awng said coming up with such songs was a struggle for some bands, who ended up exhorting their listeners to be careful of traffic. He and his group tried to create songs that fulfilled the requirement without being ridiculous or preachy, but the censorship of his other songs drove him crazy. He said: 'That's why I decided I didn't want to be a professional singer in Burma any longer. When you try to write something, you have to start thinking about the boundary first. It's not supposed to be like that.'

When the censors forced him to change his lyrics because they suspected a certain word had anti-government connotations, Mun Awng
was upset. He said that the censors don't care about the meaning or the
flow of the song. One of Mun Awng's songs, called '*Bilu si, lu si*' or 'Line
of Ogres', explained that to make good music, first you have to tune the
strings properly, and then you have to know the right frets and the right
sound. Mun Awng remembered: 'The censors didn't like it, because they
thought it meant the right person for the right job.' Mun Awng had to
change most of the lyrics and record it according to the government-
approved version. He said: 'Only people who could hear me singing in
private could know the real lyrics.'

By 1988, Mun Awng had become famous and successful, but he was fed
up with the restrictions. One day he told his producer that the next album
he made would not go through the censorship board. He remembers: 'He
looked at me like he thought I was sick.' But Mun Awng ended up doing
what he said. His next album was recorded in Thailand.

When the demonstrations broke out on 8 August 1988, Mun Awng
joined in. Two days later, his room-mate's friend was shot in the back
of the neck and a bullet went through his cheek. Mun Awng and some
friends frantically waved down a car and got him to the hospital before
the street was blocked by troops. At the hospital, Mun Awng saw many
more people who had been shot by soldiers. He said that the experience
changed his life. Once the military cracked down, he decided to head for
the Thai border. After arriving in Karen territory, he was given a quick
course in basic military training by the newly formed All Burma Students'
Democratic Front and sent out to the front lines. Thrown into battle
situations for which he was ill prepared, he began to question what he
was doing. Having to spend his days with a gun instead of a guitar also
upset him. Finally, he said, he decided he should continue the struggle
as a musician rather than as a soldier.

Convinced that the power of music could revive the spirits of democracy activists inside the country and along the border, he put together
an album called *Battle for Peace*. Composed by writers inside Burma as
well as by colleagues in the ABSDF, many of the songs memorialized the
events of 1988. A few were marching songs for demonstrators. Others
expressed hope for a new beginning.

Tapes of Mun Awng's new album were smuggled into Burma and also
played over Burmese-language radio stations broadcasting from abroad.
People in Burma copied the tapes and passed them on to friends. Some
of the songs became famous. Mun Awng even heard that when male

university students sang songs under girls' dormitory windows, some girls insisted that they would listen only if their suitors sang Mun Awng's songs.

The real proof of his impact came in December 1996 when student demonstrations broke out in Rangoon. As well-armed troops moved in on all the streets surrounding the junction where the students were gathered, the students kept up their spirits by singing the national anthem and three of Mun Awng's rallying songs. Those who didn't know the songs by heart read from lyric sheets that had been prepared and passed out by student activists. Mun Awng later saw a videotape of the demonstration. Watching a whole new generation of students empowered by his songs, he was amazed and gratified.

The military regime also recognizes the power of music to influence people and has made concerted efforts to use music to build support for their rule.[8] In particular, the authorities have persuaded famous singers to perform propaganda songs in return for special privileges. Sai Htee Hsaing, a Shan singer who entertained the 1988 pro-democracy demonstrators with progressive songs, later sang government-written songs and was provided with a house and car in return. Idolized by teenagers, Zaw Win Htut long resisted singing propaganda songs, but in 1994 he was banned from performing in public. Seeing his career disintegrating, he agreed to work with the regime in order to be able to perform again. The result was an album entitled *Maha*, which means 'great'. The songwriter was an army captain working for military intelligence, and the songs extolled Burmese imperialism under Pagan-dynasty kings, whose legacy the regime sees itself as preserving. Because of its catchy tune, the title song became a hit. Zaw Win Htut lost the respect of some of his more political fans, but even democracy supporters found themselves unconsciously humming along with his new songs.

By encouraging or intimidating popular singers to work with them, the regime both improves its ability to reach a wider audience with its message and also discourages the discontented from taking action. When students see their favourite stars belting out propaganda songs, they lose confidence in their own abilities to resist the generals.

Since the mid-1990s, the junta has also sought to win the support of the new generation by no longer actively discouraging rock and roll, and other modern forms of music. Burmese hip-hop and rap singers have become very popular, although rap has not become a dissident genre in Burma in terms of its lyrics. This is because singers of all types still face stark censorship, with words such as 'dark', 'truth' and 'beggar' not allowed in their songs. Beggars cannot officially be sung about, because acknowledging the existence of beggars would imply the regime isn't taking care of the country's citizens. In recent years, the Myanmar Music Asiayone (association), which is led by regime loyalists, has been tasked with checking lyrics before they are sent to the censorship board, to ensure that lyrics with hidden meanings do not make it through.[9]

To reach younger audiences with its propaganda, the regime established a new TV station, Myawaddy TV, in 1995. The only other channel, Myanmar TV, features stern-looking government appointees reading out lengthy government news reports in a monotone, footage of army officers attending meetings and visiting monasteries, and marching songs. Myawaddy TV, on the other hand, presents news in brief soundbites, interspersed with entertainment programmes. The entertainment programmes include contemporary music videos, Burmese movies and Chinese and Korean soap operas, which have become a big hit in Burma.

Myawaddy TV does its own recording and editing, and the authorities ensure that the performers adhere to the restrictions on behaviour and attire. They can now move when singing but they cannot dance wildly or provocatively. Similarly, while some Western-style clothing has been allowed, particularly for men, performers must dress modestly. At one point, the TV censors banned the wearing of red, deemed a political colour, and yellow, because pro-democracy activists had organized a yellow campaign in support of Aung San Suu Kyi.[10] Nor can performers bring American flags onstage. By claiming that they are safeguarding traditional Burmese culture against decadent Western influences, the top generals have garnered a certain amount of respect among the older generation. But among the younger generation, there is a strong desire to be current with international trends. They feel that in yet another area of their lives the regime is holding them back.

Although the generals have claimed the moral high ground in affirming their commitment to traditional values, the pro-democracy movement in exile has tried to subvert the regime by using a traditional form of chanting, *thangyat*, to critique the military's policies. *Thangyat* are performed during the new year festivities in April, with new lyrics being set to standardized chant rhythms each year. Such songs provide a vehicle for the expression of popular dissatisfaction with government officials and abuses of authority, and have been performed since the pre-colonial period. The military regime has forbidden independent performances of *thangyat* in the country, but activists who fled to the Indian border after 1988 have produced annual CDs condemning the regime's policies on forced labour, tourism, narcotics and other issues. The recordings have been surreptitiously sent into the country and frequently played over foreign-based Burmese-language radio broadcasts.

In addition, some comedians have used traditional *a-nyeint* performances, which combine dance and comedy routines, to satirize the regime. In a performance in Rangoon in November 2007, Say Yaung Sone and Thee Lay Thee, a troupe consisting of five men in their thirties and forties, boldly took aim at the regime's crackdown on the monks' demonstrations. The popular VCD of the performance was soon banned, but Burmese communities abroad invited them to come and perform. They took advantage of the opportunity to get out and express themselves freely, but with the knowledge that the authorities might be waiting for them with a prison van if and when they returned home.[11]

'Mad' art

Like literature, movies and music, art can be used to agitate people, so the art world has been another arena for the battle between the military regime and independent thinkers. In 1988, art students played a key role in making banners, logos and designs for the pro-democracy demonstrations and the independent newspapers and magazines that sprang up. The military subsequently put an end to this by permanently closing the fine arts club at Rangoon University. In the 1990s the regime founded the University of Culture, where some aspiring artists now study. Others have looked to private teachers for training and inspiration.

Commercial art galleries can be found in Rangoon and Mandalay and some other tourist towns, but public exhibitions come under government scrutiny. Before the exhibition opens, the censors come to inspect the paintings and ask about their meanings. In 2008, the director of the government-sponsored artists' association was in charge of censoring paintings. If there was too much red in the painting (a revolutionary colour) or the painting featured worn-out objects or decrepit buildings, it was rejected. Such scenes contradict the image the regime is trying to project of a modern nation. Nudes are not allowed, because they do not fit with traditional culture.

Similarly, under the BSPP, modern art was considered too subversive to be taught at the country's two art academies. The Culture Ministry instead urged the teachers and students to channel their creativity into forms of art that could be used to promote state-sponsored ideals. Sitt Nyein Aye, a student at the Mandalay Art Academy in the 1970s, remembered, 'The BSPP people came to the school and said, "Art for politics' sake, not art for art's sake".' The students were told that to explore abstract ideas in art was selfish. If the work couldn't be readily understood by farmers and workers (and, one supposes, the censors) it shouldn't be undertaken.

When Sitt Nyein Aye first saw examples of modern art at a book fair sponsored by the United States Information Service, he was stunned. After that, he and another classmate secretly studied modern art with two artists outside the academy. They had to hide their work from the headmaster and many of the teachers and students who derided modern art as 'mad art'.

Still, his teachers were aware of his extracurricular activities. As a result, he said, he was denied the school's top prize despite his superior talent. Sitt Nyein Aye was crestfallen. The prizewinner was sent to Europe for further studies, something he could never afford on his own. Moreover, Sitt Nyein Aye had wanted to take the prize back to his family and the monks at his village monastery to show that their confidence in him had been justified.

Sitt Nyein Aye came from a small village, and his young life was spent mostly in the monastery. The few students who wanted to continue their studies beyond primary school had to move to town. Sitt Nyein Aye's parents were farmers with no extra money for education, but monks from his village monastery supported him financially. After graduating without the prize, Sitt Nyein Aye was too upset to go back home. Instead, he made a life for himself on the streets, sketching and selling his work to passers-by. Although poor and often hungry, Sitt Nyein Aye found pleasure in remaining true to his ideals. He said: 'I didn't do any commercial work at that time. I wanted to create. I lived only for this.'

In school, Sitt Nyein Aye had been hampered by his instructors' rigidity as well as by a lack of supplies. 'Ten people had to share one water-colour cake,' he recalled. 'Oil paints were rationed out equally by colour in tiny amounts. You couldn't get more. Sometimes we needed a lot of black and only a little white, but we couldn't do anything.' When painting on the streets, there were no restrictions.

Once or twice a week, he would take his sketches to his teachers for their comments. At the time, they had no idea that he was homeless. They were happy to teach him because he was clearly so devoted to developing his abilities. And they instructed him not only in the skills of painting but also in the finer points of Buddhist philosophy. Encouraging him to deepen his thinking about all aspects of life, these teachers provided him with the kind of holistic education that epitomized traditional teaching relationships but was so lacking in the formal curriculum.

As his art developed, so did his political awareness. He wrote an article entitled 'In the dark, every cat is black', which attacked the regime for killing people's creativity and forcing them into the same mould. He said: 'They hate educated people, so they oppress all people who can rule or create or invent.' What saddened him and his teachers was that the regime made it so difficult for talented older artists to pass on their knowledge to the next generation. Instead, artists felt that they had to hide their skills and their work.

Sitt Nyein Aye is an exception, and after a few years even he began to think about his responsibilities to his parents and siblings. He decided that he had to take up commercial work to earn a decent living. But his political leanings got the better of him. Asked to design a small calendar for junior college students, he included a sketch of the Rangoon University student union building, which had been blown up by the Ne Win regime in 1962. For that, he spent two months in custody.

After his release, he threw himself into apolitical work. Soon, his studio was inundated with orders. Previously, he said, all signboards were done with coloured letters on a white background. But Sitt Nyein Aye revolution-ized commercial art in Upper Burma by incorporating a wide variety of colours, textures and designs developed from his study of modern art. Even the authorities were drawn to his work. He designed a new badge for the military and did small projects for military intelligence personnel. Although he achieved success, Sitt Nyein Aye said he still wasn't happy. He claimed: 'I had the exact opposite problem [to before]. I had a lot of money, and a lot of materials, but no time to paint my own things. So I thought, "Success is like a prison".'

Nevertheless, he used the money he made to bring a measure of pros-perity to his village. Besides donating cash and clothing, he purchased goats and cows for villagers to raise. He also opened a small art course every summer, bringing children to Mandalay to study with him. By 1988, he was beginning to move away from his commercial business in order to focus again on more creative work. But then the demonstrations broke out, and he set up an independent newspaper under the auspices of an activist monks' association. The day after the coup, he fled with a group of students to India, where he has invested his talents in producing artwork for the resistance groups' offices and publications.

Since Sitt Nyein Aye left the country, Burmese artists' interest in con-temporary forms of art has grown. But the fact that modern art by its nature takes a defiant attitude towards tradition and control makes it an obvious area of concern for the regime. And artists, because of their powerful ability to convey emotions and immortalize historical events in unforgettable images, have been subject to constant surveillance.

Nevertheless, some Burmese artists have managed to achieve international fame, and a small but growing number of galleries outside the country show their work. One artist who has painted and performed haunting pieces is Htein Lin. A former political prisoner who spent from 1998 to 2004 behind bars, he secretly made over three hundred works of art on white prison uniforms, many of which were given to him by prisoners on death row.[12] A number of the paintings reflect the gruesome nature of prison life, including hunger, sickness and criminal prisoners who voluntarily cut off their fingers in order to avoid being sent to a labour camp. A few years after he was released, he moved abroad. Galleries in London and Thailand have held showings of his prison artwork, which he had arranged to be smuggled first out of prison and then out of Burma, as well as his more recent work. He has also created silent but emotionally intense performance pieces which reflect his anguished feelings about his country.

Like writers and poets, artists who have remained in Burma sometimes organize their own private showings or do performance art pieces for friends. While anger with the regime and its endless restrictions and demands may lead to depression in some, it has only increased the spirit of defiance in others.

Performers and social work

The authorities routinely organize cash donation ceremonies for various regime-sponsored projects. Famous performers, as well as businessmen, are often informed in advance how much money they are expected to present. When entertainers seek to engage in their own social work, however, they often come under suspicion. This is particularly true if they are known to have an anti-government attitude. Nevertheless, a number of people in the entertainment industry have been motivated to work for society, particularly as the country's social and economic problems have mounted.

For instance, the actor Kyaw Thu founded the Free Funeral Services Society in Rangoon with some friends in 2001. Supported by donors at home and abroad, it has provided tens of thousands of free funerals. The organization has also financed treatment in some hospitals and set up a free clinic. In mid-May 2007, however, the organization, along with twenty-three others, was informed that it could not renew its registration. A week later, the Home Ministry said the organizations could write letters of appeal, apparently because of international pressure. Kyaw Thu offered alms to monks participating in the September 2007 demonstrations, and was briefly imprisoned afterwards, but the organization has continued its work and, together with Kyaw Thu, took an active role in cyclone relief efforts as well.[13]

According to *The Irrawaddy*, an estimated four hundred people from the entertainment world volunteered for cyclone relief work.[14] They included Zarganar, a famous comedian and film-maker who had been imprisoned for his satirical mimes and speeches. When well-known entertainers take on social causes, other citizens are motivated to take action as well.

Having a positive impact on society is the desire of many in the literary and artistic community. Today, there are more ways to distribute information, more venues for performing, and more civil society organizations operating. Small numbers of writers, journalists, artists and musicians have also had the opportunity to travel abroad, gaining exposure and a breath of fresh air. Thus the cat-and-mouse game continues as the regime tries to create new ways to control and direct the creative energies of its citizens, while members of the artistic community look for new spaces in which to express themselves and better the lives of others.

12 | Religion and magic: disappearing jewels and poltergeists

A monk cannot tell authorities about people's problems. If he does, the authorities will consider that monk to be their enemy. (A monk, Mandalay)

While many Burmese seek solace and community through their spiritual practices, the regime also penetrates the religious sphere in many ways. The ruling generals are constantly demonstrating their own piety through lavish donations to monks in a bid to shore up their moral authority. At the same time, the regime feels it must keep monks under surveillance, because the country's spiritual leaders are the main alternative voices of authority, and they have frequently intervened in the country's political crises. The regime has tried to further its ideology of national consolidation by promoting the spread of Burman-style Buddhism and reducing the population of Muslims, particularly in Northern Arakan State. Meanwhile, ordinary Burmese, as well as the regime and some opposition activists, use numerology, astrology and the advice of fortune-tellers to try to cheat fate and ensure success.

Buddhism and politics

The primary duties of Buddhist monks towards lay people are to instruct them in the philosophy and practice of Buddhism and to accept their donations, so that lay people have a chance to make merit. Although these practices are frowned on by conservative monks, many monks also engage in fortune-telling, astrology, lottery number predictions, and the giving of protective charms and incantations to lay people. They themselves may believe in the efficacy of such practices, and they may want to help their supporters, whose main concerns are with their daily lives rather than with seeking enlightenment. Others may seek to enhance their reputations through such practices.[1]

At critical points in Burma's history, monks have felt compelled to venture farther into the realm of worldly affairs to protect their religion or to call attention to injustice. In the early 1900s, monks played a leading role in organizing protests against the colonial government, particularly because they felt that Buddhism had been insulted. In the decades since

General Ne Win took over, the lay community has often looked to the monks for leadership in their struggle against unjust governance.

U Nandiya, a strict, middle-aged monk from Mandalay, put monks' participation in political affairs into a philosophical and historical perspective. In his opinion, everyone must accept the suffering that all humans face: namely, desire, sickness, ageing and death. But suffering from injustice is not natural and should be eradicated. He explained:

> If you have a headache and take aspirin, the headache will be reduced, but if you think this is your fate, then the headache isn't reduced. Also, everyone in Burma knows we need a good government and political system so that we can have a good life. So we must work for this. The Buddha never talked about fate, so we shouldn't get too confused with our fortunes. We should focus on work, knowledge, and effort.

U Nandiya gave an example from the Buddha's life to reinforce his point. He said that during his lifetime, the Buddha tried to solve social conflicts, such as a dispute over water distribution between Bihar and a neighbouring state. There are also plenty of examples from Burma's own past. He explained how during the Pagan dynasty, King Narapatisithu (AD 1173–1210) forced people to cut down trees, bake bricks and build pagodas. One of the Buddhist monks suggested to the king that he shouldn't force people to do this kind of work, but the king ignored him, so the monk said that he wouldn't stay in the kingdom because there was no justice.

What U Nandiya and many other contemporary Burmese monks hate most is the regime's forcible collection of money, including for religious purposes. Such donations should be purely voluntary, he said. Most monks, he added, also disagree with the use of forced labour and feel unhappy that people's lives are made so difficult by all the military government's demands.

When I asked U Nandiya if Buddhist monks stood for the people, he replied, 'Buddhist monks stand for justice.' But on the subject of the slingshot fights during the 1990 religious boycott, he admitted that the monks had gone too far. 'It was not appropriate to do this,' he said. 'It broke Buddhist discipline. But most who participated were very young. People supported it because they hated the military so much, but didn't dare to fight by themselves.'

Monks have also been directly affected by military rule. Ill-conceived economic policies and heavy taxation of villagers in remote areas have made it difficult for villagers to provide adequate support for the monks.

Mandalay is a monastic teaching centre, so the population of monks is quite high. In the 1990s, as many impoverished Burmese sold their homes to Chinese immigrants and moved to the outskirts of town, it became more difficult for all the monks in the city centre to collect sufficient alms. In recent years, high inflation and sudden price increases have hit residents of Rangoon and other cities hard, leaving some unable to properly feed themselves, let alone the monks. Compassion for the lay people's suffering – as well as their own – prompted many urban monks to join the 2007 marches.

Not surprisingly, successive military regimes have promoted monks who support them or who adhere to the belief that monks should not participate in political activities. Student activists, on the other hand, have tried to encourage and work with monks who feel compelled to fight against injustice. Monks realize that they risk debasing the monkhood as an institution by plunging into the dirty world of politics, but they also risk being seen as irrelevant if they remain indifferent to the plight of the people who bring them their daily sustenance.

At the same time, many Burmese are influenced by the belief that suffering in this life is a result of bad deeds in the past, so one might as well just accept the political situation as inevitable. When the time for change comes, it will happen by itself. Particularly in times of intense repression, such thinking tends to predominate. Individuals focus more on personal efforts to improve their chances for a better next life through praying, adhering to Buddhist discipline and making religious donations.

The temple represents an important space in society, and one that is generally perceived as belonging outside military control. Time spent in religious establishments often provides a respite from personal and political tensions outside. Meditation, in particular, has played an interesting role. When on the run, just released from prison or feeling stressed from the dangers of their political work, some activists have turned to monasteries and meditation centres as sanctuaries where they can regain peace of mind. Meditation has led more than a few out of their political lives and into a focus on spiritual development. Others have used the sense of calmness and stability obtained from meditating to help them ward off depression and continue their political work.

The regime is well aware that most political uprisings in Burma have been led by students or monks or a combination of the two. The students are bold and committed, but they lack clout. The monks, on the other hand, have moral authority among the people, as well as an organizational structure that allows them to mobilize quickly and widely. Thus, the junta has developed a two-pronged strategy to prevent citizens and monks from coalescing into a powerful anti-government force. First, they have tried to limit the influence of the monks, particularly in their role as advocates of the people. And second, they have used combinations of awards, gifts, surveillance and intimidation to make monks hesitant to defy the regime.

Before the military took over, monks say that they were often able to intervene if certain authorities were treating people unjustly. But now the army refuses to honour this role. Villagers and townspeople still complain to monks about their sufferings, such as having to do forced labour or pay monthly porter fees, but they know the monks cannot persuade the authorities to stop such abuses. There have even been instances of military commanders telling abbots to call on people to build feeder roads so that it will appear as if the work is a religious donation rather than forced labour.

Some monks have decided that given the country's current socio-economic crisis, they must help their communities both spiritually and materially. Some donate part of the food they receive to the very poor. A number of other monks have opened up primary schools for poor children. A few monasteries have also provided sanctuary for AIDS sufferers, who get little support from the state. All of these activities help address the day-to-day needs of the poor and sick, but the monks cannot tackle the root causes of these problems, which largely stem from misguided government policies and neglect.

Although monks are supposed to live simple lives with only a few necessary possessions, many have found it hard to reject the luxuries offered by generals and other benefactors. Lavish gifts to senior monks include TVs, VCRs and fancy cars, all of which are technically prohibited by the monks' code of discipline. The junta has also built special hospitals solely for monks, with equipment and treatment far superior to what is found in public hospitals. Those senior monks who are well supported by the authorities and rich people can lose touch with the day-to-day reality for ordinary people. According to one scholarly monk, some senior monks did not know how badly poorer people had been affected by inflation and the gas price hikes in 2007, and when they saw video footage of the violence used against the monks and other demonstrators, they thought that anti-government people had doctored the images on a computer.

The regime rewards supportive monks with large donations and religious titles. Meant to be bestowed on those who show a superior mastery of Buddhist doctrine, the titles instead often go to monks who are loyal to the regime. In some cases, they are given to senior monks whose loyalty may be in doubt, but whom the regime hopes to co-opt. Even if the monk himself continues to view the regime with distaste, others may see him as tainted by having accepted the title.

Successive military regimes have also secretly placed intelligence agents in the monasteries, so if any monks are discussing politics or meeting with political activists, their activities will be reported. The planted monks can also urge other monks to stay out of politics. In some cases, military authorities have tried to obtain representation on monastery committees as well, so that they can keep an eye on the goings-on at the monasteries.

U Nandiya described some of the other methods successive regimes have used to rein in the country's monks, who numbered about 400,000 before the September 2007 crackdown. They abolished religious associations outside the government's control and, through the state-controlled media, defamed respected monks who took anti-regime stands. 'For instance,' U Nandiya said, 'they publish "news" that the monk has drunk liquor or slept with a woman. They don't bother with ordinary monks, even if they are doing bad things.' At the same time, the senior generals look for loyal monks to promote to leadership positions on the state-controlled supreme council of monks. They rely on such monks to keep younger monks in line, although some members of the supreme council refused to be used this way during the 2007 demonstrations.

In Burma there has always been a tension between the belief that every government is bad and best avoided and the idea that the government is the defender of the Buddhist faith. As noted earlier, the legitimacy of kings in Burma and throughout South-East Asia rested in part on their fulfilling their duties as religious patrons. Over the last twenty years, the top generals and their wives have invested much of their time in the building of new monasteries, the restoration of important pagodas, and the presentation of donations to monks. In many cases, this has probably been done as a genuine expression of their faith, but there are also political motivations. The generals recognize that there is still credibility to be gained from such activities, because they are taking the lead in restoring or enhancing the greatness of Burma as a Buddhist land. At the same time, as Schober has argued, citizens become linked to the regime as participants in the rituals, and they may even feel that they owe the generals a debt of gratitude for providing the opportunity to make merit.[2]

For example, in April 1999 the military regime oversaw the completion of the restoration of the Shwedagon Pagoda, the most revered pagoda in

the country. Many civil servants and others were ordered to make donations of cash and labour for the restoration project, but few resented it.
They are intensely attached to this stunning pagoda, which symbolizes
the spiritual soul of the nation. In addition, they believe their donations
will help them achieve a higher status in their next lives, leading them
closer to their ultimate goal of nirvana. The pagoda is believed to contain
eight hairs of the Buddha which were brought to what was then a Mon
kingdom by two merchant disciples of the Buddha. Over the centuries,
the pagoda has been expanded and restored several times. According to
the regime's figures, by the end of March 1999 the call for donations had
brought in 94 pounds of gold, the equivalent of $2 million in cash, and
nearly 68,000 pieces of jewellery, which could be broken up and used to
decorate the bejewelled umbrella at the top of the pagoda.[3]

Similarly, in 1996 the military regime negotiated a lease with the Chinese government to have a tooth relic of the Buddha flown from China
to Burma for a few months. Many people in Burma were grateful to the
regime for arranging this, because they believe that the tooth relic has tremendous power and significance. The junta also oversaw the construction
of tooth-relic pagodas in Rangoon and Mandalay to house replicas of the
tooth relic, imbued through a ritual with the potency of the original.[4]

Still, many people realize that the regime has tried to use its highly
publicized religious activities to gain political legitimacy. One common
joke in Burma is that a disgruntled customer complains to the shop where
he bought his TV, 'This is supposed to be a multicolour TV but all I ever
see is green and yellow.' The meaning: the news on government-controlled
TV consists largely of military personnel, in their green uniforms, giving
donations to monks, in their yellow robes.

The disappearing jewels

Despite the authorities' apparent devotion to Buddhism, there have
been reports of military men engaged in the plunder of Buddha images
and old pagodas. When pagodas are built, the patrons and well-wishers
place gems and other valuables in a sealed treasury located under the
centre of the pagoda. The landscape of Upper Burma is dotted with old
pagodas which have fallen into disrepair. These pagodas have become
prime hunting grounds for fortune-seekers in green uniforms. In one case
in Sagaing Division, villagers were forced to dig up the treasury under
military orders. When they reached the treasury, the soldiers ordered
them to leave the area. According to one of the villagers, the soldiers then
cordoned off the pagoda, removed the valuables and took them away.[5]

A much more dramatic incident took place in Mandalay in 1997, when one of the most sacred Buddha images in Burma was mysteriously damaged. After King Bodawpaya conquered Arakan in 1784, he had the huge bronze Mahamuni Buddha image split into pieces and brought up to a site just outside Mandalay, where it was reconstructed and housed in a new temple. This image, which has become the symbol of Arakanese national identity, was revered by Arakanese, Mon and Burmans alike for centuries. It was also believed to contain a precious stone in its navel, which would give miraculous powers to its possessor.

In 1996, some Mandalay authorities insisted that it was time for a renovation. During the renovation, a mysterious hole appeared in the belly of the statue, where the gem was thought to be located. As senior monks began to investigate the case, rumours quickly spread that one of the two monks who possessed a key to the building had been forced by a military officer to open the building at night. As a result, a senior monk called monks from all the major monasteries in Mandalay to a meeting to discuss the issue. During the course of the all-day meeting, in which answers about what had happened were not forthcoming, a monk and another man suddenly came into the room to announce that a Muslim man had raped a Buddhist girl.[6]

Some of the already frustrated monks decided to take action, and headed to the Muslim man's house, which they ransacked, and went on to damage a nearby mosque. As the news spread, a frenzy of attacks on mosques broke out in Mandalay and other cities. Over the next few days, monks could be seen wielding long sticks and desecrating mosques, often while riot police passively watched the scene from a distance. There were also several reports of people seeing monks with walkie-talkies under their robes, and a few had very shiny heads, indicating they had just been shaved. In other words, it was widely believed that military men dressed as monks were involved, although many real monks also participated. In the meantime, the hype surrounding the damage done to the Mahamuni image was forgotten, and its belly was patched up. Later, it turned out that the girl had not been raped after all. As for the precious stone, no one knows whether it really was in the stomach of the Buddha, and whether or not the thieves managed to extract it.[7]

The Mahamuni incident occurred just before the annual monks' exams were scheduled to take place. Rather than provide a gathering place where the monks could discuss taking action against the regime, the authorities postponed the exams. When they were finally held a year later, the monks had to pair off and take responsibility for each other. If one monk were to engage in anti-government activities, the other one would also be in trouble. As they have done in other communities, the authorities imposed a policy of communal punishment for the acts of individuals in order to reduce the possibility of unrest.

Buddhism and the NLD

While monasteries are supposed to be neutral places, certain abbots and monasteries are perceived as being either in the SPDC or the pro-democracy camp. The monks who have been labelled as pro-regime are often seen as beholden to one or more of the generals, although perhaps the generals can draw on their power as well. The relationship between the monks who are labelled as pro-democracy and the NLD is different. The NLD cannot co-opt monks; its members can only seek guidance or solace from monks whom they respect. Aung San Suu Kyi and intellectual members of the NLD have tended to look to Buddhist insight meditation techniques as a way to develop themselves, and have sought out meditation teachers in the temples. In addition, the NLD leaders have routinely drawn on Buddhist teachings to explain their political points. Some NLD members have also been attracted to a more socially engaged form of Buddhism, and have had good relations with monks who are active in social welfare activities.[8] NLD members also hold donation ceremonies at temples, and some have made going to temples to pray for the release of Aung San Suu Kyi and other political prisoners a regular event. Supporters of Aung San Suu Kyi are known to have put her photograph on their Buddhist altars in their homes, signifying both their respect for her and their wish that she be protected by higher powers so that she can continue to lead the struggle on their behalf.

The regime has sought to prevent the NLD from gaining support among the monastic community in various ways. In late September 1996, the SLORC issued a decree forbidding NLD members from becoming ordained as monks. Monks were also told to be wary of NLD members frequenting monasteries, because the NLD was supposedly trying to encourage monks to join the anti-government movement. Lieutenant General Myo Nyunt, the then Minister of Religious Affairs, claimed: 'Although [the NLD members] are Buddhists, they are unaware of the sin of dividing the monks.'[9] This order contravened Buddhist doctrine and was generally ignored by monks. It can be seen, however, as an attempt to reverse the 1990 monks' boycott of the military, when they refused to accept offerings from or carry out ceremonies for members of the military and their families. The aim seems to have been to put a distance between the monks and the NLD, to demoralize NLD members, and perhaps to turn ordinary citizens against the NLD for purportedly politicizing the monkhood. The NLD has not directly encouraged monks to come out on its side but, as noted earlier, ordinary people have tried to ascertain the political sympathies of venerated monks.

Stories about Aung San Suu Kyi's and Lieutenant General Khin Nyunt's visits to the Thamanya abbot in the mid-1990s indicate the extent to which people are looking to the monks to support their political ideals, even if only symbolically. A devout, elderly monk from the Pa'o ethnic minority group, U Vinaya, set up a monastery on Thamanya hill 20 miles outside Pa'an, the capital of Karen State, in 1980. Over the years, he built up a large following with devotees throughout the country. A vegetarian, he was famous for his strict practice, and people believed that he had magical powers. On weekends, up to three thousand people would go to see him, including large numbers of businessmen and students from Rangoon, who hoped his blessing would guarantee success in their endeavours.

The Thamanya abbot also generously allowed Karen villagers fleeing from the civil war between the *tatmadaw* and the KNU to build huts on monastery land around the foot of the mountain. In 1996, there were several thousand Karen villagers living there, free from the food and labour demands of both the *tatmadaw* and the KNU. Some of the villagers farmed, but many worked at the monastery, preparing enormous amounts of food for the endless stream of visitors.

The Thamanya abbot never talked openly about politics, but the authorities certainly perceived him as a possible threat because of his ability to attract people. Members of the military regime, including Lieutenant General Khin Nyunt, visited him, and so did Aung San Suu Kyi. In her first trip outside Rangoon after she was released from house arrest in 1995, she headed directly to Karen State to pay her respects to the Thamanya abbot. During her visit, a picture was taken of her sitting at his feet. This picture was later copied, laminated and widely distributed by her supporters, who took it as a sign of the abbot's tacit support for her and the democracy movement. To this the abbot merely said that anyone could have their picture taken with him.

When I was travelling in Burma in 1996, I heard several apocryphal stories comparing Aung San Suu Kyi's and Lieutenant General Khin Nyunt's visits to the monastery. One version claimed that when Aung San Suu Kyi arrived at the foot of the long stairway up to the monastery, the abbot came down to welcome her. But when Lieutenant General Khin Nyunt arrived, the abbot did not descend. The abbot invited Aung

San Suu Kyi to visit again, but he did not extend the same invitation to Lieutenant General Khin Nyunt. When the general tried to give the abbot a van, he refused the gift, saying, 'Monks don't need vans. Take it back.' In another variation, it was said that when Lieutenant General Khin Nyunt got in his car to leave, it wouldn't start. He had to go back up to the abbot, who told him that only after he had got rid of his anger would the car start. Probably not one of these details is true, but they reflect people's desires for a different reality.

The military regime courted the Thamanya abbot for two reasons. Besides wanting to rein him in, they also hoped to garner more support from the Burmese populace by showing respect to a monk whom the people adored. The regime encouraged the abbot to move to Rangoon, where they could have more contact with him. He rejected the offer, saying he was perfectly happy where he was.

Still, the regime kept a close eye on him. Although guns are not supposed to be brought into any monastery, on the day I visited, armed *tatmadaw* soldiers were patrolling the nearby monastery-sponsored primary school, where an award ceremony was taking place. When I asked why there needed to be armed soldiers at a school during daylight hours, I was told that it was for the children's security. I couldn't help but wonder whether it had more to do with demonstrating that, ultimately, this territory was under the regime's rather than the abbot's control.

Later, when the abbot was hospitalized in Rangoon, he allowed the authorities to pay his medical bill, but they were infuriated when he visited Aung San Suu Kyi after he recovered.

In late 1999, the junta was caught off balance by the publicized demands of two venerated monks, U Zawtipala, the abbot of Kyakhatwaing monastery in Pegu, and U Kundalabiwuntha of Mahaghandharon monastery in Mandalay. Issuing separate appeals to both the regime and the NLD, the senior monks urged them to work together for national reconciliation. U Zawtipala, who had never been involved in politics, even offered to act as a mediator in talks between the NLD and the regime. He asked both sides to be flexible but also suggested that the government should not go against the will of the people.[10] While the NLD issued a statement declaring the party's willingness to accept the abbots' guidance, the regime suggested that the senior monks had been used by the opposition. In a written response to the appeals, the regime insisted that 'The National League for Democracy should be willing to adopt a more realistic and flexible policy.'[11] The generals ignored the call for dialogue.

During the September 2007 demonstrations, when a group of monks and civilians marched down University Avenue and stopped briefly in front of Aung San Suu Kyi's house, the top generals were very upset. The All Burma Monks' Alliance had already included political demands – namely the release of all political prisoners and a call for national reconciliation – in its statements, and, as became clear later, some of the key participants in the marches had warm relations with NLD members. The regime did not want to see an alliance emerge between the monks and the NLD and quickly took action to end the growing demonstrations. Nevertheless, the generals cannot stop thoughtful monks from recognizing that health, education, religion and politics are all linked. As one well-known monk put it, 'you can't separate them'.

Repression of Christians

Besides cultivating loyal Buddhist monks, the regime has sought to win the support of the majority Burmans by encouraging the promotion of Buddhism among non-Buddhist peoples. Throughout military rule, foreigners have been able to come to Burma to study Vipassana meditation at monasteries and meditation centres. This is a source of pride for Burmese citizens, who generally view Burmese Buddhism as the most pure form of Buddhism being practised today. With regard to the ethnic minorities in Burma, some Burman Buddhists share the military regime's perception that if all the ethnic minorities 'became' Buddhists, it would be beneficial for them personally and the country would be more unified.

While personal relations between Buddhists and Christians have generally been quite good, nationalist propaganda has negatively characterized Christians as supporters of British colonial rule. Given that large numbers among some of the ethnic resistance armies are also Christian, higher-ranking *tatmadaw* officers in particular tend to mistrust Christians and see them as a problem. Some Christians assert they have been discriminated against in obtaining promotions in government service, and particularly in the army.

Although Christians in the cities and towns in central Burma have not faced physical persecution, they have been obstructed in the practice of their religion in various ways. Endless delays in approving building permits for new religious structures are common, and there have been cases of newly built churches being pulled down even after the proper permit has been obtained.

Seemingly arbitrary forms of harassment have also been used. A member of the Myanmar Council of Churches (MCC), which represents twelve

Protestant denominations, described some of the challenges they faced in the mid-1990s. Lieutenant General Myo Nyunt, the Minister of Religious Affairs at the time, informed the council that they could no longer use the word *thoukdan kyan* for 'Proverbs', even though it had been used since the first translation of the Bible into Burmese more than one hundred years ago. The general did not want them to use this word because Buddhists used it in their doctrinal texts. The council member explained:

> Not long after, the Christians invited [Lieutenant] General Myo Nyunt to a Christmas Eve dinner in Rangoon. He gave a long speech which had been written for him and included quotes from the Bible, including sections from Proverbs. Then the MCC elders wrote a letter to the government saying that since [Lieutenant] General Myo Nyunt himself had used the word *thoukdan kyan* for Proverbs, why can't we? So then the Ministry of Religious Affairs dropped the issue.

The council member also talked about how, in 1995, the SLORC sent a letter to the Myanmar Christian Council saying that secular colleges used caps and gowns at their graduation ceremonies, so divinity colleges would have to choose some other form of attire. He said that the MCC wrote back explaining that, from medieval days in Europe, when colleges were religious institutions, gowns had been used. Secular institutions had only come later. After that, the Ministry of Religious Affairs said nothing.

In the ethnic states and remote areas, many of the authorities take a more aggressive approach. In particular, Christians in Karen and Karenni states on the eastern border and in Chin State and Sagaing Division on the western border have seen their churches burned down, their pastors arrested and *tatmadaw* soldiers disrupt services. One Chin pastor explained:

> On Sundays we can't have a full service, because they take porters that day, too. They refuse to make an exception. Sometimes they also take porters during the church service. We can't do anything. Sometimes we intercede on behalf of villagers. We say, 'Let that man be a porter two days from now.' But they never listen. They always say, 'These are orders from above.' They never understand the villagers.

In the remote Naga hills, in the late 1990s, some parents allowed their children to accompany authorities to what they were told were secular schools, only to find out later that their children had been sent to Buddhist monasteries and inducted as novice monks.

Particularly in Chin State, the authorities were upset by an evangelical

Chin group's plans to convert all Chin to Christianity by the year 2000, as part of an international Christian campaign. Since then, the authorities in some townships tried to lure Christians into becoming Buddhists by offering them exemption from forced labour as well as food allowances or money.[12] Another Chin pastor told about a Christian village of two hundred houses in Tamu township, Chin State, where the authorities went even farther. He said that besides offering food and money, some villagers were also given buffaloes and land for cultivating rice. As a result, fifty households converted, and one of the converts was then appointed by the military as the headman.

Such activities are also aimed at creating splits among the ethnic minority communities, with some people agreeing to convert – at least in name – and others refusing. As with artists and writers, conflicts develop within religious communities over what degree of cooperation is acceptable and who has gone too far. People within the community begin to view each other with suspicion, and bonds of trust are broken down. To some extent, however, the Christian community has been able to counter these pressures and maintain its vitality by putting much of its energy into church activities and social welfare work.

As in the Buddhist community, there has been an ongoing debate in the Christian community about whether the current sorry state of affairs is 'God's will' or demands action. Those pastors and church members who attribute current suffering to God's will believe that they are being punished, usually because of moral laxity in the community. For them, more disciplined behaviour and more fervent prayer are the keys to a better future. Other Christians reject this position as too passive and insist that God rewards only those who act. But because action usually means coming into confrontation with hostile authorities, following through requires strong commitment.

As a minority population, Christians have been reluctant to take a prominent role in politics in the heartland of Burma; some Christian leaders, however, have played a role aiming to make peace between the regime and the ethnic resistance armies. Church leaders in predominantly Christian ethnic minority areas have, in some cases, been outspoken. Among the armed ethnic nationalist groups where Christians are in the majority, many members have viewed their struggles as necessary to protect not only their ethnic rights but also their religion. Christian communities based in central Burma and the government-controlled parts of the ethnic states have focused on redressing social problems and encouraging personal development, somewhat along the lines of the self-actualization writers. Pastors and priests, church staff and motivated church members have worked together to organize English classes, youth leadership courses, drug rehabilitation programmes, free healthcare for the poor, and summer conferences that bring together people from various parts of the country. These activities have provided an alternative arena for the development of ideas and skills and have helped to create mutual understanding among people from different ethnic groups.

Foreign missionaries have been banned from living in Burma since the mid-1960s, but Protestant and Catholic teachers and development workers have continued to visit Burma, and a number of Burmese Christians have attended conferences and courses at religious institutions outside the country. As a result, they have been able to appeal for some financial assistance from abroad and to learn about the role of the Christian community in political movements and development programmes in other countries. Such links with the outside world have also made them feel less isolated. Some young Buddhists have observed with interest the successes of the Christians' social programmes, and there have been instances of interfaith cooperation on social welfare projects.

Exploitation of Muslims

Like the Christian community, the Muslim community is well aware of its minority status. The largest concentration of Muslims is in Northern Arakan State. Smaller Muslim populations are scattered throughout the cities, towns and rural areas of Burma, and mostly consist of the descendants of farmers, clerks and traders who came during the colonial period. While many Buddhists have Muslim friends, nationalist propaganda regarding the colonial period and the Muslim religion have been used to instil prejudice towards Muslims. Burmese have been taught to see Indians and Bengalis as having taken advantage of Burma's colonization by the British to make money and rise to positions of influence in the colonial government. At the same time, according to Islamic practice, non-Muslims who marry Muslims are expected to convert to Islam.

Throughout military rule in Burma, successive regimes have used the spectre of a Muslim takeover to whip up nationalist sentiment. In particular, when anti-regime tensions are running high, incidents of intolerable behaviour by Muslims, whether real or invented, always seem to pop up and are used to channel anger into communal conflicts.

In July 1988, pamphlets supposedly written by Muslims encouraging fellow Muslims to marry Burmese women suddenly appeared in Taunggyi and other towns where anti-military feelings were growing after the student demonstrations in Rangoon. As expected, Muslim–Buddhist conflicts broke out, and the shops and homes of Muslims were attacked and looted. Such pamphlets have shown up several times in Burma over the past ten years, including in October 1996 in Rangoon, when pamphlets appeared saying in part:

Burmese Citizens – Beware!

The Muslims living in Burma are attempting to expand their religion while destroying Buddhism in Burma by using the following ways:

1) Land: All the land in the country shall be owned by the Muslims.
2) Money: To organize Buddhists to become Muslims using the power of money.
3) Women: To organize Buddhist women to get married with Muslims using money and other ways.
4) Doctrine: To preach Muslim doctrine in every place.
5) State power: After successfully using these above methods and [the] majority of the people become Muslim, to take state power.[13]

Although many people realize that these pamphlets are intended to incite unrest, some people still fall for them every time, and the damage done leaves a legacy of bitterness.

The authorities have often prevented Muslims from building new mosques or even making repairs to historic mosques in some of the larger towns.[14] Muslims, like Christians, have also sometimes had to donate cash and labour to the building of Buddhist pagodas.

In more extreme cases, the military has sought to drive Muslims out of Burma, such as during the 1997 *tatmadaw* offensive against the Karen National Union. *Tatmadaw* soldiers looted and destroyed the mosques in many of the towns and villages where the KNU had previously operated.[15] One Muslim man was getting water from a well in front of a mosque in his village when *tatmadaw* soldiers came out of the mosque ripping up the Koran. He said, 'They threw the pieces of the Koran on the street. When the Muslim women on the street saw this, they cried and felt such pain. The soldiers said, "Don't cry! This is not a Muslim country. This is a Buddhist country! Go away!"'[16] In other cases Muslims were killed. As a result of the campaign to clear the area of Muslims, hundreds of Muslims fled with Karen villagers across the border into Thailand.

The Muslim Rohingya community in Northern Arakan State has been particularly targeted. A heavy-handed *tatmadaw* operation in the area drove 200,000 Rohingyas into Bangladesh in 1978, and a *tatmadaw-*

orchestrated forced-relocation programme in 1991 sent 250,000 Rohingyas over the border. Today, as many as 300,000 displaced Rohingya are living in Bangladesh, India and Pakistan, unable or unwilling to go back.[17] For those who remain, restrictions have tightened in recent years. Besides the fact that they are denied citizenship, Rohingya villagers in the northern districts of Rakhine State cannot travel even to another village without permission, seriously limiting their ability to work, get an education or even go to the doctor. Far worse, in some townships young Rohingya have effectively not been allowed to marry, because their marriage applications have not been processed. Those who marry unofficially can be arrested and jailed. Malnutrition is extremely high, and rice cannot be moved from one village to another without a permit. All these practices are meant to drive the Rohingya out of Burma permanently.

Among local Buddhist Rakhines and the Burmese population in general, there is little apparent sympathy for the Rohingyas' plight. The regime has been able to play off different populations against each other, and although those opposed to military rule know that they must be unified, they have often fallen victim to their own fears and prejudices. Among the exiled groups, a desire to keep the largely anti-Rohingya Arakanese organizations in their alliances led other groups to stay quiet for many years, although the policy has changed among some of the alliances in recent years. Notably, there are several Muslims from various areas of Burma in the NLD. They clearly hope that a democratic government would stop much of the discrimination they have experienced under military rule.

As much as the junta has promoted the Buddhist religion, even ethnic minority Buddhists are dissatisfied with the regime's explicitly Burman version of Buddhism. Mon and Shan monks have faced difficulties in distributing literature in their own languages, and in some cases they have been prohibited from taking Buddhist exams in their own languages. Shan people were furious when SLORC authorities took over the funeral arrangements for a famous Shan monk who died in Hsipaw in the mid-1990s. The entire ceremony was Burmanized, from the design of the structure holding the coffin to the way he was cremated. Likewise, when the regime restored a famous Shan temple in Hsipaw, the Shan-style roof was replaced with a Burmese-style one. Thus, the regime has attempted to impose a homogeneous culture that is both Buddhist and Burman, and while this policy has offended many, from members of other religions to members of other ethnic nationalities, they have found it difficult to unite in opposition.[18]

Fortune-telling and sympathetic magic

While Buddhism preaches the importance of realizing the imperma-
nence of all living things, many Burmese are attached to beliefs in the
power of spirits, the planets and magic to affect their present lives. Even
the most devout Burmese Buddhists do not necessarily deny the existence
of such forces, but insist that whether they exist or not is irrelevant in
the larger quest for enlightenment. Thus, the brother and sister spirits
whose shrine is on Mount Popa (described in Chapter 1) continue to be
propitiated in return for protection. Some of the most devoted followers
are military generals and especially their wives. This is because the pattern
of those in power removing potential rivals continues, and generals vying
for the top slots are in the most precarious positions of all.

Numerous books and magazines are devoted to fortune-telling and
astrology and sell well. Besides including stories of magical occurrences
and special powers, they feature in-depth coverage of horoscopes and
antidotes to the troubles that might befall the readers. The simplicity of
many of the *yadaya* – or cheating fate – techniques helps people feel they
can do something concrete to assert control over their lives. During the
1988 demonstrations, for instance, one mother had her sons eat bowls
of *mohingha*, a fish-and-noodle soup that was often served at funerals.
This was her own brand of cheating fate. She reasoned that if they ate
the funeral food before joining the demonstrations, they would not be
killed.

The SLORC and SPDC also apparently tried to thwart the rise of Aung
San Suu Kyi through astrological means. According to one person working
with the Education Ministry, in 1996 the regime reportedly changed the
rules for the beauty contests held at annual school sports competitions.
The officials were told to eliminate any girls whose astrological charts
predicted strong leadership potential, because this was associated with
Aung San Suu Kyi assuming power.

In March 1999, an apocryphal story about Lieutenant General Khin
Nyunt's test to predict Burma's political future was whispered from person to person in Rangoon. It went like this:

As rain fell during the recent full-moon day of the hottest and driest
month of the Burmese calendar, a story about Khin Nyunt started spreading. According to this story, Khin Nyunt climbed up to the top part of
the Shwedagon Pagoda at 4.00 a.m. He placed a lion made of mud and
a peacock made of wax at the top part of the pagoda, and vowed that the
peacock should dissolve and the lion get harder as a sign that he will

continue to rule the country. On the other hand, if Aung San Suu Kyi were going to rule the country, the lion would dissolve and the peacock would get harder. Many people thought the peacock would dissolve as the weather was very hot. But unexpectedly, it started raining around 11.00 a.m., and it lasted until the evening. Finally, the figure of the lion dissolved, while the peacock became harder.[19]

This story bolstered the spirits of the beleaguered opposition, but other tales seem to favour the regime. A 2007 story spoke of General Than Shwe's wife, Kyaing Kyaing, going to Shwedagon Pagoda in a wheelchair and circling the middle level of the pagoda, declaring, '*ma hsin bu, ma hsin bu, ma hsin bu*', meaning 'I/we won't step down, won't step down, won't step down'. I asked May Hlaing, the well-educated woman who told me this, whether it wasn't just a rumour. But she said assuredly, 'Some rumours are true.' Whether true or not, it reflects the understanding of Burmese citizens that General Than Shwe (and his wife) are determined to remain in power at all costs.

Because of the widespread belief in the potential efficacy of *yadaya*, people in Burma expect that the generals engage in such actions. As noted earlier, General Ne Win frequently turned to magic to strengthen his hold on power. Such tales, however, may also be part of 'whispering campaigns', where one side tries to derail the other by the use of rumours. This technique has been used by the authorities and people opposed to military rule, although there is no evidence that the NLD leadership has resorted to this. With facts always hard to come by, such stories spread quickly.

Choosing auspicious dates and numbers has been a subject of intense concern for the military regime and pro-democracy activists alike. According to one older male fortune-teller who takes his job quite seriously: 'The military officers think that it is better to act by calculating things according to astrology than doing things haphazardly.' He said they are right and the NLD should do the same. He thought that the NLD should use astrological calculations to determine when they should hold their meetings and undertake organizing trips, so that these would be successful. He said, 'If they have to face their enemy the SPDC, [they should calculate] what day and what time will be advantageous for them.' Although he thought that Aung San Suu Kyi herself did not consult astrologers, he was sure that others in the NLD did. He said that he certainly hoped so, because it could help them.

Moreover, the astrologer recommended that Aung San Suu Kyi should stay away from the number 8, which is not a lucky number. He said that the chances of success on an 8 date are very low. Instead she should counter the regime with 9 or 12. One prominent student activist said that a couple of fortune-tellers had also warned his group about the inauspiciousness of the number 8. Thus, if a political anniversary fell on an 8, his group dated its statement the day before or the day after.

Similarly, the exile community, and some activists inside Burma, tried to promote the idea of launching a new mass movement on '9/9/99', or 9 September 1999. Numerologically, this was an extremely auspicious date. The military regime was well prepared, however, and had posted military personnel in all public areas where people might gather. Up to five hundred activists, monks and NLD members were arrested or detained in the six weeks preceding 9/9/99. A few small protests broke out but were quickly dispersed.

In consultation with astrologers, first General Ne Win and later the SLORC chose 9 as their lucky number. Nine is also the special number of the *nats*, and thus is strongly associated with power. As a result, the regime at one point issued currency notes in denominations of 45 kyats and 90 kyats, which at least can be credited with keeping the population's maths skills up. The SLORC staged its coup on 18 September, with September being the ninth month, and the eighteenth also representing a nine, because $1 + 8 = 9$.

Likewise, the SLORC sought to guarantee that the National Convention would work in its favour by carefully putting delegates into groupings whose total numbers equalled nine. There were eighty-one NLD members plus eighteen other elected representatives from various parties. Each of these added up equals nine, and the two numbers added together ($81 + 18$) equal 99, which if added again equals 18, and $1 + 8 = 9$. Then there were 603 appointed representatives, $6 + 0 + 3 = 9$. The total number of delegates was 702, which again equals 9.

This was pointed out to me by a citizen-sleuth who revelled in uncovering the regime's magical activities. He also showed me the 1-kyat notes issued by the SLORC, which appear to have four 8s inside the numeral 1. When the bill is turned sideways, the 1 resembles a chair, which symbolizes ruling power. The meaning, he said, was that the regime had overcome the pro-democracy movement. Whether or not the regime really intended this is not the key issue. The point is that people are reading meanings into everything around them, and that the psychological battle for political ascendancy is a critical part of the struggle.

Many citizens suspect that the generals have the ability to effectively use *yadaya*, astrology and numerology to prolong their rule.[20] They may also offer such explanations when the regime seems particularly strong and they are feeling that to challenge it would be futile. Some astrologers have even suggested that one reason Burma has suffered so long under military rule is because an inappropriate date was selected for independence. U Nu's astrologers chose 4.20 a.m. on 4 January 1948. The problem was that the planet of Mars was ascendant during January, and Mars symbolizes the military. According to the fortune-teller, the astrologers couldn't ask the nationalist leaders to delay independence another month, so they had to select the least bad day in January. Again, the degree of truth of such statements is not really important. They are useful as a barometer for people's readings of the current balance of power and their confidence in their own ability to act.

Spirits of the dead

As hard as the regime tries to control the living, it must also confront the dead. In 1996, the SLORC ordered the digging up of Kyandaw cemetery in Rangoon, so it could sell the land for a large sum of money.[21] This large cemetery contained the graves of people from different faiths, and surviving family members were extremely upset about having to move the remains of their ancestors to a distant cemetery outside the city. For many it was also a big financial burden, because they had to pay the unearthing fee, transportation charges and then a reburial fee at the new site. For others, their religious beliefs forbade the exhumation.

Two years later, in June 1998, strange occurrences were reported at Myenigone junction, not far from the former cemetery. Myenigone was also where, on 21 June 1988, dozens of people were killed during an anti-government demonstration. Suddenly, on the tenth anniversary, a poltergeist was reported at the location. Plates and cups were said to have risen off tables in a tea shop, and televisions were levitating and smashing into each other in a nearby appliance store. One person even reported turning on a TV and seeing an image of blood. It was believed that the spirits of those killed in 1988 were coming back to haunt the regime.

Dismayed by this attack from an unexpected quarter, the Rangoon divisional commander hurried to the scene, where he read out an announcement telling the spirits that they had been released from their duties on earth and could move on. Such announcements are customarily read at funerals in Burma. People in the area held their own ceremonies, inviting monks to come and recite chants to drive away the spirits. While one such ceremony was taking place, it was said that donated juice bottles started moving and smashed into each other. Police and soldiers were sent to block off the area and disperse the huge crowd. In the state-sponsored *Kyemon* newspaper, an editorial accused political groups of spreading false rumours about poltergeists to stir up trouble.[22]

After a few days the situation calmed down, and the regime was able to breathe more easily again. It is exactly this kind of incident, however, which reminds the military that their hold on power is always tenuous and challenges will continue to appear, if not in the form of direct confrontations then through unexpected and even bizarre occurrences. For, ultimately, the battle to shift the balance of power in Burma is a psychological one. When the supporters of democracy feel that powerful forces are aligned with them, they may shake off their fear and act, but because psychic aspects play such a key role, nobody can predict when.

13 | The internationalization of Burma's politics

The international community's various dealings with Burma have been as politicized and complex as Burma's internal dynamics. After 1988, both the regime and the pro-democracy movement looked abroad for support and legitimacy. The regime sought military aid, foreign investment and membership in regional groupings, while Aung San Suu Kyi and other democracy activists urged the international community to do more to bring about a resolution of Burma's political crisis. Several kinds of international actors have interacted with Burmese political forces, including foreign governments and international political bodies, foreign companies, international NGOs and Burmese exiles and Burma support groups. This chapter considers the policies of various governments and other actors towards Burma and some of the debates that have arisen about foreign involvement in Burma.

Neighbouring countries' relations with Burma

While the military regime, the pro-democracy groups and the ethnic nationalist organizations looked to other governments for support, foreign governments adopted policies towards Burma which reflected a mix of self-interest, pragmatism and moral imperatives. In the case of Burma's neighbouring countries, policies changed dramatically as new opportunities emerged in Burma.

Thus, in the mid-1960s and 1970s, China strongly supported the Communist Party of Burma, but in the 1990s the Beijing government became the regime's strongest ally. After the 1988 coup, Burma's military junta was ostracized by most governments, with many initially refusing to recognize the SLORC. The generals in Rangoon were, however, able to turn to China for critical military support. Between 1990 and 1997, China furnished as much as 3 billion dollars' worth of military equipment to the *tatmadaw*.[1] Besides fighter aircraft, tanks and artillery, China sold Burma radar, signals intelligence equipment and electronic warfare equipment.[2] The Chinese armed forces also provided training for Burma's armed forces. Although some of the Chinese equipment was of poor quality and malfunctioned, the *tatmadaw* was able to boost its capacity significantly.

China assisted Burma's military in return for access to intelligence information. China was eager to keep an eye on India's military activities as well as to monitor shipping in the Indian Ocean and through the Straits of Malacca.[3] China also looked to Burma as a market for Chinese goods and an important trade route to the Indian subcontinent and the Indian Ocean. As a result, the Chinese invested in the development of ports, roads, bridges and factories in Burma.[4] Chinese consumer goods flooded Burma's markets, and as opportunities for making money expanded, the presence of Chinese in northern Burma grew rapidly, particularly in Mandalay and other towns.[5] Chinese companies from Yunnan Province have also been active in logging and mining in northern Burma. In the early 2000s, China's interests in Burma expanded to include oil and gas exploration and the planned development of pipelines to bring Burmese and Middle Eastern oil and natural gas up through Burma to landlocked south-western China.[6]

China has also been an important ally for Burma in international forums such as the United Nations, because it too opposes foreign demands to improve domestic human rights records. Nevertheless, China has its concerns with the regime as well. First, China wants to see stability along the China–Burma border and therefore would like to see the relations between the ethnic resistance groups in northern Burma and the regime improve. They are concerned that the ceasefires could break down and fighting could resume, which would have spillover effects for China. Second, the Chinese government is frustrated with the regime's gross economic mismanagement, which adversely affects Chinese business interests in the country. China sees economic development in Burma as key to raising prosperity in south-western China. Third, the Chinese government has been very concerned about the amount of heroin coming from Burma. Not only have drug addiction rates increased, but because the heroin addicts frequently share needles, HIV/AIDS infections have also spread.[7] The United Wa State Army, one of the main trafficking groups, came under pressure from China as well as the regime and banned the production of opium by farmers in its territory in 2005. Nevertheless, heroin trafficking continues to a lesser degree, as does the trafficking of amphetamines.[8]

Despite the Chinese government's concerns with the Burmese regime, Chinese leaders have perceived continued military rule as better than having a pro-West democratic government in control. They see Aung San Suu Kyi, the NLD and other democracy activists as closely linked to the USA in particular, and worry that China would lose influence if these groups came to power. In addition, China worries that a civilian government wouldn't be able to maintain political stability in Burma.

As much as the generals in Rangoon relied on support from China, they also recognized that such dependence was dangerous and did not sit well with the domestic population. As a result, the regime sought to improve ties with other governments in the region which were eager to contain China's spreading influence.

Fortuitously, from the regime's perspective, India re-evaluated its policy towards Burma in the mid-1990s and decided that it needed to improve relations with the regime. Previously, the Indian government had hoped that the democracy movement would succeed and had welcomed democracy activists who fled from Burma in the 1988–90 period. Indian leaders decided, however, that the regime was firmly entrenched and that India had other important interests it needed to pursue in Burma. First, the Indian government was very eager to put an end to the insurgency in north-east India, where armed resistance groups, some of whom had received arms and training from China in the past, were demanding an end to Indian rule.[9] India tried to end the civil war both by improving the economies of the north-eastern states and by weakening the strength of the separatist armies, many of which had sanctuaries and training camps in Burma. The Indian government needed the cooperation of the Burmese military to drive them out. Second, India was worried about China's growing influence in Burma and did not want Burma to become a client state of its arch-rival in the region. Third, as India began promoting the growth of private industry in India, the government adopted a new 'Look East' policy to expand trade with Burma and the rest of South-East Asia.

To improve relations with the Burmese regime, India began selling military equipment to the *tatmadaw*, including maritime surveillance aircraft, artillery guns and tanks. It also financed infrastructure projects that could facilitate trade and periodically shared intelligence and carried out joint operations with the Burma Army along its common border.

Since the discovery of natural gas and oil in western Burma and its territorial waters, India has been eager to purchase energy from Burma and signed a gas and oil exploration contract with the regime in 2007. In 2008, India signed two deals with the military regime to build hydropower dams along western Burma's Chindwin river to supply electricity to north-eastern India.[10]

While India has allowed the pro-democracy activists who had sought refuge in the north-east and in Delhi to remain, the government no longer publicly criticizes the regime. Nevertheless, some Indian politicians and journalists have remained outspoken in their support for the Burmese democracy movement. This is because of their ideological commitment to democracy as well as the historical links that were forged with General Aung San and other Burmese leaders during their respective national struggles. Good relations continued throughout the period of parliamentary rule in Burma, and in the early 1960s Aung San Suu Kyi attended high school in New Delhi when her mother was the Burmese ambassador to India.

The Burmese regime has shown itself to be quite adept at playing India and China off against each other, just as it plays off different groups within the country against each other. The generals have been able to take advantage of China and India's competing interests to obtain economic benefits, as well as military and political support, from both.

Like India, Thailand began reconfiguring its policy towards Burma in the mid-1990s. In the past, the Thai military quietly supported the armed ethnic nationalist groups controlling virtually all of the Burmese side of the Thai–Burma border. This was part of a cold war strategy to maintain a buffer zone that would make it more difficult for communists from China, Burma and Thailand to link up. But in the early 1990s, the communist threat faded, and ethnic resistance groups began losing ground to the far larger and better-equipped *tatmadaw*. With more *tatmadaw* troops along the border, the Thai Army was worried about *tatmadaw* incursions into Thai territory. Very little of the Thai–Burma border had been jointly demarcated, and the actual location of the borderline was in dispute in several areas. Taking a pragmatic view, and also lured by logging, fishing and other investment opportunities in Burma, Thailand's generals began to improve relations with the Burmese junta. They also cooperated in pressuring some of the ethnic nationalist armies to make ceasefire agreements with the Rangoon regime. As a result, the New Mon State Party, which depended on access to Thailand for supplies, finally agreed to a ceasefire in 1995.

Meanwhile, businessmen from Thailand were also eager to take advantage of trade and investment opportunities in resource-rich Burma and encouraged the Thai government to facilitate this. Thai governments found themselves having to balance a concern about the regime's repressive behaviour, which often resulted in refugee flows into Thailand, and the Thai business community's calls for better relations with the military regime. Such conflicts were apparent in the Thai government's handling of the Burmese embassy takeover in Bangkok in October 1999 and its reaction to the Burmese regime's subsequent unilateral closure of the Thai–Burma border. The student activists who took over the embassy told the media that they had undertaken such a drastic action only to refocus the world's attention on Burma and to demand a political dialogue between the military regime and the NLD. The Thai deputy foreign minister, M. R. Sukhumbhand Paribatra, offered himself in exchange for the hostages and was able to persuade the hostage-takers to get on a Thai military helicopter with him and to take them to a Karen-controlled area just inside Burma. Everything was quickly resolved, without any bloodshed. With regard to the hostage-takers, the Thai interior minister, Sanan Kachornprasart, told the press: 'We don't consider them to be terrorists. They are student activists who fight for democracy.'[11]

From the Thai government's perspective, they had handled the situation well, but the generals in Rangoon were outraged that the hostage-takers had been viewed sympathetically and had escaped arrest. The regime promptly revoked all Thai fishing concessions in Burmese waters and shut the border to trade. Thai businessmen demanded that the Thai government do something. Soon after, the Thai government put pressure on Burmese political activists living in Thailand to register with the United Nations High Commission for Refugees and to agree to be resettled in a third country as soon as possible. Then they began deporting hundreds of illegal Burmese migrant workers. On 23 November 1999, the Thai foreign minister flew to Rangoon to smooth relations with Burmese officials. The next day, the Burmese regime reopened the border to trade.

In the late 1990s, the Burmese regime stopped construction of the Mae Sot–Myawaddy 'Friendship Bridge' linking Thailand and Burma for almost two years until it exacted concessions from the Thai government.[12] It sought more pressure on the KNU and Burmese dissidents operating out of Thailand. Even though the full cost of the bridge construction was borne by the Thais, the regime assumed it could count on Thai businessmen to pressure the Thai government to do whatever was necessary to keep the construction on track. Of course, by delaying such projects, the regime sacrificed much-needed income too, but eliminating its political opposition, rather than improving the economy, was the regime's top priority.

In the mid- to late 1990s, the regime also used various tactics to try to reduce the refugee population along the Thai–Burma border by encouraging the Democratic Karen Buddhist Army (DKBA) to burn down refugee camps in Thailand.[13] The camps were perceived as a support to the KNU because many KNU families lived there. In addition, their existence served as evidence that Burma was not as peaceful as the regime claimed. The regime's hope was that, by burning down the camps, the Thais might feel that the best way to eliminate the border incursions would be to repatriate the refugees, and that the refugees would feel they were no worse off at home. The policy worked to a certain degree. Some refugees went back and Thai military units repatriated a few groups of refugees. Other refugees were moved to camps farther away from the border, where they would be safer from attack.

Following the election of one of Thailand's wealthiest businessmen, Thaksin Shinawatra, as prime minister in 2001, Thai policy focused far more on promoting economic interests in Burma. Shin Corp, founded by Thaksin, invested in telecommunications projects together with companies close to the regime, while the Thai and Burmese governments jointly developed plans to build hydroelectric dams on the Salween river which could produce electricity for Thailand. The Yadana and Yetagun pipelines, which were constructed in the late 1990s, were already bringing gas from Burma's Gulf of Martaban, and were seen by the Thai government as critical in fuelling the country's growing economy.

Successive Thai governments have continued to prioritize their energy interests in making policy on Burma. Nevertheless, relations between Thai and Burmese leaders have never been particularly warm. Thai history textbooks continue to emphasize past Burmese military conquests of Thailand, suggesting that Burma remains a threat to Thailand's national integrity. As if to reinforce such perceptions, the Burmese authorities erected statues of one of Burma's great empire-building kings, Bayinnaung, at two border points with Thailand. In the mid-1500s, King Bayinnaung invaded Thai territory (then known as Siam), conquering the capital and bringing back loot and war captives. The message of these statues appears to be 'Don't think we couldn't do it again'.

Thailand has hedged its bets by allowing members of the democracy movement and ethnic resistance groups to maintain a low profile in the country, although they have generally not been permitted to become legal foreign residents or Thai citizens.

Bangladesh, like other neighbouring countries, has found relations with Burma challenging. The Bangladeshi government has been extremely frustrated by the Burmese regime's refusal to take back all the Rohingya refugees and its continued harsh policies towards the Rohingya in Burma, which cause yet more Rohingya to flee to Bangladesh. Yet Bangladesh is desperate to improve its economy, so the Bangladeshi government has sought to expand trade with Burma. In November 2008, a dispute over the maritime boundary between the two countries came to a head when Burmese warships accompanying a gas exploration ship were confronted by Bangladeshi warships.[14] Both retreated, but Burma vowed to continue the exploration work in the future.

Burma's generals have insisted that no other countries have the right to interfere in Burma's domestic affairs, but they have been unwilling to admit the extent to which their policy decisions have had serious implications for their neighbours. The refugee crisis is just one example. Although most of the funding for the refugees' food and medicine is provided by outside sources, Burma's neighbouring countries, especially impoverished Bangladesh, still suffer a heavy burden. Not only do they have to provide security, but the local population is also often resentful of the refugees' presence and their use of local resources.

The failure or inability of the regime to eradicate drug production has had particularly profound consequences for Burma's neighbours. In the mid-2000s, up to 900 million amphetamine pills produced in Burma were entering Thailand annually.[15] Meanwhile, addiction to Burmese heroin expanded rapidly in the Indian border state of Manipur, which developed one of the highest rates of HIV infection in India.

Diseases were not stopped by national borders either. As the report *The Gathering Storm* documents, diseases such as filariasis (also known as elephantiasis), malaria and tuberculosis have all been inadvertently reintroduced or spread by Burmese refugees and migrant workers.[16]

South-East Asian and ASEAN relations with Burma

Singapore and Malaysia initially showed a great interest in working together with the SLORC. In the 1990s, Singapore supplied Burma's military with weapons, ammunition, training and probably the communications equipment that enabled the regime to increase its monitoring capabilities over phone, fax and data transmissions.[17] Singapore also became one of Burma's largest foreign investors, with most of its money channelled into the development of the tourism industry. Over the years, however, leaders in both Singapore and Malaysia have been frustrated by the regime's unwillingness to make even small political concessions and its gross economic mismanagement, which has made it difficult for their companies to do business in Burma.

Before Suharto's fall in 1998, Indonesia was also an important supporter of Burma's generals. The SLORC and SPDC regimes looked to Indonesia as a model of how a military-backed government could maintain control at home while also developing good relations with international financial institutions and foreign governments. Since the fall of Suharto, however, democratic politicians in Indonesia have called for the restoration of democracy in Burma.[18]

Until the mid-1990s, Burmese leaders expressed no interest in joining ASEAN. But with membership promising to lead to increased investment and a degree of protection from Western condemnation over its refusal to democratize, the SLORC began to lobby for inclusion. Although some ASEAN nations expressed concern about Burma's pariah status, they were eager to lessen China's influence over Burma. Likewise, some members opposed the West's confrontational stance towards Burma and believed they could persuade the regime to act more moderately through a policy of political and economic engagement.

Despite calls by Aung San Suu Kyi and some Western governments for ASEAN not to grant Burma full membership, Burma became a member in 1997. The Burmese regime had a song written to commemorate its inclusion in the association, and for a time the government-sponsored website, at www.myanmar.com, was called the Myanmar–ASEAN website.

Nevertheless, ASEAN suffered. The European Union (EU) refused to allow Burma to participate fully in annual EU–ASEAN meetings until the Burmese regime showed improvements in human rights and made political concessions.[19] In the late 1990s, this resulted in a number of joint meetings being postponed and much time spent on negotiations for how to include Burma in joint meetings without according it the same status as other participants. For a time, Burmese delegates were not able to participate in any joint meetings held in Europe because of the EU's visa ban on regime officials. The visa ban on the Burmese foreign minister was lifted for the 2006 Asia–Europe (ASEM) meeting, however, so that EU officials could interact with the Burmese foreign minister.

In addition, the Burmese generals refused to improve their behaviour. Burma's intransigence forced ASEAN to consider the merit of its founding principle of non-interference in other members' domestic affairs. In 1998, Thai foreign minister Surin Pitsuwan proposed a new policy of 'flexible engagement', meaning that ASEAN should be able to have frank discussions about domestic issues that have implications for other countries in the association.[20] The Philippines' foreign minister, Domingo Siazon, publicly urged the junta and the opposition to begin a political dialogue without preconditions.[21] Nevertheless, other members of ASEAN did not support the proposed 'flexible engagement' policy, and for the next few years the Asian economic crisis led ASEAN member countries to focus more on their problems at home than on regional policy issues.

According to ASEAN's system of rotating the chairmanship, Burma was supposed to take the position in 2006. In 2005, however, the USA and the EU threatened not to attend any ASEAN meetings hosted by Burma, including the ASEM meeting. The United States also said it might withhold funding to several development projects in the region if Burma took the chair. ASEAN was divided on the issue, however; some members made public their hopes that the Burmese regime would decide by itself to give up the chair. The regime at first remained defiant, but finally backed down.

After the brutal crackdown on the 2007 monks' demonstrations, ASEAN issued a statement expressing its 'revulsion' at what had happened.[22] This was the strongest statement ASEAN had ever issued on Burma. The possibility of punitive action against Burma, however, was not considered. When ASEAN drew up its charter in 2007, it decided to establish a human rights body, but in the end it was agreed that no mechanism would be created to punish member governments that violate human rights.

In 2004, interested MPs in various ASEAN countries joined together to establish the ASEAN Inter-Parliamentary Myanmar Caucus. The caucus has urged ASEAN leaders to push for genuine political reform in Burma. Given that many countries in ASEAN are not democracies, however, or are not fully democratized, the leaders of many ASEAN countries are more interested in seeing an easing of the political conflict in Burma than democracy per se.

Other Asian countries' relations with Burma

Japan has tried to persuade the regime to change its ways by offering increased development assistance in return for the regime taking specific actions. The regime has sometimes responded positively to Japan's offers, but only to the extent that it has suited them. Although Aung San Suu Kyi's release in 1995 appears to have been related to Japanese diplomatic efforts, the generals did not hesitate to put her back under house arrest once she became a threat to them.

Recognizing the importance of Japanese support, Aung San Suu Kyi tried to reach out to the Japanese public through a weekly column for the *Mainichi* newspaper in 1995 and 1996. Entitled 'Letters from Burma', it described the leading members, activities and policies of the NLD and the kinds of repression her party and ordinary people face under military rule.[23]

While Aung San Suu Kyi has the sympathy of many Japanese, the

Japanese business community has continued to lobby hard for improved relations with Burma's generals. Although the Japanese government would like to see democracy restored in Burma, Japanese officials are also worried that if they do not maintain good relations with the military regime, they will lose political and economic access to Burma. As a result, Japan has cancelled some of Burma's debt and continued to offer overseas development assistance to Burma, reducing the amount only slightly after the Japanese journalist Kenji Nagai was killed by a Burma Army soldier during the September 2007 demonstrations.

Burma is one of the few countries in the world that currently has good relations with both North and South Korea. South Korea's Daewoo International Corporation has teamed up with the regime's Ministry of Gas and Energy to engage in gas exploration in the Bay of Bengal. Meanwhile, the SPDC has been quietly purchasing weapons from North Korea for several years and officially restored relations in 2007.[24] Burma had cut off diplomatic relations with Pyongyang in 1983, after North Korean agents set off a bomb in Rangoon which killed eighteen visiting South Korean officials, including four cabinet members.

Burma has increasingly looked to Russia for weapons purchases in recent years. It has also sought to build a nuclear reactor with assistance from Russia and perhaps North Korea.[25] Russia has also been helpful to the regime by consistently opposing any UN Security Council action on Burma.

Finally, the regime has developed closer relations with the Pakistani military and, since 1989, has purchased guns and ammunition from Pakistan on several occasions.[26]

Western countries' relationships with Burma

In the 1990s and early 2000s, the United States government took the most hardline stance against Burma's generals. In part, this has been because the USA has no direct strategic interests in Burma, nor have many American corporations invested there. After the SLORC's crackdown in 1988, the United States expressed its disapproval by refusing to post an ambassador to Burma, and since then a lower-ranking chargé d'affaires has run the American embassy in Rangoon. Following Aung San Suu Kyi and the NLD's call for foreign businesses to stay out of Burma until democracy was restored, in 1997 the US Congress passed a bill forbidding any new investment by American companies. After the Depayin Massacre in 2003, Congress passed a bill banning imports from Burma. The United States also imposed a visa ban on top regime officials and their family members and, over time, expanded the list to include leading USDA officials and businessmen with close ties to the regime. In response to the 2007 crackdown, Congress passed a law blocking the import of all jewellery made from Burmese jade and rubies. This targeted sanction was aimed primarily at the regime and businesses close to the regime. The USA has also sought to rally other countries to take more coordinated action on Burma, and Canada has imposed many of the same economic sanctions that the USA has.

At the same time, the USA has provided funding for projects intended to build the capacity of democracy activists and Burmese journalists and has given financial support for education, health and humanitarian assistance inside Burma and along its borders.[27] In 2008, the USA provided an additional $18 million in assistance for Cyclone Nargis survivors via UN programmes and international NGOs.

The European Union has adopted a common position on Burma, which includes an arms embargo, a visa ban on senior military officers, their families and business people who work closely with them, and a ban on European companies investing in Burmese state-owned companies. The common position does not allow any bilateral assistance to Burma except for humanitarian and social development programmes, with the money for such programmes preferably channelled through local organizations. The EU also provides funding for humanitarian assistance for Burmese refugees. Some EU members have also funded democracy promotion, media and capacity-building programmes, primarily for Burmese organizations in exile. After the 2007 crackdown, the EU banned the import of logs, minerals and gems from Burma and prohibited European investment in Burmese companies engaged in these businesses.

The British government feels a particular responsibility to Burma, having colonized the country in the 1800s, and because Aung San Suu Kyi lived in England for many years with her British husband, Michael Aris. Along with the Burma Campaign UK, the British government encouraged Premier Oil to withdraw from Burma, which it did in 2002.[28]

When making policy towards Burma, Australia and New Zealand have tried to balance their position as Western-style liberal democracies and as geographically Asian countries. They have spoken out in support of the democracy movement and do not sell weapons to Burma, but they have been reluctant to impose economic sanctions. Over time, however, the Australian and New Zealand governments have all imposed more restrictions on Burma. Following the 2007 demonstrations, Australia refused to accept a general as the Burmese ambassador to Australia.

Since the mid-1990s, Western embassy officials, particularly American and British, have maintained regular contact with top NLD leaders and sent representatives to NLD functions. The staff of most Asian embassies, on the other hand, have generally refrained from attending NLD events, not wanting to irritate the regime.

The sanctions debate

While sanctions have been an effective tool in helping bring about change in some countries, they have not led to change in others. In the case of Burma there has been a heated debate about their value, even among people who desperately want to see change in the country.

There have been two main arguments against sanctions. The first is that they haven't worked, since many countries are not following them but are investing heavily in Burma instead. As a result, the countries that impose sanctions also lose their leverage over the regime. The second argument is that blanket sanctions, such as import bans, hurt ordinary people more than the regime. When ordinary people lose their jobs in export factories, they may not have other jobs to turn to. The families of the top authorities, on the other hand, have plenty of other sources of income.

In addition, banning Western companies from entering Burma has been criticized as mistaken on the grounds that Western companies are more likely to treat their employees well and that a Western business presence will help stimulate good business practices in Burma. By also banning Burmese companies from exporting to certain countries, it is more difficult for a middle class to develop in Burma.

Others have argued that the regime responds only to pressure, and that the sanctions have had some impact on the regime. If the regime didn't care about the sanctions, why do the top generals repeatedly talk about how they want them lifted? Moreover, the NLD leadership has called for such measures, and it is important to respect their policy recommendations, since they were elected by the people. In any negotiations with the regime, the sanctions serve as a significant bargaining chip for the NLD, which could ask the international community to remove them in return for concessions from the regime. Furthermore, the sanctions indicate to the Burmese people that people in other countries will not condone the regime's use of violence against its citizens. Supporters of sanctions also argue that it is the regime's gross economic mismanagement which is preventing the development of a middle class far more than the sanctions. Some also question whether Western corporations would really do a better job of respecting Burmese workers' rights, given that Unocal and Total did nothing to stop the *tatmadaw*'s use of forced labour in relation to the construction of the Yadana gas pipeline.[29]

Increasingly there is agreement among those who support sanctions that targeted sanctions are likely to be more effective and less punitive to the society as a whole. As a result, several Western countries have adopted sanctions that are directed only at the military government's top officials, their families and the business people who have close relations with the regime.

Nevertheless, it is increasingly clear that sanctions alone will not bring about a change in Burma, both because the regime has other supporters and because the regime is determined to maintain its hold on power.

Attempting to persuade the generals while working with them has also proven ineffective when delinked from any forms of pressure. The regime responds only when the international community adopts a coordinated approach that combines pressure and persuasion. The top generals need to feel that they have no other choice, but also that following the policy prescription will not lead to the regime's demise. For instance, the regime has been pressured into allowing UN envoys to enter the country and even agreed to appoint a liaison minister to meet with Aung San Suu Kyi, but no genuine dialogue ever took place. Without strong and sustained pressure, it seems likely that any concessions the regime makes to the international community will be minimal and often reversible.

The UN and Burma

Various UN bodies and agencies have attempted a variety of approaches in dealing with the regime, depending on their mandates.

In order to stop or at least reduce human rights abuses, the Human Rights Council has appointed a series of special rapporteurs to document human rights abuses in Burma, with the intention of shaming the regime into better behaviour. The regime often bars special rapporteurs from entry for months or even years at a time, however. The Human Rights Council and the General Assembly have passed annual resolutions condemning the regime's policies of repression and urging it to begin a dialogue with all stakeholders, but their calls have gone unheeded.

UN secretary-generals have tried to use their good offices to bring about political reform. In 1998, the United Nations' Secretariat sent a high-level representative to Burma to float the idea of providing $1 billion worth of World Bank aid to Burma if the regime would enter into a dialogue with the NLD, but the generals said no.[30]

The UN secretary-generals appointed two special envoys, first Razali Ismail, a Malaysian diplomat, and then Ibrahim Gambari, a former foreign minister of Nigeria, to make regular trips to Burma to meet with the SPDC leadership and Aung San Suu Kyi to try to facilitate a dialogue process. Over time, both found the regime unwilling to work seriously with them or to negotiate with the opposition.

Within the Security Council, there has been an ongoing debate over whether the crisis in Burma falls within the UN Security Council's mandate, which is to consider threats to international peace. The debate has been shaped by differing understandings of the mandate as well as the particular interests of some of the Security Council's permanent members. In 2005, two Nobel Peace Prize winners, Bishop Desmond Tutu and Vaclav Havel, commissioned a report called *Threat to the Peace*. The report argued that the Security Council should consider the case of Burma because other countries with similar problems had been addressed by the Council in the past. China and Russia have repeatedly insisted, however, that Burma's problems are its internal affairs and shouldn't be considered by the Security Council.

In January 2007, the USA proposed a Security Council resolution on Burma calling for the military regime to release all political prisoners, including Aung San Suu Kyi, stop attacks on ethnic groups, and speed up the transition to democracy. The resolution did not pass, as it was vetoed by China and Russia. After the 2007 crackdown on the monks, the Security Council issued two presidential statements on Burma, which are not binding. The statements called for the release of political prisoners and the relaxing of Aung San Suu Kyi's conditions of detention. On 1 May 2008, the Security Council issued another Presidential Statement calling on the regime to make the 2008 referendum and the 2010 election process inclusive and credible. In other words, Aung San Suu Kyi, the NLD and other opposition political parties should be able to participate and the campaigning, voting and vote-counting should be undertaken in a legitimate way. Nevertheless, the regime went ahead with the referendum later that month with widespread complaints about voter intimidation and vote-rigging.

Because it wants to be seen as a responsible actor on the global scene, China has in some cases urged the regime to take certain actions behind the scenes.[31] The generals have responded in instances when they are worried that the Security Council or other international actors might take harsher actions if it does not make some concessions.

The International Labour Organization (ILO), which is a member of the UN family and consists of labour and business representatives as well as government representatives, has tried to use a combination of pressure and persuasion with the regime. By threatening Burma with sanctions from its members, while also explaining to the regime how bad it looked to be using forced labour in the twenty-first century, the ILO was able to convince the regime to issue orders banning the practice. The use of forced labour has been greatly reduced in central Burma, although as of 2008 it is still widely used in parts of the ethnic states, particularly in conflict areas.

Several UN agencies work in Burma to address humanitarian problems and carry out development work to the extent that they can. For instance, UNICEF has supplied vaccines and helped expand immunization coverage to the remote areas. The World Food Programme has provided food to Rohingya families in Arakan State and to Cyclone Nargis survivors. And UNDP has introduced poverty-alleviation programmes which have had some benefits for rural communities. The UN agencies have been eager to expand their work, which they see as making a real difference in people's lives. As a result, they seek to create a good working relationship with the authorities. This has consisted of trying to persuade ministry officials and local authorities of the value of their programmes as well as generally keeping quiet in public about the regime's abuses. Some UN agency personnel have tried to push the boundaries, while others have felt that they must largely comply with the regime's demands and restrictions in order to maintain access.

The International Committee of the Red Cross (ICRC), which is linked to the UN but operates independently, pulled out of Burma in 1995 because the regime would not allow ICRC representatives to visit political detainees, but returned to the country in 1999 after negotiating a new agreement. The ICRC was able to visit prisons freely until 2005, when the regime said its personnel would have to be accompanied by USDA members, a condition the ICRC could not accept. In 2006, the regime stopped the ICRC from providing humanitarian assistance in Burma's eastern ethnic states.

The media and international campaigns

The regime's primary method of dealing with foreign journalists is to deny them visas. If the international community doesn't know what's going on in Burma, it will not take an interest and the regime will be free to act as it pleases. The regime tends to let journalists in only for specific regime-organized events, with visas valid only for a few days. A number of journalists have managed to get into Burma on tourist visas, however, and have been able to meet a wide range of people.

In 1997 and 1998, representatives of the military regime worked with two US consulting firms, Jefferson Waterman International and Bain and Associates, to improve their image abroad. The firms sought to get stories favourable to the regime placed in the press and helped organize journalists' visits to Burma to see the regime's achievements.[32] The focus was on repealing sanctions and repudiating the regime's image as a 'narco-state'.

The authorities have made great efforts to cut off Aung San Suu Kyi's access to the media. When she was first released from house arrest in 1995, the regime allowed foreign journalists to interview her, but they soon regretted it because, through the media, she became far better known internationally. When possible, Aung San Suu Kyi has tried to maintain contact with the international community by producing written statements and videotaped addresses which have been secretly taken out of Burma and presented at conferences and events abroad. During periods of house arrest, her phone line has been cut and she hasn't been able to send out statements. A notable exception was when UN Special Envoy Gambari met with her in November 2007 and took out her statement calling for the regime to begin a genuine dialogue with her about political reform.

Foreign news agencies and the Burmese exile media have increasingly relied on local Burmese stringers to write about events in Burma. At great risk to themselves, stringers have covered stories relating to the 2007 demonstrations, the problems that emerged during the cyclone relief and reconstruction, and various abuses by local authorities. Some Burmese bloggers inside and outside the country have also taken it upon themselves to report on what is going on in Burma, as did many ordinary citizens during the 2007 demonstrations and crackdown.

As discussed in Chapter 10, the exile media have done a great deal to bring news to people inside Burma. Some exile media organizations have also sought to reach an international audience by producing their news in English. *The Irrawaddy*, for instance, produces a monthly magazine in English as well as daily articles online in English and Burmese. The low cost of producing news online has also allowed smaller ethnic minority media groups to get out news about events in their areas of Burma.

Meanwhile political activists in particular put themselves at great risk if they talk to the international press. In 2008, Zarganar, the satirist and social activist, ended up in prison for criticizing the regime's slow response to Cyclone Nargis in interviews with the foreign media. Burmese and foreign activists have periodically felt the need to resort to dramatic gestures to raise international awareness. In 1989 and 1990, two sets of Burmese student activists staged plane hijackings, with the main demand being that the press publicize the situation in Burma. One plane came down in Bangkok and one in Calcutta. In both cases, no one was hurt and some of the passengers sympathized with the hijackers in the end. Both incidents received widespread coverage. In 1999, another group of Burmese students took over the Burmese embassy in Bangkok, which again received much international coverage.

Foreign activists have tried to gain media attention for Burma by getting themselves arrested in the country. A group of eighteen activists handed out pamphlets on the tenth anniversary of the 1988 uprising in Rangoon, and were held for six days before they were deported. When they returned to Bangkok, they were greeted by throngs of journalists and their story was picked up around the world. Similarly, James Mawdsley, a British citizen, made three trips into Burma during which he was arrested for distributing anti-government literature. In August 1999, he was sentenced to seventeen years in prison and served fourteen months before being released. James Mawdsley's case drew a great deal of attention to himself and Burma, and he wrote a book about his experiences as well.

Meanwhile, Burmese activists and politicians in exile, in coordination with Burma campaign groups in various countries, have sought to raise awareness and influence policy on Burma. In particular, they have pressured multinational corporations to withdraw their investments and pushed governments to adopt sanctions. Relying heavily on e-mail and the Internet to network and distribute information, the US-based Free Burma Coalition expanded to over one hundred chapters in 1996. Pepsi, Levi-Strauss, Heineken and several other companies pulled out of Burma, in part because of activists' pressure in the USA and elsewhere.

Responding to Aung San Suu Kyi's call for a tourist boycott of the regime-sponsored 'Visit Myanmar Year' in 1996/97, the Free Burma movement launched a worldwide campaign to stop travel agencies offering package tours to Burma and to urge tourists to stay away. The campaign significantly reduced tourist arrivals and embarrassed the regime. The generals had launched Visit Myanmar Year not only to make money but also to increase their acceptability at home and abroad.[33]

It should be noted that the issue of whether tourists should visit Burma or not has been controversial. Those who support tourists going argue that tourists can learn about the situation in Burma first hand and they can help the Burmese people financially by using their services and supporting their businesses. Those opposed say that the regime benefits monetarily from the taxes on hotels where tourists stay, that many abuses have taken place in relation to the development of the tourist industry, and that mass tourists, at least, will not have a chance to see the real Burma.

In the early 2000s, the US Campaign for Burma and the Euro-Burma Network of campaign groups focused on pushing for Security Council action on Burma. In the 1990s, no one expected the Security Council to take up Burma, but in 2007 Burma was on the agenda more than once, in part because of these groups' efforts.

The US Campaign for Burma has been particularly creative in how it has raised awareness of the situation in Burma. In 2007 and 2008, the campaigners urged people to put themselves under house arrest for twenty-four hours during the weekend before Aung San Suu Kyi's birthday. During this period, those under voluntary arrest should invite family and friends over to learn more about Burma, to write letters to the US government and the UN urging them to take action on Burma, and to raise money for the US Campaign for Burma's lobbying work. They also worked with American celebrities to make short videos on YouTube to educate young people in particular about the crisis in Burma.

Meanwhile, the Burmese border-based resistance organizations, which included elected parliamentarians, NLD members, student activists and ethnic nationalists, served as conduits for information in and out of the country. Besides trying to get reports about human rights abuses and political developments out to the international community, members of the border-based organizations also worked to get news about global standards on human rights and strategies for resistance into the country. Operating out of cramped offices in border towns and capital cities in Burma's neighbouring countries, Burman and ethnic minority activists participated in developing international campaigns and cultivated links with student, professional and religious groups around the world. Through lobbying trips to the United Nations and foreign capitals and speeches at international human rights conferences, they informed a wider audience about the crisis in Burma and broadened their own political understandings.

As a result of journalists', activists' and citizen reporters' efforts, and their clever use of new technologies such as cell phones, digital cameras, CDs and the Internet, there is far more international awareness about Burma today than there was twenty years ago. Still, Burma has to compete for attention with a number of other countries that are also in crisis, and it is rarely the first priority.

Foreign assistance to Burma

Along with the debate about sanctions, there has been a vigorous debate about foreign assistance.[34] What kinds of foreign assistance should be provided inside Burma and how? Is it possible to provide assistance in a way that won't benefit the regime? Will foreign assistance make a difference if the regime doesn't change its policies? These questions have been argued over by people in Burma, foreign governments, exiles, UN agencies and NGOs alike.

Before the mid-1990s few international organizations had access to Burma, and almost all humanitarian assistance went to refugees along the country's borders. Since the mid-1990s, however, the regime has begun allowing foreign organizations to set up programmes inside Burma, particularly in the fields of health, education and income generation. Given the high levels of malnutrition, preventable illnesses and poverty, many organizations were eager to do what they could to help. Yet as in other countries under authoritarian rule, international NGOs and UN programme staff have had to make difficult decisions about what kinds of compromises they would and would not be willing to make.

The first issue that came up was to what degree organizations should cooperate with the authorities. For instance, some expatriate organizations were told they had to hand over vehicles to military officers in return for being able to continue their programmes. In addition, the regime often sought to channel assistance towards organizations close to the regime. In one case, a UNDP household survey, which was given to the government's statistical office to carry out, was then farmed out to members of the USDA to administer.[35] In 1996, two international organizations financed a health-related publication put out by the Myanmar Maternal and Child Welfare Association (MMCWA). Besides health news, the funded issues also ended up including MMCWA speeches criticizing 'internal destructionists', in other words the NLD. Such actions made it difficult for organizations that wanted to help ordinary citizens but could not stop the authorities from interfering or politicizing their assistance.

When international organizations first started coming into Burma, Aung San Suu Kyi asked them to meet with the NLD to discuss their work. The regime made it clear, however, that it would not favour NGOs and UN agencies that did so. Most organizations decided that, in this case and others, it would be necessary to go along with the regime's demands if they wanted to continue to maintain access. Some tried to find creative ways to push the boundaries or refuse demands when they could.

Access was another problem. The regime generally did not allow NGOs to work in politically sensitive areas, which were the areas of greatest need. Then, in 2006, the regime introduced new guidelines for foreign NGOs, with the Burmese version of the guidelines being stricter than the English version. Foreign staff would have to apply for permission before travelling to project sites and would have to be accompanied by government staff on all visits to sites. In addition, new NGO staff would have to be chosen from a list of names suggested by the authorities.[36] While not all the restrictions have been implemented, NGOs are well aware that they walk a fine line. Médecins Sans Frontières France, which worked in conflict areas in Mon and Karen states, decided to pull out in 2006 after the authorities imposed increasingly tight travel restrictions on its staff and pressured local health authorities not to cooperate with them.[37] Since Cyclone Nargis, however, many new NGOs have been able to work in the Irrawaddy Delta though rarely in other areas.

In the 1990s, some Burmese and foreign activists argued that if the UN and foreign NGOs supported healthcare and other programmes, the regime would feel no responsibility to fund these programmes itself. Whether this was the reason or not, according to the 1999 World Bank report, state funding for both primary education and healthcare declined steadily in the 1990s.[38] Nevertheless, the international organizations operating in Burma argued that given the terrible health problems in particular, not to provide assistance would be unconscionable.

Some NGO staff point out that having an international presence in the country is important in and of itself, because of the witnessing role international NGOs can play and the dialogues they can initiate with people in and out of the government. Although international NGOs are reluctant to report publicly on abuses they see, UN and NGO staff have found some well-intentioned people within government ministries to whom they can talk. Also, some staff have worked hard to broaden the perspective of the authorities with whom they have worked.

International organizations and UN programmes have had some direct and invaluable benefits for the people they have reached. Vaccines, HIV/AIDS education and treatment and clean water have all meant that some people who would have died otherwise are still alive. Poverty alleviation and rural development have been more difficult, however, as the international organizations have no control over the regime's economic policies. They cannot stop land confiscation or inflation, nor can they prevent the authorities from ordering people to grow physic nuts or other crops that may not be the most appropriate for their areas. While it is worthwhile to continue such programmes, and also to engage in capacity-building for Burmese staff, the impact will necessarily be limited until there is a change of government or a significant shift in the way the regime operates.

Aid, then, should be provided, but with a real awareness of what can and cannot be achieved. Burmese staff should be empowered so that they can continue the work whether their organization is able to stay or not. And UN agencies and NGOs should collaborate closely so they can use a carefully calibrated combination of pressure and persuasion with the regime in order to increase access and reduce restrictions.

At the same time, cross-border assistance in the areas of relief, health and education should also be continued. Local organizations with border offices have the capability to reach areas that cannot be reached – or not regularly – from inside the country. These areas include conflict zones, ceasefire zones and remote areas that can be more easily accessed from Burma's borders.

More effective international involvement

In recent years, Western countries have begun shifting from focusing almost exclusively on punitive measures against the regime to trying to provide more assistance to people in Burma. This trend should be continued, so that there is a better balance of pressure on the regime and support for those who are living under military rule. Along with humanitarian assistance, more support should be given to Burmese civil society organizations of all types so that they can expand their activities and networks. Capacity-building programmes, short-term courses, exposure trips and other activities that will help broaden Burmese social workers', civil servants' and professionals' perspectives should also be supported. If, ultimately, change must come from within Burma, empowering Burmese is important.

Foreign governments and appropriate international organizations – as well as members of the democracy movement – should also work more on identifying and engaging in a dialogue with a broader range of contacts than just the political parties and the regime. This includes middle-ranking officers, retired military personnel, business people with connections to the regime, and others. Such dialogues could generate more ideas and perhaps a greater consensus on how to initiate reforms or persuade some in the higher ranks of the military that change is necessary and possible.

Finally, foreign efforts should continue to focus equally on restoring democracy and ethnic rights, as Burma cannot achieve lasting peace until both are resolved.

14 | Conclusion: a different Burma

In 2008, Burmese of all faiths and economic backgrounds donated money, labour and time to help the Cyclone Nargis victims. This spirit of compassion and spontaneous organizing to help others reflects the way that Burmese people would like to live. Sadly, successive regimes have often subverted this spirit by dividing people and instilling fear in order to maintain their own power. While they would like to obtain wholehearted support from the population for their rule, it is not necessary. All that is needed is for people not to resist.

The depth of opposition to military rule became clear during the 1988 pro-democracy demonstrations and the 1990 election. The large crowds that greeted Aung San Suu Kyi wherever she travelled in 2002 and 2003, and the 2007 monks' demonstrations for economic reform and national reconciliation, reflected people's continued desire for change. But the generals ignored their citizens' and the international community's appeals for a genuine political transition. They opted instead for a new constitution that institutionalizes the military's leading role in politics and ensures centralized decision-making.

It seems that the more the regime feels cornered, the more defensive it becomes. And yet when the generals feel that their control is secure, they see no need to compromise with their opponents. Thus, if the NLD and other democracy activists do nothing, they are ignored, but when they take action in order to spur the junta to make concessions, they are brutally punished. Likewise, the ethnic nationalists have found that no matter how they struggle for their political rights, whether through party politics, the National Convention or armed resistance, the regime has sought to disregard their demands and weaken their organizations whenever possible.

If large numbers of Burmese people could engage in sustained non-violent resistance activities, and if the Burmese pro-democracy groups and the ethnic nationalist organizations could adopt a shared programme of action, it is possible that the regime would find itself in a position where it had to make compromises. But since 1990, the generals have managed to isolate political activists and sow enough fear into the general population that people largely police themselves. Moreover, the generals have used threats and arrests to limit contact between the ethnic political leaders and pro-democracy leaders in Burma, making it hard for them to work closely together.

Whenever repression intensifies, many people in Burma become cynical about the possibility of effecting change and turn to fatalistic interpretations of their situation. Still, the idea of a different future is kept alive through the determined struggles of Aung San Suu Kyi and numerous other committed politicians, through student activism and monks' calls for dialogue, through writers, film-makers and artists who manage to convey a belief that change is possible despite the censors, and through news of political transformation in other former dictatorships.

Where is Burma's Ramos?

For a political transition to occur in Burma, it is likely that there will need to be a convergence of three factors: unified domestic political pressure, concerted international pressure and a powerful group in the military which decides to work with the democratic movement. A shift in approach by a military leader or faction would not necessarily have to revolve around a desire to restore democracy but could emerge out of an intra-military power struggle or a decision to work together with people from outside the military on economic reform. Once such a process started it is possible that it could take on a life of its own, as has happened in some other countries.

In South Africa, international pressure and widespread domestic resistance set the preconditions for a political transformation. But it was not until de Klerk agreed to negotiate with Mandela that change was possible. While de Klerk originally did not intend to allow a black government to come to power, the South African economy was deteriorating because of sanctions and boycotts. De Klerk finally came to the conclusion that continued intransigence would only lead the country to ruin.[1]

The Philippines offers another model where two powerful generals split away from Marcos, but not because they were committed to democracy.[2] Former defence minister Juan Ponce Enrile and General Fidel Ramos were angry about not obtaining the promotions they had hoped for. Meanwhile, Marcos's overspending and economic mismanagement had severely weakened the economy. At the same time, a people-power movement backed by the Catholic Church had formed around Corazon Aquino, the wife of slain political leader Benigno Aquino and the real winner of the February 1986 presidential election. As the situation became more unstable, Enrile and Ramos saw their chance. They set up a rebel headquarters at Camp Aguinaldo in Manila. When it became clear that the forces loyal to Marcos were going to attack, civilian demonstrators surrounded the base to protect the Enrile–Ramos faction, putting nuns in front. Many soldiers defected to the Enrile–Ramos camp, and others refused to shoot the nuns and the civilian protesters. Representatives of the US government told Marcos they would fly him out of Manila, and he complied, although he originally assumed he was being airlifted only to his home province. Instead he was taken to Hawaii.

Although Enrile and Ramos originally intended to take power for themselves, not to restore democracy, they had to work with Corazon Aquino and the democracy movement. And she, realizing the need to placate the army, agreed to share power with them. In the first three years of her administration, disgruntled groups in the military made several coup attempts. But Aquino managed to hang on, convincing Ramos in the process of the importance of maintaining a democratic system. After her term of office was over, General Ramos was elected to succeed her, and the military gradually came to accept democratic rule.

In Burma, economic mismanagement has led to high inflation and widespread poverty. A pro-democracy movement emerged in the late 1980s and has been weakened but not defeated. Furthermore, there has been a fair amount of international pressure on the regime to negotiate. But so far Rangoon's generals have refused to budge, and no de Klerk or Ramos has emerged. This is partly because international pressure has not been strong enough. The regime has been able to rely on China and India in particular for diplomatic support and large-scale investment, owing to these countries' economic and national security interests in Burma. It is also because the regime feels it has successfully been able to undermine its domestic opposition. In the Philippines and South Africa, some public opposition in the form of legal organizations and an alternative press was tolerated, but in Burma the pro-democracy movement has had virtually no legal channels for organizing and disseminating its views, and even the smallest anti-regime actions are harshly punished.

Perhaps, as a first step, the Burmese generals could be persuaded to follow the example of Vietnam or Indonesia under Suharto, liberalizing the economic sphere and allowing civilians to have a much greater role in some areas of policy-making while still retaining control of the political sphere. Although the 2008 constitution suggests there will be little change in the way the country is run, it is possible that the existence of political parties and a partly elected parliament will lead to pressures on the authorities to improve their economic policy-making and do more for the well-being of their citizens.

While the regime insists the country would fall apart if it were not in power, the example of Indonesia suggests that it need not be so. Also comprised of numerous ethnic groups and people of many faiths, Indonesia made the transition from military rule to democracy relatively smoothly. Sudden economic collapse, anger at the corruption of the Suharto regime and the suppression of student activists and other pro-democratic groups finally led large numbers of people to take to the streets. Rioting, looting and attacks on the Chinese community took place, allegedly with the support of some in the military. But when Suharto no longer had the full support of the army leadership, he was forced to step down. There were other outbreaks of violence in the following months, but the new government was able to contain this relatively quickly.

Indonesia also contended with armed insurgencies, albeit on a much more limited scale than in Burma. After democracy was restored, however, the Indonesian government was able to negotiate an autonomy agreement with the Free Aceh Movement which has held up well. Significantly, the agreement was made under the presidency of Susilo Bambang Yudhoyono, a former general. He has urged Burma's generals to follow in Indonesia's footsteps, calling for democratization and national reconciliation.

Democratization and national reconciliation

Although the regime has often said that Western-style democracy is not appropriate for Burma, liberal democratic governments have flourished in Japan and India and, more recently, in Taiwan. This suggests that democracy is not incompatible with Asian societies. Democracy takes somewhat different forms in each country in which it is practised. It is shaped by the culture and history of the people as well as by the way in which it is introduced. Democracy is never perfect, but it is a system of government that recognizes the inherent dignity of all citizens and their right to participate in decisions that affect their lives. This is what people in Burma voted for in 1990 and this is what they are still looking for today: to be able to live in dignity and to have a government that respects their needs and reflects their desires.

Moreover, many of the core values enshrined in a democratic system are also deeply rooted in Buddhism. Buddhist ideology is fundamentally broad-minded, and it insists on a detached attitude towards the world. Each person must make his or her own way towards enlightenment, and this must be done by recognizing that everything to which we cling is ultimately impermanent. If such tenets were applied to political and social relations, ideological inflexibility and racial prejudices should ideally find little support.

At the same time, Buddhist philosophy insists that individuals use their powers of reasoning to make informed decisions. As General Aung San wrote in 1935 in an essay entitled 'Burma and Buddhism', the Buddha told his followers not to believe anything merely because it was written in a religious book, often repeated or stated by people in positions of authority. Beliefs and ideas, he said, must be tested by observation and analysis, be reasonable and beneficial to all. Concerned that Burmese were slipping into a pattern of passive acceptance, General Aung San stated: 'It is therefore the bounden duty of every true Burman to revive the spirit of criticism, inherent in Buddhism, and apply it to every problem affecting Burma.'[3]

While the regime has focused on national consolidation, what is needed is a process of national reconciliation, in the sense of resolving the political demands of all stakeholders. It will be a challenging process in Burma, but, if handled correctly, it can be done. The armed ethnic nationalist organizations and the civilians in conflict areas desperately want peace. Most would be satisfied with a genuine federal system that gives them a certain degree of control over affairs in their state and the right to promote their languages and cultures. Most members of ethnic minority groups who joined political parties set up in 1988 or have stayed out of politics see their people's futures as inseparable from that of Burma as a whole and will push for moderation. If a new constitution can offer clear protection for states' rights, and the rights of smaller minorities within those states, it seems likely that a deal can be struck.

The military mindset regarding national unity will, however, have to be changed. The leading generals – and the Burmese population as a whole – must come to see that a union can be better held together by cultivating shared interests and benefits, rather than relying on the use of brute force. In this regard, new concepts, such as unity in diversity and shared sovereignty, must be introduced and valorized.

Most sensitive for the military is the issue of transitional justice. If senior officers believe that a political transition will lead to their being punished for crimes committed under past regimes, they will do all they can to prevent or derail a transition process. On the other hand, given the degree to which many people have suffered in Burma, whether in villages in conflict areas or in interrogation centres and prisons, this issue cannot simply be ignored. Those who seek political change in Burma must convince the generals that their security will be guaranteed, but

273

they must also find a way to ensure that past suffering is recognized and addressed.

While the ruling Burmese generals have treated Aung San Suu Kyi as the arch-enemy, she is probably the best person to ensure a smooth transition. Aung San Suu Kyi values the Burmese military as the institution founded by her father and understands the need to ensure its dignity. She has the trust of many ethnic leaders as well as of a large part of the general population because of her integrity. Moreover, she has continued to express a willingness to negotiate with the generals, despite everything they have done to her. Nevertheless, it is also important for the democracy movement to do more to nurture the leadership capacity of its most talented members, so that it is not overly reliant on single individuals.

The democratic movement as a whole can also benefit from developing more openness and tolerance. Rigid thinking, hierarchical power structures and a culture of mistrust have characterized not only the military regime but, in many cases, the opposition groups as well. Constructive criticism is frequently interpreted as a challenge rather than a contribution, and people may be valued more for their loyalty rather than their ability to think creatively. Having grown up in a political system that inculcated or intensified such attitudes and practices, this is not surprising. As Min Zin wrote in an article in *The Irrawaddy* news journal: 'The idea that democracy is a way of life that you must practice in your daily life, in your organization, and in your community is pretty far removed from our practice, attitude, and behavior.'[4]

Still, there are grounds for optimism. Many more Burmese than in the past have exposure to other ways of thinking than the regime's, through their travels and their attempts to educate themselves outside the formal education system. Some in the democracy movement, in literary circles and in alternative educational programmes have sought to encourage debate and dialogue and have emphasized the importance of learning from other countries' experiences. The Internet has also provided a window to the world for those who have access to it. And many in the democracy movement, in religious organizations and in other fields have sought to reach out to others and work collectively for the good of all.

A different Burma

Were Burma to achieve a political transition, what would the country be like? On the negative side, in the short to medium term, there could well be instances of political violence and communal tensions. In particular, fighting could break out between Rohingya Muslims and Arakanese

Buddhists in Arakan State and between groups that have competed for control of territory in Shan State. Civilians who have lost their land to the *tatmadaw* or other settlers may also resort to violence to get their property back if the government cannot quickly find a way to address this problem. Corruption is also likely to continue until salaries are adequate, a strong judicial system is in place to deal with breaches of the law, and a culture of intolerance for corruption is instilled.

On the positive side, what would change significantly is that people would no longer live in fear. Ideally, the size of the military would be trimmed and soldiers primarily deployed to protect borders rather than wage war against their fellow citizens. The security laws would be amended and political prisoners released. Some of Burma's beloved traditions, which have been suppressed or sanitized under military rule, could also re-emerge. *Thangyat* could again be sung during the new year's festival, public talks by well-known literary figures could be freely organized, and comedians in *anyeint* performances could satirize the leaders of the day, both to entertain their audiences and to remind the leaders of their responsibilities to those they represent.

It would be a time of exuberant hopes and tumultuous change, but as in other newly democratizing countries, it is likely that raising the standard of living would be the key issue for most people. Trying to bring about measurable improvements quickly will be one of the biggest challenges for a new government, as will trying to redress the income gap between the rich and the poor. In many ways, Burma would probably become less distinctively Burmese as it integrated into the global economy, but Burmese would also presumably feel more confident about their status within the international community. Foreign aid would flow in, and new businesses would mushroom. Civil society organizations would expand their activities and seek a role in defining government policies. There would be an explosion of newspapers, magazines, art shows, theatre and film-making, with debates raging about how best to develop the country, how to reassess social and cultural practices, and how to reconfigure political and economic relations. Universities, markets and tea shops would be teeming with people comparing ideas and saying whatever they felt like saying, without having to worry about going to jail for it. In short, Burma would no longer be a place of silence.

Notes

Introduction

1 *Integrated Household Living Conditions Survey in Myanmar*, IDEA International Institute, June 2007, p. 14.

2 Quoted in 'Yangon to the UN: thanks, but …', *Far Eastern Economic Review*, 25 December 1998.

1 Historical legacies

1 S. J. Tambiah, 'The Gallactic Polity: the structure of traditional kingdoms in Southeast Asia', *Annals of the New York Academy of Sciences*, no. 293 (July 1977), pp. 69–97.

2 For instance, Victor Lieberman, *Burmese Administrative Cycles: Anarchy and Conquest, c.1580–1760* (Princeton, NJ: Princeton University Press, 1984), p. 98, describes how King Thalun resettled Mons, Shans, Siamese, Laos, Indians and Arakanese in the agricultural areas around his capital.

3 E. R. Leach, 'The frontiers of "Burma"', *Comparative Studies in Society and History*, vol. 3, no. 1 (October 1960), pp. 49–68.

4 Father Vincenzo Sangermano, *The Burmese Empire a Hundred Years Ago* (Bangkok: White Orchid Press, 1985 [1st edn 1833]), pp. 73–4) describes the capriciousness of many kings who had rivals and subjects killed at the slightest suspicion.

5 See R. C. Temple, *The Thirty-Seven Nats* (London: W. Griggs, 1906) for different versions of this tale and further information on the role of *nats*.

6 See David I. Steinberg, *Burma: A Socialist Nation of Southeast Asia* (Boulder, CO: Westview Press, 1982), pp. 24–34, for a fuller discussion of Britain's motives.

7 See Chapter 3 of Thongchai Winichakul's *Siam Mapped: A History of the Geo-Body of a Nation* (Honolulu: University of Hawaii Press, 1994).

8 Chao-Tzang Yawnghwe, 'The Burman military: holding the country together?', in J. Silverstein (ed.), *Independent Burma at Forty Years: Six Assessments* (Ithaca, NY: Cornell University Southeast Asia Program, 1989), pp. 86–7.

9 See Dr San C. Po, *Burma and the Karens* (London: Elliot Stock, 1928) for a Karen assessment of the impact of Christianity and education on the Karens.

10 Mary Callahan, *Making Enemies: War and State Building in Burma* (Ithaca, NY: Cornell University Press, 2003), p. 35.

11 Maung Maung Pye, *Burma in the Crucible* (Rangoon: Khittaya Publishing House, 1951), pp. 15–16.

12 U Maung Maung, *From Sangha to Laity: Nationalist Movements of Burma: 1920–1940* (Australian National University Monograph on South Asia no. 4, 1980), chs 8–10.

13 Maurice Collis, *Trials in Burma* (Bangkok: Ava Books, 1996 [1938]) discusses the social aspects of discrimination; J. S. Furnivall, *Colonial Policy and Practice* (London: Cambridge University Press, 1948), discusses the economic policies that encouraged racial divisions.

14 The Karenni State was

recognized as separate from Burma during the colonial period, although it was eventually ruled like the other frontier areas. After the British had taken control of lower Burma in the mid-1850s, the British and King Mindon had signed an agreement recognizing the Karenni territory's independence in order to maintain a buffer between the British and Mindon's kingdom.

15 See Maung Maung, *Burma's Constitution* (The Hague: Martinus Nijhoff, 1959).

16 See Josef Silverstein, *Burma: Military Rule and the Politics of Stagnation* (Ithaca, NY: Cornell University Press, 1977), pp. 58–9, for more information on the restrictions placed on states by the 1947 constitution.

17 See Kin Oung, *Who Killed Aung San?* (Bangkok: White Lotus, 1996) for more details.

18 For an account of this period from a civil servant of Indian heritage, see Balwant Singh, *Independence and Democracy in Burma, 1945–1952: The Turbulent Years* (Ann Arbor: University of Michigan Center for South and Southeast Asian Studies, 1993).

19 Yawnghwe, 'The Burman military', pp. 92–4.

20 See Manning Nash, *The Golden Road to Modernity: Village Life in Contemporary Burma* (Chicago, IL: University of Chicago Press, 1965), p. 322.

21 For more information on U Nu's policies in the 1950s, see Hugh Tinker, *The Union of Burma* (London: Oxford University Press, 1957), chs 4–12.

22 Nash, *Golden Road to Modernity*, pp. 280–81.

23 Callahan, *Making Enemies*, pp. 168–9.

24 See ibid., pp. 184–90; U Thaung, *A Journalist, a General and an Army in Burma* (Bangkok: White Lotus, 1995), pp. 38–41.

25 Steinberg, *Burma*, pp. 70–1.

26 Ba Maw, *Breakthrough in Burma, Memoirs of a Revolution, 1939–1946* (New Haven, CT: Yale University Press, 1968), p. 196.

2 The Ne Win years

1 Bertil Lintner, *Outrage: Burma's Struggle for Democracy* (Bangkok: White Lotus, 1990), p. 39.

2 David Steinberg, *Burma: A Socialist Nation of Southeast Asia* (Boulder, CO: Westview Press, 1982), p. 79; David Steinberg, 'The Union Solidarity Development Association', *Burma Debate*, January/February 1997.

3 John F. Cady, *The United States and Burma* (Cambridge, MA: Harvard University Press, 1976), p. 248.

4 Steinberg, *Burma*, p. 79.

5 Josef Silverstein, 'Burmese student politics in a changing society', *Daedalus*, vol. 97, no. 1 (1968), p. 291.

6 Josef Silverstein quoted in Lintner, *Outrage*, pp. 43–4; interview with a Burmese journalist.

7 Interviews with Chins whose family members were imprisoned, and see Pu Lian Uk, 'No room for the Chin in Burman monopolized politics', *Burma Debate*, December 1994/January 1995, p. 30.

8 R. H. Taylor, 'Elections in Burma/Myanmar: for whom and why?', in R. H. Taylor (ed.), *The Politics of Elections in Southeast Asia* (Cambridge: Cambridge University Press, 1996), p. 175.

9 Lintner, *Outrage*, p. 59.

10 Cady, *The United States and Burma*, p. 253.

11 Ibid., p. 254.

12 Information on the 1969–78 protests from U Tint Zaw, a former Rangoon University professor, U Aung Saw Oo, a long-time political activist, and other activists who were involved.

13 See Andrew Selth, *Death of a Hero: The U Thant Disturbances in Burma, December 1974* (Brisbane: Griffith University Centre for the Study of Australian–Asian Relations, April 1989) for a full account.

14 Ibid., p. 15.

15 Ibid., p. 23.

16 See Bertil Lintner, *Burma in Revolt: Opium and Insurgency since 1948* (Boulder, CO: Westview Press, 1994), ch. 7; Martin Smith, *Burma: Insurgency and the Politics of Ethnicity* (London: Zed Books, 1999), chs 13 and 15.

17 See Lintner, *Burma in Revolt*, pp. 209–11; Smith, *Burma*, ch. 14.

18 Smith, *Burma*, pp. 259–60.

3 Breaking the silence

1 See Bertil Lintner, *Outrage: Burma's Struggle for Democracy* (Bangkok: White Lotus, 1990) for a full account of the 1988 demonstrations.

2 Ibid., pp. 75–7.

3 For a translation of one of Aung Gyi's letters, see *Asiaweek*, 8 July 1988. Excerpts from another letter were printed in *Asiaweek* on 12 August 1988.

4 Lintner, *Outrage*, pp. 80–81.

5 In South-East Asia, men can enter and leave the monkhood at will. In Burma, Buddhist men generally enter the monkhood once as young boys and again when they have reached the age of about twenty. Most stay only for a week or a few months, although some choose to become monks for life.

6 Lintner, *Outrage*, pp. 94–103.

7 This figure has been widely cited but never verified.

8 The British Library has a collection of nearly one hundred unofficial publications from this period. See Anna J. Allott, *Inked Over, Ripped Out: Burmese Storytellers and the Censors* (Chiang Mai, Thailand: Silkworm Books, 1994), p. 15.

9 *Asiaweek*, 9 September 1988.

10 Ibid., 2 September 1988.

11 According to Bertil Lintner, *Burma in Revolt: Opium and Insurgency since 1948* (Boulder, CO: Westview Press, 1994), p. 294, not only did the leadership of the CPB not authorize participation in the uprising but the majority of the troops (mainly Was) did not even know an uprising was happening.

12 'Going back to work, sullenly', *Asiaweek*, 14 October 1988.

13 The ten ethical rules are: generosity, morality, self-sacrifice, integrity, kindness, austerity, non-anger, non-violence, patience and harmony. For a more complete description see Aung San Suu Kyi, *Freedom from Fear and Other Writings* (London: Penguin Books, 1991), pp. 170–73.

14 A student activist told me how he and his colleagues had been given leaflets to distribute with pictures of Aung San Suu Kyi's head attached to a nude body, but they had destroyed them in disgust. He said the authorities assumed that some student groups would be happy to distribute them because they disagreed with Aung San Suu Kyi's decision to participate in the election.

15 'Bar the name, much the same', *Asiaweek*, 23 June 1989.

16 'Anniversaries of anger', ibid., 7 July 1989.

17 'Heading for a showdown', ibid., 14 July 1989.

18 Michael Aris, 'Introduction', in Aung San Suu Kyi, *Freedom from Fear*, p. xxi.

19 For a description of events at Daw Aung San Suu Kyi's compound on the day of her arrest, see 'Truth will come one day', *Burma Debate*, August/September 1995, p. 11.

20 Interview with Daw San Kyaw Zaw, 29 November 1998.

21 Lintner, *Burma in Revolt*, p. 304.

22 This figure was given in an Amnesty International report cited in ibid., p. 377. He says others put the number even higher.

23 Robert Taylor, *The State in Burma* (London: C. Hurst, 1996), p. 177.

24 See 'Burma's cheated voters', Letters to the Editor, *Asiaweek*, 10 August 1990.

25 See All Burma Students' Democratic Front, *To Stand and be Counted: The Suppression of Burma's Members of Parliament* (Bangkok, June 1998), p. 20, for the full statistics.

26 'The ides of September', *Asiaweek*, 14 September 1990.

27 Lintner, *Burma in Revolt*, pp. 311–12.

4 Military rule continues

1 Mary Callahan, *Political Authority in Burma's Ethnic Minority States* (Washington, DC: East West Center), 2007, p. 7.

2 *New Light of Myanmar*, 6 June 1996.

3 Anthony Davis and Bruce Hawke, 'Burma: the country that won't kick the habit', *Jane's Intelligence Review*, 1 March 1998.

4 Bruce Hawke, 'Narcotics – Burma's military implicated', ibid., 1 October 1998; François Casanier, 'A narco-dictatorship in progress', *Burma Debate*, March/April 1996.

5 Davis and Hawke, 'Burma'.

6 Ibid.

7 *International Narcotics Control Strategy Report* (Washington, DC: US Department of State, March 1996).

8 Kei Nemoto, 'The Japanese perspective', *Burma Debate*, August/September 1995, pp. 23–4.

9 I did not attend this event but subsequently watched a videotape of the performance.

10 See 'Human Rights Watch/Asia condemns sentencing of NLD supporters', *Human Rights Watch/Asia*, Press release, 20 March 1996.

11 Human Rights Watch/Asia reported the arrest of three men in Mandalay for distributing videos of the People's Forum. 'Human Rights Watch/Asia condemns new arrests of NLD supporters', *Human Rights Watch/Asia*, Press release, 11 January 1996.

12 *New Light of Myanmar*, 12 November 1996 (posted on the Internet).

13 The USDA was modelled on General Suharto's mass party, Golkar, in Indonesia. See David I. Steinberg, 'The Union Solidarity Development Association', *Burma Debate*, January/February 1997.

14 'SLORC chief incites mobs to crush opponents of junta', *The Nation* (Bangkok), 13 November 1996.

15 'Notification No. 6', Committee Representing the People's Parliament, 9 February 1999.

16 '183 parliament representatives remain valid in Myanmar', *Xinhua*, 18 October 1999.

17 Craig Skehan, 'Junta cut off Aris' last words', *Bangkok Post*, 31 March 1999.

18 The Karenni State Nationalities People's Liberation Front, the Shan State Nationalities People's

Liberation Organization and the Kayan New Land Party issued a joint statement, and the New Mon State Party and the Shan State Army issued individual statements. See *The BurmaNet News*, no. 1104, 25–27 September 1998, regarding the military regime's reaction and statements by some groups against the CRPP.

5 The Than Shwe years

1 Quoted in Larry Jagan, 'Burma's referendum: a done deal that may yet unravel', *Mizzima*, 2 May 2008.

2 *Preliminary Report of the Ad Hoc Commission on the Depayin Massacre* (Thailand: 4 July 2003), p. 8. See the rest of the report for witness accounts.

3 Paulo Sergio Pinheiro, *Situation of Human Rights in Myanmar: Report Submitted by the Special Rapporteur, Paulo Sergio Pinheiro*, UN Commission on Human Rights (Geneva: 5 January 2004), pp. 7–8.

4 Ibid., p. 9.

5 Ibid., p. 10.

6 'The Seven Step Road Map to Disciplined Democracy announced by Gen. Khin Nyunt', *New Light of Myanmar*, 30 August 2003.

7 Kyaw Zwa Moe, 'Game over if NC proceedings not changed, says ethnic leader', *The Irrawaddy*, 7 May 2004.

8 'A Shan veteran politician put under house arrest', AAPP, 11 February 2005.

9 Shah Paung, 'Ceasefire group says it can't trust National Convention', *The Irrawaddy*, 7 December 2006.

10 Wai Moe, 'One blood, one voice, one command', ibid., 27 June 2008.

11 Bertil Lintner, 'Myanmar's 88 Generation comes of age', *Asia Times Online*, 25 January 2007.

12 Ibid.

13 Shah Paung, 'Burmese open their hearts', *The Irrawaddy*, 9 February 2007.

14 Quoted in 'Myanmar's new capital: remote, lavish and off-limits', *International Herald Tribune*, 23 June 2008.

15 See Ministry of Health, *Health in Myanmar 2005* (Yangon, 2005), p. 61. The unofficial exchange rate in 2005 was approximately 1,000 kyat per US dollar.

16 'Myanmar's new capital offers luxury in isolation', AFP, 24 February 2007.

17 Ibid.

18 'Burma leader's lavish lifestyle aired', BBC, 2 November 2006.

19 Maung Maung Oo, 'More trouble brewing for Mandalay Beer', *The Irrawaddy Magazine*, December 2001.

20 Bertil Lintner, 'Myanmar payback time', *Jane's Defense Weekly*, 15 April 2005.

21 Ed Cropley, 'Myanmar biofuel effort raises doubts', Reuters, 12 March 2008.

22 Sean Turnell, 'Burma's economic prospects', Testimony before the Senate Foreign Relations Subcommittee on East Asian and Pacific Affairs, 29 March 2006, pp. 6, 12.

23 William Boot, 'Junta's piggy bank full as economy sinks', *The Irrawaddy Magazine*, March 2008, pp. 14–15.

24 'Thailand: deaths of Myanmar workers highlight migrant labour problems', *IRIN*, 11 April 2008.

25 Announcement of All Burma Monks' Alliance: 12th Waning Day of Wagaung, 1369 BE, Sunday, Letter no. 1/2007.

26 For an excellent account of the demonstrations and the authorities'

response, see Human Rights Watch, *Crackdown: Repression of the 2007 Popular Protests in Burma*, December 2007.

27 'Statement of the People's Alliance Formation Committee to the entire clergy and the people of the whole country', *People's Alliance Formation Committee*, 21 September 2007.

28 'Sharing Legislative Power: Article 5 B', *2008 Constitution of Myanmar*.

29 Philippe Naughton, 'UN chief Ban Ki Moon to meet Burma's "Senior General" Than Shwe', *Times Online*, 21 May 2008.

30 Ibid.

31 Ivo Daalder and Paul Stares, 'The UN's responsibility to protect', *International Herald Tribune*, 13 May 2008.

32 'Myanmar junta hands out aid boxes with generals' names', AP, 10 May 2008.

33 Glenn Kessler, 'Burma gives "cronies" slice of storm relief', *Washington Post*, 13 June 2008.

34 'Referendum 2008; Burma's road to a false democracy', *Mon Forum*, 30 April 2008, pp. 6–9 (note: the publication actually came out in May); 'Massive cheating reported from Referendum polling stations', *The Irrawaddy*, 10 May 2008.

35 'Referendum 2008', *Mon Forum*, p. 7.

6 Families

1 'Burmese general, wife disown son', *The Nation*, 26 February 1998. Lt Gen. Khin Nyunt was quoted as saying Ye Naing Win was disowned 'for his inexcusable deed'.

2 While long-time Indian residents have suffered under this system, migrant Chinese with a bit of money have found ways to purchase citizenship papers. See Dermot Tatlow, 'China's shadow', *Asiaweek*, 28 May 1999.

7 Communities

1 Written in huge letters on an elevated water tank at the Defence Services Academy in Maymyo, Shan State, among other places.

2 'Burma: stop forced evictions', Human Rights Watch press statement, 30 May 2008.

3 Karen Human Rights Group, *Summary of Forced Labor in Burma*, KHRG no. 97–S1 (7 August 1997).

4 Images Asia, Karen Human Rights Group and the Open Society Institute's Burma Project, *All Quiet on the Western Front? The Situation in Chin State and Sagaing Division, Burma* (Thailand: January 1998).

5 'Forced labour in Burma', ICFTU online press release, 7 May 1999.

6 International Labour Organization, *Resolution on Burma* (Geneva: ILO, 1999).

7 'Myanmar lashes West for ILO expulsion', Associated Press, 17 June 1999.

8 See, for example, Amnesty International, *Crimes against Humanity in Eastern Myanmar* (June 2008), pp. 20–26.

9 Amnesty International, *Myanmar Aftermath: Three Years of Dislocation in the Kayah State* (June 1999).

10 Shan Human Rights Foundation, *Dispossessed: Forced Relocation and Extrajudicial Killings in Shan State* (Thailand: 1998).

11 Ibid.

12 Shan Human Rights Foundation, *Charting the Exodus from Shan State* (Thailand: 2003), p. 6.

13 Thailand Burma Border

Consortium, *Internal Displacement and International Law in Eastern Burma* (Thailand: October 2008), p. 2.

14 Ibid., p. 2.

15 See, for example, Karen Women's Organization, *Shattering Silences* (Thailand: 2004); Shan Human Rights Foundation and Shan Women's Action Network, *License to Rape* (Thailand: 2002); Women's League of Burma, *System of Impunity* (Thailand: 2004); Women's League of Chinland, *Unsafe State* (India: 2007).

16 Christina Fink, 'Ongoing militarization in Burma's ethnic states', *Contemporary Politics*, 4(14), December 2008, p. 456.

17 Ibid.

18 Karen Women's Organization, *State of Terror* (Thailand: 2007), pp. 19–20.

19 Amnesty International, *Crimes against Humanity*, p. 2.

20 Zaw Oo and Win Min, *Assessing Burma's Ceasefire Accords* (Washington, DC: East West Center, 2007), pp. 47–50.

21 Andrew Bosson, *Forced Migration/Internal Displacement in Burma – with an Emphasis on Government-Controlled Areas* (Internal Displacement Monitoring Centre, May 2007), p. 26.

22 Ibid., p. 47.

23 Ibid., p. 47.

24 Dermot Tatlow, 'China's shadow', *Asiaweek*, 22 May 1999; Clifford McCoy, 'Seedlings of evil growing in Myanmar', *Asia Times Online*, 23 August 2007.

25 United States Commission on International Religious Freedom, *Annual Report* 2006 (May 2006), p. 105; Dennis Bernstein and Leslie Kean, 'Ethnic cleansing: rape as a weapon of war in Burma', *The Nation*, 31 May 1998.

26 'Govt, people and Tatmadaw will unitedly strive for emergence of peaceful, modern, developed democratic nation despite all obstructions', Myanmar Information Committee, Information Sheet no. D-3389(I), 28 July 2005.

27 See Brian Heidel, *The Growth of Civil Society in Myanmar* (Bangalore: Books for Change, 2006) for more detailed information.

8 The military

1 Andrew Selth, *Transforming the Tatmadaw: The Burmese Armed Forces since 1988* (Canberra: Australian National University Strategic and Defence Studies Centre, 1996), p. 132.

2 Human Rights Watch, *Sold to be Soldiers: The Recruitment and Use of Child Soldiers in Burma*, October 2007, pp. 32–44.

3 See Selth, *Transforming the Tatmadaw*, p. 50.

4 Images Asia, Karen Human Rights Group and the Open Society Institute's Burma Project, *All Quiet on the Western Front? The Situation in Chin State and Sagaing Division, Burma* (Thailand: January 1998), pp. 52–3.

5 'Burmese economy is an obstacle to aid', *New York Times*, 29 May 2008.

6 See Karen Human Rights Group, *Interviews with SLORC Army Deserters* (Thailand: 18 May 1996).

7 Human Rights Watch, *Sold to be Soldiers*, pp. 63–6.

8 See 'Better the devil you don't know', *The Irrawaddy*, July 1999, pp. 20–21.

9 Soe Myint, 'India and Burma: working on their relationship', *The Irrawaddy*, March 1999, p. 22.

10 See Chapter 7, note 15.

11 See Andrew Selth, *Burma's Intelligence Apparatus* (Canberra: Australian National University Strategic and Defence Studies Centre, June 1997), p. 28.

12 David Steinberg, 'Myanmar reconciliation – progress in the process?', in A. Salim et al. (eds), *Southeast Asian Affairs 2003* (Singapore: Institute of Southeast Asian Studies, 2005), p. 176.

13 Kyaw Yin Hlaing, 'Myanmar in 2004: why military rule continues', in C. K. Wah et al. (eds), *Southeast Asian Affairs 2005* (Singapore: Institute of Southeast Asian Studies, 2005), p. 235.

14 'The spring before Khin Nyunt's fall', *The Irrawaddy*, October 2008, p. 15.

15 Bertil Lintner, 'Velvet glove', *Far Eastern Economic Review*, 7 May 1998.

16 See Gustaaf Houtman, *Mental Culture in Burmese Crisis Politics: Aung San Suu Kyi and the National League for Democracy* (Tokyo: Tokyo University of Foreign Studies, Institute for the Study of Languages and Cultures of Asia and Africa, 1999), pp. 142–7; 'Minister U Tin Winn inspects departmental works in Monywa District', *New Light of Myanmar*, 13 August 2002; and Bob Beale, 'Further evidence for out of Asia theory', *ABC Science Online*, 28 October 2003.

17 Than Myint-U, *The River of Lost Footsteps* (New York: Farrar, Straus and Giroux, 2006), p. 158.

9 Prison

1 See All Burma Students' Democratic Front, *Tortured Voices: Personal Accounts of Burma's Interrogation Centres* (Bangkok: July 1998) for more information about interrogation centres.

2 NCGUB Human Rights Documentation Unit, *Human Rights Yearbook 1997–8: Burma*, p. 290.

3 Assistance Association for Political Prisoners (AAPP), *The Darkness We See: Torture inside Burma's Interrogation Centers and Prisons*, December 2005, p. 22.

4 See Amnesty International, *Myanmar: Justice on Trial*, 30 July 2003, pp. 19–26.

5 NCGUB Human Rights Documentation Unit, *Human Rights Yearbook 1997–8: Burma*, p. 109.

6 'Burma', in Human Rights Watch/Asia, *Human Rights Watch World Report 1999* (Human Rights Watch, 1999).

7 'Burmese gulag claims another victim', *The Irrawaddy*, 17 October 2006.

8 See Amnesty International and Human Rights Watch annual reports on Burma.

9 See the home page of the AAPP website for regular updates: www.aapp.org.

10 'Allegations contrary to present endeavours exerted by Government with goodwill for prosperity of Myanmar', Myanmar Information Committee Information Sheet no. D-3873(I), 1 December 2006.

11 Win Naing Oo, *Cries from Insein* (Bangkok: All Burma Students' Democratic Front, 1996), p. 25. Also, AAPP, *Eight Seconds of Silence: The Death of Democracy Activists behind Bars*, May 2006, p. 25.

12 AAPP, *Forced Labor of Prisoners in Burma* (Thailand: May 2002), p. 2.

13 See Amnesty International, *Myanmar: Conditions in Prisons and Labor Camps* (22 September 1995).

14 Phone interview with Ko Tate, secretary of the Assistance Association for Political Prisoners, 31 October 2008.

15 Translated by ATN.

16 The information provided here comes from interviews with Moe Aye. He has also discussed aspects of his prison experience in his self-published book, *Ten Years On: The Life and Views of a Burmese Student Political Prisoner* (Bangkok, 1999). See also Kyaw Swa Moe, 'Learning without bars', in AAPP, *Spirit for Survival* (Mae Sot, Thailand: September 2001), pp. 111–16.

17 In 1995, twenty-two political prisoners were given extra sentences after a raid of their cells turned up printed materials such as *Time* and *Newsweek* magazine articles, transcripts of foreign radio broadcasts, short stories and poems, and pro-democracy literature. Some were tortured and placed in tiny dog cells for their 'crime'. See All Burma Students' Democratic Front, *Pleading Not Guilty in Insein* (Bangkok: February 1997).

18 AAPP, *The Darkness We See*, p. 85.

19 Ibid., p. 76.

20 The regime responded to exile organizations' reports on prison conditions in 'Allegations contrary to present endeavours exerted by Government with goodwill for prosperity of Myanmar', Myanmar Information Committee Information Sheet no. D-3873(I), 1 December 2006. The statement was read out by the director-general of the Myanmar Police Force, Brigadier General Khin Yi, in a press conference the day before.

10 Education

1 Asian Development Bank, 'Myanmar', in *Asian Development Outlook 2005* (Manila: 2005), p. 107.

2 See Min Zin, 'Hard lessons', *The Irrawaddy*, July 2003, p. 11.

3 Htet Aung, 'Save our schools', ibid., June 2007.

4 UNICEF, 'At a glance: Myanmar', www.unicef.org/infobycountry/myanmar.html.

5 Thein Lwin, 'Issues surrounding curriculum development in the ethnic nationalities areas of Burma', *Burma Studies Conference* (Gothenburg, Sweden: September 2002), p. 3.

6 UNICEF, 'At a glance: Myanmar'.

7 Bertil Lintner, *Outrage: Burma's Struggle for Democracy* (Bangkok: White Lotus, 1990), p. 62.

8 Democratic Voice of Burma, 'New curriculum excludes General Aung San', 26 June 2008.

9 See Karen Human Rights Group, *The Situation of Children in Burma* (Thailand: 1 May 1996); Min Zin, 'Hard lessons', pp. 8–11.

10 'Integrate public spirit and influence and lead people to regional development', Myanmar Information Committee Sheet no. D-3578(I), 7 February 2006.

11 Monks at higher levels do engage in serious discussion of Buddhist philosophy, but for young children who attend monastery classes for only a few years, most of the learning is based on memorization.

12 Ashley South, 'Mon nationalist movements: insurgency, ceasefires, and political struggle', Paper presented at the Seminar on the Discovery of Ramadasa, Bangkok, Thailand, 10–13 October 2007, p. 19.

13 'While schools are closed', *Burma Issues*, vol. 7, no. 9 (September 1997); communication, 3 August 1999.

14 Min Zin, 'Hard lessons', p. 11.

15 This policy was originally introduced in order to fill the need

for more trained graduates in the sciences and technical fields. See Josef Silverstein, 'Burmese student politics in a changing society', *Daedalus*, vol. 97, no. 1 (Winter 1968), p. 287.

16 Communication from Aung Saw Oo, June 1999. Universities were shut down in 1962, 1963, 1969, 1970, 1974 (twice), 1975, 1976, 1987, 1988 (twice), 1991 and 1996.

17 Nwe Nwe Aye, 'Russia–Myanmar relations grow stronger', *Myanmar Times*, 13–19 February 2006; Khun Sam, 'Russia, junta begin search for uranium in northern Burma', *The Irrawaddy*, 12 June 2007.

18 See Karen Human Rights Group, *Interviews with SLORC Army Deserters*, KHRG no. 96-19 (Thailand: 18 May 1996), p. 3; Win Htein, 'Time to change the Tatmadaw's image', Mizzima News Group (posted on BurmaNet News on 26 March 2000).

19 Yeni, 'Burma's IT generation combats regime repression', *The Irrawaddy*, 7 October 2008.

20 Jane Perlez, 'A tiny window on the US, prized by those peering in', *New York Times*, 23 November 2006.

11 The artistic community

1 For a history of the development of censorship in Burma, see Anna J. Allott, *Inked Over, Ripped Out: Burmese Storytellers and the Censors* (Chiang Mai: Silkworm Books, 1994).

2 See David Brunnstrom, 'Military rule in Myanmar – a writer's tale', Reuters, 25 August 1999.

3 Yeni, 'Burma: the censored land', *The Irrawaddy*, March 2008, pp. 20–21.

4 Allott, *Inked Over, Ripped Out*, p. 31.

5 Violet Cho, 'Journalists arrested, detained for Nargis reporting', *The Irrawaddy*, 2 July 2008.

6 Videotape of the 1990 Writers' Forum.

7 Toby Hudson, 'Lights, camera – but where's the action?', *The Irrawaddy*, September 2005, pp. 38–9.

8 See Gavin Douglas, 'Who's performing what?', in Monique Skidmore (ed.), *Burma at the Turn of the 21st Century* (Honolulu: University of Hawaii Press, 2005), pp. 229–47, for an analysis of how the regime has tried to promote and standardize particular types of music in order to serve its ideological interests.

9 Aung Zaw, 'Burma: music under siege', in M. Korpe (ed.), *Shoot the Singer: Music Censorship Today* (London: Zed Books, 2004), pp. 53–4.

10 Ibid., p. 56.

11 Kyaw Zwa Moe, 'A man without a head can run Burma', *The Irrawaddy*, February 2008, pp. 12–13.

12 Jane Perlez, 'From a Burmese prison: a chronicle of pain in paint', *New York Times*, 13 August 2007.

13 Htet Aung, 'Junta reconsiders ban on social organizations', *The Irrawaddy*, 24 May 2007.

14 'Comic relief', *The Irrawaddy*, June 2008, p. 13.

12 Religion and magic

1 Guillaume Rozenberg, 'The cheaters', in M. Skidmore (ed.), *Burma at the Turn of the 21st Century* (Honolulu: University of Hawaii Press, 2005), p. 34.

2 Juliane Schober, 'Buddhist visions of moral authority and modernity in Burma', in ibid., p. 118.

3 Patrick McDowell, 'Grand pagoda being restored', AP, 19 July 1999.

4 For a more lengthy discussion of the tooth relic, see Juliane Schober, 'Buddhist just rule and Burmese national culture: state

patronage of the Chinese tooth relic in Myanma', *History of Religions*, vol. 36, no. 3, pp. 220–44.

5 Images Asia, Karen Human Rights Group and the Open Society Institute's Burma Project, *All Quiet on the Western Front? The Situation in Chin State and Sagaing Division, Burma* (Thailand: January 1998), pp. 42–3.

6 These details were provided in a confidential report written in early May 1997. A videotape of this monks' meeting and the damage done to the Mahamuni image was later circulated outside Burma.

7 See 'Burmese monks protest innocence', *The Nation*, 28 March 1997; Aung Zaw, 'Rangoon plays the Muslim card', *The Nation*, 28 March 1997; and 'Eyewitness recalls recent unrest in Burma', *The Nation*, 5 April 1997, for more details.

8 Both Gustaaf Houtman and Juliane Schober have discussed how Buddhism has been perceived and practised differently by the top generals and the NLD leadership. See Schober, 'Buddhist visions of moral authority', and Gustaaf Houtman, *Mental Culture in Burmese Crisis Politics: Aung San Suu Kyi and the National League for Democracy* (Tokyo University of Foreign Studies, 1999).

9 'Minister says opposition trying to "divide the monks"', BBC Radio (translated from a Burmese-language Radio Myanmar broadcast), 29 September 1996.

10 'Senior monk appeals to Burmese Ruling Council, opposition to hold peace talks', BBC Radio, 4 November 2000. Note: this is a translation of the DVB's Burmese-language broadcast on the subject on 2 November 1999.

11 See Min Zin, 'Taking the lead: the need for a peace movement in Burma', *The Irrawaddy*, February 2000, pp. 14–15.

12 See 'Religious persecution', *Chin Human Rights Organization* (India: February 1997).

13 Images Asia, *Report on the Situation for Muslims in Burma* (Thailand: May 1997), Appendix. Such pamphlets were also reportedly distributed by local authorities in several towns in Shan State in June 1996 and led to attacks on Muslim shops in Kalaw. Communication, June 1996.

14 US State Department, *International Religious Freedom Report 2007*, www.state.gov/g/drl/rls/irf/2007/90131.htm, September 2007.

15 See Images Asia and BurmaNet, *Nowhere to Go: A Report on the 1997 SLORC Offensive against Duplaya District (KNU Sixth Brigade) Karen State, Burma* (Thailand: April 1997), pp. 8–17.

16 Ibid., p. 11.

17 Marwaan Macan-Markar, 'Ban on marriages, another yoke on Rohingya Muslims', Inter Press Service, 6 December 2005.

18 See Houtman, *Mental Culture in Burmese Crisis Politics*, ch. 5, for what he calls the regime's 'myanma-fication' project.

19 Communication from a border source who received the information from Rangoon, April 1999.

20 See Aung Zaw, 'Shwedagon and the generals', *The Irrawaddy*, May 1999.

21 'Burmese dead are obstacle to modernization', Reuters, 3 February 1997.

22 Maung Hmat Gyauk, *Kyemon* (Rangoon), June 1998 (note: my copy of the article is undated).

13 The internationalization of Burma's politics

1 Desmond Ball, *Burma's Military Secrets: Signals Intelligence from the Second World War to Civil War and Cyber Warfare* (Bangkok: White Lotus Press, 1998), pp. 219–29.

2 Ibid., p. 219; Anthony Davis, 'Burma casts wary eye on China', *Jane's Intelligence Review*, 1 June 1999.

3 Ball, *Burma's Military Secrets*, p. 224.

4 Dermot Tatlow, 'China's shadow', *Asiaweek*, 28 May 1999.

5 Ibid.

6 Ryan Clarke and Sangeet Dalliwall, 'Sino-Indian competition for Burmese oil and natural gas', *Harvard International Review*, 4 September 2008.

7 'Myanmar told to curb the drug trade', *International Herald Tribune*, 15 February 2006.

8 Ibid.

9 Anuj Chopra, 'Why India is selling weapons to Burma', *Christian Science Monitor*, 23 July 2007; Martin Smith, *Burma: Insurgency and the Politics of Ethnicity* (London: Zed Books, 1999), p. 252.

10 William Boot, 'India's support for Burmese junta pays off', *The Irrawaddy*, 24 September 2008.

11 David Brunnstrom, 'Myanmar embassy gunmen villains then heroes', Reuters, 3 October 1999.

12 See 'Irate villagers threaten protest over stoppage of work on Moei river bridge', *The Nation*, 13 June 1995; Yindee Lertcharoenchok, 'One bridge, two different views', *The Nation*, 15 August 1997.

13 'US condemns Burma for role in camp attacks', *The Nation*, 1 February 1997; Yindee Lertcharoenchok, 'Karen refugees under threat of further attacks from Burma', *The Nation*, 6 February 1997.

14 'Burma refuses to retract from gas exploration in Bay of Bengal', *Mizzima News*, 7 November 2008.

15 Jon Ungphakorn, 'Asian states run out of patience with Myanmar', *Taipei Times*, 11 October 2005.

16 See chs 6–9 in E. Stover et al. (eds), *Gathering Storm: Infectious Diseases and Human Rights in Burma* (Berkeley: Human Rights Center University of California, July 2007).

17 William Ashton, 'Burma receives advances from its silent suitors in Singapore', *Jane's Intelligence Review*, 1 March 1998.

18 Tony Hotland, 'President SBY tells Myanmar junta to open up', *Jakarta Post*, March 2006.

19 'EU firm on Burmese stand at ASEAN meet', *The Nation*, 27 May 1999.

20 Kavi Chongkittavorn, 'ASEAN needs "flexible engagement"', *The Nation*, 20 July 1998.

21 'Siazon calls for open dialogue in Myanmar', *Straits Times*, 26 July 1998.

22 Paul Eckert, 'ASEAN voices "revulsion" at Myanmar violence', Reuters, 27 September 2007.

23 These articles were compiled into a volume: Aung San Suu Kyi, *Letters from Burma* (London: Penguin Books, 1997).

24 Clifford McCoy, 'Rogues of the world unite', *Asia Times Online*, 28 April 2007.

25 Norman Robespierre, 'Nuclear bond for North Korea and Myanmar', *Asia Times Online*, 4 October 2008.

26 William Ashton, 'Myanmar's military links with Pakistan', *Jane's Intelligence Review*, 1 June 2000.

27 US funding for such

programmes came to just under $13 million in 2007.

28 Terry Macalister, 'Premier Oil gets out of Burma', *Guardian*, 17 September 2002.

29 In the United States, two lawsuits were filed against Unocal for the company's investment in the Yadana pipeline. The federal judge found that the evidence suggested Unocal knew the *tatmadaw* was using forced labour on the project and was benefiting from this practice. Ultimately, Unocal was ordered to pay compensation to the plaintiffs, who had suffered not only forced labour but also forced relocation and other abuses.

30 'Yangon to the UN: thanks, but ...', *Far Eastern Economic Review*, 25 December 1998.

31 Joshua Kurlantzick, 'China, Burma, and Sudan: convincing argument', *New Republic Online*, 11 May 2006.

32 R. Jeffrey Smith, 'Burma's image problem is a moneymaker for US lobbyists', *Washington Post*, 24 February 1998.

33 See Christina Fink, 'Visit Myanmar Year: tourism in Burma', in Jill Forshee, with Sandra Cate and Christina Fink (eds), *Converging Interests: Traders, Travelers, and Tourists in Southeast Asia* (Berkeley: International and Area Studies, UC Berkeley, 1999).

34 For two different perspectives, see: The Burma Campaign UK, *Pro-Aid, Pro-Sanctions, Pro-Engagement: A Position Paper on Humanitarian Aid to Burma* (London: July 2006) and International Crisis Group, *Burma/Myanmar after Nargis: Time to Normalize Aid Relations* (Brussels: October 2008).

35 'Cash for USDA members participating in Household Expenditure Survey', *New Light of Myanmar*, 30 March 1996.

36 Guideline for systematic and effective plan to implement development activities with the cooperation of UN, NGOs, INGOs and international organizations (unofficial translation), cited in the Burma Campaign UK, *Pro Aid*, p. 8.

37 'Prevented from working – the French section of MSF leaves Myanmar (Burma)', *Médecins Sans Frontières*, 30 March 2006.

38 Thomas Crampton, 'Burma's debt is pushing economy to the brink – the World Bank warns', *International Herald Tribune*, 15 November 1999.

14 Conclusion

1 See, for instance, James Barber, *South Africa in the Twentieth Century: A Political History – in Search of a Nation State* (Oxford: Blackwell, 1999).

2 See Mark R. Thompson, *The Anti-Marcos Struggle: Personalistic Rule and Democratic Transition in the Philippines* (New Haven, CT: Yale University Press, 1995).

3 Aung San, 'Burma and Buddhism', *The World of Books*, vol. XXI (April 1935); reprinted in Mya Han, *General Aung San's Literary Handiwork* (Rangoon: University Historical Research Department, 1998), pp. 61–2.

4 Min Zin, 'Spiritual revolution', *The Irrawaddy*, vol. 7, no. 2 (February 1999), p. 18.

Bibliography

Note: There are no surnames in Burmese, so I have listed Burmese names alphabetically according to the first letter of the first word of their names. Some authors have used 'U' in front of their names in their publications. In such cases, I have listed them under U.

Books and academic articles

All Burma Students Democratic Front (1997) *Pleading Not Guilty in Insein* (Bangkok: self-published).

— (1998) *To Stand and be Counted: The Suppression of Burma's Members of Parliament* (Bangkok: self-published).

Allott, Anna J. (1994) *Inked Over, Ripped Out: Burmese Storytellers and the Censors* (Chiang Mai, Thailand: Silkworm Books).

Aung San Suu Kyi (1991) *Freedom from Fear and Other Writings*, ed. Michael Aris (London: Penguin Books).

Aung-Thwin, Michael (1985) *Pagan: The Origins of Modern Burma* (Honolulu: University of Hawaii Press).

Ball, Desmond (1998) *Burma's Military Secrets: Signals Intelligence from the Second World War to Civil War and Cyber Warfare* (Bangkok: White Lotus Press).

Barber, James (1999) *South Africa in the Twentieth Century: A Political History – In Search of a Nation State* (Oxford: Blackwell Publishers).

Beyrer, Chris (1998) *War in the Blood: Sex, Politics and AIDS in Southeast Asia* (London: Zed Books).

Burma Center Netherlands and Transnational Institute (eds) (1999) *Strengthening Civil Society in Burma: Possibilities and Dilemmas for International NGOs* (Chiang Mai, Thailand: Silkworm Books).

Burma Socialist Programme Party (1983) *Facts about Burma* (Rangoon: BSPP).

Cady, John F. (1958) *A History of Modern Burma* (Ithaca, NY: Cornell University Press).

— (1976) *The United States and Burma* (Cambridge, MA: Harvard University Press).

Callahan, Mary (2003) *Making Enemies: War and State Building in Burma* (Ithaca, NY: Cornell University Press).

— (2007) *Political Authority in Burma's Ethnic Minority States: Devolution, Occupation and Coexistence* (Washington, DC: East West Center).

Carey, Peter (ed.) (1997) *Burma: The Challenge of Change in a Divided Society* (London: Macmillan).

Clements, Alan and Leslie Kean (1994) *Burma's Revolution of the Spirit: The Struggle for Democratic Freedom and Dignity* (Bangkok: White Orchid Press).

Donkers, Jan and Minka Nijhuis (eds) (1996) *Burma behind the Mask* (Amsterdam: Burma Centrum Netherlands).

Fink, Christina (1999) 'Visit Myanmar Year: tourism in Burma', in Jill Forshee, with Sandra Cate and

Christina Fink (eds), *Converging Interests: Traders, Travelers, and Tourists in Southeast Asia* (Berkeley, CA: International and Area Studies, UC Berkeley), pp. 85–107.

— (2008) 'Ongoing militarization in Burma's ethnic states', *Contemporary Politics*, vol. 14, no. 4, pp. 447–62.

Furnivall, J. S. (1956) *Colonial Policy and Practice* (New York: New York University Press).

Havel, Vaclav (1987) *Living in Truth*, ed. Jan Vladislav (London: Faber and Faber).

Heidel, Brian (2006) *The Growth of Civil Society in Myanmar* (Bangalore: Books for Change).

Houtman, Gustaaf (1999) *Mental Culture in Burmese Crisis Politics: Aung San Suu Kyi and the National League for Democracy*, Study of Languages and Cultures of Asia and Africa Monograph Series no. 33 (Tokyo: Tokyo University of Foreign Studies).

Kin Oung (1996) *Who Killed Aung San?* (Bangkok: White Lotus Press).

Koenig, William J. (1990) *The Burmese Polity, 1782–1819: Politics, Administration and Social Organization in the Early Konbaung Period* (Ann Arbor: University of Michigan, Papers on Southeast Asia).

Leach, E. (1960) 'The frontiers of Burma', *Comparative Studies in Society and History*, vol. 3, no. 1, pp. 315–35.

Lehman, F. K. (1967) 'Ethnic categories in Burma and the theory of social systems', in Peter Kundstadter (ed.), *Southeast Asian Tribes, Minorities, and Nations* (Princeton, NJ: Princeton University Press), pp. 93–124.

Lieberman, Victor B. (1984) *Burmese Administrative Cycles: Anarchy and Conquest, c. 1580–1760* (Princeton, NJ: Princeton University Press).

Lintner, Bertil (1990) *Outrage: Burma's Struggle for Democracy* (Bangkok: White Lotus Press).

— (1994) *Burma in Revolt: Opium and Insurgency since 1948* (Boulder, CO: Westview Press).

Maung Aung Myoe (1998) *Building the Tatmadaw: The Organisational Development of the Armed Forces in Myanmar, 1948–98* (Canberra: Strategic and Defence Studies Centre, Australian National University).

Maung Maung (1959) *Burma's Constitution* (The Hague: Martinus Nijhoff).

Maung Maung Gyi (1983) *Burmese Political Values: The Socio-Political Roots of Authoritarianism* (New York: Praeger).

Maung Maung Pye (1951) *Burma in the Crucible* (Rangoon: Khittaya Publishing House).

Mi Mi Khaing (1943) *Burmese Family* (Bloomington: Indiana University Press).

Mya Han (1998) *General Aung San's Literary Handiwork* (Rangoon: University Historical Research Department; sections in Burmese and English).

Mya Maung (1992) *Totalitarianism in Burma: Prospects for Economic Development* (New York: Paragon House).

Nash, Manning (1965) *The Golden Road to Modernity: Village Life in Contemporary Burma* (Chicago, IL: University of Chicago Press).

Rotberg, Robert I. (ed). (1997) *Burma: Prospects for Political and Economic Reconstruction* (Cambridge, MA: World Peace Foundation).

San C. Po, Dr (1928) *Burma and the Karens* (London: Elliot Stock).

Sangermano, Father Vincenzo (1985) *The Burmese Empire a Hundred Years Ago* (Bangkok: White Orchid Press; 1st edn, 1833).

Selth, Andrew (1993) *Death of a Hero: The U Thant Disturbances in Burma, December 1974*, Australia–Asia Paper no. 49 (Brisbane: Griffith University Centre for the Study of Australia–Asia Relations).

— (1996) *Transforming the Tatmadaw: The Burmese Armed Forces since 1988* (Canberra: Australian National University Strategic and Defence Studies Centre).

— (1997) *Burma's Intelligence Apparatus* (Canberra: Australian National University Strategic and Defence Studies Centre).

— (2002) *Burma's Armed Forces: Power without Glory* (Norwalk, CT: Eastbridge).

Shway Yoe (1963) *The Burman: His Life and His Notions* (New York: W. W. Norton).

Silverstein, Josef (1968) 'Burmese student politics in a changing society', *Daedalus*, vol. 97, no. 1, pp. 274–92.

— (1977) *Burma: Military Rule and the Politics of Stagnation* (Ithaca, NY: Cornell University Press).

— (ed.) (1989) *Independent Burma at Forty Years: Six Assessments* (Ithaca, NY: Cornell University Southeast Asia Program).

Skidmore, Monique (ed.) (2005) *Burma at the Turn of the 21st Century* (Honolulu: University of Hawaii Press).

Smith, Martin (1991) *State of Fear: Censorship in Burma (Myanmar)* (London: Article 19).

— (1994) *Ethnic Groups in Burma: Development, Democracy and Human Rights* (London: Anti-Slavery International).

— (1996) *Fatal Silence? Freedom of Expression and the Right to Health in Burma* (London: Article 19).

— (1999) *Burma: Insurgency and the Politics of Ethnicity* (London: Zed Books; 1st edn, 1991).

South, Ashley (2007) 'Conflict and displacement in Burma/Myanmar', in M. Skidmore and T. Wilson (eds), *Mynamar: The State Community, and the Environment* (Canberra: Asia Pacific Press), pp. 54–81.

Spiro, Melford E. (1967) *Burmese Supernaturalism* (Philadelphia, PA: Prentice-Hall).

Steinberg, David I. (1982) *Burma: A Socialist Nation of Southeast Asia* (Boulder, CO: Westview Press).

— (1997) 'The Union Solidarity Development Association', *Burma Debate*, vol. 4, no. 1.

— (2001) *Burma: The State of Myanmar* (Washington, DC: Georgetown University Press).

Stover, Eric et al. (eds) (2007) *Gathering Storm: Infectious Diseases and Human Rights in Burma* (Berkeley: Human Rights Center, University of California).

Tambiah, S. J. (1977) 'The Gallactic Polity: The structure of traditional kingdoms in Southeast Asia', *Annals of the New York Academy of Sciences*, no. 293, pp. 69–97.

Taylor, Robert (1996) 'Elections in Burma/Myanmar: for whom and why?', in R. H. Taylor (ed.), *The Politics of Elections in Southeast Asia* (Cambridge: Cambridge University Press).

— (1987) *The State in Burma* (London: C. Hurst).

Temple, R. C. (1906) *The Thirty Seven Nats* (London: W. Griggs).

Than Myint-U (2006) *The River of Lost Footsteps* (New York: Farrar, Straus and Giroux).

Than Tun (1988) *Essays on the History and Buddhism of Burma* (Arran, Scotland: Kiscadale Publications).

Thawnghmung, A. M. (2008) *The Karen Revolution in Burma: Diverse Voices, Uncertain Ends* (Washington, DC: East West Center).

Thompson, Mark R. (1995) *The Anti-Marcos Struggle: Personalistic Rule and Democratic Transition in the Philippines* (New Haven, CT: Yale University Press).

Thongchai Winichakul (1994) *Siam Mapped: A History of the Geo-Body of a Nation* (Honolulu: University of Hawaii Press).

Tinker, Hugh (1957) *The Union of Burma* (London: Oxford University Press).

U Maung Maung (1980) *From Sangha to Laity: Nationalist Movements of Burma: 1920–1940*, Monograph on South Asia no. 4 (Canberra: Australian National University).

Venkateswaran, K. S. (1996) *Burma: Beyond the Law* (London: Article 19).

Vum Son (1987) *Zo History: With an Introduction to Zo Culture, Economy, Religion and Their Status as an Ethnic Minority in India, Burma and Bangladesh* (self-published).

Yawnghwe, Chao-Tzang (1989) 'The Burman military: holding the country together?', in J. Silverstein (ed.), *Independent Burma at Forty Years: Six Assessments* (Ithaca, NY: Cornell Southeast Asia Program).

Zaw Oo and Win Min (2007) *Assessing Burma's Ceasefire Accords* (Washington, DC: East West Center).

Personal accounts

All Burma Students' Democratic Front (1998) *Tortured Voices: Personal Accounts of Burma's Interrogation Centres* (Bangkok: self-published).

Aung San Suu Kyi (1997) *Letters from Burma* (London: Penguin Books).

— (1997) *The Voice of Hope: Conversations with Alan Clements, with contributions by U Kyi Maung and U Tin Oo* (London: Penguin Books).

Aye Saung (1989) *Burman in the Back Row* (Hong Kong: Asia 2000 Ltd).

Ba Maw (1968) *Breakthrough in Burma, Memoirs of a Revolution, 1939–1946* (New Haven, CT: Yale University Press).

Collis, Maurice (1943) *The Land of the Great Image: Being Experiences of Friar Manrique in Arakan* (New York: New Directions Books).

— (1996) *Trials in Burma* (Bangkok: Ava Publishing House; 1st edn, 1938).

Falla, Jonathan (1991) *True Love and Bartholomew: Rebels on the Burmese Border* (Cambridge: Cambridge University Press).

Lintner, Bertil (1996) *Land of Jade: A Journey from India through Northern Burma to China* (Bangkok: White Orchid Press; 1st English edn, 1990).

Mirante, Edith (1993) *Burmese Looking Glass: A Human Rights Adventure and a Jungle Revolution* (New York: Grove Press).

Moe Aye (1999) *Ten Years On: The Life and Views of a Burmese Student Political Prisoner* (Bangkok: self-published).

Sargent, Inge (1994) *Twilight over Burma: My Life as a Shan Princess* (Honolulu: University of Hawaii Press).

Singh, Balwant (1993) *Independence and Democracy in Burma, 1945–1952: The Turbulent Years* (Ann Arbor: University of Michigan Center for South and Southeast Asian Studies).

Smith Dun, General (1980) *Memoirs*

of the *Four-Foot Colonel*, Data
Paper no. 113, Southeast Asia
Program, Department of Asian
Studies (Ithaca, NY: Cornell Uni-
versity Press).

U Nu (1975) *Saturday's Son* (New
Haven, CT: Yale University Press).

U Thaung (1995) *A Journalist, a
General and an Army in Burma*
(Bangkok: White Lotus Press).

Win Naing Oo (1996) *Cries from Insein*
(Bangkok: All Burma Students'
Democratic Front).

Yawnghwe, Chao-Tzang (1987) *The
Shan of Burma: Memoirs of an Exile*
(Singapore: Institute of Southeast
Asian Studies).

Literature

Khin Myo Chit (1969) *The 13
Carat Diamond and Other Stories*
(Rangoon: Sarpay Lawka Book
House).

Ludu U Hla (1993) *The Caged Ones*,
trans. Sein Tu (Bangkok: White
Orchid Press; 1st English edn,
1986).

Ma Ma Lay (1991) *Not Out of Hate*,
trans. Margaret Aung-Thwin, ed.
William H. Frederick (Athens:
Ohio University Center for International Studies).

Maung Htin (1998) *Nga Ba*, trans.
Maw Thi Ri (New Delhi: Irrawaddy
Publications).

Mya Than Tint (1996) *On the Road
to Mandalay: Tales of Ordinary
People*, trans. Ohnmar Khin and
Sein Kyaw Hlaing (Bangkok:
White Orchid Press).

Orwell, George (1934) *Burmese Days*
(New York: Harcourt Brace).

Reports

Images Asia (1996) *'No Childhood at
All': A Report about Child Soldiers
in Burma* (Thailand: May).

— (1997) *Report on the Situation for
Muslims in Burma* (Thailand: May).

Images Asia and BurmaNet (1997)
*Nowhere to Go: A Report on the
1997 SLORC Offensive against Du-
playa District (KNU Sixth Brigade)
Karen State Burma* (Thailand:
April).

Images Asia, Karen Human Rights
Group and the Open Society
Institute's Burma Project (1998)
*All Quiet on the Western Front?
The Situation in Chin State and
Sagaing Division, Burma* (Thailand:
January).

International Labour Organization
(1999) *Resolution on Burma*
(Geneva: ILO).

Shan Human Rights Foundation
(1998) *Dispossessed: Forced Relocation and Extrajudicial Killings in
Shan State* (Thailand: April).

UNICEF (1995) *Children and Women
in Myanmar: A Situation Analysis*
(Rangoon: UNICEF).

United States Committee for Refugees (1998) *Burma Country Report
1998* (Washington, DC: US Committee for Refugees).

United States Department of Labor,
Bureau of International Affairs
(1998) *Report on Labor Practices
in Burma* (Washington, DC: US
Department of Labor).

United States Embassy, Rangoon
(1997) *Foreign Economic Trends
Report* (Rangoon: US Embassy).

*Also numerous reports by the
following organizations*

Amnesty International
Human Rights Foundation of Mon-
land
Human Rights Watch
International Crisis Group
Karen Human Rights Group
Thailand Burma Border Consortium

Websites

www.burmanet.org – *The BurmaNet News*, a daily compilation of news stories on Burma

www.irrawaddy.org – *The Irrawaddy News Online* and *The Irrawaddy News Magazine*

www.mizzima.com – *Mizzima News Online*

www.myanmar.com – gateway to the *New Light of Myanmar* and other state-sponsored publications

Index